P9-DNW-094

Frommer's®

Maine Coast

3rd Edition

by Paul Karr

Here's what the critics say about Frommer's:

"Amazingly easy to use. Very portable, very complete."
—**BOOKLIST**

"Detailed, accurate, and easy-to-read information for all price ranges."
—**GLAMOUR MAGAZINE**

"Hotel information is close to encyclopedic."
—**DES MOINES SUNDAY REGISTER**

"Frommer's Guides have a way of giving you a real feel for a place."
—**KNIGHT RIDDER NEWSPAPERS**

WILEY

Wiley Publishing, Inc.

ABOUT THE AUTHOR

Paul Karr has written, coauthored, or edited more than 25 guidebooks, including Wiley's *Vancouver and Victoria For Dummies* and *Frommer's Vermont, New Hampshire & Maine.* He has also contributed to Discover Channel/Insight Guides to Montreal, Atlanta, Vienna, Austria, and Switzerland; Wiley's Irreverent Guides to Rome and Vancouver; and *Scandinavia: The Rough Guide* while writing articles for *Sierra* and *Sports Illustrated,* among other publications. He divides his time between New England, both coasts of Canada, and Europe.

Published by

WILEY PUBLISHING, INC.

111 River St.
Hoboken, NJ 07030-5774

Copyright © 2009 Wiley Publishing, Inc., Hoboken, New Jersey. All rights reserved. No part of this publication may be reproduced, stored in a retrieval system or transmitted in any form or by any means, electronic, mechanical, photocopying, recording, scanning or otherwise, except as permitted under Sections 107 or 108 of the 1976 United States Copyright Act, without either the prior written permission of the Publisher, or authorization through payment of the appropriate per-copy fee to the Copyright Clearance Center, 222 Rosewood Drive, Danvers, MA 01923, 978/750-8400, fax 978/646-8600. Requests to the Publisher for permission should be addressed to the Permissions Department, John Wiley & Sons, Inc., 111 River Street, Hoboken, NJ 07030, 201/748-6011, fax 201/748-6008, or online at http://www.wiley.com/go/permissions.

Wiley and the Wiley Publishing logo are trademarks or registered trademarks of John Wiley & Sons, Inc. and/or its affiliates. Frommer's is a trademark or registered trademark of Arthur Frommer. Used under license. All other trademarks are the property of their respective owners. Wiley Publishing, Inc. is not associated with any product or vendor mentioned in this book.

ISBN 978-0-470-39319-2

Editor: Anuja Madar
Production Editor: Katie Robinson
Cartographer: Andrew Dolan
Photo Editor: Richard Fox
Production by Wiley Indianapolis Composition Services

Front cover photo: Acadia National Park, Hancock County: Bass Harbor Light overlooking the Atlantic Ocean Bass Harbor
Back cover photo: Maine: Close-up of lobster buoys and shop window

For information on our other products and services or to obtain technical support, please contact our Customer Care Department within the U.S. at 800/762-2974, outside the U.S. at 317/572-3993 or fax 317/572-4002.

Wiley also publishes its books in a variety of electronic formats. Some content that appears in print may not be available in electronic formats.

Manufactured in the United States of America

5 4 3 2 1

CONTENTS

4 SUGGESTED MAINE COAST ITINERARIES — 64

5 THE SOUTHERN COAST — 74

6 PORTLAND — 105

11 SIDE TRIPS FROM THE MAINE COAST   256

FAST FACTS, TOLL-FREE NUMBERS & WEBSITES   282

INDEX   293

LIST OF MAPS

ACKNOWLEDGMENTS

Gracious thanks to all who cooperated with this and previous editions, especially Wayne Curtis, who authored the original title; a boatload of editors and higher-ups at Frommer's and Wiley, including Anuja Madar, Naomi Kraus, and Mike Spring (and dozens before them); and countless unsung copy editors, designers, printers, web jockeys, sales folk, and bean-counters who ensure that books are actually assigned, edited, printed, and sold. Thanks to the many tourism officials, PR liaisons, and hotel and restaurant staff who tirelessly answered questions, arranged itineraries, checked facts, provided tours, cooked meals, made beds—and then let me do my job without trying to tell me how to do it. Thanks to the staticky web of AM radio stations crisscrossing northern New England, who kept me in the Red Sox loop throughout the short summer. If only your signals reached to Gotham . . . Thanks to Gibson, Epiphone, and Harmony for making fine guitars that travel well. And finally, this goes out to my lovely girl.

—Paul Karr

AN INVITATION TO THE READER

In researching this book, we discovered many wonderful places—hotels, restaurants, shops, and more. We're sure you'll find others. Please tell us about them, so we can share the information with your fellow travelers in upcoming editions. If you were disappointed with a recommendation, we'd love to know that, too. Please write to:

Frommer's Maine Coast, 3rd Edition
Wiley Publishing, Inc. • 111 River St. • Hoboken, NJ 07030-5774

AN ADDITIONAL NOTE

Please be advised that travel information is subject to change at any time—and this is especially true of prices. We therefore suggest that you write or call ahead for confirmation when making your travel plans. The authors, editors, and publisher cannot be held responsible for the experiences of readers while traveling. Your safety is important to us, however, so we encourage you to stay alert and be aware of your surroundings. Keep a close eye on cameras, purses, and wallets, all favorite targets of thieves and pickpockets.

Other Great Guides for Your Trip:

Frommer's Vermont, New Hampshire & Maine
Frommer's New England
Frommer's Portable Maine Coast
Frommer's Best Loved Driving Tours: New England
Frommer's Family Vacations in the National Parks
Frommer's Unofficial Guide to Campgrounds in the Northeast

FROMMER'S STAR RATINGS, ICONS & ABBREVIATIONS

Every hotel, restaurant, and attraction listing in this guide has been ranked for quality, value, service, amenities, and special features using a **star-rating system.** In country, state, and regional guides, we also rate towns and regions to help you narrow down your choices and budget your time accordingly. Hotels and restaurants are rated on a scale of zero (recommended) to three stars (exceptional). Attractions, shopping, nightlife, towns, and regions are rated according to the following scale: zero stars (recommended), one star (highly recommended), two stars (very highly recommended), and three stars (must-see).

In addition to the star-rating system, we also use **seven feature icons** that point you to the great deals, in-the-know advice, and unique experiences that separate travelers from tourists. Throughout the book, look for:

Finds	Special finds—those places only insiders know about
Fun Facts	Fun facts—details that make travelers more informed and their trips more fun
Kids	Best bets for kids and advice for the whole family
Moments	Special moments—those experiences that memories are made of
Overrated	Places or experiences not worth your time or money
Tips	Insider tips—great ways to save time and money
Value	Great values—where to get the best deals

The following **abbreviations** are used for credit cards:

AE	American Express	DISC	Discover	V	Visa
DC	Diners Club	MC	MasterCard		

FROMMERS.COM

Now that you have this guidebook to help you plan a great trip, visit our website at **www. frommers.com** for additional travel information on more than 4,000 destinations. We update features regularly to give you instant access to the most current trip-planning information available. At Frommers.com, you'll find scoops on the best airfares, lodging rates, and car rental bargains. You can even book your travel online through our reliable travel booking partners. Other popular features include:

- Online updates of our most popular guidebooks
- Vacation sweepstakes and contest giveaways
- Newsletters highlighting the hottest travel trends
- Podcasts, interactive maps, and up-to-the-minute events listings
- Opinionated blog entries by Arthur Frommer himself
- Online travel message boards with featured travel discussions

What's New Along the Coast of Maine

GREATER PORTLAND Though I reported in the last edition of this book that the Portland Public Market would close, it actually didn't—not completely, anyway. Instead, some of the merchants simply **moved the market to a new home closer to downtown.** Yes, the big public market created by benefactress Betty Noyce near the city library closed its doors in early 2007, and a new version of the market sprung from the grass roots of the old one, and while it's smaller, it's also right in the center of the city. The new Public Market House is located at 28 Monument Square. See chapter 6.

Portland's international ferry terminal has also moved, a hop, skip, and a jump north along Commercial Street. Where the old terminal for the ferry to Nova Scotia used to be located beneath the bridge to South Portland, it is now on the northern end of the Old Port waterfront, at the newly christened Ocean Gateway Pier. It's just north of the Casco Bay Lines ferry terminal.

The venerable **Black Point Inn** in Scarborough will probably *never* move. However, it did change hands recently. The new owners have sheared off the cottages from the former property, leaving management to concentrate on the main inn. What remains is as elegant as ever; the rack rates are hefty, but that's partly because they include breakfast, dinner, and a small afternoon tea service each day. See p. 108.

Finally, Portland's fine Uffa! restaurant is moving out of town, changing concepts and name, and taking its chef with it. Brunchies, drown your sorrows.

FREEPORT TO MIDCOAST MAINE The excellent little **Bowdoin College Museum of Art** (p. 137) in Brunswick has reopened to the public following a $20-million renovation.

Also in Brunswick—very nearby, in fact—the Brunswick Inn on Park Row has **added a tiny wine bar/lounge** to its already excellent property. Sip a wine or local beer in front of a fire or on the inn's porch. See p. 138.

Jessica Gorton has opened the Sweet Leaves Teahouse (© **207/725-1326**) just off Brunswick's main street. It's **a welcome addition to the downtown cafe scene.** Sweet Leaves features cheese plates, panini, great salads, tea cakes, gourmet yogurt, upscale root beer floats, and more, plus a full selection of black, green, white, and herbal teas. It's located off the main street at 22 Lincoln St., formerly the site of some very fine other restaurants. See p. 139.

However, a bit of bad news for foodies bound for Brunswick: The excellent **Starfish Grill has closed its doors,** bad news for everyone *except* the local fish population.

Moving northeast along the coast a bit, the intriguing **Solo Bistro has opened at 128 Front St. in Bath.** Right on the town's prime commercial street, it's a bistro/jazz club serving burgers, seafood, salads, sandwiches, and some fancier entrees as well. The decor is Scandinavian (the husband-and-wife owners are Danish). See p. 139.

Down a long peninsula from Bath, the venerable **Sebasco Harbor Resort** has finally gone modern—okay, a little bit modern—with the addition of a spa facility and some new suites.

MIDCOAST MAINE   No more $1 pop-corn? It's true. Sadly, the plucky little Bayview Street Cinema in downtown Camden has been shuttered, depriving the state of one of its finest independent movie houses. You'll likely have to head to Portland now to see good independent films.

However, there is an addition to the midcoast area: **a new observatory on the lovely Verona Island bridge** (U.S. Rte. 1, just outside Bucksport). It's said to be the world's highest public bridge observatory, 437 feet up with panoramic views of the surrounding mountains, lakes, and even Penobscot Bay. To get up top, enter and pay admission to adjacent Fort Knox State Park first. See p. 173.

Also new in the region: **new owners for the Camden Harbour Inn** (two Dutchmen, if you're wondering), and boy, have they transformed the place. It has gone from simple Maine boardinghouse to luxury inn in no time; the new rate structure, of course, reflects this change. See p. 167.

SIDE TRIPS FROM THE MAINE COAST Portsmouth's fine restaurant **43 Degrees** has, sadly, closed its doors.

The **Children's Museum of New Hampshire** didn't close, but it *did* move out of the immediate Portsmouth area to the small city of Dover (and change its name slightly). Contact the museum at Ⓒ **603/742-2002** (or check it out online at www.childrens-museum.org/cmnh) for new directions, the latest ticket prices, exhibition schedules, and other important details.

The Best of the Maine Coast

Humor columnist Dave Barry once suggested that Maine's state motto should be changed to "Cold, but damp," thereby emphasizing its two primary qualities.

That's cute, but it's also sort of true. Spring here tends to last just a few days or weeks; November features bitter winds alternating with gray sheets of rain; and the long winters often bring a mix of blizzards and ice storms.

Ah, but summer. Summer on the coast of Maine brings osprey diving for fish off wooded points, fogs rolling poetically in from the Atlantic, and long, timeless days when the sun rises well before visitors do. (By 8am, it can already feel like noon.) Maine summers offer a serious dose of tranquillity; a few days in the right spot can rejuvenate even the most jangled city nerves.

The trick is *finding* that right spot. Route 1 along the Maine coast is mostly an amalgam of convenience stores, tourist boutiques, and restaurants catering to bus tours. The main loop road, single beach, and most popular mountain peaks in Acadia National Park tend to get congested in summer. And arriving without a room reservation in high season? Simply a bad idea.

On the other hand, Maine's remote position and size often work to your advantage. The state has an amazing 5,500 miles of coastline, plus 3,000 or so coastal islands (admittedly, some of these are nothing more than rocks). With a little homework, you can find that little cove, island, or fishing village that isn't too discovered yet, book your room well in advance, and enjoy coastal Maine's incredibly lovely scenery without sweating any of the last-minute details.

Getting to know the locals is fun, too. They're mostly fishermen (as opposed to the farmers who colonized the rest of New England) and other seafaring folk, or the descendants of such, and today's coastal Mainers—even the transplanted ones—exhibit both a wry, dry sense of humor and a surprising gregariousness. (There's a Bait's Motel in Searsport, complete with worm-hanging-off-its-hook motif, for instance, and a tiny street called Fitz Hugh Lane in Somesville.) And fishermen's stories, of course, are the stuff of legend. Take the time to get to know some folks, and you'll smile a lot more.

Basically, your main challenge when preplanning a vacation in coastal Maine boils down to simply this: Where to start? Here's an entirely biased list of destinations—some places I enjoy returning to time and again. During my years of traveling through the region, I've discovered that places like these merit more than just a quick stop; instead, they're worth a detour or an extended stay of a few days to a week.

1 THE NATURAL WONDERS OF COASTAL MAINE

- **The Beaches of Southern Maine** (southern Maine): The flat, white-sand beaches of southernmost Maine are gorgeous and perfect for playing Frisbee,

THE BEST OF THE MAINE COAST

1

THE NATURAL WONDERS OF COASTAL MAINE

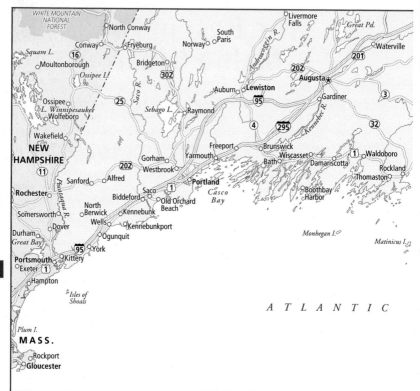

walking, tanning, kite flying, and photography. Just watch your tootsies: That water's cold. See chapter 5.

- **Casco Bay's Islands** (southern Maine): Locals call 'em the Calendar Islands for a reason: They claim there are 365 of these rocky islands dotting Casco Bay, in every shape and size. (I'd wager there are more than that, though.) Catch a mail boat from Portland harbor and see how many *you* can count. See chapter 6.

- **Rocky Peninsulas** (southern, Midcoast, and Downeast Maine): Everywhere you go—from the Cape Neddick area to just south of Portland, from Harpswell to Georgetown, from Blue Hill to

Boothbay to Schoodic Point—you'll find long fingerlings and headlands carved of sheer bedrock. Once these were mountaintops high above an ancient sea; now they comprise some of the East Coast's most beautiful scenery. Try some back-road wandering to find the best ones. Just remember that these take time to traverse. See chapters 5, 8, and 10.

- **The Camden Hills** (Midcoast Maine): They're not huge, yet this run of hills comes with a bonus you'll only understand when you get to the top: eye-popping coastal vistas of boats, villages, and islands. In the winter, you can even

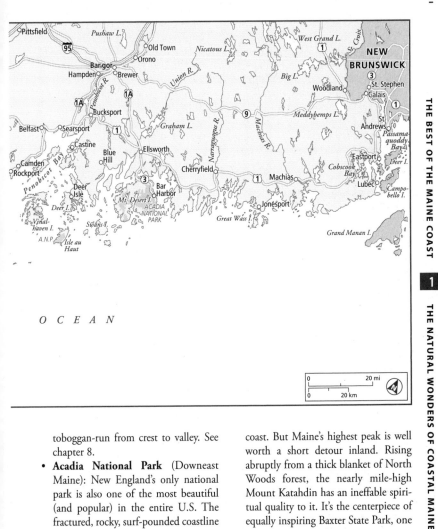

toboggan-run from crest to valley. See chapter 8.

- **Acadia National Park** (Downeast Maine): New England's only national park is also one of the most beautiful (and popular) in the entire U.S. The fractured, rocky, surf-pounded coastline here is the main attraction, but don't overlook the quiet, boreal forests and open summits of low mountains that afford spectacular coastal views, either. And don't forget to rent a mountain bike or horse-drawn carriage for further exploration. See chapter 9.
- **The Appalachian Trail and Mount Katahdin** (side trip from Downeast Maine): All right, they're not on the coast. But Maine's highest peak is well worth a short detour inland. Rising abruptly from a thick blanket of North Woods forest, the nearly mile-high Mount Katahdin has an ineffable spiritual quality to it. It's the centerpiece of equally inspiring Baxter State Park, one of the last, best wildernesses remaining in the eastern U.S. While here, don't forget to check out the Trail itself, which stretches 2,100 rugged miles from Georgia before winding uphill to the finish line here on Katahdin. These stretches in Maine include some of the most magnificent scenery in New England. See chapter 11.

2 THE BEST SMALL TOWNS

- **York Village** (southern Maine): What else can you say? It's Maine's oldest settlement, so it's got history and fine architecture. It's also got a set of beaches and a coastal trail nearby. And people just seem friendly here. See chapter 5.
- **Camden** (Midcoast Maine): This seaside town has everything—a beautiful harbor; great Federal, Queen Anne, and Greek Revival architecture; and even its own tiny mountain range affording great hikes with sweeping ocean views. With lots of elegant bed-and-breakfasts, it's a perfect base for explorations farther afield. See chapter 8.
- **Castine** (Midcoast Maine): Soaring elm trees, a peaceful harborside setting, grand historic homes, and a selection of good inns make this a great spot to soak up some of Maine's coastal ambience off the beaten path. See chapter 8.
- **Blue Hill** (Midcoast Maine): A tiny town with fine harbor views; a general

store; central green; museum; a lazy, summery feeling; and no—absolutely no—pretense nor tourist tack (so far). See chapter 8.
- **Northeast Harbor** (Mount Desert Island, Downeast Maine): Northeast has a waterside setting, sure, but also a gentle mixture of seafaring locals and art-loving summer folks, giving it an aura of a place that's still living life from a century ago. The single, sleepy main street anchors one of Mount Desert Island's best little villages. See chapter 9.
- **Eastport** (Downeast Maine): Sure, it's basically a fish-processing town, yet Eastport is making a slow transition from working-class town to (gasp) tourist destination. Don't be surprised if it gets more popular as time goes on; or see it now, and be ahead of the curve. See chapter 10.

3 THE BEST PLACES TO SEE FALL FOLIAGE

- **The Camden Hills** (Midcoast Maine): The surrounding countryside is full of blazing color, with whitewashed homes and sailboats to offset it. See chapter 8.
- **Acadia National Park** (Downeast Maine): This national park possesses some of the finest foliage in northern New England, all the more so because it's set right beside the dramatic, rocky coastline. See chapter 9.
- **Blueberry Barrens** (Downeast Maine): Downeast Maine's vast wild blueberry

fields suddenly turn a brilliant cranberry-red color each fall, practically setting the landscape ablaze with color. This is one of Maine's unappreciated scenic treasures. Wander the dirt roads northeast of Cherryfield through the upland barrens, or just drive Route 1 between Harrington and Machias past an experimental farm atop (of course) Blueberry Hill. See chapter 10.

4 THE BEST COASTAL VIEWS

- **From Hiking Trails on Monhegan:** The village of Monhegan is clustered

around the harbor of the same-named island, quite a way off the coast. The rest of the 700-acre rock is comprised of picturesque wild lands, with miles of trails crossing open meadows and tracing rocky bluffs. See chapter 7.

- **From the Deck of a Windjammer:** See Maine as many saw it for centuries—from the ocean, looking inland. Sailing ships depart from various harbors along the coast, particularly from Rockland and Camden. Spend between a night and a week exploring the dramatic shoreline. See chapter 8.

- **From Merchant's Row via Kayak:** The islands between Stonington and Isle au Haut, rimmed with pink granite and capped with the stark spires of spruce trees, are among the most spectacular on the entire East Coast. They're inaccessible by motorboat, but wonderful to explore by sea kayak if you've got the skill (or the will). Some outfitters even offer overnight camping trips on the islands. See chapter 8.

- **From Acadia's Park Loop Road:** Forming the heart of Acadia National Park, this is New England's premier oceanside drive. Start along a ridge with views of Frenchman Bay and the Porcupine Islands, then dip down along the rocky shores to watch the surf crash against the dark rocks. Plan to do this 20-mile loop at least twice to get the most out of it. See chapter 9.

- **From a Well-Located Rocking Chair:** Views are never better than when you're caught unaware—such as glancing up from an engrossing book on the front porch of an oceanside inn and catching a great sunset or angle of light on the water. This book includes many hotels and inns on the water. A list of the best porch views in Maine could run for pages, but it would certainly include those gleaned from the Beachmere Inn (in Ogunquit), the Black Point Inn (in Scarborough), Grey Havens (on Georgetown Island), East Wind Inn (in Tenant's Harbor), the Samoset Resort (outside Rockport), the Inn on the Harbor (in Stonington), the Tides Inn (in Bar Harbor), and the Claremont (in Southwest Harbor). But feel free to find your own best front porch, too.

- **New Hampshire Route 1A by Bike:** This beautiful little ride packs a sampling of all sorts of coastal scenery into a tiny slice of New Hampshire coastline running approximately from Hampton Beach. You begin among sandy beaches, then pass rocky headlands and handsome mansions before coasting into the scenic, appealing little city of Portsmouth. See chapter 11.

5 THE BEST ACTIVE VACATIONS

- **Mountain Biking at Acadia:** Oil magnate John D. Rockefeller, Jr., built the carriage roads of Mount Desert Island so that the gentry could enjoy rambles in the woods on horseback—far away from those pesky cars that were just then filling his bank accounts with huge profits. His extensive network today offers some of the most scenic and enjoyable scenic mountain biking in the U.S. Thanks, John! See chapter 9.

- **Kayaking the Coast:** With its massive and serpentine coastline and thousands of islands, most of them uninhabited, Maine is a world-class destination for those who know their way around a sea kayak. The Stonington area is considered the best spot for kayaking in Maine, but it's hard to go wrong anywhere northeast of Portland. Just beware the dangers that lurk in the form of tricky tides or weather—kayak with a guide if you're at all a novice.

- **Canoeing the North Woods:** Maine has thousands of miles of flowing rivers and streams, and hundreds of miles of shoreline along remote ponds and lakes. Happily, these are not all that far inland from the coast. Bring along a tent, sleeping bag, and cooking gear, and you're good to go: It will be just you, the stars, and the sounds of the loons. See chapter 11.

6 THE BEST DESTINATIONS FOR FAMILIES

- **York Beach** (southern Maine): This beach town is actually a set of three towns; head for Short Sands with the kids, where they can watch a taffy-pulling machine, play video games in an arcade, ogle seashells in a trinket shop, or scarf cotton candy at a small amusement park. The Long Sands section is ideal for tanning, Frisbee tossing, or kite flying, and nearby Nubble Light (a scenic lighthouse) is close to a kid-friendly ice-cream shop. See chapter 5.
- **Old Orchard Beach** (southern Maine): This place has sort of a carnival atmosphere—there are french fries, hot dogs, and fried-dough galore. Though it might be a bit much for adults, the kids will probably love it. See chapter 6.
- **Monhegan Island** (southern Maine): The mail boat from Port Clyde out to Monhegan is rustic and intriguing, the inns are a rustic overnight adventure, and the smallish island's scale is perfect for kids to explore, especially kids in the, say, 8-to-12-year-old range. See chapter 7.

7 THE MOST INTRIGUING HISTORIC HOMES

- **Victoria Mansion** (Portland): The Victorians went all out for grandiose material excess in a Trumpian-before-the-Donald sort of style. You'll find Victorian decorative arts at their zenith in this elaborate Italianate mansion, which was built during the Civil War. It's open to the public for tours throughout the summer, and then again during the Christmas season. See chapter 6.
- **Parson Fisher House** (Blue Hill): Parson Jonathan Fisher, who served as minister to the quiet town of Blue Hill in the late 18th century, was a man of extraordinary talents, from designing his own house to building his own clocks and preaching sermons in five languages (including Aramaic). As if that wasn't enough, his primitive landscape paintings of the region are surprisingly good. See chapter 8.

8 THE BEST PLACES TO REDISCOVER THE PAST

- **Sabbathday Lake Shaker Community** (New Gloucester): This is the last of the active Shaker communities in the nation and the only one that voted to accept new converts rather than die out. The 1,900-acre farm about 45 minutes outside of Portland has a number of exceptional buildings, including some dating from the 18th century. Visitors can view examples of Shaker craftsmanship and buy herbs to bring home. See chapter 6.

- **Mount Desert Island & Bar Harbor:** In the mid-1800s, America launched a love affair with nature and never looked back. See where it started, here amid surf-wracked rocks, and where some of the nation's most affluent families ventured to erect vacation "cottages," with bedrooms by the dozen. The area still offers lessons on how to design with nature as accomplice rather than adversary. See chapter 9.

- **Portsmouth** (New Hampshire): Portsmouth is a salty coastal city that also happens to possess some of the most impressive historic homes in all New England. Start at Strawberry Banke, a 10-acre compound of 42 historic buildings. Then visit some of the many other grand homes in the surrounding neighborhoods. See chapter 11.

9 THE BEST RESORTS

- **The Colony Hotel** (Kennebunkport; ✆ **800/552-2363** or 207/967-3331): This rambling, gleaming white resort dates from 1914 and has been upgraded over the years without losing any of its charm. You can play shuffleboard, putt on a putting green, or lounge in an oceanview pool. More vigorous souls cross the street to brave the cold Atlantic. See p. 100.

- **White Barn Inn** (Kennebunkport; ✆ **207/967-2321**): Much of the White Barn staff hails from Europe, and they treat guests graciously. The rooms and suites here are a delight, and the meals (served in a gloriously restored barn) are among the best in northern New England. See p. 98.

10 THE BEST BED & BREAKFASTS

- **The Captain Lord Mansion** (Kennebunkport; ✆ **800/522-3141** or 207/967-3141): You'll transcend all those "wannabe&Bs" at this genuine article, chock-full of grandfather clocks, Chippendale highboys, and other antiques. This mansion is just off the village center in Kennebunkport, perfectly situated for relaxing strolls to the beach or into town. See p. 100.

- **Grey Havens** (Georgetown Island; ✆ **800/431-2316** or 207/371-2616): This graceful, 1904-shingled home with prominent turrets sits on a high, rocky bluff overlooking the sea. Inside, it's done in mellow pine paneling, with a spacious common room where you can relax in cozy chairs in front of the cobblestone fireplace while listening to classical music. See p. 139.

- **Lindenwood Inn** (Southwest Harbor; ✆ **800/307-5335** or 207/244-5335): This place features a jovial owner, good rooms, a refreshingly laid-back and summery feel, a fine pool and deck, and proximity to one of Mount Desert Island's key lobster piers. See p. 231.

- **The Claremont** (Southwest Harbor; ✆ **800/244-5036** or 207/244-5036): The Claremont is a Maine classic, Victorian-style resort, complete with sparely decorated rooms, creaky floorboards in the halls, great views of water and mountains, and a croquet pitch. See p. 230.

11 THE BEST AFFORDABLE ACCOMMODATIONS

- **Driftwood Inn & Cottages** (Bailey Island; ✆ 207/833-5461): Where else can you find a double room at the edge of the rocky Maine coast starting at around $80? This classic shingled compound dates from 1910 and offers mostly rooms with shared bathrooms, but the views might be worth that inconvenience. See p. 141.
- **Maine Idyll Motor Court** (Freeport; ✆ 207/865-4201): The 1932 Maine Idyll Motor Court is a classic—a cluster of 20 cottages scattered about a grove of beech and oak trees. Each cottage has a tiny porch, wood-burning fireplace (birch logs provided), TV, fridge, modest kitchen facilities (no ovens), and timeworn furniture. The downside? A little highway noise. Cottages start at $63 for two. See p. 133.

12 THE BEST ALTERNATIVE ACCOMMODATIONS

- **Maine Island Trail:** About 70 remote islands along the Maine coast are open to camping, and from these remote, salty wildernesses, you'll see some of the best sunsets imaginable. See "Outdoor Activities," in chapter 3, for an introduction.
- **Windjammers** (Midcoast and Downeast Maine): Maine has the East Coast's largest fleet of windjammers, offering adventures on the high seas throughout the summer. You can explore offshore islands and inland estuaries and learn how sailors once made the best of the wind. Accommodations in private cabins are typically spartan, but you'll spend most of your time on the deck luxuriating in the stunning views. See chapter 8.

13 THE BEST RESTAURANTS

- **Hurricane** (Kennebunkport; ✆ 207/967-1111): Talented chef Brooks Mac-Donald's restaurant emphasizes local seafood and lobster with a creative flair right in Kennebunkport's Dock Square. See p. 103.
- **White Barn Inn** (Kennebunkport; ✆ 207/967-2321): The setting, in an ancient, rustic barn, is magical. The tables are draped with floor-length tablecloths, and the chairs feature Italian upholstery. The menu—and the decor—changes seasonally, but is always top-notch. See p. 104.
- **Fore Street** (Portland; ✆ 207/775-2717): Fore Street is one of New England's most celebrated restaurants, and has been previously selected as one of *Gourmet* magazine's 100 best restaurants in the U.S. Chef Sam Hayward has been getting lots of press. His secret? Simplicity: Some of the most memorable meals are prepared over an applewood grill. See p. 111.
- **Primo** (Rockland; ✆ 207/596-0770): Melissa Kelly and Price Kushner create culinary magic on two floors of a century-old home at this winning Rockland

bistro. Expect fancy treatments of foie gras, scallops, duck, steak, and more; outstanding desserts; and a long, impressive wine list. See p. 161.

14 THE BEST LOCAL DINING EXPERIENCES

- **Becky's** (Portland; © 207/773-7070): Five different kinds of home fries on the menu? It's breakfast nirvana at this local institution right on Portland's working waterfront. This is *the* favored hangout of Portland's fishermen, not to mention high school kids, businessmen, and lots of other folks. See p. 114.
- **Silly's** (Portland; © 207/772-0360): Hectic and fun, this tiny, kitschy restaurant serves up delicious finger food in a no-frills setting. Expect pita wraps, thick burgers, kabobs, hamburgers, and pizzas, among many other things. The milkshakes alone are worth the detour. See p. 116.
- **Dolphin Chowder House** (South Harpswell; © 207/833-6000): The fish chowder and lobster stew are so reasonably priced and delicious at this hidden spot—which is part of a marina at the very end of a dead-end road—that you'll want to find it. Blueberry muffins come with most meals. See p. 142.
- **Thurston's Lobster Pound** (Bernard; © 207/244-7600): It doesn't get much more local than this eatery, perched on stilts right above the lobster boats with atmospheric views on the so-called "quiet side" of Mount Desert Island. Choose your lobster from the tank at the counter, plus sides of corn on the cob, steamed clams, blueberry cake, and beer, then join the happy crowds either upstairs or down. See p. 234.

15 THE BEST DESTINATIONS FOR SHOPPERS

- **Kittery:** There are tons of outlets on Route 1 of this otherwise sleepy hamlet; you're bound to find something good at a low price at Crate & Barrel, Coach, Seiko, Gap, or wherever. See chapter 5.
- **Portland:** A city this size really ought to have more shops than it does—the Old Port, the chief shopping district, is in serious danger of becoming a bit too precious, and is pretty small—but you can still find great little boutiques and shops if you look hard enough. See chapter 6.
- **Freeport:** L.L.Bean is the anchor store for this thriving town of outlets, but you'll also find places such as Patagonia, J. Crew, Dansk, Brooks Brothers, and about 100 others. This is somehow among the most aesthetically pleasing of the outlet centers scattered around northern New England. See chapter 7.
- **Portsmouth, New Hampshire:** Downtown Portsmouth offers a grab bag of small, eclectic shops ranging from funky shoe, vintage, and toy shops to classy art galleries. The downtown is small enough to browse on foot, and you'll find a broad assortment of stuff for sale appealing to almost any taste. See chapter 11.

The Maine Coast In Depth

Boiled down to its simplest facts, the Maine coast basically consists of two regions: southern Maine—"down there," also sometimes referred to as "Vacationland" or "not Maine")—and Downeast—"up there" or "the real Maine." The two regions are as different as night and day; broadly speaking, the gourmet cuisine, fine cars, and luxury inns of the south coast gradually (and then quickly) give way to cottages, used cars tacked together with duct tape, and fried fish.

Maine's legendary aloofness is important to keep in mind when visiting the area, because getting to know the region requires equal amounts of patience and persistence. New England doesn't wear its attractions on its sleeve. It keeps its best destinations hidden in valleys and on the side streets of small villages. Your most memorable experience might be cracking open a boiled lobster at a roadside lobster pound marked by a scrawled paper sign, or exploring a cobblestoned alley that's not even on Google Maps. There's no Disneyland or Eiffel Tower here. This coast is, instead, the sum of dozens of smaller attractions and resists being defined by a few big ones.

Of course, the natural elements here—the wind, the soft hazy light, the shining or roiling seas—always seem to have the greatest draw on the traveler, and these elements are as rejuvenating as they are capricious. You're as likely to get a blue-sky day when the islands sparkle like coins in the harbor as you are 3 days of fog and spitting rain or snow. Maybe both in the same week. Attempting to understand this weather—just like trying to explore the coast as a regular tourist, hitting attraction after attraction—is pointless. It's better to just let the mood of each day catch you, cycling or driving a back road in search of something (a byway, an old house, a handmade sign advertising PIES) you've never seen before. Or, if the weather's really nasty, stay inside and do crossword puzzles; paint a watercolor; listen to the Red Sox on the local radio station. *Now* you're getting the real Maine.

Some writers believe Maine's character is still heavily influenced by Calvinism, by such ideas as *nothing can change my fate* and *hard work is the only virtue*. It's hard not to agree, but Mainers aren't completely stone-faced—there are wonderful characters, smiles, and stories to be had in abundance here. And you don't need to expect rock-hard mattresses and tasteless meals, either; as these pages demonstrate, spas, luxurious country inns, and restaurants serving London-class meals have swiftly arrived on the coastal Maine scene (displacing some of the boardinghouses and chowder houses of old). Be sure to visit these places, but also set aside time to spend an afternoon rocking in a chair and on a simple inn porch, or wandering a rocky beach path unhurriedly. You'll be glad you did.

1 THE MAINE COAST TODAY

You might be on Monhegan Island, or traveling downeast along Route 1. You'll see a few houses and a few people. A store. A pickup truck. And you'll wonder, "What do these people do to earn a living, anyway?"

Only a few decades ago, the answer was almost always this: living off the land. They might have fished the ocean, harvested their own woodlots, or managed gravel pits, but *work* here usually fell into a category that was awfully close to that of *survival.* Of course, many still do three jobs, but hardscrabble work is no longer the only game in town. Today a coastal Mainer just as likely might have once been a former editor for the *New Yorker,* a farmer who grows organic produce for gourmet restaurants, or a financial consultant who handles his clients by fax and e-mail. And you'll find *lots* of folks whose livelihood is dependent on tourism, whether it's the lone tour guide, the high school kid working the local T-shirt shop, or the tow-truck driver hauling fancy cars around Mount Desert Island after they break down. There's a lot of trickledown at work here.

This slow change in the economy is but one of the big shifts facing Maine and New England. The most visible and wracking change involves development and growth; for a region long familiar with poverty, a spell of recent prosperity and escalating property values has threatened to bring to Maine that curious homogenization already marking suburbs in the rest of the nation. Once a region of distinctive villages, green commons, and courthouse squares, coastal Maine is just starting to resemble suburbs everywhere else in a few places—a pastiche of strip malls dotted with fast-food chains, big-box discount and home-improvement stores, and the like.

While undeniably convenient, this is nothing short of shocking to longtime residents. Coastal towns have long maintained their identities in the face of considerable pressure. The region has always taken pride in its low-key, practical approach to life. In smaller communities, town meetings are still the preferred form of government. Residents gather in a public space to speak out about—sometimes forcefully—and vote on the issues of the day, such as

funding for their schools, road improvements, fire trucks, or even symbolic gestures such as declaring their towns nuclear-free. "Use it up, wear it out, make do, or do without" is a well-worn phrase that aptly sums up the attitude of many longtime Mainers—and it's the polar opposite of the designer-outlet ethos filtering in.

It's not clear how town meetings and that sense of knowing where your town ends and the next one begins will survive the slow but inexorable encroachment of Wal-Mart and Banana Republic in places like a mall-heavy area outside Portland, the shopping outlets of Kittery and Freeport, and the conglomeration of U.S. Route 1 near Bucksport and Ellsworth. In these spots, little regional identity can be found.

Meanwhile, the rest of coastal Maine is figuring out how best to balance the principles of growth and conservation—how to allow the economy to edge into the modern age without sacrificing those qualities that make Maine such a distinctive place. Development is a hot issue, but it isn't white-hot—yet. Few locals feel that development should be allowed at all costs. And few locals tend to think that the land should be preserved at all costs, either. They're not all that happy about rising property taxes and land prices—unless they happen to own a chunk of the coast, in which case they're probably putting up the FOR SALE signs as we speak.

Pinching off all development would mean that the offspring of longtime Maine families will have no jobs, and that Maine would be fated to spend its days as a sort of quaint theme park. But if development continued unabated, many of the characteristics that make this place unique—and attract tourist dollars—would vanish. Will the Maine coast be able to sustain its tourism industry if it's blanketed with strip malls and fast-food joints, making it look like every other town in America? Unlikely. The question is how to respect the conservation ethic while leaving room for growth,

Local Wisdom

Welcome to Vacationland

—former Maine state motto

Maine: The Way Life Should Be

—former Maine state motto

but that question won't be answered anytime soon.

Complicating things, Maine's economy has been quixotic, with tourism on the uptick but in no way growing steadily. The mid-1990s saw a slump, and things have been flat of late; even when the economy nosed back downward, however, resourceful locals somehow found a way to buy and fix up farmhouses and keep their pickup trucks and dogs happy. Turn over a few stones, and it's remarkable how many self-owned enterprises you'll find along this coast.

One change is all but inevitable: Property values will continue to rise as city folks increasingly seek a piece of whatever it is that makes rural Maine special. Commentators believe this change, while welcome after decades of slow growth, will bring new conflicts. The continuing rise of an information culture will make it increasingly likely that telecommuters and info-entrepreneurs will move in and settle the coast's most pristine villages, running their businesses via modem or satellite. How will these affluent newcomers feel about increased coastal development or increasing numbers of tour buses cruising their quaint harborside streets? How will locals respond to all the new money—with envy, or with open arms? And how much will the state's priceless natural resources become stressed by increased tourism or development?

Change doesn't come rapidly to the Maine coast. But there's a lot to sort out, and friction will certainly continue to build, one waterfront condo at a time. One thing is for sure: It will be interesting to see how it plays out.

2 LOOKING BACK AT MAINE

Viewed from a distance, Maine's history mirrors that of its progenitor, England. This coastline rose from a sparsely populated, inhospitable place to a place of tremendous historical importance in a relatively short time, thanks to its tremendous natural resources (such as white pine trees for ship's masts, and endless schools of fish that could be caught offshore). For a time, Maine captured a good deal of America's overseas trade and became a legitimate world industrial and marine powerhouse—not to mention a center of literary and creative thought and even fine art.

Don't believe me? That's because the party ended almost as suddenly as it began, when commerce and culture sought more fertile grounds to the west and south.

To this day, Maine refuses to separate itself from the past. When you walk through downtown Portland, layers of history pile up at every turn: modern buses and punk-rock wannabes crouching before fine church steeples dating from colonial times; oceanview parks; elaborate mansions by world-class architects that speak to the refined sensibilities of the late Victorian era.

This history is even more inescapable as you proceed up the coast and off the beaten track. Travelers in Downeast Maine—an overlooked, economically depressed area today—can still find clues to what Henry Wadsworth Longfellow called "the irrevocable past" in everything from the stone walls running through the woods to the handsome Federal-style homes once built by wealthy merchants.

Here's a brief overview of some historical episodes and trends that have shaped coastal Maine:

INDIGENOUS CULTURE Native Americans have inhabited Maine since about 7000 B.C. The state was inhabited chiefly by Algonquins and Abenakis, who lived a nomadic life of fishing, trapping, and hunting; they changed camp locations several times each year to take advantage of seasonal fish runs, wildlife movements, and the like.

After the arrival of the Europeans, French Catholic missionaries succeeded in converting many Native Americans, and most tribes sided with the French in the French and Indian War in the 18th century. Afterward, the Indians fared poorly at the hands of the British and were quickly pushed to the margins. Today they are found in greatest concentration at several reservations in Downeast Maine. Other than that, the few remnants left behind by Indian cultures have been more or less obliterated by later settlers.

THE COLONIES In 1604, some 80 French colonists spent winter on a small island on what today is the Maine–New Brunswick border. They did not care for the harsh weather of their new home and left in spring to resettle in present-day Nova Scotia. In 1607, 3 months after the celebrated Jamestown, Virginia, colony was founded, a group of 100 English settlers established a community at Popham Beach, Maine. The Maine winter demoralized these would-be colonists, as well,

and they returned to England the following year.

The colonization of the region began in earnest with the arrival of the Pilgrims at Plymouth Rock in 1620. The Pilgrims—a religious group that had split from the Church of England—established the first permanent colony, although it came at a hefty price: Half the group perished during the first winter. But the colony began to thrive over the years, in part thanks to helpful Native Americans. The success of the Pilgrims lured other settlers from England, who established a constellation of small towns outside Boston that became the Massachusetts Bay Colony. Throughout the 17th century, colonists from Massachusetts pushed northward into what is now Maine (but was once actually part of Massachusetts). The first areas to be settled were lands near protected harbors along the coast and on navigable waterways.

The more remote settlements came under attack in the 17th and early 18th centuries in a series of raids by Native Americans conducted both independently and in concert with the French. These proved temporary setbacks; colonization continued throughout New England into the 18th century.

THE AMERICAN REVOLUTION Starting around 1765, Great Britain launched a series of ham-handed economic policies to reign in the increasingly feisty colonies. These included a direct tax—the Stamp Act—to pay for a standing army. The crackdown provoked strong resistance. Under the banner of "No taxation without representation," disgruntled colonists engaged in a series of riots, resulting in the Boston Massacre of 1770, when five protesting colonists were fired upon and killed by British soldiers.

In 1773 the most infamous protest took place in Boston (and, at the time, Maine was still part of Massachusetts). The British had imposed the Tea Act, which prompted a group of colonists dressed as

American Indians to board three British ships and dump 342 chests of tea into the harbor. This well-known incident was dubbed the Boston Tea Party. Hostilities reached a peak in 1775 when the British sought to quell unrest in Massachusetts. A contingent of British soldiers was sent to seize military supplies and arrest high-profile rebels John Hancock and Samuel Adams. The militia formed by the colonists exchanged gunfire with the British, thereby igniting the revolution ("the shot heard round the world"). Hostilities formally ended in February 1783, and in September Britain recognized the United States as a sovereign nation.

While no notable battles were fought in Maine, a number of forts were established along the coast of Maine—first for the purpose of defending the British from the French, and then for the purpose of defending the new America from, well, the British. Many of these forts remain well preserved today, as state parks.

FARMING & TRADE As the new republic matured, economic growth in New England followed two tracks. Residents of inland communities survived by farming and trading in furs.

On the Maine coast, however, boatyards sprang up anywhere there was a good anchorage, and ship captains made tidy fortunes trading lumber for sugar and rum in the Caribbean. Trade was dealt a severe blow following the Embargo Act of 1807, but commerce eventually recovered, and Maine-ported ships could be encountered everywhere around the globe. Entire towns such as Searsport developed almost solely as exclusive (at the time) hometowns for the sea captains who stayed at sea for long months on these difficult journeys; many of their homes contained distinctive "widow's walks," from which their wives could watch for their returns.

The growth of the railroad in the mid–19th century was another boon. The train opened up much of the coast to trade by

connecting Maine with Boston. The rail lines allowed local resources—such as timber from the Maine woods, floated downriver to the coast via log drives—to be much more easily shipped to markets to the south.

INDUSTRY Maine's Industrial Revolution found seed around the time of the embargo of 1807. Barred from importing English fabrics, New Englanders simply pulled up their bootstraps and built their own textile mills. Other common household products were also manufactured domestically, especially shoes. Coastal towns such as Biddeford, Saco, and Topsham became centers of textile and shoe production. Today, however, industry no longer plays the prominent role it once did—manufacturing first moved to the South, then overseas.

TOURISM In the mid- and late 19th century, Mainers discovered a new cash crop: the tourist. All along the eastern seaboard, it became fashionable for the gentry and eventually the working class to set out for excursions to the mountains and the shore. Aided by the dramatic paintings of the Hudson River School painters, Acadia and the downeast coast were suddenly lifted by a tide of summer visitors; this tourism wave crested in the 1890s in Bar Harbor. Several grand resort hotels from tourism's golden era still host summer travelers in the area.

ECONOMIC DOWNTURN While the railways helped Maine to thrive in the mid–19th century, the train played an equally central role in undermining its prosperity. The driving of the Golden Spike in 1869 in Utah, linking America's Atlantic and Pacific coasts by rail, was heard loud and clear in Maine, and it had a discordant ring. Transcontinental rail meant manufacturers could ship goods from the fertile Great Plains and California to faraway markets; the coastal shipping trade was dealt a fatal blow. And the tourists, too, began to set their sights on the suddenly accessible Rockies and other stirring sites in the West.

Beginning in the late 19th century, Maine lapsed into an extended economic slumber. Families commonly walked away from their farmhouses (there was no market for resale) and set off for regions with more promising opportunities. The abandoned, decaying farmhouse became almost an icon for the Maine coast, and vast tracts of farmland were reclaimed by forest. With the rise of the automobile, the grand resorts further succumbed, and many closed their doors as inexpensive motels siphoned off their business.

BOOM TIMES   During the last 2 decades of the 20th century, much of Maine rode an unexpected wave of prosperity. A massive real-estate boom shook the region in the 1980s, driving land prices sky-high as prosperous buyers from New York and Boston acquired vacation homes or retired to the most alluring areas. In the 1990s, the rise of the high-tech industry also sent ripples from Boston north into Maine. Tourism rebounded as harried urbanites of the eastern seaboard opted for shorter, more frequent vacations closer to home.

Travelers to more remote regions, however, will discover that some communities never benefited from this boom; they're still waiting to rebound from the economic downturn earlier in the 20th century. Especially hard hit have been places such as Downeast Maine, where many residents still depend on local resources—lobsters, fish, farmland, maybe a bed-and-breakfast or crafts business on the side—to eke out a living. And, remarkably, it still works.

3 COASTAL MAINE ART & ARCHITECTURE

ARCHITECTURE   You can often trace the evolution of a place by its architecture, as styles evolve from basic structures to elaborate mansions. The primer below should help you with basic identification.

- **Colonial** (1600–1700): The New England house of the 17th century was a simple, boxy affair, often covered in shingles or rough clapboards. Don't look for ornamentation; these homes were designed for basic shelter from the elements, and are often marked by prominent stone chimneys.
- **Georgian** (1700–1800): Ornamentation comes into play in the Georgian style, which draws heavily on classical symmetry. Georgian buildings were in vogue in England at the time, and were embraced by affluent colonists. Look for Palladian windows, formal pilasters, and elaborate projecting pediments. Portsmouth, New Hampshire, has abundant examples of later Georgian styles.
- **Federal** (1780–1820): Federal homes (sometimes called Adams homes) may best represent the New England ideal. Spacious yet austere, they are often rectangular or square, with low-pitched roofs and little ornament on the front, although carved swags or other embellishments are frequently seen near the roofline. Look for fan windows and chimneys bracketing the building. In Maine, excellent Federal-style homes are found throughout the region in towns such as Kennebunkport, Bath, and Brunswick.
- **Greek Revival** (1820–60): The most easy-to-identify Greek Revival homes feature a projecting portico with massive columns, like a part of the Parthenon grafted onto an existing home. The less dramatic homes may simply be oriented such that the gable faces the street, accenting the triangular pediment. Greek Revival didn't catch on in

New England the way it did in the South, however.

- **Carpenter Gothic and Gothic Revival** (1840–80): The second half of the 19th century brought a wave of Gothic Revival homes, which borrowed their aesthetic from the English country home.

- **Victorian** (1860–1900): This is a catch-all term for the jumble of mid- to late-19th-century styles that emphasized complexity and opulence. Perhaps the best-known Victorian style—almost a caricature—is the tall and narrow Addams Family–style house, with mansard roof and prickly roof cresting. You'll find these scattered throughout the region. The Victorian style also includes squarish **Italianate** homes with wide eaves and unusual flourishes, such as the outstanding Victoria Mansion in Portland.

- Stretching the definition a bit, Victorian can also include the **Richardsonian Romanesque** style, which was popular for railroad stations and public buildings.

- **Shingle** (1880–1900): This uniquely New England style quickly became preferred for vacation homes on the Maine coast. They're marked by a profusion of gables, roofs, and porches, and are typically covered with shingles from roofline to foundation.

- **Modern** (1900–present): Maine has produced little in the way of notable modern architecture; you won't find a Fallingwater (one of Frank Lloyd Wright's best-known works, near Pittsburgh), though you might spy a surprising modernist building somewhere on an enclave of wealth such as Mount Desert Island or Cape Elizabeth—if you can get past the security.

ART New England is also justly famous for the **art** it has produced, particularly the seascapes painted on Cape Cod, along the coast of Maine, and by **Hudson River School** artists such as Thomas Cole and his student Frederic Church. Some of the other artists who have memorably painted New England landscapes and seascapes include **Winslow Homer** (1836–1910), **Fairfield Porter** (1907–75), **John Marin** (1870–1953), **Neil Welliver** (1929–2005), and **Andrew Wyeth** (born 1917), he of the iconic *Christina's World,* painted in a coastal Maine field.

To showcase these works, and the works of other local and traveling artists, there are a surprising number of excellent art museums and galleries in Maine. Consult the individual chapters for more details on local art offerings.

4 COASTAL MAINE IN POPULAR CULTURE

BOOKS Mainers have generated whole libraries, from the earliest days of hellfire-and-brimstone Puritan sermons to Stephen King's horror novels set in fictional Maine villages.

The tales of Bowdoin graduate **Nathaniel Hawthorne** (1804–64) captivated a public eager for native literature. His most famous story, *The Scarlet Letter,* is a narrative about morality set in 17th-century Boston, but he wrote numerous other books that wrestled with themes of sin and guilt, often set in the emerging republic.

Henry Wadsworth Longfellow (1807–82), the Portland poet who settled in Cambridge (another Bowdoin man), caught the attention of the public with evocative narrative poems focusing on distinctly American subjects. His popular works included "The Courtship of Miles Standish," "Paul Revere's Ride," and "Hiawatha." Poetry in the mid–19th century was the equivalent of Hollywood movies today—Longfellow could be considered his generation's Steven Spielberg (apologies to literary scholars).

Thoreau's *The Maine Woods* explored Maine (although not the coast) in detail, at a time when few white men had yet penetrated the interior of the state—and there were still significant dangers involved in doing that. His canoe trip to Katahdin was a genuine adventure.

Other regional writers who left a lasting mark on American literature include **Edna St. Vincent Millay** (1892–1950), a poet from Camden, and **Sarah Orne Jewett** (1849–1909), who wrote the indelible *The Country of the Pointed Firs.* The best-selling *Uncle Tom's Cabin,* the book Abraham Lincoln half-jokingly accused of starting the Civil War, was written by **Harriet Beecher Stowe** (1811–86) while in Brunswick.

And the former *New Yorker* scribe **E. B. White** (1899–1985) wrote many fine, wide-ranging essays and books (including children's books such as the classic *Charlotte's Web*) about rural Maine from his perch in North Brooklin, near Blue Hill, where he moved in 1939.

Finally, Maine is still the home of **Stephen King,** who is considered not so much a novelist as Maine's leading industry.

FILM & TV   Maine is frequently captured through the lens of Hollywood, thanks in equal parts to its natural beauty and, probably, the unusually high numbers of actors and actresses (John Travolta, for example) who maintain vacation homes here.

Lillian Gish's 1920 silent film ***Way Down East*** was perhaps the first movie to bring cinematic attention to the region. A host of horror films written by Maine's **Stephen King**—from *Carrie, Cujo,* and *The Dead Zone* down through to a welter of TV miniseries—make it sometimes seem like the only inhabitants of small New England towns are ghosts, creeps, and other supernatural forces. However, King also penned the short story upon which the wonderful Morgan Freeman–Tim Robbins-starring flick, ***The Shawshank Redemption*** (one of my all-time favorites), was later based. The story and film are both based in Maine, though the prison and events are completely fictional.

Several television series have been based in coastal Maine, most memorably ***Murder, She Wrote*** (1984–96), which saw crime novelist Angela Lansbury stumbling across and solving real-life crimes with seeming ease from fictional Cabot Cove.

5 EATING & DRINKING ON THE MAINE COAST

All along the coast you'll be tempted by seafood in its various forms. You can get fried clams by the bucket at divey shacks along remote coves and busy highways. The more upscale restaurants offer fresh fish, grilled or gently sautéed.

Live lobster can be bought literally off the boat at lobster pounds, especially along the Maine coast. The setting is usually rustic—maybe a couple of picnic tables and a shed where huge vats of water are kept at a low boil.

In summer small farmers set up stands at the end of their driveways offering fresh produce straight from the garden. You can usually find berries, fruits, and sometimes home-baked breads. These stands are rarely tended; just leave your money in the coffee can.

Restaurateurs haven't overlooked New England's bounty. Many chefs serve up delicious meals consisting of local ingredients—some places even tend their own gardens. Some of the fine dishes I've enjoyed while researching this guide include curried pumpkin soup, venison medallions with shiitake mushrooms, and wild boar with juniper berries.

But you don't have to have a hefty budget to enjoy the local foods. A number of regional classics fall into the "road food" category. Here's an abbreviated field guide:

- **Baked beans:** Boston is forever linked with baked beans (hence the nickname "Beantown"), but they remain amazingly popular in Maine. A local Saturday-night church supper on the coast often consists of just baked beans and brown bread at "bean hole" suppers featuring the food. There's also a famous B&M baked-bean plant in Portland.
- **Lobster rolls:** Lobster rolls consist of some pretty basic fixings: fresh lobster meat plucked from the shell, mixed with just enough mayonnaise to hold it together, and served on a hot-dog roll (preferably grilled in butter). There are fancier permutations in touristy areas, with stuff such as celery and onions mixed in, but you want this basic version: it's meatier and more succulent. You'll find the rolls almost everywhere along the Maine coast; expect to pay between $9 and $15 per roll (more in lean lobster-harvest years). One of the meatiest in Maine is served at Red's Eats, a hot-dog stand by the side of the road in downtown Wiscasset. For info on where to find some of the best *boiled* lobsters off the pier, see the box "Pier, Beer & Lobster," on p. 21).
- **Moxie:** It's hard to imagine it now, but early in the 20th century, the Maine-made soft drink Moxie outsold

Coca-Cola. Part of its allure was the fanciful story behind its 1885 creation: A traveler named Moxie was said to have observed South American Indians consuming the sap of a native plant, which gave them extraordinary strength. The drink was then helpfully "re-created" by Maine native Dr. Augustin Thompson. It's still very, very popular among old-timers in Maine, although some others say it tastes worse than cough medicine. Think Coke plus quinine, minus any sweetener.

- **Wild Maine blueberries:** You sometimes get the feeling, traveling in Downeast Maine, that the entire state's economy would implode if anything ever happened to the blueberry crop; it's grown and harvested (and added to recipes) everywhere in these parts. Look for roadside stands and diners advertising pies made with fresh berries in mid- to late summer. Also note that the tiny wild blueberries (which grow on low shrubs, often on wind-swept rocks or hilltops) are tastier than the bigger, commercially grown high-bush variety you're probably familiar with.

Finally, no survey of Maine foods would be complete without a mention of the local beer. Maine *alone* probably has more microbreweries than any other *region* in the U.S. except for the Pacific Northwest. Popular brewpubs to hit include Federal Jack's Brewpub (Kennebunkport); the Sea Dog Brewing Co. (now located in Topsham, originally in Camden); and Portland's clutch of terrific mini-breweries—at least a half-dozen, at last count, all making mighty good beer.

6 LIGHTHOUSES: A TOUR UP THE COAST

Unlike its neighbor Nova Scotia, Canada, Maine doesn't maintain, advertise, or market a "Lighthouse Trail"—but it might be a good idea to cobble one together, because

this state has quietly assembled some of the best lighthouses in the U.S. Most were built of stone in the early to mid–19th century, and nearly all were automated in

(Moments) Pier, Beer & Lobster

The best lobster restaurants are those right on the water, where there's no pretension or frills. The ingredients for a proper feed at a local lobster pound are a pot of boiling water, a tank of lobsters, some well-worn picnic tables, a good view, and a six-pack of Maine beer. Among the best on Mount Desert Island is famous **Beal's Lobster Pier** (© 207/244-3202) in Southwest Harbor, one of the oldest pounds in the area. **Thurston's Lobster Pound** (© 207/244-7600) in tiny Bernard (across the water from Bass Harbor) is atmospheric enough to have been used as a backdrop for the Stephen King miniseries *Storm of the Century;* it's a fine place to linger toward dusk, with great water views from the upstairs level. **Abel's Lobster Pound** (© 207/276-5827) on Route 198, 5 miles north of Northeast Harbor, overlooks the deep blue waters of Somes Sound; eat at picnic tables under the pines or indoors at the restaurant. It's quite a bit pricier than other lobster restaurants at first glance, but they don't charge for the extras that many other lobster joints do—and some visitors claim that lobsters here are more succulent. Then there's **Trenton Bridge Lobster Pound** ★ (© 207/667-2977) on Route 3 in Trenton (on the mainland) just before the bridge across to the Island, a personal favorite of mine. It's salty and unpretentious as all get-out. A container of their smoky lobster stew and a slice of homemade blueberry pie make for ideal takeout.

the 1960s or 1970s with very few exceptions. (Today no keepers live full time in any Maine lighthouses.) To see them all, you'd need to drive the coast bottom to top—in other words, follow the chapters of this book in geographical order—and also be in possession of a boat.

Let's forget about the boat for a minute and concentrate on those most easily seen by car; I've sprinkled references to Maine's most visible lighthouses throughout this guidebook, but henceforth, a quick primer on connecting the dots and seeing them one by one, beginning with the southern coast. (*Note:* If you're tacking on a side trip to Portsmouth, New Hampshire—described in greater detail in chapter 11—you've got a shot at even adding a few *more* lighthouses to your "seen-in-lifetime" list. See below for more on those.)

THE SOUTHERN COAST Almost from the moment you cross the state line in Kittery, you're on the scent of our imagined Lighthouse Trail. Make a beeline for Fort McClary, on the back road from Portsmouth to York (Rte. 103); from Portsmouth, simply follow State Street across the bridge to Maine, then turn right at the sign for Route 103. Follow the winding road a few miles to a sharp right-hand bend, and the park's there on the right before you round the bend. From here, you can view squat, gray-granite **Whaleback Light.** It's not much to look at, though a private boat would help you get closer; public access to the lighthouse grounds is not permitted, however.

A few miles north of Kittery, detour off Route 1 to York Beach and head for Long Sands. Here, from the comfort of nothing more than a blanket or beach chair, you can—with good eyes—spy *two* lighthouses at once.

The first one, **Nubble Light** (p. 79), is obvious at the northern end of the beach. It sticks far out on a promontory and is the archetypal Maine light. For a closer look at it, drive to the northern end of the beach and hang a right, then drive the winding cape road to the turnoff for Sohier Park (parking is free). Here, from a rock or bench, you can get almost close enough to the fabled light to touch it—don't try however; a dangerous narrow passage of water separates the viewing area from the rock-bound lighthouse. Snap a photo, then head up the hill for an ice-cream cone at Brown's, again keeping your gaze fixed on the lighthouse as you eat.

The other lighthouse visible from Long Sands, the tall, slim, ghostly **Boon Island light,** demands a perfectly clear day and binoculars or exceptional vision. Gaze out to sea, roughly in the middle of the stretch between both ends of crescent-shaped Long Sands, and its hazy outline may appear to you. Though nearly 10 miles offshore, the granite tower stands more than 13 stories tall—New England's tallest—and that's why it can be seen.

Tiny, wind-swept Boon Island itself has an appropriately murky history: When a British ship ran aground here in 1710, survivors resorted to cannibalism for nearly 3 weeks to survive until a member of the party somehow sailed ashore and fetched help. Author Kenneth Roberts wrote a popular novel, *Boon Island,* fictionalizing parts of this incident. Incredibly, the barren rock and its lighthouse was still inhabited as recently as 1978, when one of the worst winter storms in New England history destroyed all the outbuildings and part of the tower, where the keeper's family cowered for several days awaiting rescue. Soon afterward, it was automated.

It's a bit farther north to the next light. The small **Goat Island Light** lies just off the lovely little hamlet of Cape Porpoise, north of Kennebunkport. (From Dock Sq. in the center of Kennebunkport, follow coastal Rte. 9 about 2¹/₂ miles north and east to find the village.) The light has a

storied history, including its use as a command post for U.S. Secret Service agents defending the family compound of President George H. W. Bush; a keeper who did a 34-year stint of duty on the rock; a caretaker who died in a boating accident in 2002; and Maine's last lighthouse-keeping family, the Culps, who departed the light in 1990 and turned it over to automation and the care of the Kennebunkport Conservation Trust, which maintains the 25-foot tower and keeper's house and plans to restore the property further in the future. Boat visits are welcome.

At the mouth of the Saco River, where the big river enters the Atlantic at the Biddeford-Saco line, the cute little **Wood Island Lighthouse** and its keeper's house still guard this passage—though you'd never know it, as the light's almost impossible to view, except by boat. The light has a rich history, however, including tales of ghosts, murder most foul, and a keeper's dog smart enough to ring bells by himself. The Friends of Wood Island Lighthouse (www.woodislandlighthouse.org) offer summertime boat tours to the island; otherwise, its premises can't be visited by the public.

GREATER PORTLAND Greater Portland contains perhaps the finest—and most visited and photographed—lights on the whole of the Maine coast.

To view **Cape Elizabeth Light,** the southernmost light in the Portland area, head straight for Two Lights State Park (there were previously two working lights here; one was phased out). The light-keeper's home is now privately owned, but this lighthouse has a rich lore, including daring rescues of shipwrecked sailors in the boiling, stormy sea and the work of painter Edward Hopper, who featured the light in several early-20th-century paintings. It is still an important signal on this rocky part of the coast. If you're hungry after viewing it, be sure to drop by the outstanding Two Lights Lobster Shack (see the sidebar "Lucky 77: Hitting the Beaches," in chapter 6) for a bite, and also visit the small souvenir shack on the rocks.

Just to the north, **Portland Head Light** (p. 118) possesses lovely proportions, an 80-foot beveled tower, a handsome keeper's home (now a small museum), and a scenic position on a cliff before the horizon and the Atlantic. This is one of the very best lighthouses in Maine to view with the family—and one of the most popular and often photographed, as well. (Don't come here for solitude.) Hundreds of thousands of visitors come each year to the free park from which it can be viewed, just off Shore Road in Cape Elizabeth. There's also a gift shop.

From Portland Head Light, you can get a very good view of another lighthouse just offshore: the often-overlooked (probably due to its crude looks) **Ram Island Light,** built of Maine granite in 1905.

Next up, reachable by following South Portland's Broadway to its end, is the **Spring Point Light,** an amusingly shaped light that somewhat resembles a fire hydrant. But take it seriously: It guards the heavily trafficked passage between Portland Harbor and the so-called Calendar Islands, a passage critical to oil and freight transport into and out of Maine. The light is set out at the end of the narrow stone breakwater, and can be walked up to and viewed but not entered except during special open houses held periodically, when you may view the keeper's room, which is slowly being outfitted with period furnishings. There's a museum, the Portland Harbor Museum (© **207/799-6337**), on the land side of the breakwater with plenty more information about the area. The light is also adjacent to both the pretty campus of Southern Maine Community College and the ruins of Fort Preble, good places for a picnic and a walk.

Nearby around the point, the Portland Breakwater Light—locally known as **"Bug Light"**—is a smaller, squatter version of the Spring Point light sitting on land that was once an important shipbuilding complex. A small, free city park surrounds the light.

FREEPORT TO MIDCOAST From either Bath or South Freeport, you can take a boat tour to view the attractive high rock housing **Seguin Island Light** a few miles off Popham Beach. Contact Atlantic Seal Cruises (© **207/865-6112**), which runs twice-weekly tours in summertime, or the Maine Maritime Museum (© **207/443-1316**), which offers periodic cruises past the light. Due to the heavy fogs that frequently move into this area, the house sports Maine's strongest (and most valuable) lens; it's 12 feet high, and has been operating since 1857, the same year the keeper's home and stone light tower were also constructed.

Smaller, weaker **Pond Island Light, Cuckolds Light,** the **Perkins Island Light, Ram Island Light,** and the mainland-based **Squirrel Point Light** are all located in the same general vicinity as Seguin, and they can also be viewed during the Maine Maritime Museum's cruises or during other charter runs from the Boothbay Harbor waterfront. Squirrel Point's light can also be hiked to via a rough trail that begins off Bald Head Road in Arrowsic.

Also in Arrowsic, some of **Doubling Point Light**'s grounds are free to roam—reach it by crossing the huge bridge from Bath, making an immediate right onto Route 127 south, and following signs to the Doubling Point Road turnoff on the right. The light is connected to the keeper's quarters by a long causeway, which is closed to the public. Two small related lights, known as the **Range Lights,** are housed in octagonal wooden towers near the Doubling Point grounds; these lighthouse grounds are also free to visit, and the towers are architecturally singular on the coast, though unsigned and a bit difficult to find. Once again, the Maine Maritime Museum's special lighthouse cruises often pass by this set of lights.

From the Boothbay Harbor pier, it's easy to visit the handsome **Burnt Island Light** and its attractive complex of outbuildings: Catch an excursion from the pier, then settle in for one of the twice-daily summertime tours. Plan ahead, however; the tours take 2 to 3 hours apiece. Now owned by the state of Maine, the complex, still active as a navigational aid, is also home to a program of nature, arts, and even music courses—a real success story.

Before leaving Boothbay Harbor, you may wish to detour down the long peninsula to West Southport (take Rte. 27 to the turnoff for the village) to get a view of offshore **Hendricks Head Light,** now privately owned and beautifully restored.

Finally, there's the **Pemaquid Point** (in Bristol) and its museum and the **Marshall Point Lighthouse** (in Port Clyde) and its museum, both of which I describe in greater detail in chapter 7; and, offshore, there's the **Monhegan Island Light** and *its* museum (open July–Sept; ✆ 207/596-7003), which I haven't mentioned. But it's well worth a look if you're out on the island, and makes a fine, fitting end to this section of our ad hoc lighthouse trail.

PENOBSCOT BAY The Midcoast region harbors plenty of lights, though many are small and posted on offshore rocks, thus inaccessible (and unviewable) by car. However, the squat **Owls Head Light,** now owned by the Coast Guard and still active, sits on a promontory in Knox County Lighthouse Park (✆ 207/941-4014); it can be viewed by anyone who can wrangle a parking spot in the lot. (The light itself, of course, is off-limits.) Interestingly, there's a long walkway and set of stairs connecting the keeper's house to the actual light, making this one of the most visually pleasing of all Maine's lighthouses.

The southernmost light of the two in the city of Rockland is known as **Rockland Harbor Southwest Light,** and this light is fascinating: It's the only one in Maine that was built by a private citizen. A local dentist constructed the light as both an aid to ships and a kind of homage to the other Rockland light (see below), and it began blinking on and off in 1987; today it's an official navigational light and still privately held. From downtown Rockland, head south about 2 miles on Route 73 and hang a left onto North Shore Road.

The **Rockland Breakwater Light** is at the northern edge of the harbor, sitting atop a handsome brick home about a mile out on a rugged stone breakwater; it's easily viewed from the Samoset resort complex (see "Where to Stay," in chapter 8), but the grounds are only open to the public during summer weekends.

Rockport's Marine Park is a good spot to look out at the attractive keeper's house and its **Indian Island Light;** however, the light itself no longer functions. Just north in Camden, the **Curtis Island Light** is quite attractive—it sits on a private island, now owned by the city—but can only really be seen well from the deck of a sightseeing charter or windjammer cruise leaving from the harbor.

Again just north, in Lincolnville, stand on the ferry dock for a look at the **Grindle Point Light,** with its unusual squarish light tower—or, better yet, hop the ferry for an up-close look; it docks on Islesboro nearly beside the lighthouse. The light is part of a public park that includes a small museum built as a memorial to sailors.

Continuing north, pull off Route 1 at signs for Stockton Springs if you want a look at the tiny **Fort Point Light,** still active and now a state historic site. It's not the most impressive of the state's lights, however.

Castine is already attractive enough, but the presence of the **Dice Head Light** makes it even more so; the light, privately owned and resided in, features an unusual rough, conical stone tower (though the actual light is no longer atop this interesting structure). Simply follow Route 166 to its very end at the water for a look. Do not approach the tower, however; it's private property.

There are three lighthouses on or just offshore Deer Isle, but one is no longer active and the other two can only be seen from a boat cruising off the island's back shore.

Finally, the **Robison Point Light** on Isle au Haut is accessible to the public—in fact, this is the only lighthouse in Maine where you can sleep in the keeper's house (May–Oct). Contact the Keeper's House (© **207/460-0257;** www.keepershouse. com) for current rates and availability; there's no phone and no electricity, but the owners will prepare a gourmet meal for you if you wish.

MOUNT DESERT ISLAND & DOWN-EAST Mount Desert Island and its surrounding islands are home to very few lights that can be visited or viewed by the public. One that can is the **Bass Harbor Head Light,** on Mount Desert's western lobe, down Route 102A past Southwest Harbor. The complex includes a cylindrical light tower, simple keeper's house, triangular fog signal, and even a barn.

From Bass Harbor, head for another light that can be visited by the public: the **Burnt Coat Harbor Light** (also known as Hockamock Head Light). To get here, however, you'll need to catch a ferry from Bass Harbor to Swan's Island. The squared brick tower and keeper's home were built in 1872.

The downeast section of the Maine coast is rife with little ledges and lighthouses, often steeped in fog and usually off-limits to the public (and too far offshore or too indistinct to be seen anyway). The inactive **Winter Harbor Light** can be glimpsed from the Schoodic Peninsula loop road, although distantly.

The slim stone tower of the **Petit Manan Light** near Milbridge pokes an impressive 120 feet above the surrounding sea. However, it's off-limits and difficult to see anyway. You can get a better look at it while taking a tour of the Maine Coastal Islands National Wildlife Refuge (see "What to See & Do" in chapter 10).

Finally, the **West Quoddy Head Light** in Lubec is part of the state park of the same name I've described in chapter 10. This is America's easternmost point, and there's a museum on the lighthouse grounds, open daily from spring through Columbus Day. Check it out, then sit awhile to reflect on all you've seen on your lighthouse tour.

A LITTLE SOMETHING EXTRA If you decide to begin your Maine coasting in Portsmouth, New Hampshire, you can take a side trip to the coast and glimpse a few more lighthouses. The cast-iron **Fort Point Light,** part of the state's Fort Constitution Historic Site (© **603/436-1552),** is located on Route 1B near the Wentworth by the Sea resort described in "Where to Stay" in chapter 11. It can be viewed from the historic site—which is free to enter—from May through October, but can only be entered on one special open-house day each month during that season; check with the park for the open-house dates.

There's also the brick **White Island Light,** offshore in the Isles of Shoals and too far to be seen except when taking a cruise of the islands. Contact the Isle of Shoals Steamship Co. (© **800/441-4620** or 603/431-5500; www.islesofshoals.com) about periodic lighthouse cruises of the area.

For more on Maine's (and New Hampshire's) lighthouses and preservation efforts, contact the **American Lighthouse Foundation,** P.O. Box 565, Rockland, ME 04841 (© **207/594-4174;** www. lighthousefoundation.org).

Planning Your Trip to the Maine Coast

This chapter provides the nuts-and-bolts travel information you'll need before setting off for coastal Maine. Browse through this section before hitting the road to ensure you've touched all the bases.

1 VISITOR INFORMATION

For a comprehensive overview of what's what in the state, contact Maine's state office of tourism (© **888/624-6345;** www.visitmaine.com).

For local and regional information, chambers-of-commerce addresses and phone numbers are provided for each region in the chapters that follow. If you're a highly organized traveler, you'll call in advance and ask for information to be mailed to you long before you depart. (If you're like the rest of us, you'll swing by when you reach town and hope the office is still open.)

2 ENTRY REQUIREMENTS

PASSPORTS

New regulations issued by the Department of Homeland Security now require virtually every air traveler entering the U.S. to show a passport. As of January 23, 2007, all persons, including U.S. citizens, traveling by air between the United States and Canada, Mexico, Central and South America, the Caribbean, and Bermuda are required to present a valid passport. As of January 31, 2008, U.S. and Canadian citizens entering the U. S. at land and sea ports of entry from within the Western Hemisphere will need to present government-issued proof of citizenship, such as a birth certificate, along with a government-issued photo ID, such as a driver's license. A passport is not required for U.S. or Canadian citizens entering by land or sea, but you are highly encouraged to carry one.

For information on how to obtain a passport, see **"Passports"** in the **"Fast Facts"** appendix (p. 286).

VISAS

The U.S. State Department has a **Visa Waiver Program (VWP)** allowing citizens of the following countries to enter the United States without a visa for stays of up to 90 days: Andorra, Australia, Austria, Belgium, Brunei, Denmark, Finland, France, Germany, Iceland, Ireland, Italy, Japan, Liechtenstein, Luxembourg, Monaco, the Netherlands, New Zealand, Norway, Portugal, San Marino, Singapore, Slovenia, Spain, Sweden, Switzerland, and the United Kingdom. (**Note:** This list was accurate at press time; for the most up-to-date list of countries in the VWP, consult www.travel.state.gov/visa.) Canadian citizens may enter the United States without visas; they will need to show passports (if

Destination: Coastal Maine—Red Alert Checklist

- Did you make sure to book advance reservations for popular tours and restaurants you don't want to miss?
- Did you make sure your favorite attractions are open? Especially if you're traveling early or late in the season, you should call ahead for opening and closing hours if you have your heart set on seeing certain places.
- Do you have a safe, accessible place to store money?
- Did you bring identification that could entitle you to discounts, such as AAA and AARP cards, student IDs, and so on?
- Did you bring emergency drug prescriptions and extra glasses and/or contact lenses?
- Do you have your credit card PINs?
- If you have an e-ticket, do you have documentation?
- Did you leave a copy of your itinerary with someone at home?
- If renting a car, have you checked your insurance and credit card policies to see what's covered? You may be able to save money by declining the extra insurance (collision-damage waiver) offered by the rental agency.

traveling by air) and proof of residence, however. *Note:* Any passport issued on or after October 26, 2006, by a VWP country must be an **e-Passport** for VWP travelers to be eligible to enter the U.S. without a visa. Citizens of these nations also need to present a round-trip air or cruise ticket upon arrival. E-Passports contain computer chips capable of storing biometric information, such as the required digital photograph of the holder. (You can identify an e-Passport by the symbol on the bottom center cover of your passport.) If your passport doesn't have this feature, you can still travel without a visa if it is a valid passport issued before October 26, 2005, and includes a machine-readable zone, or between October 26, 2005, and October 25, 2006, and includes a digital photograph. For more information, go to **www.travel.state.gov/visa**.

Citizens of all other countries must have (1) a valid passport that expires at least 6 months later than the scheduled end of their visit to the U.S., and (2) a tourist visa, which may be obtained without charge from any U.S. consulate.

As of January 2004, many international visitors traveling on visas to the United States will be photographed and fingerprinted on arrival at Customs in airports and on cruise ships in a program created by the Department of Homeland Security called **US-VISIT.** Exempt from the extra scrutiny are visitors entering by land or those (mostly in Europe; see p. 26) that don't require a visa for short-term visits. For more information, go to the Homeland Security website at **www.dhs.gov/dhspublic**.

For specifics on how to get a visa, see **"Visas"** in the **"Fast Facts"** appendix (p. 289).

MEDICAL REQUIREMENTS

Unless you're arriving from an area known to be suffering from an epidemic (particularly cholera or yellow fever), inoculations or vaccinations are not required for entry into the United States.

Skipping the Airport Security Lines as a Registered Traveler

In 2003, the **Transportation Security Administration** (**TSA;** www.tsa.gov) approved a pilot program to help ease the time spent in line for airport security screenings. In exchange for information and a fee, persons can be pre-screened as registered travelers, granting them a front-of-the-line position when they fly. The program is run through private firms—the largest and most well-known is Steven Brill's **Clear** (www.flyclear.com), and it works like this: Travelers complete an online application providing specific points of personal information including name, addresses for the previous 5 years, birth date, social security number, driver's license number, and a valid credit card. (You're not charged the **$99 fee** until your application is approved.) Print out the completed form and take it, along with proper ID, with you to an enrollment station. (Enrollment stations can be found in more than 20 participating airports and in a growing number of American Express offices around the country.) It's at this point where it gets seemingly sci-fi. At the enrollment station, a Clear representative will record your biometrics necessary for clearance; in this case, your fingerprints and your irises will be digitally recorded.

When your application has been screened against no-fly lists, outstanding warrants, and other security measures, you'll be issued a clear plastic card that holds a chip containing your information. Each time you fly through participating airports (and the numbers are steadily growing), go to the Clear Pass station located next to the standard TSA screening line. Here you'll insert your card into a slot and place your finger on a scanner to read your print—when the information matches up, you're cleared to cut to the front of the security line. You'll still have to follow all the procedures of the day like removing your shoes and walking through the x-ray machine, but Clear promises to cut 30 minutes off your wait time at the airport.

Each time I've used my Clear Pass, my travel companions are still waiting to go through security while I'm already sitting down, reading the paper, and sipping my overpriced smoothie. Granted, registered traveler programs are not for the infrequent traveler, but for those of us who fly on a regular basis, it's a perk I'm willing to pay for.

—David A. Lytle

CUSTOMS

WHAT YOU CAN BRING INTO THE U.S. Every visitor more than 21 years of age may bring in, free of duty, the following: (1) 1 liter of wine or hard liquor; (2) 200 cigarettes, 100 cigars (but not from Cuba), or 3 pounds of smoking tobacco; and (3) $100 worth of gifts.

These exemptions are offered to travelers who spend at least 72 hours in the United States and who have not claimed them within the preceding 6 months. It is forbidden to bring into the country almost any meat products (including canned, fresh, and dried meat products such as buillion, soup mixes, and so on). Generally, condiments including vinegars, oils, spices, coffee, tea, and some cheeses and baked goods are permitted. Avoid rice products, as rice can often harbor insects. Bringing fruits and vegetables is not advised, though not prohibited. Customs will allow produce depending on where you got it and where you're going after you arrive in the U.S. Foreign tourists may carry in or out up to $10,000 in U.S. or foreign currency with no formalities; larger sums must be declared to U.S. Customs on entering or leaving, which includes filing form CM 4790. For details regarding U.S. Customs and Border Protection, consult your nearest U.S. embassy or consulate, or **U.S. Customs** (www.customs. ustreas.gov).

WHAT YOU CAN TAKE HOME FROM MAINE **Canadian Citizens:** For a clear summary of Canadian rules, write for the booklet *I Declare,* issued by the Canada Border Services Agency (© **800/461-9999**

in Canada, or 204/983-3500; www. cbsa-asfc.gc.ca).

U.K. Citizens: For information, contact **HM Customs & Excise** at © **0845/ 010-9000** (from outside the U.K., 020/ 8929-0152), or consult their website at **www.hmce.gov.uk**.

Australian Citizens: A helpful brochure available from Australian consulates or Customs offices is *Know Before You Go.* For more information, call the **Australian Customs Service** at © **1300/363-263,** or log on to **www.customs.gov.au**.

New Zealand Citizens: Most questions are answered in a free pamphlet available at New Zealand consulates and Customs offices: *New Zealand Customs Guide for Travellers, Notice no. 4.* For more information, contact **New Zealand Customs,** the Customhouse, 17–21 Whitmore St., Box 2218, Wellington (© **04/473-6099** or 0800/428-786; www.customs.govt.nz).

---

3 WHEN TO GO

THE SEASONS

The well-worn joke about the climate in coastal Maine is that it has just two seasons: winter and August. There's a kernel of truth in this, but it's also probably a ploy to keep outsiders from moving here. In fact, the ever-shifting seasons make Maine distinctive, and with one exception, the seasons are well defined.

SUMMER The peak summer season runs from July 4th to Labor Day. Vast crowds surge up the Maine coast during and between the two holiday weekends, swelling traffic on the turnpike and Route 1, and causing countless motels and inns to hang NO VACANCY signs. Expect to pay premium prices at hotels and restaurants along the coast in midseason. This should be no surprise: Summers are exquisite, in spite of the occasional stretches of fog or rain. (In Portland it tops 90°F/32°C only 4 or 5 days a year, on average.)

Maine's coastal weather is largely determined by whatever breezes are prevailing. Southerly winds bring haze, heat, humidity, fog (thick fogs occasionally linger for days), and even thunderstorms. Northwesterly winds bring cool weather and knife-sharp vistas. ('Northeasters' bring wind and storms, though these are rare in summer.) These systems tend to alternate during summer, with the heat arriving stealthily and slowly, then getting exiled by stiff, cool winds a few days later. (The change from hot to cool sometimes occurs in a matter of *minutes*.) Along the immediate coast it's often warmest in the late morning, because sea breezes typically kick up daily around lunchtime, pushing temperatures back down for the rest of the afternoons. Rain is rarely far away—some days it's an afternoon thunderstorm, sometimes it's a steady drizzle that brings a 4-day soaking. On average, about 1 day in

3 will bring at least a little rain. Travelers should come prepared for some.

Also be aware that early summer brings out black flies and mosquitoes in multitudes, a state of affairs that has ruined many a camping and hiking trip. While this is especially true inland, it applies along the coastline and on islands as well. Outdoors enthusiasts are best advised to wait until July 4 or later for long camping-out adventures unless they want to end up resembling human pincushions.

AUTUMN Don't be surprised to sense fall approaching even as early as mid-August, when you'll first notice a few leaves turning orange on the maples at the edges of wetlands. Fall comes early to Maine, puts its feet up on the couch, and hangs around for some time. The foliage season truly begins in earnest in the northern part of the region by the third week in September; in the south, it reaches its peak around mid-October.

Fall is to Maine what the Grand Canyon is to the Southwest. It's one of the great natural spectacles of the place, and when the rolling hills become saturated in brilliant reds and stunning oranges (every year's foliage is different; some years are amazing, others downright dreary), the season is almost garish. Even hardened locals still get dewy-eyed at the sight of the annual colors year after year.

Happily, thanks to Maine's low elevation and the moderating influences of ocean temperatures along the coast, foliage season tends to run even longer along the coast than it does just inland. Maine's mountains can become brown and brittle by mid-October, when coastal foliage is just hitting its stride; sometimes the tart colors even linger into the first few days of November.

Keep in mind that this is also the most popular time of year for *other* travelers, however—bus tours flock like migrating geese to all parts of New England in early October. As a result, hotels are invariably booked solid, and advance reservations are essential. Don't be surprised if you're assessed a foliage surcharge of $10 to $50 per night at some inns. Pay it and be glad you're here.

Maine also maintains a recorded **foliage hot line** and **website** to let you know where and when the leaves are at their brightest peaks. Call © **888/624-6345** for the latest updates, or log onto the state's foliage website at www.maine foliage.com.

WINTER Maine winters are like wine; some years are good, some are lousy. During a good season, mounds of light, fluffy snow blanket the deep woods and fill the ski slopes. A good winter offers a profound peace and tranquillity. The muffling qualities of fresh snow bring a great silence to the region, and the hiss and pop of a wood fire at a country inn can sound like a heavenly symphony. During these winters, exploring the powdery forest floors on snowshoes or cross-country skis is an experience bordering on the magical.

During those *other* winters, though (the lousy ones), the weather gods bring a nasty mélange of rain, freezing rain, and sleet. The woods become filled with dirty crusty snow; the cold is damp and numbing, and the sky seems perpetually cottony and bleak. In 1998, a destructive ice storm wreaked so much havoc on the woods that you can still see evidence (fallen trees) today; more than half of all Maine's homes lost power, for periods up to 2 weeks. During times like this, even the stoutest residents wish they'd been born in the Caribbean.

Things are particularly tricky along the coast during winter; a winter vacation can be spectacular (not much beats cross-country skiing at the edge of the pounding surf), but it's a venture that could as likely yield rain as snow.

Where to go during winter? Beach towns such as York Beach and Ogunquit and tourist destinations such as Boothbay

Harbor shut down almost entirely and become almost depressing in winter. Skip those. Winter visitors are better off heading for places with more substantial year-round communities and a good selection of year-round lodging and cultural attractions, such as Kennebunkport, Portland, and Camden. (A foray inland to Baxter State Park is also a fine idea in a cold clear winter; see chapter 11.)

SPRING Maine's spring seemingly lasts only a weekend or so, often appearing around mid-May but sometimes as late as June. One day the ground is muddy, the trees barren, and gritty snow is still collected in shady hollows. The next day it's in the 70s or 80s, trees are blooming, and kids are jumping off docks into the ocean. Travelers need to be crafty and alert if they

want to experience spring in Maine; it's also known as "mud season" in these parts, and many innkeepers and restaurateurs actually close up shop for a few weeks for repairs or to venture someplace a lot more cheery.

That said, April and May can offer superb days when a blue sky arches overhead and it's warm in the sun. This might be the most peaceful time of year—a good season for taking solitary walks on the beach or sitting on rocky promontories with only seagulls for company. And here's another secret: Maine hotel rooms are never cheaper than they are in springtime. Just be aware that as soon as that sun slips behind a cloud or over the horizon, it'll feel like winter again; don't leave the parka or gloves far behind.

Portland's Average Temperatures

	Jan	Feb	Mar	Apr	May	June	July	Aug	Sept	Oct	Nov	Dec
Avg. High (°F)	31	32	40	50	61	72	76	74	68	58	45	34
(°C)	−1	0	4	10	16	22	24	23	20	14	7	1
Avg. Low (°F)	16	16	27	36	47	54	61	59	52	43	32	22
(°C)	−9	−9	−3	2	8	12	16	15	11	6	0	−6

THE MAINE COAST CALENDAR OF EVENTS

JANUARY

New Year's Portland. Ring in the New Year with a smorgasbord of events and entertainment throughout downtown Portland. Events for families are scheduled in the afternoon; adult entertainment, including loads of live music, kicks off later in the evening at numerous auditoriums, shops, and churches. One admission price buys entrance to all events. December 31 and January 1.

FEBRUARY

U.S. National Toboggan Championships, Camden. A raucous and lively athletic event where being overweight is an advantage. Held at the Camden Snow Bowl's toboggan chute. Call ✆ 207/236-3438. Early February.

MARCH

Maine Boatbuilders' Show, Portland. More than 200 exhibitors and 9,000 boat aficionados gather as winter fades to make plans for the coming summer. A great place to meet boat builders and get ideas for your dream craft. Call ✆ **207/774-1067.** Mid-March.

Maine Maple Sunday. Maple sugarhouses throughout the state open their doors to visitors. Call ✆ **207/287-3491.** Fourth Sunday in March.

APRIL

Boothbay Harbor Fisherman's Festival. Local fishermen display their talents in fish filleting, clam shucking, and even lobster eating. Enjoy seafood feasts, exhibits, games, and a Blessing of

the Fleet on Sunday afternoon. Call
© **207/633-2353.** End of April.

MAY

Annual Fiddlers Contest, Ogunquit.
Rosin up your bow and whip out your
best version of Sally Goodin. Or just
come and listen to others. Call © **207/
646-6170.** Early May.

**Owls Head Spring Auto & Antique
Aeroplane Show,** Owls Head. A combination show gathering hundreds of
antique planes (no trains) and automobiles. Held at the Owls Head Transportation Museum on Route 73. Call
© **207/594-4418.** Late May.

JUNE

Old Port Festival, Portland. A block
party in the heart of Portland's historic
district with live music, food vendors,
and activities for kids. Call © **207/772-
6828.** Early June.

Market Square Weekend, Portsmouth,
N.H. This lively street fair attracts 300
vendors and revelers from throughout
southern New Hampshire and Maine
into downtown Portsmouth to dance,
listen to music, sample food, and enjoy
summer's arrival. Call © **603/436-
3988.** Early June.

Annual Windjammer Days, Boothbay
Harbor. For nearly 4 decades, windjammers have gathered in Boothbay Harbor
to kick off the summer sailing season.
Expect music, food, and a parade of
magnificent sailboats. Call © **207/633-
2353.** Late June.

JULY

Independence Day, regionwide. Communities all along the coast celebrate with
parades, greased-pole climbs, cakewalks,
cookouts, road races, and fireworks.
The bigger the town, the bigger the
fireworks. But many small coastal towns
feature seafood and/or lobster-boat racing, an unusual and fun way to celebrate
the occasion; Eastport's celebration is

particularly impressive (it's 4 days long);
see chapter 10. Check local newspapers
or contact chambers of commerce for
details. July 4.

Summer Performance Series, Portland. Relax and enjoy one of the 50 free
noontime performances in Portland's
downtown parks. Music includes classical, folk, jazz, rock, country, and children's shows. Call © **207/874-8793** for
a complete listing. July and August.

York Days, York Village. Enjoy a quintessential coastal Maine celebration complete with crafts, road races, parades,
dances, concerts, fireworks, and much
more. Call © **207/363-1040.** Late July
to early August.

AUGUST

Maine Lobster Festival, Rockland. Fill
up on the local harvest at this event
marking the importance and delectabil-
ity of Maine's favorite crustacean. Enjoy
a boiled lobster or two, and take in the
ample entertainment during this informal waterfront gala. Call © **800/LOB-
CLAW** (562-2529) or 207/596-0376.
Usually held first week of August.

Wild Blueberry Festival, Machias. A
festival marking the harvest of the
region's wild blueberries. Eat to your
heart's content. Call © **207/794-3543**
or 255-6665. Mid-August.

Blue Hill Fair, Blue Hill. A classic
country fair just outside one of Maine's
most elegant villages. Call © **207/374-
3701.** Late August.

SEPTEMBER

Windjammer Weekend, Camden.
Come visit Maine's impressive fleet of
old-time sailing ships, which host open
houses throughout the weekend at this
scenic harbor. Call © **207/236-4404.**
Labor Day weekend.

Thomas Point Bluegrass Festival,
Brunswick. New England's best roots-
music festival, held at attractive Thomas

Point Beach State Park. Bring your instrument and join a fireside song circle; guests and musicians jam and improvise late into the night. Call ⓒ **207/725-6009.** Early September.

Common Ground Country Fair, Unity. A sprawling, old-time state fair with a twist: The emphasis is on organic foods, recycling, and wholesome living. Call ⓒ **207/568-4142.** Late September.

OCTOBER

Fall Foliage Fair, Boothbay. More than 100 exhibitors display their arts and crafts at the Railroad Village; plenty of festive foodstuffs and live music, too. Call ⓒ **207/633-4727.** Early October.

Mount Desert Island Marathon, Bar Harbor. Scenic 26.2-mile race through gorgeous island scenery. Call ⓒ **207/276-4226** for more information. Mid-October.

Festival of Scarecrows and Harvest Day, Rockland. A local scarecrow-making contest, plus a farmers market and other activities, spread over a 2-week period. Call ⓒ **207/596-6256** for details. Mid-October.

OgunquitFest, Ogunquit. A 3-day pre-Halloween bash, featuring arts, crafts, costumes, and a parade. Call ⓒ **207/646-2939.** Late October.

NOVEMBER

Festival of Lights, Rockland. Horse-drawn carriages, singing, shopping, and open houses of local inns. Call ⓒ **207/596-0376** for details. Late November.

Victorian Holiday, Portland. From late November until Christmas, Portland decorates its Old Port in a Victorian Christmas theme. Enjoy the window displays, take a free hayride, and listen to costumed carolers sing. Call ⓒ **207/772-6828** or 207/780-5555. Late November to Christmas.

DECEMBER

Christmas Prelude, Kennebunkport. This scenic coastal village greets Santa's arrival in a lobster boat, and marks the coming of Christmas with street shows, pancake breakfasts, and tours of the town's splendid inns. Call ⓒ **207/967-0857.** Early December.

Candlelight Stroll, Portsmouth, N.H. Historic Strawbery Banke gets in a Christmas way with old-time decorations and more than 1,000 candles lighting the 10-acre grounds. Call ⓒ **603/433-1100.** First 2 weekends in December.

York Village Festival of Lights. This beautiful festival displays an entire York Village and York Beach lit with Christmas lights, carolers, a parade, and much more. Call ⓒ **207/363-4974.** Early December.

4 GETTING THERE & GETTING AROUND

GETTING TO MAINE

BY PLANE Several commercial carriers serve the coast of Maine, though airlines more commonly connect to Maine's airports after stopping first in New York or Boston; direct connections from other cities, such as Chicago and Philadelphia, are also available. Remember that some of the scheduled flights to Maine from Boston are aboard small propeller-driven ("prop") planes; ask the airline or your travel agent if this is an issue for you.

Portland International Jetport (abbreviation PWM) is Maine's largest airport. Discount airline **JetBlue** (ⓒ **800/538-2583;** www.jetblue.com) offers direct service between Portland and New York City's John F. Kennedy International Airport, with onward connections. The airport is also served by regular flights on

---

(Tips) Flying into Maine: The Skinny

Here's the breakdown of which airlines, at press time, flew into the Maine coast's amalgam of airstrips, airfields, and larger airports (bear in mind that this info changes constantly; check ahead to be sure):

- **Comair,** which is owned by **Delta,** flies out of Bangor, Portland, and Manchester, New Hampshire.
- **Continental** also flies out of Bangor, Portland, and Manchester.
- **JetBlue** flies into Burlington from New York's John F. Kennedy airport.
- **Northwest** flies out of Portland and Manchester.
- **Southwest** flies nonstop to Manchester from numerous destinations, including California and Hawaii.
- **United** flies out of Portland.
- **US Airways** and its subsidiaries fly into Portland, Augusta, Rockland, Bangor, and Bar Harbor.

Continental (© 800/525-0280; www.continental.com), **Delta** (© 800/221-1212; www.delta.com), **Northwest** (800/225-2525; www.nwa.com), **United Express** (© 800/241-6522; www.ual.com), and **US Airways** (© 800/428-4322; www.usair.com). For general airport information, see www.portlandjetport.org, or call © 207/874-8877.

Some savvy visitors to northern New England find cheaper fares and a wider choice of flight times by flying into Boston's Logan Airport, then renting a car or connecting by bus to their final destination. (Boston is about 2 hr. by car from Portland, less than 3 hr. from the White Mountains.)

Travelers who want to try this, however, should remember that Boston's airport can become very congested; delayed flights are endemic; and traffic can be nightmarish (Rte. 1A north toward Maine is one good Logan escape route). Then there's this: Following the September 11, 2001, terrorist attacks (two of the four doomed flights departed from Boston), increased security has led to periodic but massive delays during check-in and screening.

Discount airfares aren't normally available when flying into any of the smaller airports in Maine. One trick, if you're only visiting the southernmost section of coast: instead of Portland, check fares for Manchester, New Hampshire's airport (code: MHT), which has grown in prominence thanks to the arrival of **Southwest Airlines** (© **800/435-9792;** www.southwest.com) and offers competitive, low-cost airfares and good service. Manchester is about 1 hour from York and Kittery, and less than 2 hours from Portland, by car.

Likewise, travelers to far Downeast Maine might check on rates to the Saint John, New Brunswick (airport code: YSJ) airport, about 2 hours from Eastport by car, though it's probably not going to save you much hassle or dough.

For a fuller listing of who flies where, check the "Getting There" information at the beginning of each chapter in this book. Also see my quick-look primer, "Flying into Maine: The Skinny," in the box above.

Arriving at the Airport

IMMIGRATION & CUSTOMS CLEARANCE   Foreign visitors arriving by air, no matter what the port of entry, should cultivate patience and resignation before setting foot on U.S. soil. Clearing immigration control can take as long as 2 hours.

Long-Haul Flights: How to Stay Comfortable

- Your choice of airline and airplane will definitely affect your legroom. Find more details about U.S. airlines at **www.seatguru.com**. For international airlines, the research firm Skytrax has posted a list of average seat pitches at **www.airlinequality.com**.
- Emergency exit seats and bulkhead seats typically have the most legroom. Emergency exit seats are usually left unassigned until the day of a flight (to ensure that someone able-bodied fills the seats); it's worth checking in online at home (if the airline offers that option) or getting to the ticket counter early to snag one of these spots for a long flight. Many passengers find that bulkhead seating offers more legroom, but keep in mind that bulkhead seats have no storage space on the floor in front of you.
- To have two seats for yourself in a three-seat row, try for an aisle seat in a center section toward the back of coach. If you're traveling with a companion, book an aisle and a window seat. Middle seats are usually booked last, so chances are good you'll end up with three seats to yourselves. And in the event that a third passenger is assigned the middle seat, he or she will probably be more than happy to trade for a window or an aisle.
- To sleep, avoid the last row of any section or the row in front of an emergency exit, as these seats are the least likely to recline. Avoid seats near highly trafficked toilet areas. Avoid seats in the back of many jets—these can be narrower than those in the rest of coach. Or reserve a window seat so you can rest your head and avoid being bumped in the aisle.
- Get up, walk around, and stretch every 60 to 90 minutes to keep your blood flowing. This helps avoid **deep vein thrombosis,** or "economy-class syndrome." See the box "Avoiding 'Economy Class Syndrome,'" p. 44.
- Drink water before, during, and after your flight to combat the lack of humidity in airplane cabins. Avoid caffeine and alcohol, which will dehydrate you.

(Tips) Coping with Jet Lag

Jet lag is a pitfall of traveling across time zones. If you're flying north-south and you feel sluggish when you touch down, your symptoms will be the result of dehydration and the general stress of air travel. When you travel east-west or vice versa, your body becomes confused about what time it is, and everything from your digestive system to your brain is knocked for a loop. Traveling east is more difficult on your internal clock than traveling west because most peoples' bodies are more inclined to stay up late than to fall asleep early.

Here are some tips for combating jet lag:

- **Reset your watch** to your destination time before you board the plane.
- **Drink lots of water** before, during, and after your flight. Avoid alcohol.
- **Exercise and sleep well** for a few days before your trip.
- If you have trouble sleeping on planes, **fly eastward on morning flights.**
- **Daylight** is the key to resetting your body clock. At the website for **Outside In** (www.bodyclock.com), you can get a customized plan of when to seek and avoid light.

BY CAR Coming from Boston or the New York City area, you can take several routes to reach coastal Maine. **Interstate 95** parallels the Atlantic coast to Boston, after which it skirts the New Hampshire coast, then proceeds along the southern Maine coast for a stretch before heading north toward the Canadian border.

You'll need to break off at **Route 1** or **Route 3** at some point if you're heading to Midcoast or Downeast Maine.

If you're driving to Camden or Belfast on western Penobscot Bay, you can avoid coastal traffic by taking the turnpike to Augusta, then connecting via Route 17 (to Camden) or Route 3 (to Belfast). Those heading directly to Acadia National Park may find it most expedient to follow interstates to Bangor, then Route 1A to Ellsworth, where you can connect to Route 3 onward to Mount Desert Island.

From New York City, Interstate 95 can sometimes be congested for much of its length (see "Beating the I-95 Blues" box, below), particularly on summer weekends. It's often quicker to take **I-91** north from New Haven, Connecticut, then cutting north on **I-84** toward Boston but circumventing Beantown via **I-495** north, which then joins **I-95** again near Portsmouth, New Hampshire, and the Maine state line.

Either way, note that some stretches of I-95 are toll roads.

BY TRAIN Train service to coastal Maine is very limited, but it does exist. **Amtrak** (© **800/872-7245;** www.amtrak.com) relaunched rail service to Maine in late 2001, restoring a line that had been idle since the 1960s.

Amtrak's **Downeaster** service operates four to five times daily between North Station in Boston and Portland, Maine; if you're coming from elsewhere on the East Coast, you will need to change train stations in Boston—a slightly frustrating exercise requiring either a taxi ride through congested streets or a ride and transfer on Boston's aging subway system. The Downeaster makes stops in Haverhill, Massachusetts; Exeter, Durham, and Dover, New Hampshire; and Wells, Saco, and Old Orchard Beach, Maine.

Total travel time is about 2 hours and 25 minutes between Boston and Portland. Bikes are allowed to be loaded or off-loaded

---

(Tips) Beating the I-95 Blues

From Memorial Day through Labor Day, sometimes longer, Interstate 95 from Boston to Maine becomes sluggish (even stopped-to-a-standstill) on Friday afternoons and evenings as weekend traffic backs up at the toll gates for miles. Sunday nights bring a reverse-repeat of this scene. It might sound comical that you could be stuck immobile in a Dubai-esque gridlock here in the middle of a tidal flat in the middle of nowhere; trust me, it's not nearly so funny once you're ensnared in it. U.S. Route 1 along the coast *seems* like an escape route—but it's not. Instead, it bottlenecks at the same times of day and week, especially in spots where two-lane bridges span the local tidal rivers. There's really no cure for this condition; you can, however, do a few things to prevent the affliction from striking. To avoid the very worst of the summer tourist traffic, try to stay put on weekends and during the big summer holidays. Travel midweek or midday if at all possible. Or simply take an extra day off work and head back after the holiday crush. It'll pay handsome dividends in lowered blood pressure—and you'll save a few hours you would have wasted idling your engine going nowhere.

at Boston, Wells, and Portland. The one-way fare from Boston to Portland was $24 in 2008 (with a discount for same-day round-trips). This line also has its own website, located at www.thedowneaster. com, with fares, schedules, and other useful information.

International visitors who will use this line often in Maine can buy a **USA Rail Pass,** good for 5, 15, or 30 days of unlimited travel on **Amtrak** (© 800/USA-RAIL [872-7245]; www.amtrak.com). The pass is available online or through many overseas travel agents. See the Amtrak website for the cost of travel within the western, eastern, or northwestern United States. Reservations are generally required and should be made as early as possible.

BY BUS Express bus service is well run (if a bit spotty) in coastal Maine. You'll be able to reach the major cities and tourist destinations by bus but only a few of the smaller towns or villages. Tickets from Boston to Portland usually cost between $15 and $30 per person, one-way, depending on such factors as day of week, time of day, and how far in advance you purchase the tickets. Taking the bus requires no advance planning or reservations, but in summer it's still a good idea to buy as early as possible; often you can also save money this way.

Two major bus lines serve coastal Maine from Boston and New York City. **Greyhound** (© **800/231-2222;** www. greyound.com) serves Portsmouth, New Hampshire; Portland; Bangor; and points in between with frequent departures from Boston's South Station, connecting (in summer only) onward to Ellsworth and Bar Harbor.

Concord Coach Lines (© **800/639-3317;** www.concordcoachlines.com) also serves Portsmouth, New Hampshire; Portland; and Bangor from Boston, but does not continue onward to the smaller towns; you'll need to transfer at Bangor. However,

Concord Coach buses are a bit more luxurious (and thus slightly more expensive) than Vermont Transit's rides, sometimes entertaining travelers with movies and music piped through headphones en route.

GETTING AROUND

Maine is like much of the rest of America: A set of small cities and suburbs, strung together by transportation corridors, with a whole bunch of small towns and rural areas filling in the rest of the map. Bus, train, and regional plane services are sporadic at best. This all means you will almost certainly need to travel by car (yours, or one you have rented) if you really want to see the coast of Maine in any detail.

BY CAR The major airports in Maine (see the "Getting There & Getting Around" section, earlier in this chapter) all host national car-rental chains. Some handy phone numbers and websites are **Avis** (© 800/230-4898; www.avis.com), **Budget** (© 800/527-0700; www.budget. com), **Enterprise** (© 800/736-8222; www.enterprise.com), **Hertz** (© 800/654-3131; www.hertz.com), **National** (© 800/227-7368; www.nationalcar.com), and **Thrifty** (© 800/847-4389; www.thrifty. com). You may also find independent car-rental firms in the bigger towns, sometimes at better rates than those offered by the chains. Look in the Yellow Pages under "Automobile—Renting." Also see the "Fast Facts, Toll-Free Numbers & Websites" appendix in this book on p. 282.

A famous local joke ends with the punch line, "You can't get there from here," but you may conclude it's no joke as you try to navigate through the region. Travel can be convoluted and often confusing, and it's handy to have someone adept at map reading in the car with you if you veer off the main routes for country-road exploring.

Your Car: Do Leave Home Without It

If you're *really* green-friendly, options exist for a vacation in New England *without* a car. Here are four suggestions:

- From New York City or Boston, take an **Amtrak** (www.amtrak.com) train to Brattleboro, Vermont, and explore this small town of brick architecture, good restaurants, and quirky shops. Cross the river to hike Wantastiquet Mountain one afternoon. Another day, rent a canoe and explore the Connecticut River, or get a bike and head off into the hilly countryside. There's a canoe touring center just north of town, and a bike rental outfit or two on the main street.

- From Boston, take a Concord Coach bus directly to the **Appalachian Mountain Club's Pinkham Notch Visitor Center** (© 603/466-2721), high in the White Mountains. Spend a night or two, then backpack for 2 days across demanding, rugged mountains, staying at AMC's backcountry huts (all meals provided). At the end of your sojourn, catch the AMC shuttle back to North Conway or Pinkham Notch, and then hail the return bus back to Boston.

- Bus, fly, or train it to Portland, Maine, where you can sign up for a guided sea-kayak excursion. The **Maine Island Kayak Co.** (© 207/766-2373) on Peaks Island is reached by a quick and pleasant 20-minute ferry ride (the terminal is at the corner of Commercial and Franklin sts.) and offers trips throughout the state all summer long. You can even camp within city limits on remote Jewell Island at the edge of Casco Bay, or head out for a few days along more remote parts of the coast. Portland's museums, restaurants, and bars don't require wheels to reach, either.

- Bus or fly to Bar Harbor, Maine, and then settle into one of the numerous inns or B&Bs downtown. (There's a free shuttle bus from the airport to downtown, and other free buses running around the island from spring through late fall; the bus connects downtown Bar Harbor with more than a half-dozen routes into and around the park, making travel hassle-free.) Rent a mountain bike and explore the elaborate network of carriage roads at Acadia National Park, then cruise along picturesque Park Loop Road. Another day, sign up for a sea-kayak tour or whale-watching excursion. By night, enjoy lobster or other fine meals at Bar Harbor's fine restaurants. Mountain bikes may be easily rented along Cottage Street in Bar Harbor.

North-south travel is fairly straightforward, thanks to I-95 and Route 1. Day trips by car up and down the coast can be done quite comfortably if you consult a map and understand the distances involved. Don't underestimate the size of the Maine coast—Kittery to Eastport (the easternmost city in the United States) is 293 miles. Driving times can be longer than you'd expect due to narrow roads and zigzagging peninsulas, not to mention high-season traffic. Also beware of two-sided maps that alter the scale from one side to the other, and remember when budgeting your time that Portland is closer to New York City than it is to Madawaska at the state's extreme northern tip.

If you're a connoisseur of back roads and off-the-beaten-track exploring, the *Maine Atlas and Gazetteer,* produced by DeLorme Mapping (© **800/642-0970** or 800/561-5105) in Yarmouth, is an invaluable tool. It offers an extraordinary level of detail, right down to logging roads and canoe launch sites. DeLorme's atlases are available at many local book and convenience stores and at the company's headquarters and map store in Yarmouth, a few minutes north of Portland and just off I-95.

Traffic is generally light compared to most urban and suburban areas along the East Coast.

If you're still in doubt about a route, use a Web service such as **Google Maps** (maps.google.com), **MapQuest** (www.mapquest.com), or **Yahoo! Maps** (maps.yahoo.com). These handy websites calculate distances and driving directions from any point in the country to any other point. Type in where you want to start and where you want to go, and the online software calculates the total distance and provides detailed driving instructions, along with maps if you want them. Before departing, you can plot your route and print out a daily driving itinerary.

Also, if you're visiting from abroad and plan to rent a car in the United States, keep in mind that foreign driver's licenses are usually recognized in the U.S., but you should get an international one if your home license is not in English.

Here are some representative distances between points:

New York City to	
Bar Harbor, Maine	493 miles
Portland, Maine	319 miles
Boston, Massachusetts, to	
Bar Harbor, Maine	281 miles
Portland, Maine	107 miles
Portsmouth, New Hampshire	56 miles
Portland, Maine, to	
Eastport, Maine	250 miles
Bar Harbor, Maine	174 miles
Manchester, New Hampshire	95 miles
Camden, Maine	85 miles
York, Maine	45 miles
Kennebunk, Maine	27 miles
Burlington, Vermont, to	
Portland, Maine	232 miles
North Conway, New Hampshire, to	
Bar Harbor, Maine	216 miles
Portland, Maine	65 miles

(Tips) Beware: Moose X-ing

Driving across the northern tier of Maine, you'll often see MOOSE CROSSING signs, complete with silhouettes of the gangly herbivores. These are not placed here to amuse the tourists. In Maine, the state with the most moose (an estimated 30,000, at last count), crashes between moose and cars are increasingly common.

These encounters are usually more dramatic than deer-car collisions. For starters, the large eyes of moose don't reflect in headlights like those of deer, so you often come upon them with less warning when driving late at night. Moose can weigh up to 1,000 pounds, with almost all of that weight placed high atop spindly legs. When a car strikes a moose broadside in the road, it usually knocks the legs out and sends a half-ton of hapless beast right through the windshield. Need we dwell on the results of such an encounter? I thought not. In 1998 alone, the state of Maine recorded 859 crashes involving moose, with 247 injuries and five fatalities. When in moose country, drive slowly and carefully.

BY BUS As I have already mentioned in the "Getting to Maine" section earlier in this chapter, express bus service *into* the region is quite good, but beware of trying to travel *within* Maine by bus. Quirky schedules and routes may send you well out of your way, and what may seem like a simple trip could take hours.

Traveling north-south between towns along a single bus route (for example, Portland to Bangor) is feasible, but east-west travel across Maine is, by and large, impractical.

Again, for information on travel within northern New England, contact either **Greyhound** or **Concord Coach Lines** (see earlier in this chapter, in "Getting to Maine") for service in New Hampshire and Maine. **C&J Trailways** (© 800/258-7111; www.ridecj.com) also runs some services through Maine to Boston.

BY PLANE Service between airports in Maine is sketchy at best. You can find limited direct flights between some cities (such as Portland to Bangor), but for the most part, you'll have to backtrack to Boston and fly out again to your final destination. Convenient, it's not. See the "Getting There & Getting Around" section, earlier in this chapter, for details.

Also good to know: **US Airways** (© 800/428-4322; www.usair.com) and its commuter subsidiaries handle many of the scheduled flights to Rockland and Bar Harbor, while **Quoddy Air** (© 207/853-0997), based in Eastport, offers a charter service to airports in and around Downeast Maine.

BY TRAIN As I noted above, **Amtrak** (© 800/872-7245; www.amtrak.com) provides limited rail travel on the southernmost coast of Maine. See the "Getting to Maine" section, earlier in this chapter, for details.

5 MONEY & COSTS

Here's a scene I've seen repeated dozens of times in Maine. It's late Saturday afternoon, maybe early in July. A young (or

not-so-young) couple has driven up from the city by car or motorcycle, "just for the day," in sparkling clear weather. But something magical has happened. They've fallen in love with each other all over again, and with the quaint lovely Maine-ness of (insert town here). They've decided to stay for the night in a feather bed, eat a nice meal, and maybe watch the sun set over the (ocean/mountains/lake) and have a beer, and head home tomorrow morning fully assured that all is right with the world.

Except that here they stand, before a tourist information center staff member, looking despondent (or even desperate) as the staffer holds a phone in one hand, waiting for an answer.

"Isn't there *anything* cheaper?" pleads one of the lovebirds. "No, and that's a good price," responds the person behind the desk as kindly as possible. "You won't find anything better. Now, do you want me to book it, or not?"

Yes, travelers are in for a little sticker shock on the coast of Maine, at least during peak travel seasons. In midsummer, there's simply no such thing as a cheap motel room in places such as Portland, Camden, or Bar Harbor. Even no-frills mom-and-pop motels can and do sometimes happily charge $100 a night or more for a bed that could fairly be described as a notch above car-camping. Blander-than-bland chain hotels demand even more.

To be fair, innkeepers in some of these tourist areas must reap nearly all their annual profits in what amounts to just a 2- or 3-month season each year, so that's one reason for the approaching-bank-stickup rates. It's not like they enjoy your misery (I don't think).

Anyhow, take heart. Except during peak foliage season and holidays, the cost of rooms, meals, and day-to-day expenses is generally a lot less here than you'd pay in a major non–New England city. You can find excellent entrees at upscale, creative restaurants for around $20, comparing favorably with similar dishes at big-city restaurants that would top $30.

Still, lodging here is more expensive than in almost any other rural part of the United States (see above about the paucity of cheap motels), and planning can prove tricky for budget travelers.

So you'll need money to enjoy yourself here. It's always advisable to bring money in a variety of forms on a vacation: a mix of cash, credit cards, and traveler's checks. You should also exchange enough petty cash to cover airport incidentals, tipping, and transportation to your hotel before you leave home, or withdraw money upon arrival at an airport ATM.

MONEY

The most common bills in the U.S. are the $1 (a "buck"), $5, $10, and $20 denominations. There are also $2 bills (seldom encountered), $50 bills, and $100 bills (the last two are usually not welcome as payment for small purchases).

Coins come in seven denominations: 1¢ (1 cent, or a penny); 5¢ (5 cents, or a

---

Tips   Easy Money

You'll avoid lines at airport ATMs by exchanging at least some money—just enough to cover airport incidentals and transportation to your hotel—before you leave home.

When you change money, ask for some small bills or loose change. Petty cash will come in handy for tipping and public transportation. Consider keeping the change separate from your larger bills, so that it's readily accessible and you'll be less of a target for theft.

Travel in the Age of Bankruptcy

Airlines go bankrupt, so protect yourself by **buying your tickets with a credit card.** The Fair Credit Billing Act guarantees that you can get your money back from the credit card company if a travel supplier goes under (and if you request the refund within 60 days of the bankruptcy). **Travel insurance** can also help, but make sure it covers against "carrier default" for your specific travel provider. And be aware that if a U.S. airline goes bust mid-trip, a 2001 federal law requires other carriers to take you to your destination (albeit on a space-available basis) for a fee of no more than $25, provided you rebook within 60 days of the cancellation.

nickel); 10¢ (10 cents, or a dime); 25¢ (25 cents, or a quarter); 50¢ (50 cents, or a half dollar); the gold-colored Sacagawea coin, worth $1; and the rare silver dollar.

ATMS

Nationwide, the easiest and best way to get cash away from home is from an ATM (automated teller machine), sometimes referred to as a "cash machine" or "cashpoint." The **Cirrus** (© **800/424-7787;** www.mastercard.com) and **PLUS** (© **800/ 843-7587;** www.visa.com) networks span the country; you can even find them in remote regions. Look at the back of your bank card to see which network you're on, then call or check online for ATM locations at your destination. Be sure you know your personal identification number (PIN) and daily withdrawal limit before you depart. *Note:* Remember that many banks impose a fee every time you use a card at another bank's ATM, and that fee can be higher for international transactions (up to $5 or more) than for domestic ones (where they're rarely more than $2). In addition, the bank from which you withdraw cash may charge its own fee. To compare banks' ATM fees within the U.S., use **www.bankrate.com**. For international withdrawal fees, ask your bank.

CREDIT CARDS & DEBIT CARDS

Credit cards are the most widely used form of payment in the United States: **Visa**

(Barclaycard in Britain), **MasterCard** (Eurocard in Europe, Access in Britain, Chargex in Canada), **American Express, Diners Club,** and **Discover.** They also provide a convenient record of all your expenses, and they generally offer relatively good exchange rates. You can withdraw cash advances from your credit cards at banks or ATMs, provided you know your PIN.

Visitors from outside the U.S. should inquire whether their bank assesses a fee on charges incurred abroad, usually 1% to 3%.

It's highly recommended that you travel with at least one major credit card. You must have one to rent a car, and hotels and airlines usually require a credit card imprint as a deposit against expenses.

ATM cards with major credit card backing, known as **debit cards,** are now a commonly acceptable form of payment in most stores and restaurants. Debit cards draw money directly from your checking account. Some stores enable you to receive "cash back" on your debit-card purchases as well. The same is true at most U.S. post offices.

TRAVELER'S CHECKS

Traveler's checks are widely accepted in the U.S., and that includes the most heavily touristed areas of New England (Boston and Cape Cod, for example), but foreign visitors should make sure that they're denominated in U.S. dollars; foreign-currency checks are often difficult to exchange.

At smaller destinations, such as backwoods camps in Maine, you might find they are not accepted—if in doubt, please check in advance.

You can buy traveler's checks at most banks. Most are offered in denominations of $20, $50, $100, $500, and sometimes $1,000. Generally, you'll pay a service charge ranging from 1% to 4%.

The most popular traveler's checks are offered by **American Express** (☎ **800/807-6233,** or 800/221-7282 for cardholders—this number accepts collect calls, offers service in several foreign languages, and exempts Amex gold and platinum cardholders from the 1% fee) and **Visa** (☎ **800/732-1322**). AAA members can obtain Visa checks for a $9.95 fee (for checks up to $1,500) at most AAA offices or by calling ☎ **866/339-3378.** Call ☎ **800/223-9920** for information on MasterCard traveler's checks.

If you do choose to carry traveler's checks, keep a record of their serial numbers separate from your checks in the event that they are stolen or lost. You'll get a refund faster if you know the numbers.

6 HEALTH

Mainers, by and large, consider themselves a healthy bunch, which they ascribe to clean living, brisk northern air, vigorous exercise (leaf raking, snow shoveling, and so on), and a sensible diet. Other than picking up a germ that may lead to a cold or flu, you shouldn't face any serious health risks when traveling in the region.

Exceptions? Well, yes—you may find yourself at higher risk when exploring the outdoors, particularly in the backcountry. A few things to watch for when venturing off the beaten track:

- **Poison ivy:** The shiny, three-leafed plant is common throughout the region. If touched, you may develop a nasty, itchy rash that will seriously erode the enjoyment of your vacation. The reaction tends to be worse in some people than others. It's safest to simply avoid it. If you're unfamiliar with what poison ivy looks like, ask at a ranger station or visitor information booth for more information. Many have posters or books to help with identification.
- **Giardia:** That crystal-clear stream coursing down a backcountry peak may seem pure, but it may be contaminated with animal feces. Gross, yes, and also dangerous. Giardia cysts may be present in some streams and rivers. When ingested by humans, the cysts can result in copious diarrhea and weight loss. Symptoms may not surface until well after you've left the backcountry and returned home. Carry your own water for day trips, or bring a small filter (available at most camping and sporting-goods shops) to treat backcountry water. Failing that, at least boil water or treat it with iodine before using it for cooking, drinking, or washing. If you detect symptoms, see a doctor immediately.
- **Lyme disease:** Lyme disease has been a growing problem in New England since 1975 when the disease was identified in the town of Lyme, Connecticut, and some 14,000 cases are reported nationwide annually. The disease is transmitted by tiny deer ticks—smaller than the more common, relatively harmless wood ticks. Look for a bull's-eye-shaped rash (3–8 in. in diameter); it may feel warm but usually doesn't itch. Symptoms include muscle and joint pain, fever, and fatigue. If left untreated, heart damage may occur. It's more easily treated in early phases than later, so seek medical attention as soon as any symptoms are noted.

- **Rabies:** Since 1989, rabies has been spreading northward from New Jersey into New England. The disease is spread by animal saliva and is especially prevalent in skunks, raccoons, bats, and foxes. It is always fatal if left untreated in humans. Infected animals tend to display erratic and aggressive behavior. The best advice is to keep a safe distance between yourself and any wild animal you may encounter. If bitten, wash the wound as soon as you can and immediately seek medical attention. Treatment is no longer as painful as it once was, but still involves a series of shots.

Those planning longer excursions into the outdoors may find a compact first-aid kit with basic salves and medicines very handy to have along. Those traveling mostly in the towns and villages should have little trouble finding a local pharmacy, Rite Aid, or Wal-Mart to stock up on common medicines (such as calamine lotion or aspirin) to aid with any minor ailments picked up along the way.

WHAT TO DO IF YOU GET SICK AWAY FROM HOME

If you suffer from a chronic illness, consult your doctor before your departure. Pack **prescription medications** in your carry-on luggage, and carry them in their original containers, with pharmacy labels—otherwise they won't make it through airport security. Visitors from outside the U.S. should carry generic names of prescription drugs. For U.S. travelers, most reliable healthcare plans provide coverage if you get sick away from home. Foreign visitors may have to pay all medical costs upfront and be reimbursed later. See "Medical Insurance," under "Insurance," in the appendix.

If you get sick, consider asking your hotel concierge to recommend a local doctor—even his or her own. You can also try the emergency room at a local hospital. Many hospitals also have walk-in clinics for emergency cases that are not life-threatening; you may not get immediate attention, but you won't pay the high price of an emergency room visit. There are large, good hospitals and clinics in the cities of coastal Maine, as well as many small towns. Check with your hotel or the local tourism office if you're concerned about proximity to hospitals.

If you suffer from a chronic illness, consult your doctor before your departure. For conditions like epilepsy, diabetes, or heart problems, wear a **MedicAlert**

Avoiding "Economy Class Syndrome"

Deep vein thrombosis, or "economy-class syndrome" (as it's known in the travel world), is a blood clot that develops in a deep vein. It's a potentially deadly condition (yes, deadly) that can be caused by sitting in cramped conditions—such as an airplane cabin—for too long. During a flight (especially a long-haul flight), get up, walk around, and stretch your legs every 60 to 90 minutes to keep your blood flowing. Other preventative measures include flexing of your legs while sitting, drinking lots of water, and avoiding alcohol and sleeping pills. If you have a history of deep vein thrombosis, heart disease, or another condition that puts you at high risk, some experts recommend wearing compression stockings or taking anticoagulants when you fly; ask your physician about the best course before traveling. Some symptoms of deep vein thrombosis include leg pain, a red swelling, or shortness of breath. If you feel anything like this after a very long flight or train ride, think seriously about being safe rather than sorry, and head for a clinic or hospital.

identification tag (© **888/633-4298;** www.medicalert.org), which will immediately alert doctors to your condition and give them access to your records through MedicAlert's 24-hour hot line.

Pack **prescription medications** in your carry-on luggage, and carry prescription medications in their original containers, with pharmacy labels—otherwise they won't make it through airport security. Also carry copies of your prescriptions in case you lose your pills or run out. Don't forget an extra pair of contact lenses or prescription glasses.

For domestic trips, most reliable healthcare plans provide coverage if you get sick away from home.

7 SAFETY

Maine boasts some of the lowest crime rates in the country. The odds of anything bad happening during your visit here are very slight. But all travelers are advised to take the usual precautions against theft, robbery, and assault.

Travelers should avoid any unnecessary public displays of wealth. Don't bring out fat wads of cash from your pocket, and save your best jewelry for private occasions. If you are approached by someone who demands money, jewelry, or anything else from you, do what most Americans do: Hand it over. Don't argue. Don't negotiate. Just comply. Afterward, immediately contact the police by dialing © **911** from almost any phone.

The crime you're statistically most likely to encounter is theft of items from your car. Don't leave anything of value in plain view, and lock valuables in your trunk. Better still, keep them with you at all times.

Late at night you should look for a well-lighted area if you need gas or you need to step out of your car for any reason. Also, it's not advisable to sleep in your car late at night at highway rest areas, which can leave you vulnerable to robbers.

Take the usual precautions against leaving cash or valuables in your hotel room when you're not present. Many hotels have safe-deposit boxes. Smaller inns and hotels often do not, although it can't hurt to ask to leave small items in the house safe.

8 SPECIALIZED TRAVEL RESOURCES

TRAVELERS WITH DISABILITIES

Most disabilities shouldn't stop anyone from traveling to the coast of Maine. Thanks to provisions in the Americans with Disabilities Act, most public places are required to comply with disability-friendly regulations. Almost all public establishments (including hotels, restaurants, museums, and so on, but not including certain National Historic Landmarks) and at least some modes of public transportation provide accessible entrances and other facilities for those with disabilities.

The **America the Beautiful—National Park and Federal Recreational Lands Pass—Access Pass** (formerly the **Golden Access Passport**) gives visually impaired or permanently disabled persons (regardless of age) free lifetime entrance to federal recreation sites administered by the National Park Service, including the Fish and Wildlife Service, the Forest Service, the Bureau of Land Management, and the Bureau of Reclamation. This may include national parks, monuments, historic sites, recreation areas, and national wildlife refuges.

The America the Beautiful Access Pass can only be obtained in person at any NPS facility that charges an entrance fee. You need to show proof of a medically determined disability. Besides free entry, the pass also offers a 50% discount on some federal-use fees charged for such facilities as camping, swimming, parking, boat launching, and tours. For more information, go to www.nps.gov/fees_passes.htm, or call the United States Geological Survey (USGS), which issues the passes, at © **888/ 275-8747.**

For more on organizations that offer resources to travelers with disabilities, go to frommers.com.

GAY & LESBIAN TRAVELERS

Though coastal Maine isn't exactly a hot-bed of gay culture, it has been rapidly growing as a gay travel destination, and many gays and lesbians now live and travel here. Larger cities tend to be more accommodating to gay travelers than smaller towns, but many small coastal towns now also show gay and lesbian presence. In general, gay and lesbian travelers should feel very comfortable in all vacation areas of coastal Maine.

Portland is now home to a substantial gay population. The city hosts a sizable Pride festival early each summer that includes a riotous parade and a dance on the city pier, among other events. In early 1998, Maine narrowly repealed a statewide gay-rights law that had been passed earlier by the state legislature. In Portland, however, the vote was nearly four to one against the repeal and in support of equal rights. Portland also has a municipal ordinance that prohibits discrimination in jobs and housing based on sexual orientation.

Ogunquit is hugely popular among gay travelers, a longtime (even historic) gay resort area that features a lively beach-and-bar scene in the summer. In the winter it's still active but decidedly more mellow. Several Ogunquit B&Bs are owned by gay entrepreneurs. A website, **www.gay ogunquit.com**, is a good place to find information on locally gay-owned inns, restaurants, and nightclubs.

SENIOR TRAVEL

Mention the fact that you're a senior when you make your travel reservations. Although all the major U.S. airlines except America West have canceled their senior discount and coupon book programs, many hotels still offer lower rates for seniors. In most cities people over the age of 60 qualify for reduced admission to theaters, museums, and other attractions and discounted fares on public transportation.

Maine is well suited to older travelers, with a wide array of activities for seniors and discounts commonly available. Members of **AARP** (formerly known as the American Association of Retired Persons), 601 E St. NW, Washington, DC 20049 (© **888/687-2277;** www.aarp.org), get discounts on hotels, airfares, and car rentals. AARP offers members a wide range of benefits, including *AARP The Magazine* and a monthly newsletter. Anyone 50 and over can join.

The U.S. National Park Service offers an **America the Beautiful—National Park and Federal Recreational Lands Pass—Senior Pass** (formerly the **Golden Age Passport**), which gives seniors 62 years or older lifetime entrance to all properties administered by the National Park Service—national parks, monuments, historic sites, recreation areas, and national wildlife refuges—for a one-time processing fee of $10. The pass must be purchased in person at any NPS facility that charges an entrance fee. Besides free entry, the America the Beautiful Senior Pass also offers a 50% discount on some federal-use fees charged for such facilities as camping, swimming, parking, boat launching, and tours.

For more information, go to www.nps.gov/fees_passes.htm, or call the United States Geological Survey (USGS), which issues the passes, at © **888/275-8747.**

FAMILY TRAVEL

The family vacation is a rite of passage for many households, one that in a split second can evolve into a *National Lampoon* farce. However, it can be among the most pleasurable and rewarding times of your life.

Families will have little trouble finding fun, low-key things to do with kids in Maine. The natural world seems to hold tremendous wonder for the younger set—an afternoon exploring mossy banks and rocky streambeds can be a huge adventure. Older kids may like the challenge of climbing a mountain peak or learning to paddle a canoe in a straight line, and the beach is always good for hours of afternoon diversion.

Some recommended destinations for families in Maine include York Beach and Acadia National Park. Be sure to ask about family discounts when visiting attractions. Many places offer a flat family rate that costs less than paying for each ticket individually. Some parks and beaches charge by the carload rather than the head count.

To locate accommodations, restaurants, and attractions that are particularly kid friendly, see the "Kids" icon throughout this guide.

Frommer's Family Vacations in the National Parks, by Charles Wohlforth, includes useful material on traveling with kids to Acadia National Park in Maine and Cape Cod National Seashore in Massachusetts.

TRAVELING WITH PETS

No surprise: Some places allow pets, some don't. I've noted inns that allow pets, but even here I don't recommend showing up with a pet in tow unless you've cleared it over the phone with the innkeeper. Note that many establishments have only one or two rooms (often a cottage or room with exterior entrance) set aside for guests traveling with pets, and they won't be happy to meet Fido if the pet rooms are already occupied. Also, it's increasingly common for a surcharge of $10 or $20 to be charged to pet owners to pay for the extra cleaning. On the positive side, all **Motel 6** hotels accept pets as a matter of policy, and so (surprisingly) do some upscale inns.

Keep in mind that dogs are prohibited on hiking trails and must be leashed at all times on federal lands administered by the National Park Service (this includes Acadia National Park in Maine). Pets are allowed to hike off-leash in the White Mountains National Forest in New Hampshire and the Green Mountain National Forest in Vermont. No pets of any sort are allowed at any time (leashed or unleashed) at Baxter State Park in Maine. Other Maine state parks do allow pets on a leash.

STUDENT TRAVEL

Check out the **International Student Travel Confederation (ISTC)** (www.istc.org) website for comprehensive travel services information and details on how to get an **International Student Identity Card (ISIC),** which qualifies students for substantial savings on rail passes, plane tickets, entrance fees, and more. It also provides students with basic health and life insurance and a 24-hour help line. The card is valid for a maximum of 18 months. You can apply for the card online or in person at **STA Travel** (© **800/781-4040** in North America; 132 782 in Australia; 0871 2 300 040 in the U.K.; www.statravel.com), the biggest student travel agency in the world; check out the website to locate STA Travel offices worldwide. If you're no longer a student but are still under 26, you can get an **International Youth Travel Card (IYTC)** from the same people, which entitles you to some discounts. **Travel CUTS** (✆ **800/592-2887;** www.travelcuts.com) offers similar services for both Canadians and U.S.

residents. Irish students may prefer to turn to **USIT** (✆ **01/602-1904;** www.usit.ie), an Ireland-based specialist in student, youth, and independent travel.

9 SUSTAINABLE TOURISM

Sustainable tourism is conscientious travel. It means being careful with the environments you explore and respecting the communities you visit. Two overlapping components of sustainable travel are **eco-tourism** and **ethical tourism.** The **International Ecotourism Society** (TIES) defines eco-tourism as responsible travel to natural areas that conserves the environment and improves the well-being of local people. TIES suggests that eco-tourists follow these principles:

- Minimize environmental impact.
- Build environmental and cultural awareness and respect.
- Provide positive experiences for both visitors and hosts.
- Provide direct financial benefits for conservation and for local people.
- Raise sensitivity to host countries' political, environmental, and social climates.
- Support international human rights and labor agreements.

You can find some eco-friendly travel tips and statistics, as well as touring companies and associations—listed by destination under "Travel Choice"—at the **TIES** website, www.ecotourism.org. Also check out **Ecotravel.com,** which lets you search for sustainable touring companies in several categories (water-based, land-based, spiritually oriented, and so on).

While much of the focus of eco-tourism is about reducing impacts on the natural environment, ethical tourism concentrates on ways to preserve and enhance local economies and communities, regardless of location. You can embrace ethical tourism by staying at a locally owned hotel or shopping at a store that employs local workers and sells locally produced goods.

Responsible Travel (www.responsible travel.com) is a great source of sustainable travel ideas; the site is run by a spokesperson for ethical tourism in the travel industry. **Sustainable Travel International** (www.sustainabletravelinternational.org) promotes ethical tourism practices, and manages an extensive directory of sustainable properties and tour operators around the world.

In the U.K., **Tourism Concern** (www. tourismconcern.org.uk) works to reduce social and environmental problems connected to tourism. The **Association of Independent Tour Operators (AITO)** (www.aito.co.uk) is a group of specialist operators leading the field in making holidays sustainable.

Volunteer travel has become increasingly popular among those who want to venture beyond the standard group-tour experience to learn languages, interact with locals, and make a positive difference while on vacation. Volunteer travel usually doesn't require special skills—just a willingness to work hard—and programs vary in length from a few days to a number of weeks. Some programs provide free housing and food, but many require volunteers to pay for travel expenses, which can add up quickly.

Before you commit to a volunteer program, it's important to make sure any money you're giving is truly going back to the local community, and that the work you'll be doing will be a good fit for you. **Volunteer International** (www.volunteer international.org) has a helpful list of

(Tips) **It's Easier Being Green**

Here are a few simple ways you can help conserve fuel and energy when you travel:

- Each time you take a flight or drive a car greenhouse gases release into the atmosphere. You can help neutralize this danger to the planet through "carbon offsetting"—paying someone to invest your money in programs that reduce your greenhouse gas emissions by the same amount you've added. Before buying carbon offset credits, just make sure that you're using a reputable company, one with a proven program that invests in renewable energy. Reliable carbon offset companies include **Carbonfund** (www.carbonfund.org), **Terra-Pass** (www.terrapass.org), and **Carbon Neutral** (www.carbonneutral.org).
- Whenever possible, choose nonstop flights; they generally require less fuel than indirect flights that stop and take off again. Try to fly during the day—some scientists estimate that nighttime flights are twice as harmful to the environment. And pack light—each 15 pounds of luggage on a 5,000-mile flight adds up to 50 pounds of carbon dioxide emitted.
- Where you stay during your travels can have a major environmental impact. To determine the green credentials of a property, ask about trash disposal and recycling, water conservation, and energy use; also question if sustainable materials were used in the construction of the property. The website **www.greenhotels.com** recommends green-rated member hotels around the world that fulfill the company's stringent environmental requirements. Also consult **www.environmentallyfriendlyhotels.com** for more green accommodations ratings.
- At hotels, request that your sheets and towels not be changed daily. (Many hotels already have programs like this in place.) Turn off the lights and air conditioner (or heater) when you leave your room.
- Use public transport where possible—trains, buses, and even taxis are more energy-efficient forms of transport than driving. Even better is to walk or cycle; you'll produce zero emissions and stay fit and healthy on your travels.
- If renting a car is necessary, ask the rental agent for a hybrid, or rent the most fuel-efficient car available. You'll use less gas and save money at the tank.
- Eat at locally owned and operated restaurants that use produce grown in the area. This contributes to the local economy and cuts down on greenhouse gas emissions by supporting restaurants where the food is not flown or trucked in across long distances. Visit **Sustain Lane** (www.sustainlane.org) to find sustainable eating and drinking choices around the U.S.; also check out **www.eatwellguide.org** for tips on eating sustainably in the U.S. and Canada.

questions to ask to determine the intentions and the nature of a volunteer program.

ANIMAL-RIGHTS ISSUES

Whale-watching is increasingly popular in New England, particularly in downeast parts of Maine. For those who may be concerned about the sensitivity of the

Frommers.com: The Complete Travel Resource

Planning a trip or just returned? Head to **Frommers.com,** voted Best Travel Site by *PC Magazine*. We think you'll find our site indispensable before, during, and after your travels—with expert advice and tips; independent reviews of hotels, restaurants, attractions, and preferred shopping and nightlife venues; vacation giveaways; and an online booking tool. We publish the complete contents of over 135 travel guides in our **Destinations** section, covering more than 4,000 places worldwide. Each weekday, we publish original articles that report on **Deals and News** via our free **Frommers.com Newsletters.** What's more, **Arthur Frommer** himself blogs 5 days a week, with cutting opinions about the state of travel in the modern world. We're betting you'll find our **Events** listings an invaluable resource; it's an up-to-the-minute roster of what's happening in cities everywhere—including concerts, festivals, lectures, and more. We've also added weekly **podcasts, interactive maps,** and hundreds of new images across the site. Finally, don't forget to visit our **Message Boards,** where you can join in conversations with thousands of fellow Frommer's travelers and post your trip report once you return.

animals to these visits, there are a number of animal-rights organizations that provide good information. The organization **Tread Lightly** (www.treadlightly.org) is one. For more specific information about the current status of various species of whales, visit the **Whale and Dolphin Conservation Society** (www.wdcs.org).

10 PACKAGES FOR THE INDEPENDENT TRAVELER

Package tours are simply a way to buy the airfare, accommodations, and other elements of your trip (such as car rentals, airport transfers, and sometimes even activities) at the same time and often at discounted prices.

One good source of package deals is the airlines themselves. Most major airlines offer air/land packages, including **American Airlines Vacations** (© 800/321-2121; www.aavacations.com), **Delta Vacations** (© 800/221-6666; www.deltavacations.com), **Continental Airlines Vacations** (© 800/301-3800; www.covacations.com), and **United Vacations** (© 888/854-3899; www.unitedvacations.com). Several big **online travel agencies**—Expedia, Travelocity, Orbitz, Site59, and Lastminute.com—also do a brisk business in packages.

Travel packages are also listed in the travel section of your local Sunday newspaper. Or check ads in the national travel magazines such as *Arthur Frommer's Budget Travel Magazine, Travel + Leisure, National Geographic Traveler,* and *Condé Nast Traveler.*

> **Tips Ask Before You Go**
>
> Before you invest in a package deal or an escorted tour:
> - Always ask about the **cancellation policy.** Can you get your money back? Is a deposit required?
> - Ask about the **accommodations choices and prices** for each. Then look up the hotels' reviews in a Frommer's guide and check their rates online for your specific dates of travel. Also find out what types of rooms are offered.
> - Request a complete **schedule.** (Escorted tours only)
> - Ask about the **size** and demographics of the group. (Escorted tours only)
> - Discuss what is included in the **price** (transportation, meals, tips, airport transfers, and so on). (Escorted tours only)
> - Finally, look for **hidden expenses.** Ask whether airport departure fees and taxes, for example, are included in the total cost—they rarely are.

11 ESCORTED GENERAL-INTEREST TOURS

Escorted tours are structured group tours, with a group leader. The price usually includes everything from airfare to hotels, meals, tours, admission costs, and local transportation.

Despite the fact that escorted tours require big deposits and predetermined hotels, restaurants, and itineraries, many people derive security and peace of mind from the structure they offer. Escorted tours—whether they're navigated by bus, motorcoach, train, or boat—let travelers sit back and enjoy the trip without having to drive or worry about details. They take you to the maximum number of sights in the minimum amount of time with the

least amount of hassle. They're particularly convenient for people with limited mobility, and they can be a great way to make new friends.

On the downside, you'll have little opportunity for serendipitous interactions with locals. The tours can be jampacked with activities, leaving little room for individual sightseeing, whim, or adventure—plus they often focus on the heavily touristed sites, so you miss out on many a lesser-known gem.

For more information on escorted general-interest tours, including questions to ask before booking your trip, see www.frommers.com.

12 SPECIAL-INTEREST TRIPS

One rewarding way to spend a vacation is to learn a new outdoor skill or add to your knowledge while on holiday. You can find plenty of options in Maine, ranging from formal weeklong classes to 1-day workshops.

There are lots of options; here are a couple of the most popular:

- **Fly-fishing in Maine.** What says Maine more than L.L.Bean? The world-famous outdoors-store's educational offerings are growing by leaps and bounds, and

(Value) **For Those Who Love Historic Homes**

Historic New England is a nonprofit foundation that owns and operates 36 historical properties around New England, ranging from places built in the 17th century to the present, including a number of properties profiled in this book. Members get into all of the organization's properties for free, and receive a number of other benefits including a subscription to *Historic New England* magazine; a guide to the group's properties; and invitations to members-only events and other perks. Memberships cost $45 per year for individuals, $55 for households. For more information on Historic New England and its properties, visit the group's website at www.historicnewengland.org, or call the organization's Boston headquarters at (C) **617/227-3957.**

are highly recommended by travelers of all ages. Among the many options, the intriguing fly-fishing outings ((C) **800/ 343-4552**) are worth a look. There's a good catalog available by mail or by wandering into the flagship store (open 24 hr.) on Main Street in Freeport. L.L.Bean also offers a number of shorter workshops on various outdoor skills through its **Outdoor Discovery Program;** call (C) **888/552-3261.**

• **All About Birds.** Budding and experienced naturalists can expand their understanding of marine wildlife while residing on 333-acre Hog Island in Maine's wild and scenic Muscongus Bay through the **Maine Audubon Society,** 20 Gilsland Farm Rd., Falmouth, ME 04105 ((C) **207/781-2330;** www.maine audubon.org). You're brought by boat, then stay on the island for 3 to 7 nights. Famed birder Roger Tory Peterson once taught birding classes here, and I can personally vouch for Maine Audubon's other outdoors and educational programs, too. Call or visit their lovely headquarters near Portland.

Indeed, Maine especially lends itself to outdoorsy adventures that combine fresh air and exercise with Mother Nature as your instructor in Maine's vast, beautiful classroom. For special-interest trips that are even more active than these two, see my next section, "The Active Traveler."

13 THE ACTIVE TRAVELER

Coastal Maine is a superb destination for those who don't consider it a vacation unless they spend some time far away from their cars. Hiking, canoeing, and skiing are among the most popular outdoor activities, but you can also try rock climbing, sea kayaking, mountain biking, road biking, sailing, winter mountaineering, and snowmobiling. In general, the farther north you go in the region, the more remote and wild the terrain becomes. For pointers on where to head, see "Outdoor Activities," below. More detailed information on local services is included in each regional section.

GENERAL ADVICE

The best way to enjoy the outdoors is to head to public lands where the natural landscape is preserved. Wild areas in coastal Maine include **Acadia National Park**'s various sections, **Cobscook Bay State Park,** and (a bit inland) **Baxter State Park.** You can often find adventure-travel outfitters and suppliers in towns around the perimeter of these areas.

To find real adventure, plan to stay put. I'd advise prospective adventurers to pick just one area, then settle in for a few days or a week, spending the long summer days exploring locally by foot, canoe, or kayak. This will give you the time to enjoy an extra hour lounging at a rocky beach, or to spend an extra day camped by a cove. You'll also learn a lot more about the area. Few travelers ever regret planning to do too little on their vacations. A lot of travelers regret attempting to do too much.

OUTDOOR ACTIVITIES

BEACHGOING Swimming at Maine's ocean beaches is for the hardy. The Gulf Stream, which prods warm waters south toward the Cape Cod shores, veers toward Iceland south of Maine and leaves the state's 5,500-mile coastline washed by a brisk Nova Scotia current, an offshoot of the arctic Labrador current. During summer, water temperatures along the south coast may top 60°F (16°C) during an especially warm spell where water is shallow, but it's usually cooler than that.

Maine's best beaches are found mostly between the New Hampshire border and Portland. Northeast of Portland a handful of fine beaches await—including popular **Reid State Park** (p. 141) and **Popham Beach State Park** (p. 141)—but rocky coast defines this territory for the most part. The southern beaches are beautiful but rarely isolated. Summer homes occupy the low dunes in most areas; mid-rise condos give **Old Orchard Beach** a "mini-Miami" air.

Some of the best swimming beaches in the region can be found at **Ogunquit,** which boasts a 3-mile-long sandy strand (some of which has a mildly remote character), and **Long Sands Beach** (p. 80) and **Short Sands Beach** (p. 80) at York. Long Sands possesses great views of the sea and a nearby lighthouse plus great walking at low tide (at high tide, the sand disappears completely), while Short Sands has a festive, carnival atmosphere. Both lie right on Route 1A. There are also a number of fine beaches in the greater **Portland** area; for a primer on the very best, see chapter 6.

If you love swimming but aren't especially keen on shivering, head inland to the sandy beaches at Maine's wonderful lakes, where the water is tepid by comparison. A number of state and municipal parks offer access. Among the most accessible to the coast is **Sebago Lake State Park** (✆ **207/693-6613**), about 20 miles northwest of Portland; a small admission fee is charged.

BIKING In southern Maine, **Route 103** and **Route 1A** offer pleasant scenery for bikers as well. Offshore, bring your bike to the bigger islands for car-free cruising. In Casco Bay I recommend two islands for cycling. Rustic **Chebeague Island** offers a pleasantly wooded excursion (the path cuts through forests to the sea), while more populous **Peaks Island** (p. 119) has a few cafes, more culture, and the advantage of a bicycle-rental shop near the ferry dock. Both are flat, and both are conveniently connected to Portland by Casco Bay Lines ferries. (Peaks is a much shorter ferry ride, if time matters.)

Serious mountain biking is also available in parts of coastal Maine, for those who like to get technical on two wheels. Your best bet is to consult area bike shops for the best trails, which are typically a matter of local knowledge.

The Maine Department of Transportation (DOT) publishes a booklet, *Explore Maine by Bike,* describing 25 popular bike trips around the state; log on to **www. exploremaine.org/bike** to get it. The Maine DOT also publishes a map marked up with state biking information, including traffic volumes and road shoulder conditions along popular routes. Order it by e-mailing bikeinfo@maine.gov or by calling the DOT at ✆ **207/624-3252.**

BIRDING Birders from southern and inland states should lengthen their life lists along the Maine coast, which attracts migrating birds cruising the Atlantic flyway (there are warblers galore in spring) and boasts populations of numerous native shorebirds, such as plovers (including the threatened piping plover), terns, whimbrels, sandpipers, and dunlins. Gulls and terns are frequently seen; you'll see a surfeit of herring and great black-backed gull, along with the common tern. Less frequently seen are Bonaparte's gull, the laughing gull, the jaeger, and the arctic tern.

For a recording of recent sightings of rare birds, call ℭ **207/781-2332.**

CAMPING For information about state parks, many of which offer camping, contact the **Department of Conservation,** State House Station #22, Augusta, ME 04333 (ℭ **207/287-3821**). To make camping reservations at most state park campgrounds, call during business hours on a weekday between February and early September (ℭ **800/332-1501** in Maine or 207/287-3824).

Maine also has more than 200 private campgrounds spread throughout the state, many offering full hookups for RVs. For a guide to the private campgrounds, contact the **Maine Campground Owners Association** (ℭ **207/782-5874;** www.campmaine.com), 10 Falcon Rd., Ste. #1, Lewiston, ME 04240. Campsites get booked quickly for summer weekends, so call ahead for reservations.

FISHING Anglers from all over the Northeast indulge their grand obsession on Maine's 6,000 lakes and ponds and its countless miles of rivers and streams. And deep-sea-fishing charters are available at many of the harbors along the Maine coast, with options ranging from inshore fishing expeditions for stripers and bluefish to offshore voyages in search of shark, cod, and pollock. Prices might typically range from $25 per person for day trips to $395 to charter an offshore boat for the day. Visitor information centers and chambers of commerce listed in this guide will be able to match you up with the right boat to meet your needs.

Saltwater fishing in Maine requires no license. For freshwater fishing, nonresident **licenses** are $52 for the season or $23 for 3 days. One-, 7-, and 15-day licenses are also available. Fees are reduced for juniors (ages 12–15); no license is required for those 11 and under. Licenses are available at many outdoor shops and general stores throughout the state or by mail from the address below. For a booklet of fishing regulations, contact the **Department of Inland Fisheries and Wildlife,** State House Station #41, Augusta, ME 04333 (ℭ **207/287-8000;** www.state.me.us/ifw).

GOLFING Most of southern Maine's best courses are private, but a few are open to the public. Try Kennebunkport's **Cape Arundel Golf Club** (ℭ 207/967-3494), which is favored by a certain ex-president when he's in town.

HIKING Southern Maine's walks are not hikes but rather less-demanding strolls; many of these are a matter of local knowledge. Two fine pathways skirt the water in **York** (see chapter 5), and even in **Portland** (see chapter 6) you can saunter on well-maintained (and heavily used) recreational pathways along about 5 miles of tidal waters.

SEA KAYAKING Sea kayakers nationwide migrate to Maine for world-class sea kayaking. Thousands of miles of deeply indented coastline and thousands of offshore islands have created a wondrous kayaker's playground. Paddlers can explore protected estuaries far from the surf or test their skills and determination with excursions across choppy, open seas to islands far offshore. It's a sport that can be extremely dangerous (when weather shifts, the seas can turn on you in a matter of minutes), but can yield plenty of returns with the proper equipment and skills.

The nation's first long-distance water trail, the **Maine Island Trail,** was created here in 1987. This 325-mile waterway winds along the coast from Portland to Machias, incorporating some 70 state and privately owned islands on its route. Members of the Maine Island Trail Association, a private nonprofit group, help maintain and monitor the islands and in turn are granted permission to visit and camp on them as long as they follow certain restrictions (for example, no visiting designated islands during seabird nesting season). The association seeks to encourage low-impact, responsible use of these natural treasures, and joining is a good idea if you'll be doing some kayaking. The MITA guidebook, published annually, provides descriptions of all the islands in the network and is free with association membership (note that the guide is available only to members).

For membership details, contact the **Maine Island Trail Association,** 58 Fore St., Ste. 30-3, Portland, ME 04101 (✆ **207/ 761-8225;** www.mita.org).

The islands and protected bays around **Portland** make for great kayaking, as do the cliffs, parks, and beaches just south of the city—though surf can be rough at times. Make sure you're experienced enough to handle it.

For novices, a number of kayak outfitters take guided excursions ranging from an afternoon to a week. Outfitters include the **Maine Island Kayak Co.** on Peaks Island (✆ **207/766-2373;** www.maine islandkayak.com) in the Portland area and **Maine Sport Outfitters,** located in Rockport (✆ **800/722-0826** or 207/236-8797; www.mainesport.com).

FINDING YOUR WAY

Travelers used to hire guides to ensure they could find their way out of the woods. With development encroaching on many once-pristine areas, it's now helpful to have guides to find your way *into* the woods and away from civilization and its long reach. Clear-cuts, second-home developments, and trails teeming with weekend hikers are all obstacles to be avoided. Local knowledge is the best way to find the most alluring, least congested spots.

Travelers have three options: Hire a guide, sign up for a guided trip, or dig up the essential information yourself.

HIRING A GUIDE Guides of all kinds may be hired throughout the region, from grizzled fishing hands who know local rivers like their own homes to young canoe guides attracted to the field because of their interest in the environment. Alexandra and Garrett Conover of Maine's **North Woods Ways,** 2293 Elliotsville Rd., Willimantic, ME 04443 (✆ **207/997-3723**), are among the most experienced in the region. The couple offers canoe trips on northern Maine rivers (including a Thoreau's Maine Woods trip), and are well versed in North Woods lore.

Maine has a centuries-old tradition of guides leading "sports" into the backwoods for hunting and fishing, although many now have branched out to include recreational canoeing and more specialized interests, such as bird-watching. Professional guides are certified by the state; you can learn more about hiring Maine guides by contacting the **Maine Professional Guides Association,** P.O. Box 336, Augusta, ME 04332. The association's website (www.maineguides.org) features links to some of its members.

Elsewhere, contact the appropriate chambers of commerce for suggestions on local guides.

GUIDED TOURS Guided tours have boomed in recent years, both in number and variety. These range from 2-night guided inn-to-inn hiking trips to weeklong canoe and kayak expeditions, camping each night along the way. A few reputable outfitters to start with include the following:

- **Country Walkers,** P.O. Box 180, Waterbury, VT 05676 (© **800/464-9255** or 802/244-1387; www.country walkers.com), has a glorious color catalog (more like a wish book) outlining supported walking trips around the world. Among the offerings: walking tours in coastal Maine. Trips run 4 or 5 nights and include all meals and lodging at appealing inns.

- **Maine Island Kayak Co.,** 70 Luther St., Peaks Island, ME 04108 (© **800/796-2373** or 207/766-2373; www.sea kayak.com), has a fleet of seaworthy kayaks for camping trips up and down the Maine coast. The firm has a number of 2- and 3-night expeditions each summer and has plenty of experience training novices.

- **New England Hiking Holidays,** P.O. Box 1648, North Conway, NH 03860 (© **800/869-0949** or 603/356-9696; www.nehikingholidays.com), has an extensive inventory of trips, including extended excursions on the Maine coast. Trips typically involve moderate day hiking coupled with nights at comfortable lodges.

- **Vermont Bicycle Touring,** P.O. Box 711, Bristol, VT 05442 (© **800/245-3868;** www.vbt.com), is one of the more established and well-organized touring operations, with an extensive bike tour schedule in North America, Europe, and New Zealand. VBT offers several trips in Maine, including a 6-day Acadia trip with some overnights at the grand Claremont Hotel.

GETTING MORE INFORMATION

Guidebooks to the region's backcountry are plentiful and diverse. L.L.Bean in Freeport, Maine, has an excellent selection of guidebooks for sale, as do many local bookshops throughout the region. An exhaustive collection of New England outdoor guidebooks for sale may be found online at **www.mountainwanderer.com**. The **Appalachian Mountain Club,** 5 Joy St., Boston, MA 02108 (© **617/523-0636;** www.outdoors.org), publishes a number of definitive guides to hiking and boating in the region.

Map Adventures, P.O. Box 15214, Portland, ME 04112 (© **207/879-4777**), is a small firm that publishes a growing line of good recreational maps covering popular local areas including the Camden Hills and Acadia National Park. See what they offer online at **www.mapadventures.com**.

Local outdoors clubs are also a good source of information, and most offer trips to nonmembers. The largest of the bunch is the Appalachian Mountain Club (see address above), whose chapters run group trips almost every weekend throughout the region, with northern New Hampshire especially well represented.

---

14 STAYING CONNECTED

TELEPHONES

Maine's **area code** is **207** throughout. For more information on using telephones for local and international calls in Maine, see "Telephones" in the appendix on p. 287.

CELLPHONES

Just because your cellphone works at home doesn't mean it'll work on the back roads of Maine—or even at that rustic country B&B, thanks to our nation's (and the region's) fragmented and competing cellphone coverage systems and the mostly rural nature of the state. You may or may not be within your roaming area, even if you have a national calling plan. It's a good bet that your phone will work in the region's major cities, so look over your wireless company's coverage map on its website before heading out to be sure; T-Mobile, Sprint, and Nextel are particularly weak at covering rural areas.

If you need to stay in touch at a destination where you know your phone won't work, **rent** a phone that will from **InTouch USA** (© **800/872-7626;** www.intouchglobal.com) or from some rental car desks; just be aware that you'll pay $1 a minute or more for airtime anytime you use the phone.

If you're not from the U.S., you might be a bit appalled at the poor reach of the **GSM (Global System for Mobile Communications) wireless network,** which is used by much of the rest of the world. Your phone will probably work in most major U.S. cities; it definitely won't work in many rural areas. To see where GSM phones work in the U.S., check out www.t-mobile.com/coverage. And you may or may not be able to send SMS (text messaging) home.

Need to rent a cellphone? Check at Logan Airport in Boston or smaller airports such as Portland's. Or head for the business district of the city or town you're visiting.

VOICE-OVER INTERNET PROTOCOL (VOIP)

If you have Web access while traveling, consider a broadband-based telephone service (in technical terms, **Voice-over Internet protocol, or VoIP**) such as Skype (www.skype.com) or Vonage (www.vonage.com), which allow you to make free international calls from your laptop or in a cybercafe. Neither service requires the people you're calling to also have that service (though there are fees if they do not). Check the websites for details.

INTERNET & E-MAIL

WITH YOUR OWN COMPUTER More and more hotels, resorts, airports, cafes, and retailers are going Wi-Fi (wireless fidelity), becoming "hotspots" that offer free high-speed Wi-Fi access or charge a small fee for usage. Wi-Fi is even found in campgrounds, RV parks, and even entire towns. Most laptops sold today have built-in wireless capability. To find public Wi-Fi hotspots at your destination, go to **www.jiwire.com**; its Hotspot Finder holds the world's largest directory of public wireless hotspots.

For dial-up access, most business-class hotels in the U.S. offer dataports for laptop modems, and a few thousand hotels in the U.S. and Europe now offer free high-speed Internet access.

Wherever you go, bring a **connection kit** of the right power and phone adapters, a spare phone cord, and a spare Ethernet

---

(Tips   Hey, Google, Did You Get My Text Message?

It's bound to happen: The day you leave this guidebook back at the hotel for an unencumbered stroll through Portland, you'll forget the address of the lunch spot you had earmarked. If you're traveling with a mobile device, send a text message to © **46645 (GOOGL)** for a lightning-fast response. For instance, type "lobster portland maine," and within 10 seconds you should receive a text message with an address and phone number. This nifty trick works in a range of search categories: Look up weather ("weather portsmouth"), language translations, currency conversions ("10 usd in pounds"), movie times ("harry potter 04101"), and more. If your search results are off, be more specific ("anthony's pier boston"). For more tips and search options, see www.google.com/intl/en_us/mobile/sms/. Regular text message charges apply.

Online Traveler's Toolbox

Savvy travelers know that it's a great idea to use online resources when planning a trip. Here are a few websites we keep bookmarked:

- **Airplane Food** (www.airlinemeals.net)
- **Airplane Seating** (www.seatguru.com)
- **Maps** (maps.google.com or www.mapquest.com)
- **MasterCard ATM Locator** (www.mastercard.com)
- **Time and Date** (www.timeanddate.com)
- **Universal Currency Converter** (www.xe.com/ucc)
- **Visa ATM Locator** (www.visa.com)
- **Weather** (www.intellicast.com or www.weather.com)

network cable—or find out whether your hotel supplies them to guests.

WITHOUT YOUR OWN COMPUTER Most major airports have **Internet kiosks** that provide basic Web access for a per-minute fee that's usually higher than cybercafe prices. Check out copy shops such as **FedEx Kinko's,** which often offer computer stations with fully loaded software as well as Wi-Fi access.

Portland has a couple of cybercafes, which are a good value for quick e-mail checking (figure a $3 minimum charge); in small towns, though, it's hit-or-miss (usually miss). Fortunately, coastal Maine's **public libraries** are superb at offering Internet access, nearly always for free (you

may need to submit a driver's license, library card, or other piece of identification as a deposit). The local library in a large coastal town such as York, Kennebunk, or Belfast could prove vital in a pinch—but be courteous, and do not overstay your welcome.

Youth hostels normally offer at least one computer from which you can access the Internet, though they're practically nonexistent in Maine nowadays.

Avoid **hotel business centers,** which often charge exorbitant rates, unless you're desperate and have no other choice.

For help locating cybercafes and other establishments where you can go for Internet access, please see "Internet Access" in the "**Fast Facts**" appendix (p. 282).

15 TIPS ON ACCOMMODATIONS

"The more we travel," said an unhappy couple one morning at a nameless New England inn, "the more we realize why we go back to our old favorites time and again." The reason for their chagrin? They had been forced to switch rooms at 2am when rain had begun dripping right onto them through the ceiling. I hasten to add that this story is not an isolated incident.

Small, quaint inns here often come with their own drips, creaks, and quirks.

Maine is famous for its plethora of country inns and bed-and-breakfasts (B&Bs), which offer a wonderful alternative to the sort of cookie-cutter, chain-hotel rooms that line U.S. highways from coast to coast. But (as the unhappy couple learned) there are reasons why some people *prefer*

Fun Facts Inn vs. B&B: Everybody Wins

The difference between an inn and a B&B may be confusing for some travelers, since the gap between the two narrows by the day. A couple of decades ago, inns were full-service affairs, whereas B&Bs consisted of private homes with an extra bedroom or two and a homeowner looking for a little extra income. These old-style B&Bs still exist around the region. I've occupied a few evenings sitting in a well-used living room watching Tom Brokaw with the owner, as if visiting with a forgotten aunt.

Today, B&Bs are more commonly professionally run affairs, where guests have private bathrooms, a separate common area, and attentive service. The owners have apartments tucked away in the back, prepare sumptuous breakfasts in the morning (some B&Bs offer "candlelight breakfasts"), and offer a high level of service. All of the B&Bs in this guide are of the more professionally run variety (although several or more still have shared bathrooms). Other guidebooks are available for those searching for home-stay lodging.

The sole difference between inns and B&Bs—at least as defined by this guide—is that inns serve dinner (and sometimes lunch). B&Bs provide breakfast only. Readers shouldn't infer that B&Bs are necessarily more informal or in any way inferior to a full-service inn. Indeed, all of the places listed in "The Best Bed & Breakfasts" in chapter 1 have the air of gracious inns that just happened to have overlooked serving dinner. That's true for many of the other B&Bs listed in this guide; and with a little luck, you'll stumble into Ralph Waldo Emerson's idea of simple contentment: "Hospitality consists in a little fire, a little food, and an immense quiet," he wrote in his journal.

the cookie-cutter hotels. In a chain hotel, you can be reasonably sure that water won't drip through your ceiling in the middle of the night. Likewise, the beds will be firm, the sink will be relatively new, and you'll have a TV, telephone, and counter space next to the bathroom sink.

Every **inn** and **B&B** listed in this guide yields a decent, and often a high-quality, experience. Just keep in mind that each place is different, and you need to match the personality of the place with your *own* personality. Some inns are more polished and fussier than others; this is a rural area, so a lot of them (even some calling themselves "resorts") lack basic amenities to which business travelers have grown accustomed in chain hotels. (In-room phones and air-conditioning lead the list.)

SURFING FOR HOTELS

In addition to the online travel booking sites **Travelocity, Expedia, Orbitz, Priceline,** and **Hotwire,** you can book hotels through **Hotels.com; Quikbook** (www.quikbook.com); and **Travelaxe** (www.travelaxe.net).

HotelChatter.com is a daily webzine offering smart coverage and critiques of hotels worldwide. Go to **TripAdvisor.com** or **HotelShark.com** for helpful independent consumer reviews of hotels and resort properties.

It's a good idea to **get a confirmation number** and **make a printout** of any online booking transaction.

SAVING ON YOUR HOTEL ROOM

The **rack rate** is the maximum rate that a hotel charges for a room. Hardly anybody pays this price, however, except in high season or on holidays. To lower the cost of your room:

- **Ask about special rates or other discounts.** You may qualify for corporate, student, military, senior, frequent flier, trade union, or other discounts.
- **Dial direct.** When booking a room in a chain hotel, you'll often get a better deal by calling the individual hotel's reservation desk rather than the chain's main number.
- **Book online.** Many hotels offer Internet-only discounts, or supply rooms to Priceline, Hotwire, or Expedia at rates much lower than the ones you can get through the hotel itself.
- **Remember the law of supply and demand.** Resort hotels are most crowded and therefore most expensive on weekends, so discounts are usually available for midweek stays. Business hotels in downtown locations are busiest during the week, so you can expect big discounts over the weekend.

- **Look into group or long-stay discounts.** If you come as part of a large group, you should be able to negotiate a bargain rate. Likewise, if you're planning a long stay (of at least 5 days), you might qualify for a discount of 1 free night for a 7-night stay; buy 6, get 1 free.
- **Sidestep excess surcharges and hidden costs.** Many hotels have the unpleasant practice of nickel-and-diming their guests with opaque surcharges. When you book a room, ask what is included in the room rate, and what is extra. Avoid dialing direct from hotel phones, which can have exorbitant rates. And don't be tempted by the room's minibar offerings: Most hotels charge through the nose for water, soda, and snacks. Finally, ask about local taxes and service charges, which can increase the cost of a room by 15% or more.
- There are a small handful of **all-inclusive** resorts in Maine. The term "all-inclusive" means different things at different hotels; here, it means three

> **(Tips) Nail Down That Cancel Policy!**
>
> When making reservations, it's essential that you get down (in writing, via printed-out website promise, by e-mail) some confirmation of your hotel's or inn's exact **cancellation policy.** Since they're going to take your credit card as a deposit in almost every case, you'll need this information in case your trip is way-laid for any reason at all.
>
> There's an amazing variety of policies out there. Some places give you all your money back if you cancel early enough; a cutoff of **24 hours before arrival is standard** as a deadline, but some lodging establishments require 1 week's advance notice of a cancellation, and some will let you cancel at 6pm on the *day of arrival.* Some properties refund all your deposit back even if you missed the deadline (mostly very small places do this, when they know they can sell the room again). Most properties **keep 1 night's fee** if you missed the deadline. And a few give you nothing back, no matter what.
>
> As you can see, **policies range from generous to outrageous.** One Frommer's reader canceled a reservation at a Vermont motel 2 days before arriving because a hurricane had just veered into her home state. "Sorry," she was told, "cancellations must be made 1 week in advance." Give me a break.

(Tips) Renting a House or Cottage

Renting a house or cottage in Maine for a week is another good option, particularly outside the summer high season, though there really isn't a centralized resource for doing so. You get the comforts of having your own kitchen or kitchenette and not worrying about parking, checkout times, or untimely "room service" knocks on your door. For a nice house with an ample supply of bedrooms and an unobstructed ocean view, expect to pay anywhere from $2,000 to $10,000 per week; a simpler cottage will run you less but might still cost more than you expected. Do a Web search for Maine house or cottage rentals, or go to a nationwide rent-by-owner website such as www.vrbo.com. While these certainly aren't the only choices along the Maine coast, they'll give you a good head start.

meals daily and use of the resort's sports equipment (such as canoes and kayaks).

- Carefully consider your hotel's meal plan. If you enjoy eating out and sampling the local cuisine, it makes sense to choose a Continental plan (also known as B&B), or a European plan, which doesn't include any meals and allows you maximum flexibility. If you're more interested in saving money, opt for a **Modified American plan (MAP),** which includes breakfast and dinner, or the American plan, which includes all three meals (pretty rare in this region). If you must choose a MAP, see if you can get a free lunch at your hotel if you decide to do dinner out.

- **Book an efficiency.** A room with a kitchenette allows you to shop for groceries and cook your own meals. This is a big money saver, especially for families on long stays.

- **Consider enrolling in hotel "frequent-stay" programs,** which are upping the ante lately to win the loyalty of repeat customers. Frequent guests can accumulate points or credits to earn free hotel nights, airline miles, in-room amenities, merchandise, tickets to concerts and events, or discounts on sporting facilities. Perks are awarded not only by many chain hotels and motels (Hilton HHonors, Marriott Rewards, Wyndham ByRequest, to name a few), but some individual inns and B&Bs. Many chain hotels partner with other hotel chains, car-rental firms, airlines, and credit card companies to give consumers additional incentives to return.

- **Ask if the hotel charges extra for additional guests** (beyond two). The room rates published in this guide are all for two people sharing one room. Most places charge $10 and up per extra guest sharing the room. Don't assume that children traveling with you can stay for free—usually they can, but ask first about extra charges—and don't assume that every room can hold more than two.

- **Ask about a minimum stay requirement and discounts for multiday stays.** Many inns now require guests to book a minimum of 2 nights or more during the busiest times (holiday weekends, peak ski season, peak fall foliage season). These policies are mentioned in the following pages if known, but check anyway. And they might not apply if you walk in off the street; innkeepers develop sudden amnesia when faced with a chance to sell an empty room on a Saturday night despite a policy against such a stay.

Tips for Digital Travel Photography

- **Take along a spare camera—or two.** Even if you've been anointed the "official" photographer in your travel group, encourage others to bring their own cameras to provide fresh perspective—and backup. Your photographic "second unit" can include you in a few shots so you're not the "invisible person" on the trip.
- **Stock up on digital film cards.** At home, it's easy to copy pictures from your memory cards to your computer as they fill up. During your travels, cards seem to fill up more quickly. Take along enough digital film for your entire trip or, at a minimum, enough for at least a few days' of shooting. At intervals, you can copy images to CDs. Many camera stores and souvenir shops offer this service, and a growing number of mass merchandisers have walk-up kiosks you can use to make prints or create CDs while you travel.
- **Share and share alike.** There's no need to wait until you get home to share your photos. You can upload a gallery's worth to an online photo sharing service. Just find an Internet café where the computers have card readers, or connect your camera to the computer with a cable. You can find online photo sharing services that cost little or nothing at **www.clickherefree. com**. You can also use America Online's Your Pictures service, or commercial enterprises that give you free or low-cost photo sharing such as Kodak's EasyShare gallery (**www.kodak.com**), Snapfish (**www.snapfish.com**), or Shutterfly (**www.shutterfly.com**).
- **Add voice annotations to your photos.** Many digital cameras allow you to add voice annotations to your shots after they're taken. These serve as excellent reminders and documentation. One castle or cathedral may look like another after a long tour; your voice notes will help you distinguish them.
- **Experiment.** Travel is a great time to try out new techniques. Take photos at night, resting your camera on a handy wall or other support as your self-timer trips the shutter for a long exposure. Try close-ups of flowers, crafts, wildlife, or maybe the exotic cuisine you're about to consume. Discover action photography—shoot the countryside from trains, buses, or cars. With a digital camera, you can experiment and then erase your mistakes.

—From *Travel Photography Digital Field Guide,* 1st Edition (Wiley & Sons, 2006)

LANDING THE BEST ROOM

Somebody has to get the best room in the house; it might as well be you (or me). You can start by joining the hotel's frequent-guest program, which may make you eligible for upgrades. A hotel-branded credit card usually gives its owner "silver" or "gold" status in frequent-guest programs for free. Always ask about a corner room—they're often larger and quieter, with more windows and light.

When making your reservation, also ask if the hotel is renovating; if it is, request a room away from the construction. If you're a light sleeper, request a quiet room away from vending and ice machines, elevators, restaurants, bars, and discos. (*Never* book a room over the bar or function room on a Fri or Sat night, no matter how often reservations staff try to tell you that "things quiet down around midnight." They don't.) Ask for a room that has most recently been renovated or redecorated.

If you aren't happy with your room when you arrive, ask for another one. Most lodgings will be willing to accommodate you.

Also ask the following questions before you book a room:

- What's the view like? Cost-conscious travelers might be willing to pay less for a back room facing the parking lot if they don't plan to spend much time in their room. But you're here to see mountains and ocean views, so, you might well be willing to pay the extra cash for the great view.

- Does the room have air-conditioning, heaters, ceiling fans? Do the windows open?

- How far is your hotel (and room) from the beach, ski resort, apple orchard, or whatever you came to see? If it's really far, does the hotel provide a map for drivers?

SERVICE CHARGES

Rather than increase room rates in the face of rising competition, hotels, inns, and B&Bs are increasingly tacking on nickel-and-dime fees to their guests' bills. Most innkeepers will tell you about these fees when you reserve or check in; a few will surprise you at checkout.

The most common surcharge is an involuntary "service charge" of 10% to 15%. Coupled with state lodging taxes (even "sales-tax-free" New Hampshire hits tourists with an 8% levy), that bumps the cost of a bed up by nearly 25%. (The rates listed in this guide don't include service charges or sales tax.)

Other charges may include a pet fee ($10 or more per day extra), a foliage-season surcharge ($10–$50 per room), and a "resort fee" (of 15%–20% tax at certain resorts). Some hotels even tack on a $1 per day fee for the presence of an in-room safe, whether it is used or not.

Suggested Maine Coast Itineraries

Many travelers look at a coast-of-Maine trip as their only chance in a lifetime to see this part of the world. They try to race around the region seeing everything from Kittery to Portland to Acadia, plus even (maybe) a moose in the Maine Woods along the way . . . all in less than a week.

Trust me: That's nothing but a formula for disappointment, and has all the makings of a trip on which you'll probably end up seeing the inside of your windshield more than anything else. The coast of Maine has very few attractions that lend themselves to snap-a-photo tourism. Instead, it's best seen by moving slowly—on foot, in a canoe, on a bike, driving the back roads. The happiest visitors to this region tend to be those who stay more or less in one place or region, getting to know that place especially well through a series of carefully crafted day trips.

With that in mind, here are a few itineraries to use as a starting point; feel free to mix and match, improvise, or even devise your own. The first tour shows you the best of the entire Maine coast, but it takes from 1 to 2 weeks to do right; don't try to compress it into a couple of days. A second set of tours focuses on the city of Portland, Maine's cultural capital, geared toward the perspective of those traveling with families. I have devised three separate itineraries, according to how much time you have available. Finally, a third tour takes visitors through the often-neglected Bath-Brunswick area, focusing on the museums, art, and historic homes that reside there.

If you have somehow gotten to Maine without a car, and won't have time to rent or borrow one during your visit, see my suggestions for touring the coast without a vehicle in "Your Car: *Do* Leave Home Without It" in chapter 3.

THE REGIONS IN BRIEF

Southern Maine From the state line at Kittery to the Freeport-Bath-Brunswick area, Maine's southern coast features most of the state's best beaches and beach resorts. It's also home to the region's largest and most vibrant city, Portland. In addition, I recommend dipping a few miles south of the Piscataqua River to experience the adjacent New Hampshire coast and its anchor city of Portsmouth (which I will cover separately in chapter 11). For the purposes of this guidebook, I have divided southern Maine into three

chapters: Kittery to the Kennebunks; Portland; and Freeport to Monhegan Island.

Midcoast Maine Midcoast Maine begins, depending on whom you ask, somewhere around the big bridge in downtown Bath and ends somewhere around Bucksport or Ellsworth. In between, you'll discover more rocky headlands, bays, and coves than you ever dreamed existed, as well as quaint villages with names such as Blue Hill, Camden, and Rockport and even some small hills and mountains. For the purposes of this book, I have shoehorned this entire, wonderfully scenic region into one action-packed chapter.

Downeast Maine   Maine's rocky coast is the stuff of legend, art, and poetry, and in Downeast Maine—which goes from the Ellsworth area all the way up the coast to the Canadian border—you'll find plenty of empty back roads and room to roam, not to mention rocky islands, foggy mornings, lobster boats aplenty, and a breathtakingly beautiful national park. In this book, I have dedicated one entire chapter to MDI (as Mount Desert Island is known by locals)—and that chapter is necessarily dominated by Acadia National Park. A second chapter treating the rest of Downeast Maine details the quieter

pleasures of exploring north and east from the MDI area up to the Canadian border.

Side Trips from the Maine Coast Once you've reached the Maine coast, it's worth exploring some dandy nearby areas and attractions, as well. In my final chapter, I describe three such side trips: first, heading a few miles south to experience small-town Portsmouth, New Hampshire, and its lovely surrounding coastline; second, pushing inland from Belfast or Bangor to sample the Great North Woods of Maine, which could legitimately be called the Northeast's last bit of untrammeled wilderness; and third, pressing north across the Canadian border an hour by car or boat to experience a lovely slice of coastal New Brunswick.

1 THE BEST OF THE MAINE COAST IN 2 WEEKS

Maine's coast tends to confound hurry-up tourists—there are simply too many dead-end peninsulas to backtrack along, and too many inlets that cleave the coast too far inland. You must sometimes drive great distances just to get from one rocky, wave-beaten point to the next, so finding a single home base and fanning out from there is the best strategy. Most of this route heads north along U.S. Route 1, which can be a bit slowpokey in high summer season, but take heart: You'll have more time to soak up the views, which are pretty good for stretches, particularly once you get north of Bath.

Day ❶: York ★★
Drive into Maine from the south on I-95, and head immediately for **York Village ★** (the first exit; p. 78). Spend some time snooping around the historic homes of the **Old York Historical Society,** and stretch your legs on a walk through town or the woods.

Drive northward through **York Beach ★★** (stocking up on saltwater taffy at the Goldenrod); stay near the beach.

From York, drive 20 miles north on the Maine Turnpike (I-95) or U.S. Route 1 to find:

Day ❷: The Kennebunks ★★ & Ogunquit ★★
The Kennebunks are definitely worth a day if you enjoy the old blue-blood New England quaintness and luxury accommodations. There are some pretty fancy inns and bed-and-breakfast establishments in these parts.

Kennebunk, the lesser-known of the twin towns (they're separated by a slim tidal river), is a mixed bag of attractions, with the so-called **Wedding Cake House** ★, a very good public beach, a monastery (yes, really), and a natural-products factory store, among other things to see and do. See p. 96.

Across the river in **Kennebunkport,** you can stroll the leafy town, gawk at George Bush the elder's summer home (from a short distance away; those Secret Service guys mean business), and have a relaxed dinner at a fine restaurant. There are also a small shopping district and plenty of pleasure boats and yachts moored in the area. See p. 96.

While staying in the area, be sure to visit **Ogunquit** for its beaches, ocean views, summery atmosphere, and the small but truly excellent **Ogunquit Museum of American Art** ★★★. Also hit the antiques shops lined up along Route 1 as you trend northward if you're so inclined. See p. 86.

From the Kennebunks, drive 27 miles north either on the Maine Turnpike (I-95, exiting onto Rte. 295 and following signs) or U.S. Route 1 to the Greater Portland area.

Days ❸, ❹ & ❺: Portland ★★★

Plan to stay in **Portland** or on a nearby beach for up to 3 days, shopping for jewelry, souvenirs, or even kites or toys; taste-testing chowder recipes and microbrewed beers; and just generally soaking up the salty air and atmosphere.

And don't forget to take a walk along the **Eastern Promenade** ★★ or a day cruise on a local ferry, either. See p. 117.

From Portland, drive north 17 miles on I-295 or U.S. Route 1 to the Freeport area. There's a Maine state tourist information facility on Route 1 just north of Yarmouth, stocked with brochures and staff (daytime hours).

Day ❻: Freeport & Surrounding Areas

Head north early to beat the shopping crowds at the outlet haven of **Freeport.** (You can't leave too early for **L.L.Bean**—it never closes!) See p. 122.

From Freeport, continue northward to **Brunswick,** home to **Bowdoin College** ★ (p. 135) and its two small but excellent museums. Then press a few miles farther north to atmospheric **Bath** ★, with plenty of ancient sea captains' homes, a shipyard, and the **Maine Maritime Museum & Shipyard** ★ (p. 138). Stay in a B&B in any of the three towns.

From Freeport, drive about 70 miles north along U.S. Route 1 to the Camden-Rockland-Rockport area; summer traffic congestion can slow this to a 2-hour-plus stretch. Wiscasset (about halfway to Camden) and Waldoboro (home of Moody's Diner) make two nice stopping points along the way.

Days ❼ & ❽: Camden ★★ & Penobscot Bay ★★

Heading north from the Bath-Brunswick area, detour down to **Pemaquid Point** ★★ for a late picnic and to watch the surf roll in. Then head back to Route 1 and set your sights on the Camden-Rockland area, the commercial heart of the **Penobscot Bay** region. See p. 155.

Rockland ★, which comes first, is the workaday half of the equation. You'll find funky cafes, an excellent museum, and good restaurants. See p. 156.

Nearby **Rockport** ★ is a tiny harbor town with superb views and a tiny, artsy main street. See p. 164.

Finally, head a few miles north to wander around **Camden's** ★★ downtown, poke into shops and galleries, hike up one of the impressive hills at **Camden Hills State Park** ★★, hop a ferry to an island (North Haven and Islesboro are both great for biking), sign up for a daylong sail on a windjammer, or just spend a long afternoon unwinding on the deck of a local restaurant. It's also fun to grab an ice cream or hot dog down by the harbor.

From Camden, drive U.S. Route 1 40 miles north to state Route 15, turn south, and drive 12 more miles to:

Day ❾: Blue Hill ★★ & Deer Isle ★★

Have dinner and find accommodations in scenic **Blue Hill.** There are good views here, and the mixture of a Maine fishing town with bookshops and restaurants is quite appealing. Also take a spin around the peninsula to even smaller towns such as **Blue Hill Falls** and **Brooklin,** where you'll see boatyards, old-fashioned general stores (post offices included), and Maine ingenuity holding it all together. *This* is the real Maine. See p. 180 and 185.

Continue an additional 18 miles south on Route 15 to **Deer Isle.** The roads here are great for aimless drives, but aim anyway for **Stonington** ★ at the far end of the peninsula. If distant **Isle au Haut** ★★, visible from the town docks, makes you pine for an offshore adventure, plan a boat trip for early the next morning; secure lodging in Deer Isle; and adjust your schedule accordingly. Otherwise, explore the area by car or sign up for a kayak tour with **Old Quarry Charters** (p. 184).

From Stonington, backtrack 18 miles on Route 15 to Blue Hill, then follow Route 172 north 14 miles to U.S. Route 1. Follow Route 1 just a short distance before bearing right onto Route 3 (following signs to Acadia National Park), and continue 6 miles to the bridge to Mount Desert Island. Cross the bridge and follow Route 3 about 10 more miles to Bar Harbor.

Days ⑩, ⑪, ⑫ & ⑬: Bar Harbor ★ & Acadia National Park ★★★

Bar Harbor is the most convenient, if not the prettiest, base for exploring **Mount Desert Island** ★★, which is well worth at least 4 days on any Maine itinerary. You might want to plan at least 2 nights in Bar Harbor, especially if you're here with your family: This town provides access to comforts and services such as a movie theater, souvenir shops, bike and kayak rentals, free shuttle buses fanning out all over the island, and numerous kinds of restaurants that other island towns don't have. Yes, it's a lot more developed (perhaps too much so) than the rest of the island, but think of it as a supply depot.

Hike, bike, boat, or do whatever you have to do to explore the island and this national park—in my humble opinion, one of America's finest. What it lacks in

"bigness," it more than makes up for with intimate contact with nature. Explore at your own pace, via a beginner's kayak trip down the eastern shore, a hike out to Bar Island, or a mountain bike trip along one of the many carriage roads built by the Rockefeller family: Only bicycles and horses are allowed on these roads, making them a good respite from the island's highways, which—almost unbelievably—*do* get crowded in summer.

The scenic **Park Loop Road** ★★★ offers a good introduction to what's in store for you later (crashing waves, big mountains, drop-dead gorgeous views). Make sure to buy a park pass that lasts more than 1 day.

While exploring the rest of the island, hit some of the towns off the beaten track, too. **Northeast Harbor** ★ and **Southwest Harbor** ★ are both fishing villages that have been transformed by tourism into small centers of art, music, and shopping . . . but they still have local grocery stores where fishermen slush in to shop for slickers and Wonder Bread, too.

The things you wanted to do, but didn't have time for? Do them on your last day in Acadia. Cap off your visit with a cold-water dip at Sand Beach and tea and popovers at **Jordan Pond House** ★★ (p. 204). Maybe watch a sunrise from the top of Cadillac Mountain, take a quick last hike up The Bubbles, or paddle a canoe on Long Pond. Or just enjoy one last lobster from atop a wooden pier before setting off back south.

From Bar Harbor, follow Route 3 10 miles back to the island bridge, cross it, and continue 6 miles to Route 1. Follow Route 1 a mile south to junction with Route 1A, then turn onto Route 1A and continue about 25 miles to Bangor.

Day ⑭: Bangor ★ & Home

Heading home, you don't need to head south on Route 1 again. In fact, it's far quicker to bypass the coast and use Interstate 95—part of which comprises the Maine Turnpike (a toll road)—to get home. On the way, you might want to stop in **Bangor,** especially if you're a big fan of horror writer Stephen King. His house is pretty obvious once you get downtown. There are several museums in and around the city, as well; it's the only place that passes for a cultural center in the vastly empty spaces of inland northern Maine, so stock up (and fuel up) while you've got the chance.

From Bangor, take the Maine Turnpike (I-95) south 180 miles to the state line at Kittery. With no stops, it takes less than 3 hours.

2 PORTLAND FOR FAMILIES IN 1 DAY

A family can easily spend a pleasant 3 days exploring the cobblestones, shops, museums, and attractions of Portland. Day 1 of this tour begins in the city's emerging Arts District, which is home to a number of museums, and then makes its way to Portland's historic Old Port.

❶ Portland Museum of Art ★★★

Located on Congress Square, Portland's outstanding museum of art is almost directly in the center of the city proper, making it a good jumping-off point for a tour of the rest of Portland. Make a deal with your kids: If they behave during a trip to the art museum, they'll be rewarded with a couple of hours in their own museum (just next door). Or simply split your party up, sending teens and college-age family members to the art museum while younger kids and a lucky adult muck about in the Children's Museum. See p. 118.

❷ Children's Museum of Maine ★

Kids will love the opportunity to run from exhibit to exhibit in their own museum. In addition to its legendary camera obscura, the museum also sports permanent and rotating exhibits of interactive stuff such as a firehouse pole and mock space shuttle. Be sure to check out the Explore Floor, which offers a series of interactive science exhibits focusing on Maine's natural resources. See p. 117.

As you exit the Children's Museum, turn right on Free Street. At Oak Street, cross the street and continue half a block down Free Street to the back entrance of the:

❸ L.L.Bean Outlet Store

Fans of L.L.Bean shouldn't miss its Portland outlet, located in the Arts District a few blocks away from the museums. The outlet sells both kids' and adults' clothes; the best deals are usually the (very) slightly damaged or imperfect goods, which can often be had for a steal. See p. 122.

Either backtrack to your car or, if it's a nice day, consider hoofing it down to the Old Port. Continue left (as you leave the outlet's back door) down Free Street 4 short blocks to Temple Street. Turn right, continue a short half a block to the traffic light and intersection, then make a left on Middle Street (also called Spring St.). Continue straight 1 block to Exchange Street and find yourself in the heart of:

❹ The Old Port ★★★

Spend the rest of the day exploring the historic Old Port. If you haven't stopped for lunch yet, you'll find plenty of options in the Old Port, particularly along Commercial Street. **Exchange Street** is the key shopping address, though the other cobblestone side streets and the harbor area are also nice.

In summer, free concerts are sometimes held in a small park, and the city's tourist office—stocked with free info—is down at the bottom on Commercial Street. Kids will enjoy the ice-cream shops, boats, and knickknacks.

One of the best shops is **Northern Sky Toyz,** parked on the Old Port's busiest corner at 388 Free St. It's my go-to stop for Frisbees, but you can also find plenty more kids' (and adults') toys there, too, some of them rather unconventional.

Don't miss a seafood feed of lobster, fish, or clam chowder at a place such as **Gilbert's Chowder House,** 92 Commercial St. (p. 115). There are plenty of choices for all of these in town.

COFFEE BREAK
There's an Internet cafe at 37 Exchange St. called **Java Net Café** (☏ **207/773-2469**), with coffee, a young vibe, and Internet terminals for sending e-cards back home to the envious. If you need coffee but don't need e-mail, **Breaking New Grounds** (☏ **207/761-5637**) is just down the block at 13 Exchange St. Their coffee drinks are more creative, the feel even more bohemian, and it's more a slice of artistic Portland.

3 PORTLAND FOR FAMILIES IN 2 DAYS

On day 2 of your Portland stay, you'll focus on tiny trains and the islands dotting Casco Bay. Kids will love riding a tiny choo-choo back and forth along the waterfront, while adults enjoy the island vistas, sea breezes, and dreams of second homes.

If you're driving, think about parking in the ferry terminal garage for this tour—it's expensive, but unavoidable if you're out on the islands. To begin the tour, walk downhill to the base of the Old Port: the waterfront boulevard known as Commercial Street. Turn left and continue past the ferry docks to the:

❶ Maine Narrow Gauge Railroad Co. & Museum ★

This combo of a mini–choo-choo and museum is inexpensive and fun for the kiddies. Admission to the museum is free and educational, while the (*very* slow) train ride traces the foot of the cliffs framing Portland's east end. Parents will be popping the No-Doz, but, hey, at least it's short. See p. 117.

From the railroad, backtrack along Commercial Street 1 block to the ferry terminal, where you can:

❷ Take a Ferry to an Island

One of the don't-miss experiences of a Portland visit is a cruise around Casco Bay on a **Casco Bay Lines** (p. 119) ferry that departs from a terminal at the foot of Franklin Arterial (across from the blockish Hilton Garden Inn). You can take anywhere from a 20-minute run to a half-day mail-boat cruise. Two of my recommended

destinations are **Peaks Island**—a favorite among mothers pushing baby strollers, for its easy-to-cruise streets with Portland views—and **Long Island,** with an excellent beach.

From the ferry terminal, it's an uphill hike to the next stop; those with small children will want to drive. Exit the ferry terminal and turn right on Commercial Street. Loop around left to India Street, then take the first right onto Fore Street. The street will change its name to Eastern Promenade and open up some good views. At the top, you have two choices: Take the high road, and park for free on the street in front of the long grassy slope leading down to the water, or angle downhill to the right, where boats await. Either way, you've reached:

❸ The Eastern Promenade ★★

Young and old alike enjoy the sunrises, sunsets, picnics, sailboat views, swing sets, and ball fields of the Eastern Promenade, a 68-acre hillside park with broad, grassy slopes extending down to the water and superb views of Casco Bay and its islands. It's one of Portland's true gems. See p. 117.

From the Eastern Promenade, with the water on your right, continue by car or foot a few more blocks to Congress Street. You'll find this corner easily: There's a statue marking it. Turn left on Congress. You'll go up a slight rise, and after about 7 blocks, at the crest of the hill at 138 Congress St., find the:

❹ Portland Observatory ★

Kids like checking out the stupendous views from the top of this distinctive, shingled observatory, built in 1807 to signal ship arrivals into the city's port. (It's also locally called the Munjoy Hill Observatory, if you're asking directions.) It's said to be the last working maritime signal tower in the nation and was designated as a National Historic Landmark in 2006. It's open from spring through fall to tours. See p. 117. 393192 INDD

4 PORTLAND FOR FAMILIES IN 3 DAYS

You'll spend day 3 of your stay in Portland having a ball on the beach and taking in some action at a Portland Sea Dogs baseball game. Remember that some of these activities depend on good weather. Portland's summer temperatures are normally lovely—but in case Mother Nature doesn't cooperate, I've also added some backup plans. (Also, be sure to consult a daily paper, television, or the website www.seadogs.com to make certain the Sea Dogs are actually playing a home game.)

From downtown Portland, begin at Monument Square downtown (that's the square surrounded by the Portland Public Library, office buildings, and an open square, which sometimes holds a farmers market). Here you'll find the:

❶ Public Market House

This new market house at 28 Monument Sq. replaced the bigger Portland Public Market nearby, and is now your best bet for one-stop picnic shopping while in downtown Portland. The complex includes a cheese shop, a beer-and-wine vendor, a florist, and a bakery. It's open daily year-round.

With picnic packed, head up to Congress Street. Turn left and continue ½ mile to State Street. Turn left on State and continue downhill, following signs for Route 77. Bear right and cross a big bridge into South Portland; stay the course for several traffic lights until you reach a right turn at Ocean Street (Rte. 77). Turn right and continue about 6 more miles to reach:

❷ Cape Elizabeth

On a sunny summer day, you can't go wrong with any of a number of beaches and lighthouses out Route 77 in the quiet suburb of Cape Elizabeth and its associated areas. Be sure to bring a swimsuit, sunscreen, and a camera.

Kids especially enjoy the **Two Lights** and **Portland Head Light** lighthouses, and everyone likes the eats at Two Lights Lobster Shack (a separate outbuilding dispenses ice-cream treats for lobster-a-phobes). There's also romping around in the sand and surf on Scarborough and Willard beaches nearby.

Weather's too inclement? No worries. After doing this Cape Elizabeth circuit inside your car, as you're returning to Portland, do not turn left on Broadway for the bridge back to Portland but instead turn *right* on Broadway and continue about 1½ miles to the good **Portland Harbor Museum** (⌘ 207/799-6337). Featuring artifacts and a history of the fort, plus lectures on such topics as local lighthouses, it's open daily spring through fall.

Backtrack the way you came: From Cape Elizabeth, drive 6 miles along Route 77 to South Portland, then cross the big bridge. After a few blocks, turn left (from the two left lanes) onto High Street and continue uphill 4 blocks to Congress Street. Turn left at the light and continue about 1 mile downhill along Congress until you reach the Maine Medical Center parking garage (on the left). Park here, cross busy Congress Street, walk 2 blocks downhill, and turn right to find Hadlock Field, home of the:

❸ Portland Sea Dogs ★★★

If your kids tend more toward the teens and they're crazy about baseball, an outing at Hadlock Field can't be beat; it's one of the better minor league parks at which I've ever attended a ballgame. And there's a bonus for New Englanders: The Sea Dogs are the minor-league club for the Boston Red Sox, with a chance to catch up-and-coming talent. Yankee fans, deal with it. See p. 120.

FILL 'ER UP
You'll likely fill up on peanuts, popcorn, and hot dogs at the game. If you're looking for a healthy bite before or after the contest, the surrounding industrial district doesn't seem promising at first. However, one of my favorite Thai restaurants in Maine just happens to sit a few blocks away from the park. **Seng Thai** (✆ **207/879-2577**) is at 921 Congress St. Too experimental for you? The bar/red-sauce restaurant **Sportsman's Grill,** 911 Congress St. (✆ **207/772-9324**), is half a block away. Both places are also handy in case the game's rained out.

5 BATH & BRUNSWICK FOR CULTURE LOVERS

This tour takes in the often-neglected Bath-Brunswick sliver of the Maine coast, which is usually passed by but is in fact packed with colonial history, brick buildings, great residential architecture, and a fistful of good little museums.

Our tour starts at the Brunswick town green, in the center of town. From here, walk 1 block to the:

❶ Federal Street District, Brunswick ★

Just a block off the main street, Federal Street is several eras removed from the present. This is where the town's wealthy first set up shop, and a stroll down the long, straight thoroughfare produces plenty of **Greek Revival, Victorian,** and **Federal-style homes** to please the eye. Many of these architectural gems were designed by Samuel Melcher III, a local architect and master builder of the 19th century who also worked on Bowdoin College nearby (see below).

The Parker Cleaveland house at **no. 75 Federal** is a good example of Melcher's work; a pathbreaking Bowdoin mineralogy professor, Cleaveland lived here for nearly half a century.

TIME FOR A CUPPA
When in downtown Brunswick and needing a quick snack and some java, look no farther than the **Bohemian Coffee House** (✆ **207/725-9095**) at 4 Railroad Ave., close to the large Hannaford's grocery store (itself set back in a plaza from the town green on Maine St.). Yes, they have free wireless Internet access. And a patio. And their own homemade gelato. Gelato? 'Nuff said.

❷ Bowdoin College Campus ★

Just up the street from no. 75 Federal, you come upon the campus of **Bowdoin College,** which is built around a lovely and expansive central green in classic Ivy style. (In fact, Bowdoin is considered a "little Ivy.") Among the famous folks to have taught or studied here: Nathaniel Hawthorne, Olympic marathon gold medalist Joan Benoit Samuelson, Henry Longfellow, and Civil War Gen. Joshua Chamberlain.

The campus buildings, mostly constructed in the 19th century—the oldest dates from 1802—are remarkable. Sturdy little **Massachusetts Hall** ★, still my favorite building, originally contained the entire Bowdoin campus within its walls. **Winthrop Hall,** close by, was the first of the line of brick dormitories that march in a prim line away from **Hubbard Hall** (1934), a drippingly Gothic library.

Memorial Hall, also close to Massachusetts Hall, was constructed of stone in the late 19th century but is now overshadowed by the Pickard and Wish theaters, whose performances are open to the public.

The steepled granite **chapel** is worth peeking inside if it's open. Designed by Richard Upjohn, it's unmistakably the visual focal point of the campus.

❸ Bowdoin College Museum of Art ★★

On the Bowdoin College campus, within a McKim, Mead, and White–designed structure, this jewel of a museum holds work from big-shot Maine artists such as the **Wyeths, Marsden Hartley, Winslow Homer,** and **John Singer Sargent.** And admission is free.

The **exterior** was designed to echo Brunelleschi's Renaissance Piazzi Chapel in Florence. The interior isn't too shabby, either: Look up at the **central dome** as you enter, where four murals were painted by LaFarge and others to symbolize the great European cultural centers of Rome, Florence, Venice, and Athens.

The **Winslow Homer Collection** ★ consists not only of Homer paintings but also memorabilia and even some of his painting tools—a must-see for true art buffs. In addition to all the New England landscape artists mentioned above, the museum's collections also hold European treasures such as the **cassone panel** *Nymphs of Fiesole,* recently attributed to

the important 15th-century Renaissance artist Fra Angelico (who apparently painted it when he was a teenager). Look for other permanent or visiting work by such artists as Corot, Magritte, Picasso, and Braque. See p. 137.

❹ Peary-MacMillan Arctic Museum ★★

Bowdoin's "other" museum is equally splendid, yet in a different way. Beyond the fascinating historical items pertaining to Peary and MacMillan's historic journeying to the North Pole (Peary alone donated some 5,000 photographs and a glass lantern from his travels), there's also a growing collection of Inuit artifacts, arts, and crafts here. See p. 138.

From Brunswick, head northeast 8 miles on U.S. Route 1 or slower Bath Road to reach Bath and its historic district.

❺ Bath Historic District ★★

Bath was once sea-captain-central for these parts, and many built their lovely Greek Revival, Federal, and Georgian homes on the brow of a hill overlooking the harbor. **Washington, Hill, and Middle streets** are the best lanes to explore; many of the homes now house excellent bed-and-breakfast inns.

There's a striking Gothic Revival **church** (1843) at 880 Washington St., now home to the local historic preservation organization; noted Maine architect John Calvin Stevens did some interior work here about a half century later.

And just try to miss the oversize, Gothic Revival **Chocolate Church,** now home to a local arts organization. It's dipped in paint the color of . . . well, you can guess, I think.

You'll find a few antiques shops and a bookshop on nearby **Front Street,** the heart of the commercial district that has somehow managed to retain a still-part-of-yesteryear look.

DINING IN STYLE

While hotfooting it among Bath's and Brunswick's museums and historic homes, you're sure to wilt from hunger at some point. Thank goodness, then, for **Mae's Café,** 160 Centre St. (*C* **207/442-8577**), in a wonderful old house in downtown Bath. In addition to serving two to three meals a day, they offer great baked goods such as pecan-studded sticky buns, pies, and cookies.

❻ Maine Maritime Museum & Shipyard ★

One of Maine's two primary maritime museums (there's another north along Rte. 1 in Searsport), this one offers plenty for the kids, but also adults who appreciate seafaring history. It's housed in a former shipyard and is chock-full of art, artifacts, and exhibits on marine-related topics such as boat building and lobstering. There's a nice gift shop here, too, and the museum sometimes operates boat trips along the Kennebec River. See p. 138.

❼ Wiscasset ★★

Many call this the cutest village in Maine. There's certainly no arguing that there are plenty of fine buildings to poke through (though no museums) in a relatively small area here. More than two dozen structures in this tiny town are listed on, or have been nominated to, the National Register of Historic Places, including **Castle Tucker ★** (p. 144), which isn't really a castle, and the elegant 1807 **Nickels-Sortwell House,** 121 Main St. (*C* **207/882-6218**), a hard-luck shipbuilder's home and former hotel, which you can tour for a small admission fee; it contains great period furnishings. Afterward, stroll the lanes and waterfront and see whether you can find the former U.S. Customs house, old jail, so-called "Octagon House," and brick schoolhouse, too. See p. 143.

The Southern Coast

Maine's southern coast runs roughly from the state line at Kittery to Portland, and is the primary destination of most travelers to the state. (These statistics include many day-trippers from the Boston area). While it takes some doing to find privacy or remoteness here, there are at least two excellent reasons to come: the long, sandy beaches and a sense of history in the coastal villages . . . some of them, anyway.

Thanks to quirks of geography, nearly all of Maine's sandy shores occur along this stretch of coastline. It's not hard to find a relaxing spot whether you prefer dunes, the lulling sound of breaking waves, or a carnival-like atmosphere in a beach town. Waves depend on the weather; during a good Northeast blow, they pound the shores, rise above the roads, and threaten beach houses built decades ago. During balmy midsummer days, though, the ocean can be gentle as a farm pond, its barely audible waves lapping timidly at the shore as the tide creeps in, inch by inch, covering tidal pools full of crabs, snails, and starfish.

One thing all the beaches here share in common: They're washed by the chilled waters of the Gulf of Maine, which makes for, er, invigorating swimming. Though the beach season is generally brief and intense, running only from July 4th to Labor Day, some towns are making an effort to stretch the tourist season out into fall.

(Fun Facts) Maine: A Recent Discovery? Hardly!

Think Maine is your little secret getaway? Think again: This coast has seen wave after successive wave of visitation, beginning at least 3 centuries ago when European newcomers tried to settle it, only to be driven off by Native Americans. (It's also locally believed that Vikings may have touristed—er, pillaged?—the region even longer before that.) By the early 19th century, the Maine coast had become well colonized and blossomed into one of the most prosperous places in all the U.S. Shipbuilders constructed brigantines and sloops, using stout pines and other trees floated downriver from Maine's North Woods; ship captains built huge, handsome homes in towns such as Searsport, Kittery, Bath, and Belfast; and merchants and traders built vast warehouses to store the booty from the excursions, as well as their own grandiose homes.

Then things quieted down for a while . . . until landscape artists "rediscovered" Maine, bringing a fresh influx of city dwellers in their wake in the mid-to-late 19th century from Boston, New York, and Philadelphia, seeking relief from the heat and congestion of the city. They built huge, shingled estates facing the sea in places such as Bar Harbor and Camden. Then, at the beginning of the 20th century, a newly moneyed emerging middle class (a third wave?) showed up to discover Maine yet again, building smaller, less expensive bungalows by the shore in places such as York Beach, Kennebunk Beach, and Old Orchard Beach. The next arrival? That's you, dear reader.

Kittery is 60 miles N of Boston and 266 miles NE of New York City

Driving into Maine from the south, as most travelers do, **Kittery** ★ is the first town to appear after crossing the big bridge spanning the Piscataqua River from New Hampshire. Once famous for its (still operating) naval yard, Kittery is now better known for its dozens of factory outlets.

"The Yorks," just to the north, are three towns that share a name, but little else. In fact, it's rare to find three such well-defined and diverse New England archetypes within such a compact area. **York Village** ★ is full of 17th-century American history and architecture in a compact area, and has a good library. **York Harbor** ★★ reached its zenith during America's late Victorian era, when wealthy urbanites constructed cottages at the ocean's edge; it's the most relaxing and scenic of the three. Finally, **York Beach** ★★ is a fun beach town with amusements, taffy shops, a small zoo, gabled summer homes set in crowded enclaves, a great lighthouse, and two excellent beaches with sun, sand, rocks, surf, surfers, fried-fish stands, and lighthouse views.

Just outside York Village, the protrusion of land known as **Cape Neddick** ★★ is an excellent back-road route to Ogunquit, *if* you can find it (go past the police station in Short Sands, then bear right at the sign for the Cape Neddick Lobster Pound).

ESSENTIALS
Getting There
Kittery is accessible from either **Interstate 95** or **Route 1,** with well-marked exits. Coming from the south, the Yorks are reached most easily by heading for (but not taking) the Maine Turnpike; follow I-95 to a point just south of the turnpike exit, then exit to the right ("last exit before tolls"). Coming from the north, pay your toll exiting the turnpike and then take the first exit, an immediate right.

Amtrak (© **800/872-7245;** www.amtrak.com) operates four to five Downeaster trains daily from Boston's North Station (which does not connect to Amtrak's national network; you must take a subway or taxi from Boston's South Station first) into southern Maine, stopping outside Wells, about 10 miles away from the Yorks; a one-way ticket costs $19, and the trip takes 1³/₄ hours. From Wells, though, you'll need to phone for a taxi or arrange for a pickup to get to your final destination.

No bus lines serve the stretch of Maine between Portland and Kittery. However, several competing bus lines run regular buses daily from Boston's South Station to downtown Portsmouth, New Hampshire, which is very close to Kittery (you can actually walk over a bridge into Maine from Portsmouth). The two chief carriers are **Greyhound** (© **800/231-2222;** www.greyhound.com)—which has absorbed former competitor Vermont Transit—and **C&J Trailways** (© **800/258-7111;** www.cjtrailways.com). For more details, see "Getting There" in the Portsmouth, New Hampshire, section of chapter 11. Taking a bus from New York City's Port Authority to Portsmouth costs about $45 one-way and takes about 6¹/₂ hours; from Boston, figure a fare of $17 or $18 one-way and a 1-hour ride.

From mid-June through Labor Day, a trackless trolley (a bus gussied up to look like an old-fashioned trolley) links the two beaches (Short Sands and Long Sands) in York and provides a convenient way to explore both without having to be hassled with feeding parking meters and risking tickets. The "trolley" costs $1.50 each way. An all-day pass on a longer, circular sightseeing route through the Yorks costs $8 per adult, $4 for kids age 3 to 10; hop on at well-marked stops. The chief advantage of this route is that it passes Nubble Light (see below), a very scenic point that is too far for most folks to get to from the beaches.

Visitor Information

The **Kittery Information Center** (© 207/439-1319) is at a well-marked rest area on I-95. It's full of info and helpful staff; has a pet exercise area and copious vending machines; and is open daily from 8am to 6pm in summer, from 9am to 5:30pm the rest of the year.

The **Greater York Region Chamber of Commerce** (© 207/363-4422) also operates another helpful **visitor center,** one that mirrors the shape of a stone cottage. It's set back from Route 1, right across from the Maine Turnpike exit 1 (beside the Stonewall Kitchen headquarters). In peak season, it's open Monday to Saturday from 9am to 5pm and Sundays from 10am to 4pm; from Labor Day through June, it's open weekdays 9am to 4pm and Saturdays from 10am to 2pm.

A trackless **trolley** runs back and forth between Short Sands and Long Sands, providing a convenient way to explore without having to be hassled with parking. Hop on the trolley (© 207/363-9600; www.yorktrolley.com) at one of the well-marked stops; it's $1.50 each way, $3 to sit on board for the entire loop without debarking. The trolley makes a circle through the Short Sands business district before heading out to Long Sands and proceeding all the way to the Libby's and Camp Eaton campgrounds at the far southern end of that beach, before turning around again. (It does not travel to Nubble Light, however.) The trolley operates from late June through Labor Day daily on the half-hour, from about 9:30am until around 10:15pm.

EXPLORING KITTERY & YORK

Kittery has become a shopping mecca thanks to the establishment of colonies of little factory outlet shopping malls clustered along both sides of U.S. Route 1, about 4 miles south of York. More than 100 of these outlets flank the highway, in more than a dozen strip malls. It's aesthetically ugly, but if you're looking to score a deal, you just might find it beautiful.

(Fun Facts) Father of Our Country; Flop As a Wharf Owner

John Hancock is justly famous for his oversize signature on the Declaration of Independence, his tenure as governor of Massachusetts, and the insurance company and tall Boston building that were named for him. What's not so well known is his involvement as a proprietor of **Hancock Wharf,** a failed wharf-and-warehouse enterprise that went bust. Hancock never actually set foot on the wharf, but for years locals believed he used it to stash arms, contraband, and/or goods he didn't want taxed by those tax-happy British. It now appears that wasn't the case, but it still makes for one of the many intriguing sites and stories in the **York Village** section of downtown York. (See p. 75 for more details on this neighborhood.)

Surprisingly, the wharf has a happy ending: It's more famous today than it was then, the only 18th-century warehouse still standing on the York River. It has been designated a National Historic Site, and the York Historical Society sometimes uses it to launch or receive the occasional historic boat passing through town.

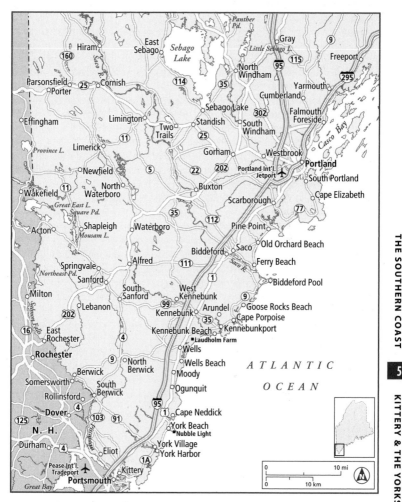

Name-brand retailers with factory shops here purveying cut-rate designer stuff include Coach, Orvis, Samsonite, Gap, Eddie Bauer, Banana Republic, Calvin Klein, Brookstone, and Polo Ralph Lauren, among many others. On rainy summer days, lots of people (including your author) have been spotted whiling away hours here. Parking can be tight on a particularly busy day.

Information on current outlets is available from the **Kittery Outlet Association.** Call © **888/548-8379** (that spells KITTERY, by the way), or visit the website at www.the kitteryoutlets.com.

Only have time for one set of outlets? For a comparison between the outlets here and the ones about an hour north in Freeport, see "Tale of the Tags: Freeport vs. Kittery," in chapter 7.

Kittery has no true town center, but is instead made of several disconnected villages (all of them quite old) and a long, skinny shopping strip. On the waterfront, the historic **Portsmouth Naval Shipyard** faces Portsmouth, New Hampshire. This active shipyard isn't open to the public (for security reasons), but you can visit the engaging displays at the **Kittery Historical & Naval Museum** (© **207/439-3080**) nearby to learn a bit about the history of submarines, the shipyard's specialty. It's open June through Columbus Day (early Oct), Tuesday to Saturday, 10am to 4pm. Admission is $3 for adults, $1.50 for children, and $6 for a family. Find it by taking U.S. Route 1 to the Kittery traffic circle, then exiting for Route 236 south; that's Rogers Road.

From Kittery, an attractive alternative route north to York follows winding Route 103—perfect for driving, though a bit busy and narrow for biking. This road passes through the historic, lost-in-time village of Kittery Point, where homes seem to be just inches from the roadway and there are not one but *two* historic forts; both are parks open to the public.

York is split into several village centers, described above; the best for walking around in is **York Village ★★**, a fine destination for those curious about early American history. First settled in 1624, the village opens several homes to the public.

For a duck's-eye view of the local terrain, visit **Excursions Coastal Maine Outfitting Co.** on Route 1 in Cape Neddick (© **207/363-0181;** www.excursionsinmaine.com). This outfitter offers daily ($35–$65) and weekly sea-kayak rentals and tours ($60 per adult for a guided half-day excursion) along the local coastline. For more dramatic paddling, ask about sunrise, sunset, full-moon, and overnight kayaking trips. The shop is located on Route 1, between Ogunquit and York; go north 5 or 6 miles from York's information hut near the turnpike exit.

Tip: Portsmouth, New Hampshire, makes a very worthwhile side trip once ensconced in Kittery or the Yorks—in fact, if you're seeking culture, arts, coffee shops, and top-flight restaurants, it's a much better base than either of those towns. Best of all, it's just a half-mile from Kittery, a few minutes' drive from the Yorks. I've described this city as a side trip in chapter 11.

DISCOVERING LOCAL HISTORY

Old York Historical Society ★★★ York's local historical society oversees the bulk of the town's collection of historic buildings, some of which date to the early 18th century, and most of which are astonishingly well preserved or restored. Tickets are available to eight Old York–operated properties in all; one good place to start is at the **Jefferds Tavern ★**, across from the handsome **old burying ground ★**. Changing exhibits document various facets of early life. Next door is the School House, furnished as it might have been in the 19th century. A 10-minute walk along lightly traveled Lindsay Road brings you to **Hancock Wharf,** next door to the **George Marshall Store.** Also nearby is the Elizabeth Perkins House, with its well-preserved Colonial Revival interiors. Finally, there are two "don't-miss" buildings in the society's collection: the **Old Gaol ★★**, which still has its (now-musty) dungeons, was built in 1719 as a jail to hold criminals, debtors, and other miscreants. It's the oldest surviving public building in the United States. Then, just down the knoll from the jail, is the **Emerson-Wilcox House ★**, built in the mid-1700s and periodically added onto through the years. It's a virtual catalog of architectural styles and early decorative arts.

TWO WONDERFUL WALKS

Two local strolls will allow visitors to stretch their legs and get the cobwebs out of their heads.

York Harbor and York Village are connected by a quiet pathway that follows a river and passes through gently rustling woodlands. **Fisherman's Walk ★** departs from below Edward's Harborside Inn, near the Stage Neck Inn. (There's limited parking at tiny York Harbor Beach.) Follow the pathway along the river, past lobster shacks and along lawns leading up to grand shingled homes. Cross Route 103 and walk over the **Wiggly Bridge** (said to be, not implausibly, the smallest suspension bridge in the world), then head into the woods. You'll soon connect with a dirt lane; follow this and you'll emerge at Lindsay Road near Hancock Wharf (see above). The entire walk is about a mile long and, depending on your pace, will take a half-hour to 45 minutes.

Also departing from near York Harbor Beach is the **Cliff Walk ★★**, a scenic little trail that follows rugged terrain along rocky bluffs and offers sweeping views of the open ocean as well as glimpses of life in some of the town's grandest cottages. The far end of this trail has been destroyed by ocean waves and has not been rebuilt; you'll have to retrace your steps back to the beach. The pathway remains the subject of recent disputes between the town and landowners seeking to limit access. Check signs for any new restrictions on trespassing before you set off.

Finally, there's the small peninsula ending at an island capped by the scenic **Nubble Light ★★★** lighthouse. This lighthouse, probably one of the most photographed in the world, is undeniably attractive—and absolutely free to view from the safety of a parking lot set across the swift little inlet that separates it from the mainland. There's little walking to be done, but this is a terrific spot for a picnic; walk a minute uphill to **Brown's Ice Cream ★★** for some of Maine's best homemade ice cream for dessert. (The lighthouse is lit up for the holiday season around Thanksgiving each year. If you happen to be here in late November inquire about the shuttle from Short Sands Beach out to the vantage point.) For information on additional lighthouses, see "Lighthouses: A Tour Up the Coast," in chapter 2.

Ⓕinds Wheeling It to the Sayward-Wheeler House

If you'd like to get a taste of York's long history, but lack the stamina for the full-court Old York visit, here's your best option: stop by the **Sayward-Wheeler House ★** in York Harbor, run by the group **Historic New England.** In this well-preserved merchant's home dating from 1760, you'll find booty (such as fine china) plundered during the 1745 Siege of Louisbourg, which routed the French out of Nova Scotia. The home is open weekends only, from June through October; tours are given hourly from 11am to 4pm. Admission is $5. For information, call the house (✆ **207/384-2454**) or the organization's office in Boston (✆ **617/227-3956;** www.historicnewengland.org).

(Tips) History Takes a Detour to South Berwick

It's tiny, it's not on the tourist map, and it's not on the coast, yet little South Berwick, Maine, provides a worthwhile detour back into Maine's colonial—and literary—history. Think about taking a few hours to explore it if raindrops happen to be pelting York Beach and ruining your beach outing.

The two most important structures in town are the late-18th-century **Hamilton House,** 40 Vaughan's Lane (© **207/384-2454**)—a solid riverside home, with fine gardens and lawns—and its contemporary, the **Sarah Orne Jewett House,** 5 Portland St. (© **207/384-2454**), a 1774 Georgian where the famous Maine author lived. (Her desk overlooks the village's main crossroads.) Both homes are open to the public from June through mid-October, on slightly different schedules. Hamilton House is open Wednesday to Sunday from 11am to 5pm, while the Jewett House is open Friday through Sunday (same hours); tours are offered on the hour at each property. Admission costs $8 per person to get into Hamilton House, just $5 per person to enter the Jewett House.

If you're looking for some nature, drop by one of the area farms or orchards, or take the kids to **Vaughan Woods State Park** (© **207/384-5160**), down Old Fields Road just off Route 236 (a bit south of the town center). Set along the quiet Salmon Falls River, the park features picnic areas and a hiking trail through groves of old-growth pine and hemlock. It's open Memorial Day to Labor Day; the admission fee is $2 per adult, $1 per child age 5 to 11, free for children 4 and under.

For golfers, the outstanding **The Links at Outlook** golf course (© **207/384-GOLF** [4653]; www.outlookgolf.com) on Route 4 is a fine, links-style track of bent grass fairways and greens. The greens fees for 18 holes will run you around $50 per person in high summer season; it's cheaper on weekdays, afternoons, and in spring and fall.

From York, South Berwick is quickly reached via Route 91 (which shoots west off Rte. 1 just south of the Maine Tpk. interchange for York). It's a ride of about 20 minutes.

BEACHES

York Beach actually consists of *two* beaches, **Long Sands Beach** ★★ and **Short Sands Beach** ★, separated by a rocky headland. Both have plenty of room for sunning and Frisbees when the tide is out. When the tide is in, though, both become narrow and cramped. Short Sands fronts the honky-tonk town of York Beach, with its candlepin bowling, taffy-pulling machine, and video arcades. It's a better pick for families traveling with kids who have short attention spans. Long Sands runs along Route 1A, directly across from a line of motels, summer homes, and convenience stores. Parking at *both* beaches is metered in summer; pay heed, as enforcement is strict and you must pay until 9pm, 7 days a week. (At the end of summer, they decapitate the meters—literally—and parking is subsequently free and plentiful until the next Memorial Day.)

Public restrooms are available at both beaches; other services, including snacks, are provided by local restaurants and vendors.

York Beach has a large supply of no-frills motels facing Long Sands Beach, with rooms ranging from very basic to suites with private seaside decks and kitchenettes. Reserve ahead during high season. Among those with simple accommodations are the **Anchorage Inn** (© 207/363-5112; www.anchorageinn.com), the **Grand View Inn Motel** (© 207/363-3838; www.grandview-york.com), and the **Sunrise Motel** (© 800/242-0750; www.sunrisemotel.net), all directly across the road from the water.

Campers lack good options around here, but might head for **Dixon's Campground** (© 207/363-3626), which has a mix of wooded tenting and RV sites set back from busy Route 1 (just north of York proper) for $26 to $38 per night. There's a 3-night minimum on holiday weekends; it's open from mid-May through Columbus Day.

In the Yorks

Dockside Guest Quarters ★   David and Harriet Lusty established this quiet retreat in 1954, and recent additions (mostly new cottages) haven't changed the friendly, maritime flavor of the place a bit. Situated on an island connected to the mainland by a small bridge, the inn occupies nicely landscaped grounds shaded by maples and pines. Five rooms are in the cozy main house, built in 1885, but the bulk of the accommodations are in small, shared town-house-like cottages constructed between 1968 and 1998 by the water. These are simply furnished but bright and airy; most have private decks overlooking the Harbor. Several also have woodstoves, a fireplace, and/or kitchenettes (you pay quite a bit extra for kitchenette units). The lawn is a good place to sit with a chair; the inn also maintains a simple restaurant and offers boat tours of the harbor, which leave from its own dock.

Harris Island (P.O. Box 205), York, ME 03909. © 888/860-7428 or 207/363-2868. Fax 207/363-1977. www. docksidegq.com. 25 units. Mid-June to mid-Oct $121–$216 double; $173–$276 cottage rooms; May to mid-June and mid-Oct to Dec $98–$125 double, $104–$197 cottage rooms. Rates include breakfast. 2-night minimum stay in summer. DISC, MC, V. Closed Jan–Apr and closed weekdays in May, Nov, and Dec. Drive south on Rte. 103 from Rte. 1A in York Harbor; cross bridge over York River, turn left and follow signs to end. **Amenities:** Restaurant; rowboats; bike rentals; badminton; croquet; laundry service; boat tours. *In room:* A/C, TV, kitchenette (some units), fireplace (some units).

Edwards' Harborside Inn ★ (Finds)   Work your way downhill off Route 1A toward the sprawling Stage Neck Inn and the public beach, and before you get there you'll come across a beautifully kept home on the water, with a private dock and a lawn whose

---

(Moments)   **Jam Sessions in York**

Need a souvenir but too weak with hunger to shop another minute? At **Stonewall Kitchen's** flagship store, on Stonewall Lane (© 207/351-2712)—just behind the huge tourist information complex at the corner of Route 1 and the access road leading to and from I-95 and the Maine Turnpike—you can sample from among the company's delicious jams and spreads before tucking into a soup-and-sandwich special from the on-site deli (see "Where to Dine," below). Then, hunger and birthday lists both satisfied in one fell swoop, keep browsing through a good selection of handy kitchen accessories: knives, lobster bibs, graters, and the like. Staff is friendly and helpful. It's open daily; the shop closes at 6pm, while the cafe closes at 3pm.

Adirondack chairs possess wonderfully quaint views of fishing boats. Ten units vary from simple to elegant (the York Suite is also known as the "Spoil Me Suite," with its tiled Jacuzzi and water views on all sides); all are lovely and homey, with touches such as chocolates. Add in a fireplace in winter, hearty hospitality, board games for relaxing, and splendiferous views from the front rooms, and you've discovered a cozy sort of place you might never want to leave.

Stage Neck Rd. (P.O. Box 866), York Harbor, ME 03911. ℭ **800/273-2686** or 207/363-3037. www.edwards harborside.com. 13 units (3 with shared bathroom). July–Aug and holidays $240 double, $350 suite; May–June and Sept–Oct $170–$200 double, $240–$270 suite; Nov–Apr $130–$160 double, $220–$250 suite. Rates include breakfast. Rates do not include 8% percent hotel service charge or 7% Maine state tax. Minimum stay some times of year. MC, V. *In room:* A/C.

Union Bluff Hotel ★   With its turrets, dormers, and porches, the Union Bluff has the look of an old-fashioned, 19th-century beach hotel; it's a surprise to learn it was built in 1989. Inside, the hotel is generic and modern; rooms have oak furniture, wall-to-wall carpeting, and small refrigerators. You can throw a stone to Short Sands Beach, T-shirt shops, a bowling alley, and a game arcade (great for kids). There are more rooms in a motel annex next door, but stick with the main inn, whose best units are top-floor suites with beach vistas (some even have Jacuzzis or fireplaces). There's also a simple wood-paneled lounge and a restaurant. It's amazing how low rates plummet here midweek and off season, when this hotel becomes among the most inexpensive places to stay in southern Maine. However, parking is very tight on the hotel's little street; big-riggers will need to park in the adjacent pay lot.

8 Beach St. (P.O. Box 1860), York Beach, ME 03910. ℭ **800/833-0721** or 207/363-1333. www.unionbluff. com. 61 units. Mid-May to late Oct $69–$249 double; $139–$329 suite; rest of the year $49–$129 double, $99–$189 suite. Packages available. AE, DISC, MC, V. **Amenities:** 2 restaurants; pub. *In room:* A/C, fridge (some units), Jacuzzi (some units), fireplace (some units).

York Harbor Inn ★★   This summery compound sits on a hillside overlooking a lovely bay and beach, far from the honky-tonk of Short and Long Sands. The main inn's 22 rooms are simplest, though this building has a good restaurant and convivial basement pub. Adjacent Harbor Hill Inn contains the best units: all have Jacuzzis, gas fireplaces, heated bathrooms, CD players, and sea views, plus a hot tub out back. Nearby Harbor Cliffs is also a good choice, with breakfast included and a variety of room styles. The newest addition is actually the oldest building: the 1730 Harbor Crest Inn, a half-mile up the road, with wonderful common areas, porches, a variety of color schemes, king-size beds, big Jacuzzi tubs, and black-and-white tiled bathrooms. The dining room is justly regarded for the views and the work of chef Gerry Bonsey, who offers truffle-scented gnocchi, fish dishes, and lobster-stuffed chicken breast.

Rte. 1A (P.O. Box 573), York Harbor, ME 03911. ℭ **800/343-3869** or 207/363-5119. Fax 207/363-7151. www. yorkharborinn.com. 54 units. May–Oct $149–$349 double and suite (weekend rates may be higher); Nov–Apr $99–$349 double and suite (weekend rates may be higher). Packages available. Some rates include breakfast. AE, DISC, MC, V. **Amenities:** Restaurant; bar. *In room:* A/C, TV, dataport, iron/ironing board.

WHERE TO DINE

In addition to the choices below, there are plenty of fried-fish joints but also several options that go beyond the usual takeout fare. On Route 1 in Kittery, not far north of the island bridge to Portsmouth, the **Beach Pea Baking Co.** (ℭ **207/439-3555**) turns out outstanding sandwiches, breads, and pastries. Eat at one of the tables outside or on the front porch. Open until 6pm, it's closed Sunday.

Packing a Picnic to York

In York the best place for a picnic is on the beach—any of them. **Long Sands** (p. 80) and **Short Sands** (p. 80) are best: The former has views of a lighthouse and boats far out to sea; the latter is more compact and surrounded by quaintly appealing arcades, hotels, and grand summer homes. Parking can be tight at both—and tickets are written with regularity. Bring lots of quarters.

Speaking of that lighthouse, **Nubble Light** (p. 79) is hard to beat for the quintessential Maine postcard-view picnic. Reach it from Long Sands. If you need sweets, stock up at the **Goldenrod** (below), a real live working candy shop just a block off Short Sands beach. For a bite, I like the **Long Sands General Store** (*(C)* 206/363-5383), near the northern end of Long Sands beach, with pizzas, sandwiches, and other essential picnicking supplies.

York Village harbors **Fazio's,** 38 Woodbridge Rd. (turn just before the town library; *(C)* 207/363-7019), a good Italian family restaurant with atmosphere. Directly on Long Sands in York Beach, **Sun & Surf** (*(C)* 207/363-2961) has a takeout window proffering fried seafood and ice cream—but also a dining room with standout ocean views and an increasingly sophisticated menu that now incorporates steaks, salads, pastas, tuna, and lamb.

If you're hankering for nothing more complicated than simple Chinese takeout, have no fear. **Chun Ping Lau** (*(C)* 207/439-6055) is a friendly place just north of the Kittery outlets on Route 1 serving amazingly inexpensive Cantonese and Szechuan combo plates of mapo tofu, cashew chicken, egg rolls, and the like.

In Kittery

Bob's Clam Hut FRIED SEAFOOD   Operating since 1956, Bob's manages to retain an old-fashioned flavor—despite now being surrounded on all sides by factory outlet malls, and with prices that have steadily escalated out of the "budget eats" category. It still does one thing very well: fries up the best heaps of clams and other seafood for miles, sides them with french fries and coleslaw in baskets, and puts them out with tremendous efficiency. Order at the window, get a soda, and stake out a table inside or on the deck (with its lovely view of, er, Rte. 1) while waiting for your number to be called. The food is surprisingly light, cooked in cholesterol-free vegetable oil; the onion rings are especially good. To ensure that your diet plans are irrevocably busted, Bob's also serves ice cream at an adjacent scoop shop. Now that's overkill.

Rte. 1 (west side), Kittery. *(C)* 207/439-4233. Reservations not accepted. Sandwiches $4–$13; dinners $8–$29. AE, MC, V. Memorial Day to Labor Day Mon–Thurs 11am–8pm, Fri–Sat 11am–9pm, Sun 11am–7:30pm; opening hours vary in off season.

In the Yorks

Goldenrod Restaurant (Kids) TRADITIONAL AMERICAN   Follow the neon to this beach-town classic—a York summer institution ever since it opened in 1896. It's easy to find: Look for visitors gawking through plate-glass windows at ancient machines hypnotically churning out taffy (millions of pieces a year). The restaurant, across from the candymaking operation, is low on frills but big on atmosphere: Diners sit on stout oak furniture around a stone fireplace or elbow-to-elbow at an antique soda fountain. Breakfast offerings are New England standards, and for lunch you can eat soups, burgers, and overpriced sandwiches. But what saves the place is the candy counter, where throngs line up to buy boxes of wax-wrapped taffy "kisses" (check the striping on each candy for its flavor; I like molasses and peppermint), almond-pocked birch bark, and other penny-candy treats. The shakes, malts, and sundaes are on the sweet side.

Railroad Rd. and Ocean Ave., York Beach. ✆ **207/363-2621.** www.thegoldenrod.com. Lunch and dinner entrees $4–$15. MC, V. Memorial Day to Labor Day daily 8am–10pm (until 9pm in June); Labor Day to Columbus Day Wed–Sun 8am–3pm. Closed Columbus Day to Memorial Day.

Lobster Cove ★ SEAFOOD/FAMILY FARE   Right across the street from the pounding surf of Long Sands Beach, dependable Lobster Cove is a good choice when the family is too tired to drive far in search of a feed. And a "feed" is what you'll get here. Breakfast consists of standard, inexpensive choices such as omelets, pancakes, and eggs Benedict. Lunch runs to burgers and sandwiches, but dinner is prime time, when a standard shore dinner of lobster, corn on the cob, clam chowder, and steamed clams is hefty and good. Lobster pie is an old-fashioned New England favorite. They also do lobster rolls, clam rolls, steaks, broiled seafoods, and traditional Maine desserts such as wild blueberry pie and warm bread pudding with whiskey sauce.

756 York St., York (south end of Long Sands Beach). ✆ **207/351-1100.** Main courses $7–$21. AE, MC, V. Daily 7:30am–9pm.

Stonewall Kitchen Café ★★ CAFE   Stonewall Kitchen's York-based gourmet foods operation has taken a step forward with this quality, inexpensive cafe, smartly located in its York headquarters/store right beside the local tourist information office. The cafe serves simple, hearty items such as fish chowder, changing soups, lobster rolls (and lobster BLTs), muffulettas (a New Orleans–style, olive-salami sandwich), turkey wraps with cranberry spread, and much more. Check the board to find out what's on daily. Finish with a dessert such as a lemon square, brownies, or fresh-baked cookies. The cafe kitchen also prepares gourmet meals to go.

Stonewall Lane (set back from U.S. Rte. 1), York. ✆ **207/351-2719.** www.stonewallkitchen.com. Sand-wiches and salads $7–$11. AE, DC, DISC, MC, V. Mon–Sat 8am–3pm (takeout until 5pm); Sun 9am–3pm (takeout until 5pm).

2 OGUNQUIT

15 miles NE of Kittery

Ogunquit (oh-GUN-quit) is a busy little beachside town that has attracted vacationers and artists for more than a century. Although it's certainly notable for the abundant and elegant summer-resort architecture, Ogunquit is probably most famous for the 3^1/$_2$-mile white-sand beach, backed by grassy dunes, that dominates the town. This beach serves as the town's front porch, and most everyone drifts over there at least once a day when the sun is shining. As a bonus, a wonderful walking trail known as the Marginal Way begins at the beach, then climbs the cliffs above tide pools to great views back onto the sand and ocean.

Ogunquit's fame as an art colony dates to around 1890, when Charles H. Woodbury arrived and declared the place an "artist's paradise." He was soon followed by artists such as Walt Kuhn, Elihu Vedder, and Yasuo Kuniyoshi, not to mention Rudolph Dirks, author of the "Katzenjammer Kids" comic. (During the latter part of the 19th century, the town later found another sort of fame as a quiet destination for regional gay travelers; today, many local enterprises here are still owned by gay proprietors.)

Despite its architectural grace and civility, the town is narrow—there's only one main street—and can become seriously overrun with tourists (and their cars) during peak summer season, especially on weekends. If you don't like crowds, try to visit in the shoulder seasons or simply visit another destination along the coast. Other advice: If you arrive early in the morning, stake out a spot on the long beach.

A pre-Halloween festival in late October, the **Ogunquit Fest,** offers 3 days of arts, crafts, costumes, and a parade; it's best for families with kids. Call © **207/646-2939** for more information.

ESSENTIALS
Getting There
Ogunquit is right on U.S. Route 1, exactly midway between York and Wells—which means it's a long way to either of the nearest convenient turnpike exits. Take either exit 7 (York) or exit 19 (Wells) off the Maine Turnpike, a toll road. Proceed to U.S. Route 1 and follow it north from York or south from Wells, turning seaward (left if you're traveling south, right if you're coming from the south) at the confusing intersection at the center of town (see below) and follow Shore Road to reach Perkins Cove and the bulk of the shops, accommodations, and eateries. Or, for the best beach access, take the other prong of the intersection to Beach Street.

Visitor Information
The **Ogunquit Welcome Center,** P.O. Box 2289, Ogunquit, ME 03907 (© **207/646-2939;** www.ogunquit.org), is on U.S. Route 1, south of the village center. It's open daily 9am to 5pm Memorial Day to Columbus Day (until 8pm weekends during the peak summer season), and Monday to Saturday during the off season—and it has restrooms.

Getting Around
Ogunquit centers on a 3-way intersection that seems fiendishly designed to cause massive traffic foul-ups in summer. Parking in and around the village is tight and relatively expensive for small-town Maine ($6 per day or more in various lots). As a result, Ogunquit is best navigated on foot or by bike.

ⓘTips Take the Trolley

A number of trackless "trolleys" (© **207/646-1411**)—buses painted to look like trolleys—with names such as *Dolly* and *Ollie* (you get the idea) run all day from mid-May to Columbus Day between Perkins Cove and the Wells town line to the north, with detours to the sea down Beach and Ocean streets. These trolleys are very handy in this traffic-congested village, kids love 'em, and they stop everywhere. (There's a map of stops posted online at **www.ogunquit.com/trolley.cfm.**) Rides cost $1.50 one-way (children free), or you can buy a day pass for $5 per adult and $3 per child 9 and under; it's worth it, simply to avoid the hassles of driving around and parking.

THE SOUTHERN COAST

5

OGUNQUIT

The village center is good for an hour or two of browsing among the boutiques, or sipping a cappuccino at one of the several coffee emporia. From the village, you can walk to scenic Perkins Cove along **Marginal Way** ★★★, a gorgeous mile-long oceanside pathway that departs across from the Seacastles Resort on Shore Road. En route, it passes tidepools, pocket beaches, and rocky, fissured bluffs, all worth exploring. This is one of Maine's best public trails. The seascapes can be spectacular, but the Way can also get extremely crowded during fair-weather weekends or toward sunset. Early morning is a good time to avoid crowds.

Perkins Cove ★, accessible either from Marginal Way or by driving south on Shore Road and veering left at the Y-shaped intersection, is a small, well-protected harbor that attracts many visitors and is often heavily congested. A handful of galleries, restaurants, and T-shirt shops cater to the tourist trade from a cluster of quaint buildings between harbor and sea. (If teeming crowds and tourist enterprises are *not* the reason you came to Maine, steer clear of Perkins Cove.) An intriguing pedestrian drawbridge is operated by whoever happens to be handy.

Not far from the cove is the lovely, newly relocated **Ogunquit Museum of American Art** ★★★, 543 Shore Rd. (✆ **207/646-4909;** www.ogunquitmuseum.org), one of the best—and most beautiful—small art museums in the nation (that's not just me talking; the director of New York's Metropolitan Museum of Art said so, too). It's only open in summer and early fall, however. Set back from the road in a grassy glen overlooking the rocky shore, the museum's spectacular view initially overwhelms the artwork as visitors walk through the door. But stick around for a few minutes—the changing exhibits in this architecturally engaging modern building of cement block, slate, and glass will get your attention soon enough; its curators have a track record of staging superb shows and attracting national attention, and the permanent collection holds work by seascape master Marsden Hartley and many members of the Ogunquit Colony, including Woodbury, Hamilton Easter Field, and Robert Laurent. The museum is open from July to October, Monday to Saturday from 10:30am to 5pm and Sundays from 2 to 5pm. Admission costs $7 for adults, $5 for seniors, and $4 for students; it's free for all children 11 and under.

(**Moments**) **Doing Doughnuts in Wells**

Cruising the Wells-Ogunquit axis, foodies will want to check out venerable **Congdon's Doughnuts Family Restaurant & Bakery** ★★, 1090 Post Rd. (which is just U.S. Rte. 1; ✆ **207/646-4219**). Clint and Dot "Nana" Congdon moved to Maine and opened a family-style restaurant in 1945; Nana's sinkers proved so popular that she relocated the whole operation to Wells 10 years later and went into the doughnut business full-time. Chocolate-chocolate is ever-popular, but you can't go wrong with almost anything else among the dozens of choices—pillowy raised doughnuts; filled blueberry doughnuts; butter crunch, honey-dipped, sugar twist, and chocolate honey doughnuts . . . or one of the seasonal specials such as maple, apple, or pumpkin doughnuts. You can also eat diner meals here, most of which involve fried food and/or breakfast fare. Despite a newish drive-through window, this place retains its original character (and that includes the local characters dining inside). The secret? They use lard. Congdon's is open daily, except Wednesdays, year-round from 6am to 2pm.

For evening entertainment, head for the **Ogunquit Playhouse** ★ ($\textit{C}$ 207/646-2402), a 750-seat summer-stock theater right on U.S. Route 1 (just south of the main town intersection) with an old-style look that has garnered a solid reputation for its careful, serious attention to stagecraft. The theater has entertained Ogunquit since 1933, attracting noted actors such as Bette Davis, Tallulah Bankhead, and Sally Struthers. Performance tickets generally cost in the range of $30 to $45 per person.

Another evening alternative is the tiny summer-stock **Booth Theatre,** at the Betty Doon Motor Hotel, Village Square ($\textit{C}$ 207/646-8142). Summer season runs for 11 weeks; each Sunday night features a magic show. Recent shows have included favorites such as *Snoopy!* and *Kiss Me Kate.* Tickets are inexpensive.

BEACHES

Ogunquit's **main beach** ★★ is more than 3 miles long, though its width varies with the tides. This beach appeals to everyone: the livelier scene at the south end near the town itself; the more remote and unpopulated stretches to the north, with their sand dunes; and the clusters of summer homes that lie beyond. The most popular access point is the foot of Beach Street, which runs into Ogunquit Village. This beach ends at a sandy spit, where the Ogunquit River flows into the sea; here you'll find a handful of informal restaurants. It's also the most crowded part of the beach. Less congested options are **Footbridge Beach** (turn on Ocean Ave. off Rte. 1 north of the village center) and **Moody Beach** (turn on Eldridge Ave. in Wells). Restrooms and changing rooms are maintained at all three beaches.

The cost of parking at the beach in Ogunquit varies quite a bit: It costs $12 per day at Obeds; $15 per day at North Beach, Footbridge Beach, and the Lower Lot; $4 per hour at Main Beach; and $3 per hour at Perkins Cove. (Private lots a few blocks from Perkins Cove charge a flat $7–$8 per day.)

A SIDE TRIP TO LAUDHOLM FARM

About 8 miles north of Ogunquit (bear right from Rte. 1 onto Rte. 9 just north of the beach town of Wells) is **Laudholm Farm** ★ ($\textit{C}$ 207/646-4521), a historic saltwater farm owned by the nonprofit Laudholm Trust since 1986. The 1,600-acre property was originally the summer home of 19th-century railroad baron George Lord, but is now used for estuarine research. The farm has 7 miles of trails through diverse ecosystems, which range from salt marsh to forest to dunes. A visitor center in the regal Victorian farmhouse will get you oriented. Tours are available, or you can explore the grounds on your own. Parking costs $2 per adult ($10 per car maximum) daily from Memorial Day through Labor Day, $1 per guest 6 to 16; it's by donation the rest of the year. There's no admission charge to the grounds or visitor center. The trails are open daily from 7am to dusk; the visitor center is open 10am to 4pm Monday to Saturday and noon to 4pm on Sunday (closed weekends in the off season, also closed mid-Dec to mid-Jan).

The farm is reached by turning east from Route 1 on Laudholm Farm Road at the blinking light just north of Harding Books. Bear left at the fork, then turn right into the farm's entrance.

WHERE TO STAY

In addition to the selections below, there are many family-owned budget to moderately priced motel operations around town. Simply cruising Route 1 can yield dividends (don't forget your AAA card if you're a member). In July and August you'll be hard-pressed to find a bargain, but try the following three economical choices first for a combination of affordability and amenities.

The family-friendly **Colonial Village Resort** (© 800/422-3341; www.colonial villageresort.com) on Route 1 is not a resort—but with two pools, a Jacuzzi, tennis court, free doughnuts, coin-op laundries, a few weekly rental cottages and apartments, and free rowboats to get you across the tidal river to the beach, it's almost a steal for families on the go most of the year. Most rooms contain kitchenettes consisting of stovetops, micro-waves, and full-size refrigerators. It's usually open from April until December, with double rooms starting as low as $44; summer rates, however, begin at $160.

Just a few steps from Ogunquit's main downtown intersection is the meticulously maintained **Studio East Motel,** 267 Main St. (© 207/646-7297; www.studioeastmotel.com). It's open April to mid-November, with peak-season rates running from $99 to $169 double. The rooms are basic, but all have refrigerators, telephones, and televisions, and there are a few two-bedroom suites. Microwaves are available for free to those staying 3 nights or more. And the quiet **Riverside Motel,** 50 Riverside Lane (© 207/646-2741; www.riversidemotel.com), has great marina views and Wi-Fi, as well as a convenient footbridge leading directly over the tidal inlet to Perkins Cove, which saves you the park-ing hassles and fees. Rooms here run $70 to $190 double, depending on the season.

Another upscale choice in addition to those listed below is **Terrace by the Sea,** 23 Wharf Lane (© 207/646-3232; www.terracebythesea.com), with great sea views, a nice heated outdoor pool, and excellent customer service. Eight of the motel-style rooms have kitchenettes. From late May through October, rates range from $69 to $242 double; in the shoulder seasons (late Mar to late May and Nov to mid-Dec), they range from $52 to $182 double. Children 5 and under are welcome in the off season. The inn is closed from early December through late March.

Above Tide Inn   This nicely sited inn rises from where a lobster shack once stood, until a 1978 blizzard took it to sea. That fact (and the inn's name) should suggest its great setting: on a lazy tidal river between town and the main beach, which is an easy stroll away. It's right by the start of Marginal Way, the town's popular walking path. Location is the prime draw here, since rooms are a bit smaller and darker than one might expect at a beach property. If the weather's good, you're in luck—each room has its own outdoor sitting area, most connected to the room (though two tables are reserved on a front deck for guests in back that don't face the water). Room no. 1 has a nice view of the river. Remember that this inn doesn't accept small children or pets.

66 Beach St. (P.O. Box 1288), Ogunquit, ME 03907. © 207/646-7454. www.abovetideinn.com. 9 units. Mid-June to Labor Day $170–$250 double; mid-May to mid-June and Labor Day to Columbus Day $110–$180 double. Rates include continental breakfast. 3-night minimum stay in summer. MC, V. Closed Columbus Day to mid-May. No children. *In room:* A/C, TV, fridge, no phone.

Beachmere Inn ★★ (Kids)   In a sea of strip motels and condos, Beachmere's got personality. Operated by the same family since 1937, this quiet, well-run inn sprawls across a scenic lawn where repeat visitors have reclined for decades. Nearly every unit has an amazing view up the beach, and all have kitchenettes. The original Victorian section dates from the 1890s and is the most fun; it's all turrets, big porches, angles, and bright beachy interiors. Next door is the modern Beachmere South, with spacious rooms and plenty of private balconies or patios—those on the end have knockout views. A new wing (Beachmere West) was added in 2008, with small spa, exercise, and children's play areas; units here have big bathrooms and sitting rooms. The adjacent Marginal Way footpath

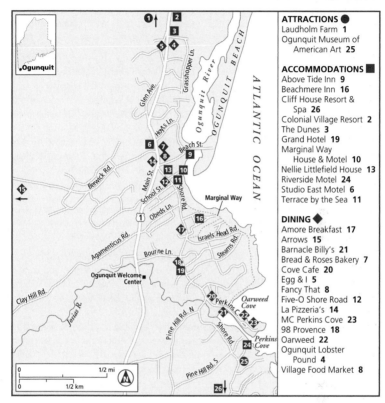

ATTRACTIONS ●
Laudholm Farm **1**
Ogunquit Museum of
American Art **25**

ACCOMMODATIONS ■
Above Tide Inn **9**
Beachmere Inn **16**
Cliff House Resort &
Spa **26**
Colonial Village Resort **2**
The Dunes **3**
Grand Hotel **19**
Marginal Way
House & Motel **10**
Nellie Littlefield House **13**
Riverside Motel **24**
Studio East Motel **6**
Terrace by the Sea **11**

DINING ◆
Amore Breakfast **17**
Arrows **15**
Barnacle Billy's **21**
Bread & Roses Bakery **7**
Cove Cafe **20**
Egg & I **5**
Fancy That **8**
Five-O Shore Road **12**
La Pizzeria's **14**
MC Perkins Cove **23**
98 Provence **18**
Oarweed **22**
Ogunquit Lobster
Pound **4**
Village Food Market **8**

THE SOUTHERN COAST

5

OGUNQUIT

is terrific for walks and beach access, and groups might inquire about several off-property cottages a short walk away.

62 Beachmere Place, Ogunquit, ME 03907. 📞 **800/336-3983** or 207/646-2021. Fax 207/646-2231. www.beachmereinn.com. 73 units. June–Aug $170–$250 double, cottage $145–$390; May and Sept to mid-Oct $95–$234 double, $75–$280 cottage; Apr and mid-Oct to early Dec $75–$170 double, $60–$210 cottage. Rates include continental breakfast. 3-night minimum in summer. AE, DC, DISC, MC, V. Closed early Dec to Mar. **Amenities:** Pub; exercise room; spa; Jacuzzi; sauna; conference room. *In room:* A/C, kitchenette.

Cliff House Resort and Spa ★★ This set of modern buildings replaced a former grand hotel, and now offers some of the best hotel-room ocean views in Maine: nearly a 360-degree panorama, in some cases. There are a number of different styles of rooms, most with comforts such as digital televisions and recliners; other updates include new beds and furniture in the Cliffscape wing and a covered corridor linking all terraces and guest rooms with the dining areas. A vanishing-edge pool fronting the sea does indeed seem to disappear into the blue yonder, and there's an upscale restaurant with knockout vistas. The state-of-the-art spa and fitness facility dispenses a wide range of soothing treatments and exercise programs.

Shore Rd. (P.O. Box 2274), Ogunquit, ME 03907. ℭ **207/361-1000.** Fax 207/361-2122. www.cliffhouse maine.com. 200 units. July–Aug $275–$350 double; mid-Apr to June and Sept to early Dec $155–$295 double. Meal plans available. 3-night minimum stay July–Aug and holiday weekends; 2-night minimum other weekends. Packages available. AE, DISC, MC, V. Closed early Jan to late Mar. **Amenities:** Restaurant; bar; indoor pool; 2 outdoor pools; fitness center; spa; Jacuzzi; room service. *In room:* A/C, TV, hair dryer.

The Dunes ★★   This classic motor court (built around 1936) has made the transition into the modern luxury age more gracefully than any other vintage motel I've seen. It has one six-unit motel-like building, but most of the rooms are in gabled cottages of white clapboard and green shutters; these have full kitchens and bathrooms. Plenty of old-fashioned charm remains in many of the units, with vintage maple furnishings, oval braided rugs, maple floors, knotty pine paneling, and louvered doors. Most of the cottages also have wood-burning fireplaces. The complex is set on 12 acres, wedged between busy Rte. 1 and the ocean, but somehow stays quiet and peaceful; Adirondack chairs overlook a lagoon, and guests can borrow a rowboat to get across to the beach.

518 U.S. Rte. 1 (P.O. Box 917), Ogunquit, ME 03907. ℭ **888/295-3863.** www.dunesmotel.com. 36 units. Summer $100–$285 double, $180–$335 cottage; spring $75–$190 double, $130–$255 cottage. July–Aug 1-week minimum stay in cottages; 3-night minimum stay in motel. All other weekends, 2-night minimum stay in motel. MC, V. Closed Nov to late Apr. **Amenities:** Outdoor pool; watersports equipment rental. *In room:* A/C, TV, dataport, fridge, coffeemaker.

Grand Hotel ★ Value   The modern Grand Hotel, built in 1990, seems a bit out of place in Victorian Ogunquit, but the hotel centers on a three-story atrium and consists entirely of two-room suites. The modern rooms have a generic, chain-hotel character, but each has a private deck from which to enjoy the Maine air (no ocean views). All rooms also have refrigerators, TVs, microwaves, and VCRs (with tapes available for rent), making it a good deal for families. The top-floor penthouses are airy and bright, with cathedral ceilings and Duraflame-log fireplaces. The hotel is about a 10-minute walk to the beach, and guests can use a nearby health club. Other nice touches: Parking (one car per party) is underground and connected to the rooms by elevator, and there's a small indoor pool.

276 Shore Rd. (P.O. Box 1526), Ogunquit, ME 03907. ℭ **800/806-1231** or 207/646-1231. www.thegrand hotel.com. 28 suites. Late June to Labor Day $139–$269 double; late Mar to late June and Labor Day to mid-Nov $59–$219 double. Rates include continental breakfast. 2- or 3-night minimum on weekends, holidays, and other peak season dates. DISC, MC, V. Underground parking. Closed mid-Nov to late Mar. Children accepted in some suites. **Amenities:** Indoor pool; Jacuzzi. *In room:* A/C, TV, kitchenette, fridge, fireplace (some units).

Marginal Way House and Motel ★   This old-fashioned, nothing-fancy compound centers on a four-story, mid-19th-century guesthouse with summery, basic rooms and white-painted furniture; the whole affair is plunked down on a large, grassy lot on a quiet cul-de-sac, and it's hard to believe you're smack in the middle of beehive-busy Ogunquit. But it's true: both the beach and the village are just a few minutes' walk away. Room no. 7 is among the best, with a private porch and canopy and ocean views. The main house is surrounded by four contemporary buildings that lack charm, yet the motel-style rooms here are generally comfortable and bright. All rooms have refrigerators and none have phones; one- and two-bedroom efficiencies are available for longer stays, and rooms on higher-floors are most desirable.

Wharf Lane (P.O. Box 697), Ogunquit, ME 03907. ℭ **207/646-8801.** www.marginalwayhouse.com. 30 units (1 with private bathroom down hall). Early June to Labor Day $82–$199 double; mid-Apr to early June and early Sept to mid-Oct $49–$159 double. Minimum stay requirements on some weekends. MC, V. Closed mid-Oct to mid-Apr. Pets allowed in off season only; advance notice required. *In room:* A/C, TV (most units), fridge, no phone.

Nellie Littlefield House ★ This 1889 home stands impressively at the edge of Ogunquit's compact commercial district. This prime location and the handsome Queen Anne architecture are the main draws here. All rooms are carpeted and feature a mix of modern and antique reproduction furnishings; several have refrigerators. Four rooms to the rear have private decks, although views are limited—mostly looking onto the motel next door. The most spacious room is the third-floor J. H. Littlefield suite, with two TVs and a Jacuzzi. The most unique unit? The circular Grace Littlefield room, located in the upper turret and overlooking the street. The basement features a compact fitness room with modern equipment.

27 Shore Rd. (P.O. Box 1341), Ogunquit, ME 03907. ✆ **207/646-1692.** www.visit-maine.com/nellielittle fieldhouse. 8 units. June–Sept $108–$230 double; Mar–May and Oct–Dec $85–$170 double. Holiday rates higher. Rates include full breakfast. 3-night minimum on high-season weekends and holidays. DISC, MC, V. Closed Jan–Feb. Children 13 and over are welcome. **Amenities:** Fitness center. *In room:* A/C, TV, fridge (some units), Jacuzzi (few units).

WHERE TO DINE

The main strip, where Route 1 converges with Perkins Cove Road, is packed with a tremendous variety of bakeries, coffee shops, markets, and restaurants, and this has got to be the latest-open-hours town in Maine: Amazingly, many places stay open until 10 or 11pm in summer. Among them is **Bread & Roses Bakery,** 246 Main St. (✆ **207/ 646-4227**), whose kitchen skillfully turns out cupcakes, peanut-butter-and-chocolate cake, raspberry mousse, cookies, and the like; there's outdoor seating as well. **Fancy That** (✆ **207/646-4118**) is a cafe nearby with sandwiches, hot panini, slices of Boston cream and other pies, and a Wi-Fi–equipped patio great for people-watching. The **Village Food Market,** 230 Main St. (✆ **207/646-2122** or 877/646-2122), stocks good wines, ready-to-go meals, and staples, and it also has a small deli; try the house red-eye coffee.

There are also myriad breakfast-only places scattered about the town. In addition to the excellent Amore (below), check out the reliable **Egg & I,** 501 Main St. (Rte. 1; ✆ 207/646-8777), and the little **Cove Café,** 4 Oarweed Rd. (✆ **207/646-2422**), near Perkins Cove. Or, if you're not in the mood for a fancy dinner, **La Pizzeria**'s, 239 Main St. (✆ **207/646-1143**), sandwiches, meatballs, and pizza pies are as dependable as the name—plus it's friendly and stays open later than just about anyplace else in Maine (usually until 11pm in summer). It's closed in winter.

There are also several lobster pounds packed into and around the little downtown, most of them seasonal (sometime in Apr through Labor Day or Columbus Day). Try the **Ogunquit Lobster Pound** (504 Main St.; ✆ **207/646-2516**), **Oarweed** (65 Perkins Cove Rd.; ✆ **207/646-4022**), or **Barnacle Billy's** (Perkins Cove; ✆ **800/866-5575** or 207/646-5575).

Amore Breakfast ★ ⒱alue BREAKFAST It's breakfast-only at this honey little Shore Road spot halfway between Main Street and Perkins Cove, but what a breakfast it is. This is *not* the place for dainty pickers and waist-watchers. (But, hey, you're on vacation, right?) Look for numerous variations on the eggs Benedict theme (including a popular one with a big hunk of lobster on top), plus Belgian waffles, wonderful bananas Foster–style French toast with pecans outside and cream cheese inside, and more than a dozen types of yummy omelets. Coffee is from a small-batch San Diego coffee roaster. And they've got heart, too: Annual benefit meals are held, with the proceeds going to care packages for a Dominican orphanage. Italian owner Leanne Cusimano deserves (and gets local) kudos.

178 Shore Rd. ✆ **866/641-6661** or 207/646-6661. www.amorebreakfast.com. Breakfast items $4.95–$13. MC, V. Summer daily 7am–1pm; off season closed Wed–Thurs.

What Could Be Finer . . . Than a Maine Diner?

One thing you'll notice as you traverse the Maine coast is a preponderance of diners.

What gives? This isn't New Jersey, after all, yet the humble diner remains as much a culinary staple of coastal Maine as the lobster shack—probably more so, in fact. Locals congregate daily in their kaffeeklatsches on the diner stools; expect a steady stream of hunting caps, thick accents, doughnuts and eggs, and Red Sox or Patriots talk (depending on the season). You'd do well to sample one or two of them while on the road. Here are a few that are easily reached if you're taking Route 1.

From the New Hampshire state line heading north, your first opportunity on Route 1 comes rather quickly, almost on top of the town line that separates York from Kittery a few miles north of the Kittery outlets. **York's Best Seafood** (© **207/439-3401**) has been serving heralded fried clams and other local diner favorites in this location (though under several names) since 1945, and remains a steady favorite among locals.

Heading north from York to Ogunquit along Route 1, you could easily blow right by the reddish-hut icon that is **Flo's Steamed Hot Dogs** (no phone) in Cape Neddick—it's a couple of miles north of York, in the middle of nowhere, at a bend in the road—without noticing. But if you crave a winner of a wiener, screech to a halt in the dirt parking lot and give it a whirl. You'll probably wait in the line, which resembles an assembly line: The steamed dogs here are cheap and good, but they can only do them 50 at a time. If your dog is number 51, bring a paperback. There are only six seats inside, so you'll probably have to eat in the car. Go anyway. And get your dogs with Flo's special sauce.

Arrows ★★★ NEW AMERICAN   When owner/chefs Mark Gaier and Clark Frasier opened Arrows in a gray farmhouse outside town in 1988, they quickly put Ogunquit on the national culinary map (and it's still ranked among the nation's top 15 by *Gourmet* magazine). They've done so not only by creating an elegant and intimate atmosphere, but by serving up some of the freshest, most innovative cooking in New England. The emphasis is on local products—often very local. The salad greens are grown in gardens on the grounds, and much of the rest is produced or raised locally. The food transcends traditional New England fare and is deftly prepared with exotic twists and turns. The menu changes nightly, but among the more popular recurring appetizers is the house-cured prosciutto—hams are hung in the restaurant to cure in the off season. Entrees might include some interpretation of lobster; wild salmon in four preparations (including a portion steamed with pine needles); roasted squab in a "crystal lantern" with tangerine and fermented black beans; or halibut cooked three ways. The wine list is top-rate. Note that there is a moderate dress code: jacket preferred for men, no shorts allowed.

41 Berwick Rd. © **207/361-1100.** www.arrowsrestaurant.com. Reservations strongly recommended. Main courses $42–$44; tasting menus $95–$135. MC, V. July to Labor Day Tues–Sun 6–9:30pm; rest of the

A little farther north, also on Route 1 but in Wells, the **Maine Diner** (℃ 207/ **646-4441**) is a classic, though perhaps getting a little too famous for its own good. (They'll page you when a table is ready.) But worry not, there's a reason why they've just passed the "four million served" mark. The lobster pie and hot lobster roll are famous and delicious, as is a plate of baked scallops. Red flannel hash? Pot roast? They've got it—as well as the "Clam-o-rama," a sampler of clam items. They serve wine and beer here, too—very unusual.

An entire book could be written about **Moody's Diner** (℃ 207/832-7785) in Waldoboro—in fact, it has. This is *the* place to stop on Route 1 when traversing north toward Acadia and points beyond. From the sublime cream pies to the only-in-Maine specials (boiled dinner on Thurs, haddock with egg sauce on Fri, and, of course, baked beans on Sat), the place simply serves food you can find almost nowhere else in the state. The old food ways are disappearing that fast. Finish with Indian pudding or one of those mile-high pies—walnut cream and rhubarb are two good choices, though any of them will satisfy. The prices, too, seem nearly locked in 1948, when Moody's opened.

Finally, way farther downeast, I'd be remiss if I didn't mention the two **Helen's** restaurants, one on Route 1 in Ellsworth just north of the Route 3 split (℃ 207/667-2433), and another, truly timeless one (expect sweet ladies waiting on you) on Main Street in downtown Machias (℃ 207/255-8423). Though neither eatery is, strictly speaking, a diner, they serve up some of the very best home-cooked meals and pies in all of the great state o' Maine, in fine old diner tradition. Look for seasonal specials such as turkey with the fixin's, pork with fiddleheads, or just order a piece of the marvelous seasonal blueberry, strawberry, chocolate cream, or other widely renowned pies.

year, call ahead for open hours or check website. Closed Jan–Mar. Turn uphill at the Key Bank in the village; the restaurant is 2 miles on your right.

Five-O Shore Road ★★ SEAFOOD/NEW AMERICAN   A fine choice if you're looking for a more casual alternative to the more formal restaurants listed, Five-O is one of those spots where just reading the menu is a decent evening's entertainment. Chef Zachary Crosby has transformed a formerly Caribbean-inspired menu into one that roams around the map: you might eat a chargrilled filet or rope-caught local mussels, but also duck nachos, escargot with shallots, local mussels roasted with almonds, wild salmon poached in a lobster-saffron bullion, mole-spiced pork, or fresh haddock stuffed with seafood. Of course, you can get a Maine lobster in season, too, perhaps served over a bed of mussels steamed with bleu cheese, sweet cream, and cracked pepper. There's also a cool cocktail lounge and club, and a strong wine list. Is this Maine or Manhattan? Either way, it's a winner.

50 Shore Rd. ℃ **207/646-5001.** www.five-oshoreroad.com. Reservations strongly recommended in summer. Main courses $24–$33. AE, DISC, MC, V. Valet parking. Memorial Day to Labor Day daily 5–9pm; call for hours outside peak season.

A good spot for bread and snacks in southern Maine is **Borealis Breads** (© 207/ 641-8800), between Ogunquit and Kennebunkport on the east side of U.S. Route 1 in a strip mall just north of the turnoff to Wells Beach. (Look for the Aubuchon hardware store.) You'll find a good selection of hearty, warm-from-the-oven breads, plus sandwiches, local specialties, and macaroons. Open until 6pm daily, it's a good pit stop before an afternoon on the beach.

MC Perkins Cove ★★ SEAFOOD/NEW AMERICAN   The loss of the original Hurricane in Ogunquit could have been a serious blow to Ogunquit diners, but chef-partners Mark Gaier and Clark Frasier of Arrows (see above) opened this bistro in its place, which manages to be fun rather than stuffy. Expect big food, even on the "small" plates: lobster rolls, chopped salads, oysters on half shell, and crab cakes give way to more sophisticated starters such as cockle clams in coconut milk and Thai herbs, fish chowder spiked with bacon, or corn-fried calamari. Entrees might include steamed lobster, sesame-grilled trout, Kobe burgers, grilled tuna, or hanger steak, plus one of the so-labeled "evil carbos" (french fries, onion rings, and so forth). Desserts are wonderful: brown-butter brownies with vanilla ice cream, burnt orange caramel, and candied orange peel; mini whoopee pies; a bittersweet chocolate cake with chocolate sauce and pistachio crème anglaise; or peppermint stick ice cream with cookies.

Perkins Cove. © 207/646-6263. www.mcperkinscove.com. Reservations recommended. Lunch entrees $8–$19; dinner entrees $24–$33. DC, DISC, MC, V. June–Sept daily 11:30am–2pm and 5:30–11pm; Feb–May and Oct–Dec closed Tues. Closed Jan.

98 Provence ★★ FRENCH   Chef Pierre Gignac incorporates local ingredients such as lobster in his French bistro-style menu; he has gained a solid local following as a result. Start with appetizers such as escargot stew, shepherd's pie made with duck, fisherman's soup, or a shallot–foie gras tart. If you still have room, move on to veal mignon, pork shank, spring lamb loin with rosemary crust and a garlic cream, roast duck, or halibut served with salmon caviar. (This is *not* a place to count calories.) A fixed price table d'hôte menu features set meals such as vichyssoise, stewed chicken, and lemon tart; mussels with bleu cheese, monkfish, and pineapple tart; and soft-shell crab with halibut confit and Provence-style nougat, served frozen. The summery, classy interior decor is as close as you'll get in New England to Provence.

262 Shore Rd. © 207/646-9898. www.98provence.com. Reservations recommended. Main courses $21–$30; table d'hôte menus $29–$39. AE, MC, V. Summer Wed–Mon 5:30–9:30pm; off season Thurs–Mon 5:30–9pm.

3 THE KENNEBUNKS ★★

10 miles NE of Ogunquit

"The Kennebunks" consist of the side-by-side villages of **Kennebunk** and **Kennebunkport,** both situated along the shores of small rivers and both claiming a portion of rocky coast. The region was first settled in the mid-1600s and flourished after the American

Revolution, when ship captains, boat builders, and prosperous merchants constructed imposing, solid homes. The Kennebunks are famed for their striking historical architecture and expansive beaches; make time to explore both.

A quick primer: Kennebunk proper begins just south of the Kennebunk River bridge, stretching south and inland to the junction of Route 9 and U.S. Hwy. 1. This is where you'll find the White Barn Inn, Tom's of Maine, and a few fast-food joints. The town also includes, a few miles to the east, the beachside community of Kennebunk Beach.

Kennebunkport's compact, trim downtown begins across the Kennebunk River, on the north side, and extends eastward to take in both million-dollar oceanfront homes (including the Bush family estate at Walker's Point) and the fishing village of Cape Porpoise.

While summer is the busy season along the coast, winter has its charms: The grand architecture is better seen through leafless trees. When the snow flies, guests find solace in front of a fire at one of the inviting inns.

ESSENTIALS
Getting There

Kennebunk is just off exit 25 of the Maine Turnpike; follow signs east into town. You can also get here by taking U.S. 1 from York and Ogunquit. To reach Kennebunkport, exit for Kennebunk and continue through town on Port Road (Rte. 35) 3¹/₂ miles. At the traffic light, turn left and cross the small bridge.

Visitor Information

The **Kennebunk-Kennebunkport Chamber of Commerce,** 17 Western Ave. (P.O. Box 740), Kennebunk, ME 04043 (℃ 800/982-4421 or 207/967-0857), can answer questions year-round by phone or at its offices on Route 9 next to the H.B. Provisions grocery store. The **Kennebunkport Information Center** (℃ 207/967-8600), operated by an association of local businesses, is off Dock Square (next to Ben & Jerry's) and is open daily in summer and fall.

The local trolley (actually a bus) makes several stops in and around Kennebunkport and also serves the beaches; it stops once per hour from 10am until 5pm. The fare comes in the form of a day pass costing $11 per adult or $6 per child ages 3 to 14; it includes unlimited trips. Call ℃ 207/967-3686, or check www.intowntrolley.com for details.

EXPLORING KENNEBUNK

Kennebunk's downtown is inland, just off the turnpike, and is a dignified, small commercial center of white clapboard and brick. The **Brick Store Museum ★**, 117 Main St. (℃ 207/985-4802), hosts shows of historical art and artifacts throughout the summer, switching to contemporary art in the off season. The museum is housed in a historic former brick store—yes, a store that once sold bricks—and three adjacent buildings. The buildings have been renovated and all have the polished gloss of a well-cared-for gallery. Admission is free (though a $3 donation is suggested), and tours cost $5 per person. The museum is open Tuesday to Friday 10am to 4:30pm and Saturday from 10am to 1pm.

Tom's of Maine (℃ 800/FOR-TOMS [367-8667] or 207/985-2944), a natural-toothpaste maker, is headquartered here. Tom and Kate Chappell sell their all-natural toothpaste and other personal-care products worldwide, but they are almost as well known for their green, socially conscious business philosophy. Tom's factory outlet sells firsts and seconds of its own products, as well as a selection of other natural products. The shop is at Lafayette Center (corner of Main and Water sts.), a historic industrial building converted to shops and offices. It's open Monday to Saturday 10am to 5pm. There's another store nearby at 1 Storer St.

When en route to or from the coast, be sure to note the extraordinary homes that line Port Road (Rte. 35). This includes the famously elaborate **Wedding Cake House ★**, which you should be able to identify all on your own. Local lore claims that the house was built by a guilt-ridden ship captain who left for sea before his bride could enjoy a proper wedding cake.

EXPLORING KENNEBUNKPORT

Kennebunkport is the summer home of former President George Bush (the elder), whose family has summered here for decades, and it has the tweedy, upper-crust feel that one might expect of the place. This historic village, whose streets were laid out during days of travel by boat and horse, is subject to traffic jams. If the municipal lot off the square is full, go north on North Street a few minutes to the free long-term lot and catch the trolley back into town. Or walk back—it's a pleasant walk of 10 or 15 minutes from the satellite lot back to Dock Square.

Dock Square has a pleasantly wharflike feel to it, with low buildings of mixed vintages and styles, but the flavor is mostly clapboard and shingles. The boutiques in the area are attractive, and many feature creative artworks and crafts. But Kennebunkport's real attraction is found in the surrounding blocks, where the side streets are lined with one of the nation's richest assortments of Early American homes. The neighborhoods are especially ripe with examples of Federal-style homes; many have been converted to B&Bs (see "Where to Stay," below).

Aimless wandering is a good tactic for exploring Kennebunkport, but at the least make an effort to stop by the **Richard A. Nott House,** 8 Maine St. (© **207/967-2751**), during your travels. Situated on Maine Street at the head of Spring Street, this imposing Greek Revival house was built in 1853 and is a Victorian-era aficionado's dream. It remained untouched by the Nott family through the years and was donated to the local historical society with the stipulation that it remain forever unchanged. Tours run about 40 minutes; it's open mid-June to mid-October 1 to 4pm Tuesday to Friday, and Saturday 10am to 1pm. Admission is $5 for adults, free for children.

(Finds **The Beach at Parson's Way**

It's certainly one of the most attractive *approaches* to a beach in Maine, and Parson's Beach itself is lovely and much less crowded than others in the area. Find the beach by heading south on Route 9 from Dock Square in Kennebunkport, through the traffic light; just after you cross a marsh and the Mousam River, hang a left onto Parson's Beach Road.

You'll drive down a country lane lined with maples. At the end, there's limited parking, though you can also park on the north side of the highway if it's full. This is not the best beach on the southern Maine coast for swimming—it's rocky at the mouth of the river—but it's great for lounging and reading. Be on your best behavior here. (Don't trample the dunes, don't take stuff from the tide pool, and so on.) You have to cross private land to reach the beach, and signs ominously proclaim that access can be denied at any time if the landowner so chooses.

For a clear view of the coast, sign up for a 2-hour sail aboard the schooner *Eleanor* ★ (at the Arundel Wharf Restaurant, Kennebunkport; ② 207/967-8809), a 55-foot gaff-rigged schooner, built in Kennebunkport in 1999 after a classic Herreshoff design. If the weather's willing, you'll have a perfect view of the Bush compound and Cape Porpoise. Fare is about $40 per person.

Ocean Drive from Dock Square to **Walkers Point** ★ and beyond is lined with opulent summer homes overlooking surf and rocky shore. You'll likely recognize the Bush family compound right out on Walkers Point when you arrive. If it's not familiar from the time it has spent in the national spotlight, look for crowds with telephoto lenses. If they're not out, look for a shingle-style secret service booth at the head of a driveway. That's the place. There's nothing to do here, though, but park for a minute, snap a picture, and then push on.

The Seashore Trolley Museum ★   A short drive north of Kennebunkport is a little local marvel: a scrap yard masquerading as a museum. (The "world's oldest and largest museum of its type." Um, okay.) Quirky and engaging, the museum was founded in 1939 to preserve a disappearing way of life, and today the collection boasts more than 200 trolleys, including specimens from Glasgow, Moscow, San Francisco, and Rome. Naturally, there's also a streetcar named *Desire* from New Orleans. About 40 of the cars still operate, and the admission charge includes rides on a 2-mile track. Other cars, some of which still contain early-20th-century advertising, are on display outdoors and in vast storage sheds.

195 Log Cabin Rd., Kennebunkport. ② 207/967-2800. www.trolleymuseum.org. Admission $8 adults, $5.50 children 6–16, $6 seniors. Late May to mid-Oct daily 10am–5pm; weekends only May and late Oct. Closed Nov–May (except May weekends). Head north from Kennebunkport on North St. for 1¾ miles; look for signs.

BEACHES

The coastal area around Kennebunkport is home to several of the state's best beaches. Southward across the river (technically, this is Kennebunk, though it's much closer to Kennebunkport) are **Gooch's Beach** and **Kennebunk Beach** ★. Head eastward on Beach Street (from the intersection of routes 9 and 35), and you'll soon wind into a handsome colony of eclectic shingled summer homes. The narrow road twists past sandy beaches and rocky headlands. It may be congested in summer; avoid gridlock by exploring on foot or by bike.

(Tips)   Biking to the Beach

Finding a parking spot is often difficult, and all beaches require a parking permit, which you can get at the town offices or from your hotel. You can avoid the hassle by renting a bike and leaving your car at your inn or hotel. A good spot for rentals is **Cape-Able Bike Shop** (② 207/967-4382), which rents a variety of bikes by the half-day, day, or week. There are also mountain bikes, along with kid trailers and baby seats. (Helmets and locks are free with rentals.) The bike shop is just north of downtown Kennebunkport at 83 Arundel Rd. (turn north on North Rd. rather than following Rte. 9 north). Some inns in town also rent bikes to guests; others provide free bikes for guests, with no strings attached (except that you have to return the bike, obviously). Ask when you book your room. The local trolley also offers beach access (see above).

Packing a Picnic in the Kennebunks

Kennebunk Beach is a fine spot for a picnic, with long sands and good waves. Watch your parking meter here, however. This is away from the downtown, and there are no shops on the beach. So, to pick up supplies, you'll need to backtrack (or plan ahead). Try **H.B. Provisions** (✆ **207/967-5762**), in a grand old country store building back near the bridge.

Farther up the coast, the unlikely city of Biddeford has a few good spots, including **Rotary Park,** with river views, and **Fortunes Rock Beach.**

Goose Rocks Beach ★, north of Kennebunkport off Route 9 (watch for signs), is a good choice for those who like their crowds light and prefer beaches to beach scenes. You'll find an enclave of beach homes set amid rustling oaks just off a fine sand beach. Just offshore is a narrow barrier reef that has historically attracted flocks of geese, hence the name.

WHERE TO STAY
Very Expensive
White Barn Inn ★★★   The White Barn pampers its guests to no end, and is perhaps the state's best hotel (with its best dining room; see "Where to Dine," below). Upon checking in, guests are shown to a parlor and served a drink, while valets gather luggage and park cars. The atmosphere is distinctly European, with an emphasis on service. Rooms are individually decorated in an upscale country style. Nearly half the rooms have wood-burning fireplaces, while the suites (in an outbuilding across from the main inn) are spectacular; each has a separate color theme and most have flatscreen televisions, whirlpools, or similar perks. There are plenty of unexpected niceties such as fresh flower and turndown service. A handful of cottages, on the Kennebunk River across the road, are cozy and nicely equipped with modern kitchens and bathrooms.

Ocean Ave. (1/4 mile east of junction of routes 9 and 35; P.O. Box 560-C), Kennebunk, ME 04043. ✆ 207/967-2321. Fax 207/967-1100. www.whitebarninn.com. 25 units, 4 cottages. $280–$540 double; $565–$785 suite; $630–$1,260 cottage. Rates include continental breakfast and afternoon tea. 2-night minimum weekends; 3 nights holiday weekends. AE, MC, V. Valet parking. **Amenities:** Outdoor heated pool; free bikes; concierge; conference rooms; limited room service (breakfast only); in-room massage. *In room:* A/C, TV, safe, Jacuzzi (some units), fireplace (some units).

Expensive
Beach House Inn ★★   This is a good choice if you'd like to be close to the people-watching, dog-walking action on and above Kennebunk Beach. The inn was built in 1891 but has been extensively modernized and expanded; in 1999 it was purchased by the folks who own the White Barn Inn (see above) and gussied up with down comforters, pillows, and other upgrades. The rooms here aren't necessarily historic, but they are carpeted and most have Victorian furnishings and accenting, plus nice framed photographs of beach landscapes. Suites have panoramic views of the ocean. But the main draw here might be the lovely porch, where you can stare out at the pebble beach across the road and idly watch the bikers and in-line skaters. The inn has bikes and canoes for guests to use and provides beach chairs and towels.

THE SOUTHERN COAST

5

THE KENNEBUNKS

211 Beach Ave., Kennebunk, ME 04043. ℭ **207/967-3850.** Fax 207/967-4719. www.beachhseinn.com. 35 units. Late June to mid-Sept $255–$390 double; early to late June and mid-Sept to Oct $185–$399 double; Nov–Dec $155–$300 double. Rates include continental breakfast and afternoon tea. Packages available. 2-night minimum on weekends. AE, MC, V. Closed Jan–May. **Amenities:** Bikes; canoes. *In room:* TV.

Captain Jefferds Inn ★★   This 1804 Federal home was fully redone in 1997, and the innkeepers have done a superb job. Fine antiques abound, and guests will need persuading to emerge from their rooms once they've settled in. Among the best are the Assisi, with a restful sitting area and some rather unique interior decorating. Three of the units now have televisions, while the Winterthur and Baxter both have whirlpool tubs. The price range reflects the varying room sizes, but even the smallest rooms—like the Katahdin, with views of the town—are comfortable and exceed the usual Maine B&B experience. Bright common rooms on the first floor offer nice lounging spaces, and an elaborate breakfast is served before a fire on cool days or outside on the terrace if good summer weather permits.

5 Pearl St. (P.O. Box 691), Kennebunkport, ME 04046. ℭ **800/839-6844** or 207/967-2311. Fax 207/967-0721. www.captainjefferdsinn.com. 15 units. Memorial Day to Oct $160–$365 double; rest of the year $125–$330 double. Rates include full breakfast. 2-night minimum weekends. AE, MC, V. Dogs in carriage house only, $30 per pet, by advance reservation. *In room:* A/C, TV (some units), hair dryer, Jacuzzi (some units).

The Captain Lord Mansion ★★★   The Captain Lord is one of the most architecturally distinguished inns in Maine, housed in a pale-yellow Federal-style home on a shady lawn above the river. This is the genuine article, with grandfather clocks, Chippendale highboys, a broad brick fireplace . . . and also a conference room with a sofa and TV. Up the elliptical staircase are the rooms, furnished in splendid antiques and gas fireplaces. Among the best: the Excelsior, a large corner room with a massive four-poster bed, love seat, and a two-person Jacuzzi; the Hesper, with a big stained-glass window in the bathroom; and the Merchant, a spacious first-floor suite that pampers you with a large Jacuzzi, NordicRider bike, and foot massager. Four rooms are in the Garden House annex, a gray clapboard home behind the main inn, where guests are served breakfast at a long table in the colonial-style kitchen; this building is less opulent but still well appointed.

Pleasant St. and Green St. (P.O. Box 800), Kennebunkport, ME 04046. ℂ **800/522-3141** or 207/967-3141. Fax 207/967-3172. www.captainlord.com. 20 units. $149–$379 double; $249–$499 suite. Rates include full breakfast. 2-night minimum weekends and holidays year-round (some holidays 3-night minimum). DISC, MC, V. No children 11 and under. **Amenities:** Lounge; conference room. *In room:* A/C, fridge, hair dryer, fireplace.

The Colony Hotel ★★   One of a handful of oceanside resorts that has preserved the classic New England vacation experience, this mammoth white Georgian Revival (from 1914) lords over the ocean and the mouth of the Kennebunk River. All rooms in the three-story main inn have been renovated recently; they're bright and cheery, simply furnished in summer-cottage antiques. Rooms in two of the three outbuildings carry over the rustic elegance of the main hotel; the exception is the East House, a 1950s-era motel at the back edge of the property with uninteresting motel-style rooms. Staff encourages guests to socialize downstairs in the lobby, on the porch, on the putting green, or at a shuffleboard court that's lighted for nighttime play.

140 Ocean Ave. (P.O. Box 511), Kennebunkport, ME 04046. ℂ **800/552-2363** or 207/967-3331. Fax 207/967-8738. www.thecolonyhotel.com/maine. 123 units. $99–$625 double. Rates include breakfast. 3-night minimum on summer weekends and holidays in main hotel. AE, MC, V. Closed late Oct to mid-May. Pets allowed ($25 per pet per night). **Amenities:** Restaurant; lounge; heated saltwater pool; putting green; bike rentals; library; room service. *In room:* A/C (some units), TV (some units), safe.

Maine Stay Inn and Cottages ★   Innkeepers Janice and George Yankowski have maintained a strong sense of history in their 1860 home and its associated cottages; the decor here is traditional, without going overboard. The common room is comfortably furnished—be sure to note the exceptional staircase in the main hall—and the cottages, arrayed along the property's perimeter, are just as appealing. Constructed during the 1950s, they've since been updated with small kitchens, and many now have gas or wood fireplaces and other amenities as well. The inn is happy to accommodate kids in these cottages (there's a minimum age of 6 in the main building). Towels, umbrellas, chairs, and town parking passes make for easy beachgoing. The full breakfast is very good—it includes spinach frittata and fresh fruit—and can be delivered to your room or your cottage if you like. Stressed? Some rooms even have Jacuzzis.

34 Maine St. (P.O. Box 500-A), Kennebunkport, ME 04046. ℂ **800/950-2117** or 207/967-2117. Fax 207/967-8757. www.mainestayinn.com. 17 units. $109–$319 double and cottage. Rates include full breakfast. 2-night minimum stay on weekends; 3 nights on major holiday weekends. AE, MC, V. *In room:* A/C, TV/VCR, kitchenette (some units), coffeemaker, hair dryer, Jacuzzi (some units), fireplace (some units).

Old Fort Inn ★★   The sophisticated Old Fort Inn sits on 15 acres in a quiet, picturesque neighborhood of late-19th-century summer homes 2 blocks from the ocean. Guests check in at a tidy antiques shop and park around back at the large carriage house, an interesting amalgam of stone, brick, shingle, and stucco. Rooms here all have creature comforts, yet retain the charm of yesteryear: They are solidly wrought and delightfully decorated with antiques and reproductions. About half of the rooms have in-floor heated tiles in the bathrooms; all have welcome amenities such as robes, refrigerators, Aveda bath products, discreet self-serve snack bars, microwaves, and sinks. There are two large suites in the main house; light-filled no. 216 faces east and looks out over the pool. A full buffet breakfast is also served in the main building.

Old Fort Rd. (P.O. Box M), Kennebunkport, ME 04046. ✆ **800/828-3678** or 207/967-5353. Fax 207/967-4547. www.oldfortinn.com. 16 units. High season $175–$395 double; low season $125–$295 double. Rates include full breakfast and 1 hr. free tennis. 2-night minimum weekends and July to Labor Day; 3-night minimum holiday weekends. AE, DC, DISC, MC, V. **Amenities:** Heated outdoor pool; tennis court; laundry service and self-serve laundry; dry cleaning. *In room:* A/C, TV, minibar, fridge, coffeemaker, hair dryer, iron/ironing board.

The Tides Inn Just across the road from Goose Rocks Beach, the Tides Inn is a clapboard-and-shingle affair dating from 1899 that retains a seaside-boardinghouse feel even if it is beginning to tire a bit. Past guests have included Teddy Roosevelt and Sir Arthur Conan Doyle. Rooms tend toward the small side, though you can hear the lapping of surf from most of them. Certain rooms have bay windows and excellent ocean views; ask for one of those when booking. The parlor has a TV and chess, while the inn's pub features a woodstove and dartboard. The dining room offers upscale traditional dining (steaks, fish) in a Victorian setting. Breakfast is offered here, as well, but it's not included in room rates.

252 King's Hwy., Goose Rocks Beach, Kennebunkport, ME 04046. ✆ **207/967-3757.** www.tidesinnbythesea.com. 22 units (4 share 2 bathrooms). Early June to Labor Day $195–$325 double; off season $145–$225 double. Extra charge for parties up to 4. 3-night minimum stay in peak season (mid-June to Labor Day and all weekends). AE, MC, V. Closed mid-Oct to mid-May. **Amenities:** Restaurant; pub. *In room:* No phone.

Moderate

Franciscan Guest House ★ (Finds) This former dormitory on the 200-acre grounds of St. Anthony's Monastery is a unique lodging choice. The 60 or so rooms are institutional, basic, and clean, with private bathrooms; guests can stroll the lovely riverside grounds or walk to Dock Square, about 10 minutes away. There's also a decent pool. It's not nearly as inexpensive as it used to be, though—the brothers have wised up to modern capitalism, and rates have escalated as a result. (They even have suites now.) Nevertheless, the place is still a fairly good bargain, especially given the fine walking trails and its position close to local beaches and restaurants.

28 Beach Ave. (P.O. Box 980), Kennebunk, ME 04046. ✆ **207/967-4865.** www.franciscanguesthouse. com. 60 units. $69–$129 double; $89–$279 suite. MC, V. Closed mid-Oct to mid-May. **Amenities:** Outdoor pool. *In room:* A/C, TV, no phone.

Lodge at Turbat's Creek (Value) This classy and unusually clean motel sits in a quiet residential neighborhood about a 5-minute drive from Dock Square. It's a good value in a town that usually gives you sticker shock. The grounds are attractive and endowed with Adirondack chairs; the inn also supplies free mountain bikes for guests who want to cruise to town, and there's a big, seasonally open heated pool as well. Rooms, on two floors, are standard motel size. They're decorated in rustic pine furniture and painted cheerfully. The continental breakfast can be taken outside, on the lawn, in good weather.

7 Turbat's Creek Rd. (P.O. Box 2722), Kennebunkport, ME 04046. © **877/594-5634** or 207/967-8700. www.kingsportinn.com/turbatshome.htm. 26 units. $89–$179 double; holidays $129–$189 double. Rates include continental breakfast. AE, MC, V. Closed Dec–Mar (but open briefly in early Dec). From Dock Sq., drive to top of hill, turn right on Maine St., turn left at 1st fork, and turn right at 2nd fork. Pets allowed; inquire before arriving. **Amenities:** Heated outdoor pool; free use of mountain bikes. *In room:* A/C, TV, dataport, hair dryer, fridge.

The Yachtsman Lodge & Marina ★★   The White Barn Inn took over this river-front motel in 1997 and made it an appealing base for exploring the southern Maine coast. Within walking distance of Dock Square, nice touches abound, such as down comforters, granite-topped vanities, high ceilings, CD players, and French doors that open onto patios just above the river. Every room is located on the first floor and is similarly appointed, but while standard motel size, their simple, classical styling is far superior to anything you'll find at a chain motel.

Ocean Ave. (P.O. Box 2609), Kennebunkport, ME 04046. © **207/967-2511.** Fax 207/967-5056. www.yachtsmanlodge.com. 30 units. $189–$369 double. Rates include continental breakfast. 2-night mini-mum stay on weekends and holidays. AE, MC, V. *In room:* A/C, TV/VCR, dataport, fridge, coffeemaker, hair dryer, iron.

WHERE TO DINE

Those looking for a quick lobster have a couple of options in the Kennebunkport area, although the prices tend to be a bit more expensive than at other casual lobster spots farther north along the coast. **Nunan's Lobster Hut** (© **207/967-4362**), Route 9 north of Kennebunkport at Cape Porpoise, is a classic lobster shack, often crowded with diners and full of atmosphere, which helps make up for disappointments such as potato chips (rather than a baked potato) served with the lobster dinner. No reservations are taken, nor are credit cards accepted; it's open daily for dinner, starting at 5pm in summer.

There's also **Cape Porpoise Lobster Co.,** 15 Pier Rd. (© **800/967-4268** or 207/967-4268), a compact spot overlooking the sparkling water. There's limited outdoor dining, but most everything is served on Styrofoam plates, so beware of rogue winds that strive to dump your meal on your lap. No reservations are taken; credit cards are accepted. It's usually open daily from 9am to 7pm for breakfast, lunch, and dinner in season; it's closed from late fall to around Memorial Day.

Federal Jack's Restaurant and Brew Pub BREWPUB   This light, airy, and mod-ern restaurant, named after a schooner built at Cape Porpoise a century ago, is in a retail

---

ⓘMoments   Packing a Picnic on Cape Porpoise

Cape Porpoise ★★ is a lovely little village, nearly forgotten by time, between Kennebunk and Biddeford. (And you've got to love the name.) It makes for a superb day trip or bike ride. While in the village, think about packing a picnic and taking it to the rocks where the lobster boats are tied up; watch the fishermen, or train your binoculars on Goat Island and its lighthouse. Drop by **Bradbury Broth-ers Market** (© **207/967-3939**) for basic staples, or the **Cape Porpoise Kitchen** (© **207/967-1150**) for gourmet-style prepared meals, cheeses, and baked goods. The village has two good lobster shacks (see "Where to Dine," below), a handful of shops, and even a postage-stamp–size library.

complex sitting a bit uneasily among boatyards lining the south bank of the Kennebunk River. From the second-floor perch (look for a seat on the spacious three-season deck in warmer weather), you can gaze across the river toward the shops of Dock Square. The upscale pub menu features regional fare with a creative twist and also offers standards such as hamburgers, steamed mussels, and pizza. This is good bet for a basic meal without any pretensions; locals keep a sharp eye on the specials board, which can include a grilled crab and havarti sandwich. The restaurant is best known for its Shipyard ales, lagers, and porters, which they've been brewing since 1992 and are among the best in New England.

8 Western Ave., Lower Village (south bank of Kennebunk River), Kennebunk. © **207/967-4322.** www.federaljacks.com. Main courses (lunch or dinner) $2.95–$16; lobster dinners priced to market. AE, DISC, MC, V. Daily 11:30am–9pm (bar to 1am); Sun brunch served 10:30am–2pm.

Grissini ★★ TUSCAN   Grissini is a handsome trattoria gone upscale. Oversize Italian advertising posters line the walls of a soaring, barn-like space, and burning logs in the handsome stone fireplace take the chill out of a cool evening. In fact, everything seems larger than life, including the plates, flatware, and water goblets. Meals are likewise luxuriously sized and nicely presented and include a wide range of pastas and pizza served with considerable flair. Expect delicious upscale treatments of gnocchi, lasagna, and pastas revved up with the likes of goat cheese, plus main courses such as risotto with smoked bacon and Gorgonzola; wood-grilled salmon, chicken, and steak; spicy lamb shank with chorizo; and lobster with cream cheese, scallops, and wild mushrooms. For those without completely empty stomachs, a changing "grotta" menu offers lighter fare of pizzas, ciabatta sandwiches, crepes, and glasses of wine. Desserts include panna cotta and tiramisu.

27 Western Ave., Kennebunk. © **207/967-2211.** www.restaurantgrissini.com. Reservations encouraged. Entrees $14–$28; grotta menu $8–$14. AE, MC, V. Sun–Fri 5:30–9pm; Sat 5–9:30pm. Closed Wed Jan–Mar.

Hurricane ★★ AMERICAN/ECLECTIC   Originally an offshoot of Brooks and Luanne MacDonald's award-winning Ogunquit restaurant, this is now the only Hurricane still blowing. The late open hours are a boon in early-closing Maine. Lunch might start with a cup of lobster chowder, the "Ice Cube" (a block of iceberg lettuce with bleu cheese dressing, toasted pecans, roasted pears, and croutons), a lobster Cobb salad, a bento box of shrimp, or pepper-seared tenderloin carpaccio; the main course could be a gourmet sandwich, some pan-roasted halibut over coconut purple rice, tuna burgers, a muffuletta sandwich, or seared diver-caught scallops. Dinner entrees run to such items as lobster cioppino, grilled veal chops, "stuffed" risotto, roasted chicken on a cheddar biscuit, rack of lamb with a white-bean ragout, or baked or boiled lobster. Finish with a vanilla bean crème brûlée, Key lime tart with coconut rum sauce, a raspberry/lemon panna cotta, or a course of cheeses.

29 Dock Sq., Kennebunkport. © **207/967-1111.** www.hurricanerestaurant.com. Reservations recommended. Main courses $15–$45; small plates $8–$22. AE, DC, DISC, MC, V. Daily 11:30am–10:30pm (winter to 9:30pm).

Pier 77 Restaurant ★★ CONTEMPORARY NEW ENGLAND   Long a tony restaurant with a wonderful ocean view, Pier 77 was recently renovated and renamed by husband-and-wife team Peter and Kate Morency. The food, drawing on Peter's training at the Culinary Institute of America and 20 years in top kitchens in Boston and San Francisco, is more contemporary and skillful than almost anything else in Maine. The menu has traditional favorites (filet mignon, lobster in the rough) along with slightly more adventurous dishes, such a trio of duck courses and a tomato-y seafood stew. The restaurant has earned *Wine Spectator*'s awards of excellence since 1993.

77 Pier Rd., Cape Porpoise (Kennebunkport). © **207/967-8500.** www.pier77restaurant.com. Reservations recommended. Main courses $14–$25. AE, MC, V. Memorial Day to Labor Day daily 11:30am–2:30pm and 5–10pm; off season, call for hours.

White Barn Inn ★★★ REGIONAL/NEW AMERICAN   The White Barn Inn's (see earlier in this chapter) classy dining room attracts gourmands from New York, Boston, and beyond. In a rustic barn attached to the inn, with a soaring interior and an eclectic collection of country antiques displayed in a hayloft, chef Jonathan Cartwright changes up the menu frequently, but always incorporates local ingredients: a lobster spring roll of daikon, carrots, snow peas, and Thai sauce, or some locally caught pan-seared diver scallops to start; an *intermezzo* course of fruit soup or sorbet; and a main course such as pan-seared filet of salmon, grilled chicken breast over creamed spinach, or simply steamed lobster over fettuccine with cognac coral butter sauce. The tasting menu runs to seasonal items such as variations of oyster; sautéed smoked haddock rarebit; Quebec foie gras roulade; or peekytoe crab. Service is astonishingly attentive and knowledgeable, capping the experience.

Beach Ave., Kennebunkport. © **207/967-2321.** Reservations recommended. Fixed-price dinner $91; tasting menu $125 per person. AE, MC, V. Mon–Thurs 6:30–9:30pm; Fri 5:30–9:30pm. Closed 2 weeks in Jan.

Portland

Maine's largest city, Portland sits on a hammerhead-shaped peninsula extending into scenic Casco Bay. It's easy to drive right past it on I-295, admiring the skyline at 60 miles an hour, and be on your way to the villages and headlands farther up the coast. After all, one doesn't usually think of urban life when envisioning a vacation in Maine.

But Portland is well worth an afternoon's detour or even a weekend stay. This historic city has plenty of charm—especially the renovated (and touristed) Old Port, with its brick sidewalks and cobblestone streets. Travelers who stop here are also rewarded with ferries to offshore islands, boutique shops, historic homes, architectural treasures, graceful neighborhoods, and top-shelf dining. Portland is the culinary mecca of northern New England, blessed with an uncommonly high number of excellent restaurants for a city its size.

Actually, it feels more like a large town than a small city. Strike up a conversation with a resident, and you're likely to get an earful about how easy it is to live here. You can buy gourmet coffee, see art-house movies, and get good Vietnamese or Thai food to go. There's even some terrific residential architecture. Yet Portland is still compact enough that you can walk from one end to the other. Despite its outward appearance of being an actual metropolis, the city has a population of just 65,000. Traffic isn't bad at all. And there's a salty tang to local culture that you'll occasionally still glimpse in the waterfront bars and chowder houses.

Like most New England cities, Portland has been forced to reinvent itself every couple of generations as economic and cultural trends overturn old paradigms. The city was a center for maritime trade in the 19th century, when a forest of ship masts obscured the view of the harbor. It's been a manufacturing hub, with locomotive factories, steel foundries, and fish-packing plants. It's been a mercantile center, with impressive downtown department stores and a slew of wholesale dealers.

Today, as a sprawling, could-be-anywhere mall in South Portland siphons off much of the commercial business, this city is bent on reshaping its downtown core as a tourist destination, regional center for the arts, and incubator for high-tech startups.

The verdict is still out on whether Portland's current reincarnation as a mini-Boston (down to the fish market, train station, and beloved local baseball nine) will succeed.

But unlike so many other deteriorating downtowns, Portland's has few vacant storefronts. Office space is in short supply, and there's a brisk urban vitality that often eludes cities many times its size. A recent wave of immigration from Africa and Asia has given this formerly white-bread town a shot in the cultural arm, too; the city's art museum is outstanding for a community this size; and an arts college brings a youthful spirit to the streets. Best of all, there's always an offshore island to escape to when cruise ships on the waterfront unload a few too many fellow tourists for your taste.

1 ORIENTATION

106 miles N of Boston and 317 miles NE of New York City

GETTING THERE

BY CAR   Coming from the south by car, downtown Portland is most easily reached by taking exit 44 off the Maine Turnpike (I-95, which is a toll road), then following I-295 (which is free) a few miles into town. Exit I-295 onto Franklin Arterial (exit 7), then continue straight uphill and downhill until you arrive at the city's ferry terminal in the Old Port. Turn right onto Commercial Street and continue a few blocks to parking meters and the visitor center (see below).

BY TRAIN   **Amtrak** (© **800/872-7245;** www.amtrak.com) runs the daily Downeaster service from Boston's North Station to Portland (passengers from other cities must change stations from South Station to North Station in Boston by taxi or subway). The train makes four to five round-trips daily, for about $23 one-way. Downtown is a short city bus ride or a 30- to 45-minute walk from the station.

BY BUS   Two big carriers, **Concord Coach Lines** (© **800/639-3317** or 207/828-1151; www.concordcoachlines.com) and **Greyhound** (© **800/231-2222;** www.greyound. com), provide bus service to Portland from Boston and Bangor. The Vermont Transit bus terminal is at 950 Congress St., about a mile downhill from, and south of, the downtown core. Concord Coach, which is a few dollars more expensive, has movies and headsets on its trips; its terminal is inconveniently set on Thompson Point Road (a 35-min. walk from downtown), but it is served by city buses and taxis.

BY PLANE   **Portland International Jetport** (© **207/874-8877**; www.portlandjetport. org), airport code PWM, is the largest airport in Maine. It's served by flights from AirTran (© 800/247-8726; www.airtrain.com), Continental (© 800/523-3273; www.continental. com), Delta (© 800/221-1212; www.delta.com), JetBlue (© 800/538-2583; www.jetblue. com), Northwest (© 800/225-2525; www.nwa.com), United Express (© 800/864-8331; www.ual.com), and US Airways (© 800/428-4322; www.usair.com). The airport has grown in fits and starts in recent years (ongoing construction and tight parking can be frustrating at times), but is still quite easily navigated; car rentals are available, and a taxi to the city center runs about $15.

VISITOR INFORMATION

The **Convention and Visitor's Bureau of Greater Portland,** 245 Commercial St., Portland, ME 04101 (© **207/772-5800** or 772-4994; www.visitportland.com), stocks a large supply of brochures and is happy to dispense information about local attractions, lodging, and dining. The center is open year-round, weekdays from 8am to 5pm and shorter hours on Saturday, depending on the season. There are three more tourist information kiosks scattered around town: one at the **Portland International Jetport** (© **207/775-5809**), open daily until 10:30pm; one in **Deering Oaks Park** near the Forest Ave. exit off I-295, open at least 6 days a week year-round; and one ad hoc kiosk that opens up outside the **cruise ship terminal** on Commercial St. for 4 hr. after any cruise ship arrives.

Portland also has a free weekly newspaper, the *Portland Phoenix,* offering good listings of local events, films, nightclub performances, and the like. Copies are widely available at restaurants, bars, and convenience stores.

The city of Portland is divided into two areas: on-peninsula and off-peninsula. (There are also the islands, but more on that below.) Most travelers are destined for the compact peninsula, which is home to the downtown and where most of the city's cultural life and retail activity takes place.

Viewed from the water, Portland's peninsula is shaped a bit like a swaybacked horse or the hammerhead on a shark, with the **Old Port ★★★** lying in the belly near the waterfront and the peninsula's two main residential neighborhoods (Munjoy Hill and the West End) topping gentle rises overlooking downtown. Congress Street, Portland's main artery of commerce, connects these two neighborhoods. The western stretch of Congress Street (roughly btw. Monument Sq. and State St.) is home to Portland's emerging **Arts District ★**, where you can find the handsome art museum, several theaters, the campus of the Maine College of Art (located in an old department store), the original L.L.Bean outlet, and a growing number of restaurants and boutiques.

PARKING

Parking is notoriously tight in the Old Port, and the city's parking enforcement is notoriously efficient. Several parking garages are convenient to the Old Port, with parking fees less than $1 per hour; you can also park in some residential neighborhoods, often for a maximum of 2 hours. Read signs carefully for news of nighttime street-sweeping hours; you *will* be towed (don't ask how I know; I just do) if you run afoul of them.

SPECIAL EVENTS

New Year's Portland rings in January with a smorgasbord of events and entertainment throughout downtown Portland. Events for families are scheduled in the afternoon; entertainment more oriented for adults—including loads of live music—kicks off later in the evening at numerous locales, including auditoriums, shops, and churches. The emphasis is on enjoying New Year's without alcohol. One admission button buys entrance to all events.

The **Old Port Festival** (© **207/772-6828**) takes place in early June, when tens of thousands of revelers descend upon the historic Old Port section to herald the arrival of summer. Several blocks of the Old Port are blocked to traffic, and the throngs order food and buy goods from street vendors. Several stages provide entertainment, ranging from kids' singalongs to raucous blues. Admission is free.

2 WHERE TO STAY

In addition to the lodgings listed below, there are tons of chain hotels and motels in and around the city. Check around the Maine Mall (in South Portland) for the largest agglomeration; you'll find all the usual names there, in various price ranges; see below for a few suggestions.

If you're looking for something more central (and you should), Hilton runs a hotel across the street from the main ferry dock in the Old Port neighborhood. The **Hilton Garden Inn** (65 Commercial St.; © **207/780-0780**) is convenient to restaurants, bakeries, and pubs—not to mention the islands of Casco Bay. You'll pay for the privilege of being in the heart of the waterfront, though: Double rooms mostly run from about $189 up to $369 per night.

The **Holiday Inn by the Bay,** 88 Spring St. (© **800/345-5050** or 207/775-2311), offers great views of the harbor from about half the rooms, along with the usual chain-hotel creature comforts. Peak-season rates are approximately $180 for a double.

Budget travelers seeking chain hotels typically head toward the area around the Maine Mall in South Portland, about 8 miles south of the attractions of downtown. Try **Days Inn** (© **207/772-3450**) or **Coastline Inn** (© **207/772-3838**). The new **Extended Stay America** (2 Ashley Dr., Scarborough; © **207/883-0554**) is a few minutes' drive south of the Maine Mall and 6 miles from downtown Portland and features in-room kitchenettes. Doubles start at about $55 nightly in the off season, $85 in summer.

VERY EXPENSIVE

Black Point Inn Resort ★★

Located 10 miles south of Portland (about 15 min. from downtown), the Black Point Inn is a Maine classic even if it is a lot smaller than it used to be. The property reopened in 2007 under new ownership, having dispensed with one of its pools and all of the cottages (slashing the inn's room count by more than two-thirds); but those rooms that did remain open were updated. Situated on 9 acres with views along the coast both north and south, this was built as a summer resort in 1873 on the same attractive rocky point memorialized by landscape painter Winslow Homer. What remains is still as elegant as ever, and the expansive porch (with its constant sea breezes) thankfully remains. Rates are charged per person, and are hefty, but do include breakfast, dinner, and a trimmed-down afternoon tea service daily.

510 Black Point Rd., Prouts Neck, ME 04074. © **207/883-2500.** Fax 207/883-9976. www.blackpointinn.com. 25 units. $380–$520 double; $480–$580 suite. Rates include full breakfast, afternoon tea service, and dinner. Packages available. AE, DC, DISC, MC, V. Free valet parking. Closed Nov–Apr. **Amenities:** Heated outdoor pool; fitness room; Jacuzzi; sauna; children's program (summers); limited room service; massage; babysitting; laundry service; dry cleaning. *In room:* A/C, TV/DVD, hair dryer, iron, safe.

Inn by the Sea ★★★

Not so much an inn as a luxury retreat, Cape Elizabeth's best hotel has made the successful transition from relaxed seaside getaway to destination resort. Yet they've done it while retaining a wonderful sense of place: suites and dining areas emphasize Maine-themed art and foods, while summery gardens and ocean views tantalize through the windows. An expansive, lovely spa was added in 2008, as were a walk-in *cave,* fireplace rooms, and bi-level spa suites with double Jacuzzis. A further set of cottages (town-house-like suites) in an outbuilding add full kitchens and extra bedroom or bathroom space. Especially welcome is this inn's move toward green practices: It's the first hotel in Maine to burn biofuels, operate carbon neutrally, and employ printed-paper key cards. Recycled materials and low-flow toiletry also predominate. Need still more green? A walkway leads to one of Maine's best beaches.

40 Bowery Beach Rd., Cape Elizabeth, ME 04107. © **800/888-4287** (outside Maine) or 207/799-3134. Fax 207/799-4779. www.innbythesea.com. 57 units. July–Aug $399–$789 suite; May–June and Sept–Oct $289–$609 suite; Nov–Apr $189–$369 suite. Packages available. AE, DC, DISC, MC, V. Pets welcome in some units. **Amenities:** Lounge; restaurant; heated outdoor pool; fitness room; spa; Jacuzzi; sauna; room service. *In room:* A/C, TV/DVD, kitchenette, fridge, coffeemaker, hair dryer, iron/ironing board.

EXPENSIVE

Portland Harbor Hotel ★★

Situated adjacent to Portland's busy nightlife on the corner of Fore and Union streets, only steps from a long row of bars and restaurants, this semicircular town-house-like structure—designed to fit in with the brick facades prevailing throughout the Old Port—appeals to the boutique crowd with its many amenities.

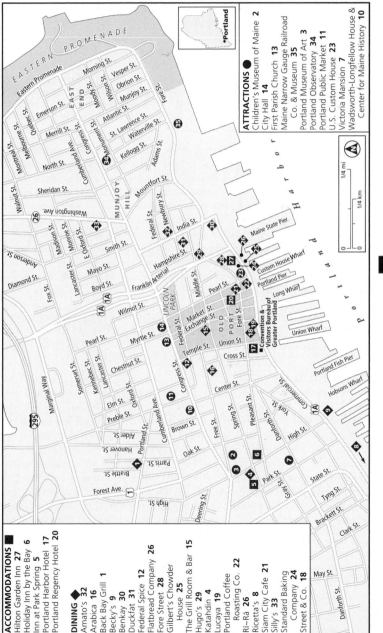

PORTLAND

6

WHERE TO STAY

ATTRACTIONS ●
Children's Museum of Maine **2**
City Hall **14**
First Parish Church **13**
Maine Narrow Gauge Railroad
  Co. & Museum **35**
Portland Museum of Art **3**
Portland Observatory **34**
Portland Public Market **11**
U.S. Custom House **23**
Victoria Mansion **7**
Wadsworth-Longfellow House &
  Center for Maine History **10**

ACCOMMODATIONS ■
Hilton Garden Inn **27**
Holiday Inn by the Bay **6**
Inn at Park Spring **5**
Portland Harbor Hotel **17**
Portland Regency Hotel **20**

DINING ◆
Amato's **32**
Arabica **16**
Back Bay Grill **1**
Becky's **9**
Benkay **30**
Duckfat **31**
Federal Spice **12**
Flatbread Company **26**
Fore Street **28**
Gilbert's Chowder
  House **25**
The Grill Room & Bar **15**
Hugo's **29**
Katahdin **4**
Lucaya **19**
Portland Coffee
  Roasting Co. **22**
Ri-Rá **26**
Ricetta's **8**
Siam City Cafe **21**
Silly's **33**
Standard Baking
  Company **24**
Street & Co. **18**

The interior courtyard throws off European ambience; large, exquisite rooms are furnished with comfy queen- and king-size beds and spacious work desks. Even the standard rooms are outfitted with big, deep bathtubs in granite-faced bathrooms; armoires; comfy duvets and down coverlets; two-line phones; and big TVs with 70 channels each. Deluxe rooms and suites add Jacuzzis and sitting areas, and many units look out onto the attractive garden area. The front desk now rents bicycles inexpensively for local sightseeing. Remember that the proximity to so many bars means some late-night weekend noise.

468 Fore St., Portland, ME 04101. ℂ **888/798-9090** or 207/775-9090. Fax 207/775-9990. www.portland harborhotel.com. 100 units. Mid-May to mid-Oct $229–$249 double, $329 suite; off season $159–$179 double, $259 suite. Packages available. AE, DC, DISC, MC, V. Valet parking in garage $10 per day. **Amenities:** Dining room; bar; fitness center; concierge; limited room service; dry cleaning; bike rental. *In room:* A/C, digital TV, Internet, hair dryer, safe, Jacuzzis (some).

Portland Regency Hotel ★★★   Centrally located on a cobblestone courtyard in the middle of the trendy Old Port, the Regency boasts one of the city's premier hotel locations. But it's got more than location—this is also one of the most architecturally striking and better-managed hotels in southern Maine. Housed in an 1895 brick armory, the hotel is thoroughly modern and offers attractive rooms, appointed and furnished with all the expected amenities. There are several types of rooms and suites, each fitted to the place's unique architecture; for a splurge, ask for a luxurious corner room with a handsome (nonworking) fireplace, sitting area, city views out big windows, and a Jacuzzi. Staff is professional, the small health club is among the best in town (it includes a sauna and hot tub), and the downstairs level conceals a restaurant and a **bar** ★ that's the best quiet place in town to sip a drink.

20 Milk St., Portland, ME 04101. ℂ **800/727-3436** or 207/774-4200. Fax 207/775-2150. www.theregency. com. 95 units. Early July to late Oct $249–$269 double, $289–$389 suite; off season $159–$219 double, $209–$329 suite. AE, DISC, MC, V. Valet parking $8 per day. **Amenities:** Restaurant; bar; fitness club w/ aerobics classes; spa; Jacuzzi; sauna; courtesy car to airport; business center; conference rooms; limited room service; babysitting (with prior notice); dry cleaning (Mon–Fri). *In room:* A/C, TV, minibar, safe.

MODERATE

Inn at Park Spring ★   This small, tasteful B&B is located on a busy downtown street in a historic brick home that dates back to 1835. It's well located for exploring the city on foot. The Portland Museum of Art is just 2 blocks away, the Old Port is about 10 minutes away, and great restaurants are all within easy walking distance. Guests can linger or watch TV in a front parlor, or chat at the communal dining table in the adjacent room. The rooms are all corner rooms, and most are bright and sunny. Especially nice is Spring, with its great morning light and wonderful views of the historic row houses on Park Street, and Gables, on the third floor, which gets abundant afternoon light and has a nice bathroom.

135 Spring St., Portland, ME 04101. ℂ **800/437-8511** or 207/774-1059. www.innatparkspring.com. 6 units. Mid-June to Oct and holidays $149–$175 double; rest of the year $99–$165 double. 2-night minimum weekends. Rates include full breakfast and off-street parking. AE, MC, V. No children 9 and under. *In room:* A/C, hair dryer, iron/ironing board.

3 WHERE TO DINE

Portland is nothing if not a city of creative cheap eats, so don't neglect local bakeries and coffee shops when trolling for quick or economical meals. My favorite bakery in New

England, hands-down, is **Standard Baking Company** ★★, 75 Commercial St. (© 207/ 773-2112), across from the ferry terminal and behind the new Hilton Garden Inn hotel. Allison Bray and Matt James bake some of the best sticky buns (with or without nuts) and focaccia I've tasted, plus top-rate breads, brioche, cookies, and more. There's good coffee, too. The bakery is open 7am to 6pm daily except Sundays, when it closes at 5pm.

Among the many coffee shops around the city, I frequent both **Arabica,** 16 Free St. (© 207/879-0792), with house-roasted beans and a good choice of teas, plus pie, bagels, scones, and even toast with peanut butter; and **Portland Coffee Roasting Co.,** 111 Commercial St. (© 207/761-9525), with inventive coffee drinks, a daily trivia quiz, and a display case of fun snacks such as sushi and energy bars.

For a pizza, head to **Flatbread Company** (see below); **Angelone's** (© 207/775-3114; 788 Washington Ave.), which makes outstandingly authentic local pies; or **Ricetta's** (© 207/775-7400; 29 Western Ave., South Portland), tucked into a small shopping mall en route to the larger Maine Mall.

For takeout or a picnic, **Supper at Six** ★, 16 Veranda St., near Back Cove and Washington Avenue (© 207/761-6600), fixes great sandwiches. (Try the Darcy, made with chicken with Thai chili sauce.) They also do a variety of to-go gourmet meals. It's open weekdays only.

Portland also claims to be the original home of the Italian sandwich—which may have been the original sub sandwich in America—and locals maintain the best example can still be found at the purported inventor of this creation, **Amato's,** 71 India St. (© 207/ 773-1682), in what's left of Portland's Italian neighborhood.

EXPENSIVE

Back Bay Grill ★★ NEW AMERICAN   Back Bay Grill has long been one of Portland's best restaurants, with an upscale, contemporary ambience; the only trouble is getting there (it's near the central post office, far off the tourist track). Chef Larry Matthews bought the place from founder Joel Freund in 2002, and his menu is revamped seasonally, emphasizing local produce and meats. Diners might start with Maine crab cakes in a Thai chili aioli sauce, beef carpaccio, crispy duck confit, or roasted acorn squash soup. Among main courses, look for lamb sausages, grilled filet mignon in redwine sauce, monkfish with pesto-whipped potatoes, or salmon crusted in horseradish and served with roasted beets and basmati rice. The fresh pastas are memorable, as well, such as hand-rolled fettuccini with truffles or lobster tortellini with lobster foam.

65 Portland St. © **207/772-8833.** www.backbaygrill.com. Reservations recommended. Main courses $17–$33. AE, DC, DISC, MC, V. Mon–Thurs 5:30–9:30pm; Fri–Sat 5:30–10pm.

Fore Street ★★ CONTEMPORARY GRILL   Fore Street has emerged as one of Maine's most celebrated restaurants. Chef Sam Hayward cooks with local and organic ingredients whenever possible, and avoids overly fancy presentations. As a result, the dining space and menu both center the kitchen's wood-fired brick oven and grill. Hayward's menu changes nightly; the best entrees include spit-roasted pork loin and chicken, grilled hanger steak, and smoky wood-roasted mussels (a big hit). Finish with the signature chocolate soufflé cake, a chocolate peanut butter torte, or gelato; dessert items are often accented with seasonal Maine fruits and berries. The soft lighting against the brick walls, maple floors, and coppery tables lends an intimate glow to the place; though it can be hard to get a reservation in summer, management sets aside a few tables each night for walk-ins.

288 Fore St. © **207/775-2717.** www.forestreet.biz. Reservations recommended. Main courses $13–$29. AE, MC, V. Mon–Thurs 5:30–10pm; Fri–Sat 5:30–10:30pm; Sun 5:30–9:30pm.

Hugo's ★★★ ECLECTIC/NEW AMERICAN   The resurrection of Hugo's is nothing short of amazing. Not so long ago the place was fading, but chef Rob Evans and partner Nancy Pugh changed all that. Trained in star kitchens (French Laundry, the Inn at Little Washington), Evans brought a philosophy of buying local ingredients and crafting unusual, exciting menus. He recently switched to a small-plate style of service here, offering everything from a simple Caesar salad or steak tartare to Long Island duck and pan-fried arctic char. A tasting menu expands the journey to 5 courses, and a chef's menu (by advance reservation only) runs to 12. Dessert could be a goat-cheese cheesecake, a plum Linzer torte with green tea froth, or a bittersweet chocolate parfait. A good tapas menu is served at the bar, as well, and the partners also run a great Belgian fries-and-milkshakes shop, Duckfat, just down the street.

88 Middle St. ℂ **207/774-8538.** www.hugos.net. Reservations strongly recommended (required for Chef's Menu). Plates $10–$21 each; tasting menu $75. AE, MC, V. Tues–Thurs 5:30–9pm; Fri–Sat 5:30–9:30pm.

Street & Co. ★★★ MEDITERRANEAN/SEAFOOD   Dana Street's intimate brick-walled bistro specializes in seafood, and it's the city's best. You pass an open kitchen as you're seated, then watch talented chefs perform their magic in the tiny space. The fish is as fresh as can be (the docks are close by, after all). Looking for lobster? This place offers it in interesting configurations, such as grilled and served over linguine in a buttery garlic sauce. Other fine choices include tuna, mussels, or the grilled catch of the day. Reservations are definitely recommended, although some tables are set aside for walk-ins; it can't hurt to check if you're just getting into town. During summer, outdoor seating is available at a few scattered tables in the alley (which is not as bad as it sounds).

33 Wharf St. ℂ **207/775-0887.** Reservations recommended. Main courses $14–$24. AE, MC, V. Mon–Thurs 5:30–9:30pm; Fri–Sat 5:30–10pm. Lounge opens 30 min. earlier.

MODERATE

Beale Street BBQ ★ (Finds) BARBECUE   Beale Street BBQ owner Mark Quigg once operated a takeout grill on Route 1 near Freeport, but author Stephen King got wind of his cooking; soon he was catering movie shoots and opening a restaurant. Of all the barbecue joints in Maine, this is probably my favorite: It's got an appealing roadhouse atmosphere, friendly staff, and great smoked meats. Check the board for daily specials, which usually include a fish entree as well as Creole and Cajun offerings; I love the barbecue sampler ("All You Really Need to Know About BBQ"), your choice of pulled pork, chicken, or beef brisket; sweet, crunchy corn bread; a half slab of ribs; a quarter chicken; delicious spicy smoked links; and a mound of barbecued beans and coleslaw. Two people can comfortably split it. There's another, fancier location (ℂ **207/442-9514**) at 215 Water St. in Bath (see chapter 7).

75 Broadway (from Portland, cross Casco Bay Bridge and turn right onto Broadway), South Portland. ℂ 207/767-0130. Reservations not accepted. Main courses $9–$18. MC, V. Daily 11:30am–10pm (Sun to 9pm in winter).

Benkay ★ (Value) JAPANESE/SUSHI   Among Portland's sushi restaurants, Benkay is hippest, usually teeming with a lively local crowd lured by the affordable menus. Chef Seiji Ando trained in Osaka and Kyoto; his sushi, sashimi, and maki rolls deliver a lot for the price, and there's a wide range of choices and combinations. Standard Japanese bar-food items such as tempura (deep-fried vegetables), *gyoza* (dumplings), teriyaki, *katsu* (fried chicken or pork cutlets), and udon (thick noodles) are also served. It stays open pretty late, too—after midnight Friday and Saturday, which is handy in early-closing

Portland. For dessert, consider the green tea ice cream: deliciously bitter . . . and good for you. Sort of.

2 India St. (at Commercial). (C) **207/773-5555.** www.sushiman.com. Reservations not accepted. Main courses $7.95–$17. AE, MC, V. Mon–Thurs 11:30am–2pm and 5–9:30pm; Fri 11:30am–2pm and 5pm–12:30am; Sat 5pm–12:30am; Sun 5–9:30pm.

Flatbread Company ★ PIZZA   This upscale, hippie-chic pizzeria—an offshoot of the original Flatbread Company in Waitsfield, Vermont—might have the best waterfront location in town. It sits on a slip overlooking the Casco Bay Lines terminal, so you can watch fishermen and ferries while you eat. (Picnic tables are set out on the deck in fair weather.) The inside brings to mind a Phish concert, with Tibetan prayer flags and longhaired staffers stoking wood-fired ovens and slicing nitrate-free pepperoni and organic vegetables. The laid-back, smoky atmosphere really makes the place; the pizza is quite good, too.

72 Commercial St. (C) **207/772-8777.** Reservations accepted for parties of 10 or more. Pizzas $12–$15. AE, MC, V. Mon–Tues 5–9pm; Wed–Sun 11:30am–9pm.

The Grill Room & Bar ★★ AMERICAN   It replaced the popular Natasha's, but the Grill Room is off to a good start: good food, served unpretentiously. Chef Harding Lee Smith, a Portland native, left Back Bay Grill to open this mecca to meat. Most items are cooked on the open kitchen's wood-fired grills, but there's more than steak here: yummy seared-tuna sandwiches on ciabatta and thin-crust pizzas, for example. Of course, you can always get a steak (porterhouse, rib-eye, sirloin; the works) or a piece of grilled fish or chicken, and you're encouraged to do so: There's a card of tasty sauces from "zippy" to "brandy cream" for pairing. The outdoor tables in Tommy's Park are ideal in summer, yet my favorite feature of the place is its bar area, with personable barkeeps, good beers on tap, and Red Sox on the flatscreen. This is fast becoming one of my favorite local bites.

84 Exchange St. (C) **207/774-2333.** Appetizers and pizzas $7–$12; entrees $13–$27. AE, DISC, MC, V. Daily 11am–2:30pm and 5–10pm (Sun to 9pm).

Katahdin ★★ CREATIVE NEW ENGLAND   Long a favorite of local Portlanders in the know, Katahdin is a lively spot that prides itself on eclectic cuisine. Chef Becky Lee Simmons' nightly specials range from the basic to the elaborate, from dayboat-caught sea scallops with smoked bacon and green pea tendrils to Maine shrimp in a buttery fondue with housemade gnocchi to roast duck with a citrusy confit. There's a good selection of wines, too. (Reservations aren't accepted, so order a glass—or one of the restaurant's famous martinis—while waiting at the bar to score a table.)

106 High St. (C) **207/774-1740.** www.katahdinrestaurant.com. Reservations not accepted. Main courses $12–$18. DISC, MC, V. Tues–Thurs 5–9:30pm; Fri–Sat 5–10:30pm.

Rí~Rá ★ IRISH PUB   This Old Port pub is styled after an Irish pub, though it's fancier than all that. They've got the decor right: the doors were imported from a pub in Kilkenny, and the back bar and counter are from others in County Louth. So far, so good, but there's no smoke and the Patriots and Sox are on TV instead of soccer—oh, well. Upstairs beyond the pub is a dining room with a view of the docks; look for smoked turkey wraps, fish and chips, meatloaf, shepherd's pie, and Guinness bread pudding, plus a few more upscale dishes such as crab-filled salmon, Derrybeg pork (which is glazed with apricot, mustard, and cider), and *broxty,* a scallion-potato pancake topped with parsley sauce and meat.

72 Commercial St. (C) **207/761-4446.** www.rira.com. Main courses $9–$20. AE, MC, V. Mon–Sat 11:30am–10pm; Sun 11am–10pm.

Packing a Picnic

Portland and its surrounding area is so stuffed with picnic spots you might need a week to sample them all.

For starters, don't miss the **Eastern Promenade** (p. 117), a hilltop park with expansive views of Casco Bay and its myriad (more than one for each day of the year) islands. Some have favorably compared this view with San Francisco's; even if that's stretching it a bit, you can't go wrong here watching the weather and light come and go.

The **Western Promenade** (p. 117), reached across town via Congress Street, has distant westerly views of the White Mountains (you can just make out the massive outline of Mount Washington on a clear day). The mall, airport, and paper mill in the foreground make for uninspiring scenery—but it's still a great spot for sunsets. There are a few benches, and in summer the free musical performances held here are of a pretty high caliber.

If you enjoy scenes of a gritty working waterfront, the **Casco Bay Lines** ferry terminal on Commercial Street (at the foot of Franklin Arterial) has plenty of benches.

If you seek a more tranquil water view, **Back Cove** loops around from Forest Avenue to Washington Avenue. Stopping places are scattered about the circular path around the cove, which in good weather is full of joggers, baby strollers, and walkers. A full loop takes about an hour.

Siam City Cafe ★ THAI   This cafe sits on a once-neglected stretch of Fore Street in the Old Port, around the corner from the Regency hotel. Thai food here is creatively presented; meals might start with a spring roll filled with shrimp, rice vermicelli, and vegetables, or some deep-fried lobster egg rolls. For the main course, try out the house version of pad Thai—a mélange of rice stick noodles, shrimp, scallops, lobster, crunchy roasted peanuts, scrambled egg, crisp bean sprouts, and scallions—or one of the curries (red, green, or *massaman*) made with chicken, scallops, shrimp, or tofu. Unexpectedly, there's also an extensive wine list featuring a healthy selection of reds and whites. Service is energetic, and the changing dessert specials are very good, including a surprisingly good chocolate mousse.

339 Fore St. ⓒ **207/773-8389.** Entrees $12–$22. AE, MC, V. 11:30am–2pm and 5–9pm.

INEXPENSIVE

Becky's BREAKFAST/LUNCH   This Portland institution resides in a squat concrete building at the not-so-quaint end of the waterfront. It's been written up in *Gourmet* magazine, but that's where the comparison to "fine dining" ends; this is a diner, Maine-style, complete with drop ceilings, fluorescent lights, and scruffy counters, booths, and tables. It opens early (4am) for the local fishermen grabbing a cup of joe and some eggs before heading out onto (or in from) the water; later in the day, it attracts high school kids, businessmen, and just about everyone else. The menu is extensive, offering what you'd expect: sandwiches, fried haddock, corn dogs, tuna melts, and milky bowls of chowder with just-caught fish. It's notable for its breakfasts, too, including more than a dozen omelets, eggs any way you want 'em, pancakes, French toast, and five types of home fries.

Just a few miles north of Portland along Route 1 in Falmouth, the Maine Audubon Society's **Gilsland Farm Sanctuary** is one of the best picnic spots I've found. Gaze out on grassy fields, wildflowers, and tidewater. Afterward, explore the society's intriguing displays, demonstration projects, and gift shops; this is clearly an organization that cares deeply about the state's natural resources. What the heck? Become a member while you're there.

And, of course, the beaches and parks in Cape Elizabeth (south of Portland, reached via Rte. 77) are all superlative picnic spots. **Two Lights State Park** and **Fort Williams Park** (which includes oft-photographed Portland Head Light) both offer sweeping vistas of lighthouses and craggy waves crashing onto dramatic rocks; **Crescent Beach State Park** is a very pleasing, sandy crescent, reached by a walk through beach roses. There's a concessions stand, too. A bit farther south, **Scarborough Beach Park** is another good choice. It's a long, sandy beach.

For picnicking supplies in metro Portland, I like **Supper at Six** for sandwiches (open weekdays only) and **Standard Baking Company** for sweets and coffee; (p. 111). Cape Elizabeth has a few general stores good for stocking up pre-beach; they're heavy on sodas, beer, and candy, but you can also score an Italian sandwich or an ice-cream treat at most.

390 Commercial St. ✆ **207/773-7070.** www.beckysdiner.com. Breakfast items $2.25–$7.50; lunch and dinner items $2–$8. AE, DISC, MC, V. Daily 4am–9pm.

Federal Spice ⓥ WRAPS/GLOBAL   Tucked in a drab location across from the city's main post office, this has been one of Portland's prime go-to places for a quick, cheap bite ever since I can remember. Located beneath a parking garage just off Temple Street, it's a breezy, informal little room with very limited seating; plan to take out. There are quesadillas, salads, and soft tacos, along with wraps full of interesting fillings such as jerk chicken, pumpkin rice, and Thai-curried slaw. The sweetish yam fries are an unusual side-dish choice when they're on the menu.

225 Federal St. ✆ **207/774-6404.** Main courses $3–$7. V. Mon–Sat 11am–6pm.

Gilbert's Chowder House CHOWDER/SEAFOOD   Gilbert's is a very popular waterfront spot with tourists, and is nautical without taking the theme too far. The reasonable prices keep locals coming, too. The chowders are okay, if unspectacular; other choices include fried clams, haddock sandwiches, and various seafood you can order either broiled or fried. There's also a basic lobster dinner with corn on the cob and a cup of clam chowder. Limited microbrews are on tap, and they serve decent cheesecake for dessert, among other choices.

92 Commercial St. ✆ **207/871-5636.** Reservations not accepted. Chowders $2.50–$9.75; sandwiches $2.25–$9.95; main courses $6.95–$23. AE, DISC, MC, V. Mon–Thurs 11am–10pm; Fri–Sat 11am–11pm; Sun 11am–9pm (closed earlier in winter).

(Fun Facts   To Market, To Market . . . Once Again

The Portland Public Market has just moved—and the local library almost did, too. It's been an interesting couple years for the city's public market, which was originally conceived and funded by the late benefactress Betty Noyce in the 1990s. A few blocks downhill from Portland's main drag, the 37,000-square-foot space was, for a short while, one of the best and hippest places in northern New England to pick up a coffee in the morning, a sandwich at lunch, a lobster and some vegetables to cook for dinner, and other gourmet goods. Sadly, the market closed its doors in 2007 and the property was sold after Noyce's nonprofit foundation determined it could no longer subsidize the lower-than-market rents being charged to food vendors. The market appeared to have dissolved for good, and city residents were understandably disheartened.

But a small consortium of vendors banded together and bought a building in the center of the city, rechristening it the **Public Market House** (at 28 Monument Sq.). Today the market thrives once more. The vacant former market building? City voters defeated a 2007 referendum that would have purchased the space and converted it into a new city library. But stay tuned.

Silly's ★ (Finds) (Kids) ECLECTIC/TAKEOUT   Silly's is the favorite cheap-eats joint for hip Portlanders. Situated on a commercial street near the Eastern Promenade, the interior is informal, bright, and funky, with mismatched 1950s dinettes and a hodge-podge back patio beneath trees. There's also a weird fascination with Einstein here; like Einstein, the menu is creative. The place is noted for its roll-ups ("fast Abdullahs"), a series of tasty fillings piled into soft tortillas. I like the shish kabob with feta and the sloppy "Diesel" made with pulled pork and coleslaw. Fries are hand-cut, burgers big and delicious, and there's beer on tap. Newer menu additions include a slop "bucket," which has a messy, layered-burrito feel. Don't overlook the dessert menu of cookies, pies, ice creams, cakes, and big milkshakes: Silly's whips 'em up with peanut butter, tahini, bananas, malt, and anything else you can imagine, even some things (cranberry sauce, marshmallow crispies) you can't.

40 Washington Ave. (C) **207/772-0360.** www.sillys.com. Most items $5–$13; pizzas to $18. MC, V. Tues–Sun 11:30am–9pm.

4 EXPLORING THE CITY

Any visit to Portland should start with a stroll around the historic **Old Port** ★. Bounded by Commercial, Congress, Union, and Pearl streets, this area near the waterfront has the city's best commercial architecture, a mess of boutiques, fine restaurants, and one of the thickest concentrations of bars on the eastern seaboard. (The Old Port tends to transform as night lengthens, with crowds growing younger and rowdier.) The narrow streets and intricate brick facades reflect a mid-Victorian era; most of the area was rebuilt following a devastating fire in 1866. **Exchange Street** is the heart of the Old Port, with other attractive streets running off and around it.

Just outside the Old Port, don't miss the **First Parish Church,** 425 Congress St., a beautiful granite meetinghouse with an impressively austere interior that has changed little since 1826. A few doors down the block, Portland's **City Hall** is at the head of Exchange Street. Modeled after New York City's, it was built from granite in 1909. In a similarly regal vein is the **U.S. Custom House,** 312 Fore St. near the Old Port. The fine woodwork and marble floors here date to 1868.

The city's finest harborside stroll is along the **Eastern Prom Pathway ★,** which wraps for about a mile along the waterfront beginning at the Casco Bay Lines ferry terminal at the corner of Commercial and Franklin streets. This paved pathway is suitable for walking or biking, and offers expansive views of the islands and boat traffic on the harbor. The pathway skirts the lower edge of the **Eastern Promenade ★★,** a 68-acre hillside park with broad, grassy slopes extending down to the water. Little East End Beach is also here, but the water is often off-limits for swimming (look for signs). The pathway continues on to Back Cove Pathway, a 3¹/₂-mile loop around tidal Back Cove.

Atop Munjoy Hill, above the Eastern Promenade, is the distinctive **Portland Observatory ★** (② **207/774-5561**), a quirky shingled tower dating from 1807, used to signal the arrival of ships into port. Exhibits inside provide a quick glimpse of Portland's past, but the real draw is the expansive view from the top of the city and the harbor. It's open daily (when flags are flying from the cupola) from Memorial Day through Columbus Day, 10am until 5pm; the last tour leaves at 4:30pm. Admission is $6 for adults and $4 for children age 6 to 16.

On the other end of the peninsula is the **Western Promenade ★.** (Follow Spring St. westward to Vaughan; turn right and then take your first left on Bowdoin St. to the prom.) This narrow strip of lawn atop a forested bluff has views across the Fore River, which is lined with less-than-scenic light industry, to the White Mountains in the distance. It's a great spot to watch the sun set. Around the Western Prom are some of the grandest and most imposing houses in the city that include a wide array of architectural styles, from Italianate to shingle to stick.

THE TOP ATTRACTIONS: FROM LIGHTHOUSES TO LONGFELLOW

Children's Museum of Maine ★ Kids   The centerpiece exhibit in Portland's kids' museum is its camera obscura, a room-size "camera" located on the top floor of this stout, columned downtown building next to the art museum. Children gather around a white table in a dark room, where they see magically projected images that include cars driving on city streets, boats plying the harbor, and seagulls flapping by. This never fails to enthrall, providing a memorable lesson in the workings of lenses—ours, and a camera's. That's just one attraction; there are plenty more, from a simulated supermarket checkout counter to a firehouse pole to a mock space shuttle that kids pilot from a high cockpit.

142 Free St. (next to the Portland Museum of Art). ② **207/828-1234.** www.childrensmuseumofme.org. Admission $6. Free 5–8pm 1st Fri of each month. AE, MC, V. Mon–Sat 10am–5pm; Sun noon–5pm. Closed Mon fall–spring. Discounted parking at Spring St. parking garage.

Maine Narrow Gauge Railroad Co. & Museum ★ Kids   In the late 19th century, Maine was home to several narrow-gauge railways, operating on rails 2 feet apart. Most of these versatile trains have disappeared, but this nonprofit organization is dedicated to preserving the examples that remain. There's a small fee for admission to the museum, which is waived if you purchase a more expensive ticket for the short ride on the little train that chugs along Casco Bay at the foot of the Eastern Promenade. Views of the islands are outstanding; the ride itself is slow-paced and yawn-inducing, but young ones probably will enjoy it. Bring the video camera.

58 Fore St. **℃ 207/828-0814.** www.mngrr.org. Museum admission $2 adults, $1 seniors and children 3–12; train fare (includes free museum admission) $10 adults, $9 seniors, $6 children 3–12, free for children 2 and under. Memorial Day to Columbus Day daily 11am–4pm (trains run on the hour); rest of the year weekends only 10am–4pm. From I-295, take Franklin Arterial exit to Fore St.; turn left and continue to museum on right.

Portland Head Light & Museum ★★

A short drive (15–20 min. depending on traffic) from downtown Portland, this 1794 lighthouse is one of the most picturesque in the nation. You'll probably recognize it from advertisements, calendars, or posters. The light marks the entrance to Portland Harbor and was occupied continuously from its construction until 1989, when it was automated and the graceful keeper's house (1891) was converted to a small town-owned museum focusing on the history of navigation. The lighthouse itself is still active, thus closed to the public; but visitors can stop by the museum or browse for lighthouse-themed gifts in a gift shop. The surrounding grounds of Fort Williams Park are great for picnics.

In Fort Williams Park, 1000 Shore Rd., Cape Elizabeth. **℃ 207/799-2661.** www.portlandheadlight.com. Free admission for grounds; museum admission $2 adults, $1 children 6–18. Park grounds daily year-round sunrise–sunset (until 8:30pm in summer); museum daily Memorial Day to Columbus Day 10am–4pm, weekends only mid-Apr to mid-May and mid-Oct to late Dec. From Portland, follow State St. across bridge to South Portland; bear left on Broadway. At 3rd light, turn right on Cottage Rd. (Rte. 77), which becomes Shore Rd.; follow several more miles to park on left.

Portland Museum of Art ★★★

This bold, modern museum was designed by I.M. Pei & Partners in 1983, and it features selections from its own fine collections along with a parade of touring exhibits. (Summer exhibits are usually targeted at a broad audience.) The museum is particularly strong in American artists with Maine connections, including Winslow Homer, Andrew Wyeth, and Edward Hopper, and it has fine displays of Early American furniture and crafts. The museum shares the Joan Whitney Payson Collection with Colby College (the college gets it one semester every other year), which includes wonderful European works by Renoir, Degas, and Picasso. Special exhibitions have brought the landscape paintings of Frederic Church, art by Native American high school students from northern Maine, and a mysterious *Mona Lisa* that may have been a preparatory study for the famous work. Guided tours are given daily at 2pm.

7 Congress Sq. (corner of Congress and High sts.). **℃ 207/775-6148.** www.portlandmuseum.org. Admission $10 adults, $8 students and seniors, $4 students 6–17. (Free admission Fri 5–9pm.) Year-round Tues–Sun 10am–5pm (Fri to 9pm); Memorial Day to mid-Oct also Mon 10am–5pm.

Victoria Mansion ★★ (Finds)

Widely regarded as one of the most elaborate Victorian brownstone homes ever built in the U.S., this mansion (also known as the Morse-Libby House) is often mentioned in books on American architecture. It's a remarkable display of high Victorian style. Built between 1858 and 1863 for a Maine businessman who had made his fortune in New Orleans, the towering, slightly foreboding home is a prime example of Italianate style. Inside, craftsmen and artisans have gone to town with murals and other detailing. The decor is somber, but the home offers an engaging look into a bygone era. It's a must for architecture buffs. The weeks leading up to Christmas bring an annual round of special tours and events.

109 Danforth St. ☎ **207/772-4841**. www.victoriamansion.org. Admission $10 adults, $9 seniors, $3 children 6–17, free for children 5 and under. Christmas slightly higher. May–Oct Mon–Sat 10am–4pm, Sun 1–5pm; late Nov to Dec Tues–Sun 11am–5pm. Tours twice per hour. Closed Nov and Jan–Apr. From the Old Port, head west on Fore St., and veer right on Danforth St. at light near Giobbi's restaurant; proceed 3 blocks to the mansion, at the corner of Park St.

Wadsworth-Longfellow House & Center for Maine History The Maine Historical Society's "history campus" includes three widely varied buildings along busy Congress Street in downtown Portland. The austere brick Wadsworth-Longfellow House dates from 1785 and was built by Gen. Peleg Wadsworth, father of noted poet Henry Wadsworth Longfellow. It's furnished in an early-19th-century style, with many samples of Longfellow family furniture on display. Adjacent to the home is the Maine History Gallery, in a garish postmodern building, formerly a bank. Changing exhibits here explore the rich texture of Maine history. Just behind the Longfellow house is the library of the Maine Historical Society, a popular destination among genealogists.

489 Congress St. ☎ **207/774-1822**. www.mainehistory.org. $7 adults, $6 seniors and students, $3 children 6–18. Longfellow House May–Dec Mon–Sat 10:30am–4pm, Sun noon–4pm.

ON THE WATER

The 3¹/₂-mile **Back Cove Pathway** ★ loops around Portland's Back Cove, offering attractive views of the city skyline across the water, glimpses of Casco Bay, and a bit of exercise. The pathway is the city's most popular recreational facility; after work in summer, Portlanders flock here to walk, bike, jog, and windsurf (there's enough water 2¹/₂ hr. before and after high tide). Part of the pathway shares a noisy bridge with I-295, and it can be unpleasant at a dead low tide; when the tides and the weather cooperate, however, it's a nice spot for a walk. The main parking lot is located across from Hannaford Plaza at the water's edge. Take exit 6 (Forest Ave. north) off I-295; turn right at the first light on Baxter Boulevard. At the next light, turn right again and park in the lot ahead on the left.

Another fine place to take in a water view is the **Eastern Prom Pathway** ★, which wraps for about a mile along the waterfront between the Casco Bay Lines ferry terminal and the **East End Beach** (the path continues onward to connect with the Back Cove Pathway). The paved pathway is suitable for walking or biking and offers wonderful views out toward the islands and the boat traffic on the harbor. The easiest place to park is near the beach and boat ramp. From downtown, head east on Congress Street until you can't go any farther; turn right, and then take your first left on the road down the hill to the water's edge.

Casco Bay Lines Six of Casco Bay's islands have year-round populations and are served by scheduled ferries from downtown Portland. Except for Long Island, the islands are part of the city of Portland. The ferries provide an inexpensive way to view the bustling harbor and get a taste of island life. Trips range from a 20-minute (one-way) excursion to **Peaks Island** (the closest thing to an island suburb, with 1,200 year-round residents) to the 5¹/₂-hour cruise to **Bailey Island** (connected by bridge to the mainland south of Brunswick) and back. All of the islands are well suited for walking; Peaks Island has a rocky back shore that's easily accessible via the island's paved perimeter road (bring a picnic lunch). There's also a bike rental outfit a few blocks from the island's ferry dock. **Long Island** has a good hidden beach. **Cliff Island** is the most remote of the six-pack, with a sedate turn-of-the-20th-century character.

Commercial and Franklin sts. ☎ **207/774-7871**. www.cascobaylines.com. Fares vary depending on the run and the season; summer rates $6–$9 round-trip. Frequent departures 6am–10pm.

Eagle Island Tours ★   Eagle Island was the summer home of famed arctic explorer and Portland native Robert E. Peary, who claimed in 1909 to be the first person to reach the North Pole. (His accomplishments have been the subject of exhaustive debates among arctic scholars, some of whom insist he inflated his claims.) In 1904, Peary built a simple home on a remote, 17-acre island at the edge of Casco Bay; in 1912, he added flourishes in the form of two low stone towers. After his death in 1920, his family kept up the home; they later donated it to the state, which has since managed it as a state park. The home is open to the public, maintained much as it was when Peary lived here. Eagle Tours takes one trip daily from Portland. The 4-hour excursion includes a 1¹/₂-hour stopover on the island.

Long Wharf (Commercial St.) ✆ **207/774-6498.** www.eagleislandtours.com. $26 adults, $24 seniors, $15 children 3–12 (includes state park fee). One departure per day at 10am, daily late June to Labor Day, weekends June and Sept.

Ferries to & from Nova Scotia

A trip to Portland can serve as a springboard for an excursion to Atlantic Canada. The most hassle-free way to link the two is by ferry, saving hours of driving time and providing a relaxing minicruise along the way.

Bay Ferries (✆ **877/359-3760** or 207/761-4228; www.catferry.com) operates a seasonal Portland-to-Yarmouth ferry known as *The Cat* (short for catamaran), which claims to be the fastest ferry in North America. The boat's dock has been relocated; it now departs from the new Ocean Gateway Pier at the northern end of Commercial Street (just north of the Casco Bay Lines ferry terminal) three to four mornings a week (Fri, Sat, and Sun, plus Thurs in mid-summer) at 8am, from June through mid-October; a second ferry heads back to Portland four to five afternoons per week. Crossing times vary, but count on about 5¹/₂ hours, less than half the time of the previous overnight service. Tickets presently cost $99 per adult or $65 per child age 6 to 13; normal-size passenger vehicles cost $164 each way, with additional charges for RVs, trucks, buses, and the like. Round-trips during the same day are discounted.

MINOR LEAGUE BASEBALL

Portland Sea Dogs ★★★   A Double-A team affiliated with the Boston Red Sox (a perfect marriage in baseball-crazy northern New England), the Sea Dogs play through summer at Hadlock Field, a small stadium near downtown that still retains an old-time feel despite aluminum benches and other updating. Activities are geared toward families, with lots of entertainment between innings and food that's a few notches above your basic hot dogs and hamburgers. (Try the french fries and grilled sausages, for instance.) You might even catch a rising star: Josh Beckett, Brad Penny, Jonathan Papelbon, and many others did time here before making it to "the show."

Hadlock Field, 217 Park Ave. (P.O. Box 636), Portland, ME 04104. ✆ **800/936-3647.** www.seadogs.com. Season runs Apr to Labor Day.

SHOPPING

Aficionados of antique and secondhand furniture stores love Portland. Good browsing can be enjoyed along Congress Street; try the stretches between State and High streets in the arts district, or from India Street to Washington Avenue on Munjoy Hill. About a dozen shops of varying quality (mostly low-end) can be found in these two areas.

(Moments)   **Lucky 77: Hitting the Beaches**

One of the supreme pleasures of visiting the Portland area is the opportunity to sample some of its many great beaches and lighthouse and ocean views. Even within Portland city limits, you can laze on the Eastern Promenade's tiny **East End Beach** (see above) for free; though I wouldn't swim there—a waste-water treatment plant looms nearby—you can take in great views. Across the bridge in South Portland, **Willard Beach ★** is a good neighborhood beach: small, with friendly locals, dogs, and tidal rocks to scramble over. There's plenty of parking here.

For the best of the out-of-town beaches and views, though, strike out for **Cape Elizabeth,** a moneyed suburb just south. (From Portland's State St., cross the Rte. 77 bridge going south, then follow signs.) You can choose from a trio of good beaches as you meander along Route 77, a lovely lane that occasionally recalls England with its sweeping views of marsh, ocean, or cultivated field.

Two Lights State Park ★★ ((©) **207/799-5871**) is impressively scenic, and has the advantage of a decent lobster-and-seafood hut beside it: **Two Lights Lobster Shack ★★**, open April through October. The lobsters are smallish, lobster rolls meaty, clam chowder pretty good, and the views are sublime. Farther south on 77, **Crescent Beach State Park ★★★** ((©) **207/799-5871**) is a lovely mile-long curve of sand with ample parking, barbecue pits, picnic tables, and a snack bar. Both charge a fee from Memorial Day to Columbus Day. The town-operated **Fort Williams State Park ★**, located on Shore Road in Cape Elizabeth just off Route 77, is a bit harder to find but offers free access and supreme views of both the ocean and the much-photographed **Portland Head Light ★★** (see "Exploring the City," earlier in this chapter). Two to 3 miles farther south, turn left onto Route 207 for two more options: **Scarborough Beach Park ★**, on the left, another long strip of clean sand and dunes with changing facilities ($3.50 for access in summer) or—a bit farther along, on the right at the end of Ferry Road—quieter **Ferry Beach,** which is free and has good views of Old Orchard to the south.

More serious antiques hounds may choose to visit an **auction house** or two. Two or three times per week, you'll be able to find an auction within an hour's drive of Portland. A good source of information is the *Maine Sunday Telegram.* Look in the classifieds for listings of auctions scheduled for the following week.

For new items, the Old Port, with its dozens of boutiques and storefronts, is well worth browsing. It's especially strong in contemporary, one-of-a-kind clothing that's a world apart from generic stuff you'll find at a mall. Artisan and crafts shops are also well represented.

Abacus Gallery   A wide range of bold, inventive crafts of all varieties—from furniture to jewelry—is displayed on two floors of this centrally located shop. Even if you're not in a buying frame of mind, this is a great place for browsing. 44 Exchange St. © **207/772-4880.**

Allen & Walker Antiques ★   This is a great stop for New England, American, and Oriental items ranging from period oil paintings to antique furniture to sake sets . . . and much more. You just never know what you'll find here on a given day, and both Allen and Walker really know their stuff. 600 Congress St. 📞 **207/772-8787.**

Amaryllis Clothing Co.   Portland's original creative clothing store, Amaryllis sells unique clothing for women, plus accessories such as lingerie, belts, and jewelry. It's as comfortable as it is elegant: Colors are rich, patterns are unique, and some items are designed by local artisans. 41 Exchange St. 📞 **207/772-4439.**

D. Cole Jewelers   Jewelers Dean and Denise Cole produce lovely handcrafted gold and silver jewelry that's always attractive, and often surprisingly affordable. Browse through elegant traditional designs, as well as more offbeat ones, at the bright, low-pressure shop; the staff is extremely helpful. 10 Exchange St. 📞 **207/772-5119.**

Folia Jewelry   Original, handcrafted jewelry by owner Edith Armstrong (and some of Maine's top designers) is nicely displayed at this tasteful shop in the heart of the Old Port. The rings are especially arty and nice. 50 Exchange St. 📞 **207/761-4432.**

Green Design Furniture   This inventive shop sells beautiful mission-inspired furniture, crafted of cherry and other woods, that disassembles for easy storage and travel. 267 Commercial St. 📞 **866/756-4730** or 207/775-4234.

Harbor Fish Market   This classic waterfront fish market would be worth a trip just to see the mounds of fish just caught in Casco Bay, but it's also a great spot for takeout lobsters (packed for travel, they easily last 24 hr.) or smoked fish for a picnic. 9 Custom House Wharf (across from Pearl St.). 📞 **207/775-0251.**

LeRoux Kitchen   You'll find kitchen gadgets, made-in-Maine food products, and a good selection of wines at this Old Port shop. 161 Commercial St. 📞 **207/553-7665.**

L.L.Bean Outlet Store   Sporting goods retailer L.L.Bean opened its downtown Portland factory outlet in 1996. Look for last year's Bean fashions, returns, and slightly damaged goods, plus a small selection of first-run, nearly full-price items. 542 Congress St. 📞 **207/772-5100.**

Maine Potters Market   Maine's largest pottery collective has been in operation for 2 decades, and it's open daily. You can select from a variety of distinctive styles crafted by local potters; shipping is easily arranged. 376 Fore St. 📞 **207/774-1633.**

Stonewall Kitchen   Stonewall is a frequent winner at trade shows for its delicious mustards, jams, and sauces: ginger peach tea jam, sun-dried tomato and olive relish, maple chipotle grill sauce, and so on. Browse (and sample the goods) at its Old Port store, which also features frequent cooking classes. 182 Middle St. 📞 **207/879-2409.**

5 PORTLAND AFTER DARK

BARS & MUSIC

Portland is usually lively in the evenings, especially on summer weekends when the testosterone level in the Old Port seems to rocket into the stratosphere, with young men and women prowling the dozens of bars and spilling out onto Fore Street and the surrounding alleys and streets.

(Moments)   **A Hundred Beers Old**

The **Great Lost Bear** (540 Forest Ave.; ℂ **207/772-0300**) has the best brew selection in all of northern New England, 50 to 60 on offer at any given moment, including most of the numerous local brews crafted in Maine. Some of the choicest ales are even dispensed from one of three cask-conditioned hand pumps. As if that weren't enough, every Thursday the bartender show-cases a particular brewer or style—a good way to get educated about the nuances of good beer. To find the Bear, head about 2 miles out on Forest Avenue (*away* from the Old Port), or ask a local for directions.

Among the Old Port bars favored by locals are **Three-Dollar Dewey's,** at the corner of Commercial and Union streets (the popcorn is free); atmospheric **Gritty McDuff's Brew Pub** ★, on Fore Street at the foot of Exchange Street, where you'll find live music and a cast of regulars quaffing great beers brewed on-site; and the slightly rowdy Irish pub **Brian Ború,** on Center Street, with a rooftop patio. All three bars are casual and pubby, with guests sharing long tables with new companions.

Beyond the active Old Port bar scene, a number of clubs offer a mix of live and recorded entertainment throughout the year. As is common in other small cities where there are more venues than attendees, the clubs have come and gone, sometimes quite rapidly. Check the city's free weekly *Portland Phoenix* for current venues, performers, and showtimes.

FILM

Downtown Portland is still blessed with two downtown movie houses, enabling travelers in the mood for a flick to avoid the disheartening slog out to the boxy, could-be-any-where mall octoplexes. **Nickelodeon Cinemas,** 1 Temple St. (ℂ **207/772-9751**), has six screens showing first- and second-run films at reasonable prices. The **Movies** ★, 10 Exchange St. (ℂ **207/772-9600** or 207/772-8041), is a compact art-film showcase in the heart of the Old Port featuring a lineup of foreign and independent films of recent and historical vintage.

PERFORMING ARTS

Portland has a growing creative corps of performing artists. Theater companies typically take the summer off, but it doesn't hurt to call or check the local papers for special per-formances.

Portland Stage Company ★   The most polished and consistent of the Portland theater companies, Portland Stage offers crisply produced shows starring local and imported equity actors in a handsome, second-story theater just off Congress Street. About a half-dozen shows are staged throughout the season, which runs from October to May. Recent productions have included *Proof, Arcadia, Fences, Noises Off,* Shakespeare's *Much Ado About Nothing,* and *Augusta* (a drama about small-town Maine). Performing Arts Center, 25A Forest Ave. ℂ **207/774-0465.** www.portlandstage.com. Tickets $25–$35 adults, discounts for students and seniors.

Portland Symphony Orchestra ★★   The well-regarded Portland Symphony, now headed by Robert Moody, offers a variety of performances throughout the season (typically Sept–May), ranging from pops concerts to Mozart; half the orchestra are Mainers, the rest New Englanders, and all are talented. Summer travelers should consider a Portland detour the week of July 4th, when the "Independence Pops" is held (weather permitting) at various sites around southern Maine, including the grounds of the Portland Head Lighthouse in Cape Elizabeth. There are also special Christmas shows. 477 Congress St. © 207/842-0800 for tickets or 773-6128 for information. www.portlandsymphony.com. Tickets $16–$57, discounts for students and seniors.

6 SIDE TRIPS

OLD ORCHARD BEACH

About 12 miles south of Portland is the unrepentantly honky-tonk beach town of Old Orchard Beach, which offers considerable stimulus for the senses (not to mention bikers, fried dough, and French Canadians aplenty). This venerable Victorian-era resort is famed for its amusement park, pier, and long, sandy beach, which attracts sun worshipers from all over. Be sure to spend time and money on the stomach-churning rides at the beachside amusement park of **Palace Playland** (© **207/934-2001**), and then walk on the 7-mile-long beach past the mid-rise condos that sprouted in the 1980s like a scale-model Miami Beach.

The beach is broad and open at low tide; at high tide, space to plunk your towel down is at a premium. In the evenings teens and young adults dominate the town's culture, spilling out of the video arcades and cruising the main strip. For dinner, do as the locals do and buy hot dogs, pizza, and cotton candy—save your change for the arcades.

Old Orchard is just off Route 1 south of Portland. The quickest route is to leave the turnpike at exit 36 in Saco and then follow I-195 and the signs to the beach. Don't expect to be alone here: Parking is tight, and the traffic can be horrendous during the peak summer months.

SEBAGO LAKE & DOUGLAS HILL

Maine's second-largest lake is also its most popular. Ringed with summer homes, Sebago Lake attracts thousands of vacationers to its cool, deep waters.

You can take a tour of the outlying lakes and the ancient canal system between Sebago and Long lakes on the *Songo River Queen II,* a faux-steamship berthed in the town of Naples (© **207/693-6861**). Running from July through Labor Day, the 1-hour trips cost $8 for adults, $6 for children age 12 and under. Longer tours and group rates are also available. Or just lie in the sun along the sandy beach at bustling **Sebago Lake State Park** (© **207/693-6613**), on the lake's north shore (the park is off Rte. 302; look for signs btw. Raymond and South Casco). The park has shady picnic areas, a campground, a snack bar, and lifeguards on the beach (entrance fee charged). It can be uncomfortably crowded on sunny summer weekends; it's best on weekdays. Bring food and charcoal for barbecuing at the shady picnic areas off the beach. The park's campground has a separate beach (you need not camp to enjoy it, though), is a distance from the day-use area, and is less congested during good weather. It books up early in the season, but you might luck into a cancellation if you need a spot to pitch your tent.

To the west of the lake, the rolling wooded uplands are very attractive. The closest prominent rise to Portland with public access is **Douglas Mountain,** whose summit is capped with a medieval-looking 16-foot stone tower. The property is open to the public; the summit is reached via an easy .25-mile trail from the parking area. Look for wild blueberries at the end of July and the beginning of August.

SABBATHDAY LAKE SHAKER COMMUNITY ★

Route 26, from Portland to Norway, is a speedy highway that runs past new housing developments and through hilly farmland. At one point the road pinches through a cluster of stately historic buildings that stand proudly beneath towering shade trees. That's the **Sabbathday Lake Shaker Community** (© 207/926-4597; www.shaker.lib. me.us), the last active Shaker community in the nation. The half-dozen or so Shakers living here today still embrace their traditional beliefs and maintain a communal, pastoral way of life. The bulk of the community's income comes from the sale of herbs, which have been grown here since 1799.

Tours are offered a half-dozen times daily from Memorial Day through Labor Day, providing a look at the grounds and several buildings, including the graceful 1794 meetinghouse. Exhibits in the buildings showcase the famed furniture handcrafted by the Shakers and include antiques made by Shakers at other U.S. communes. You'll learn plenty about the Shaker ideology, with its emphasis on simplicity, industry, and celibacy. After your tour, browse the gift shop for Shaker herbs and teas. The introductory tour lasts 1 hour and 15 minutes ($6.50 for adults, $2 for children 6–12, and free for children 5 and under).

The Shaker village is about 45 minutes from Portland. Head north on Route 26 (Washington Ave. in Portland). The village is 8 miles from exit 63 (Gray) of the Maine Turnpike; after exiting, follow signs into the center of downtown Gray, then follow Route 26 north right to the village.

Freeport to Monhegan Island

Veteran Maine travelers contend that this part of the coast, long known as the "Midcoast" (one word, please), is fast losing its native charm—it's too commercial, they say, too developed, too highfalutin' . . . in short, too much like the *rest* of the United States. These grousers have a point, especially along U.S. Route 1. But get off the main roads, and you'll swiftly find pockets of another Maine, some of the most pastoral and picturesque meadows, mountains, peninsulas, and harbors in the entire state.

The coast is best reached via U.S. Route 1, which you catch in **Brunswick** by taking exit 28 from I-295. Going north, some highlights of the coastal route include the shipbuilding town of **Bath,** pretty little **Wiscasset,** and the Boothbay region on the southern end of the Midcoast; the lovely Pemaquid peninsula; lost-in-time **Monhegan Island;** and finally the power trio of **Camden, Rockland,** and **Rockport** at the northern end of the Midcoast (which are covered in chapter 8).

Beyond local tourist huts and chambers of commerce, the best source of information for the midcoast region in general is found at the **Maine State Information Center** (✆ **207/846-0833**) just off exit 17 of I-295 in Yarmouth, which isn't really *in* the Midcoast—but you'll almost certainly pass through to get there. This state-run center is stocked with hundreds of brochures, and is staffed with a helpful crew that can provide information about the entire state but that is particularly well informed about the middle reaches of coast. It's open daily from 8am to 6pm (8:30am–5pm in winter), and the attached restroom facilities are always open.

1 FREEPORT

123 miles NE of Boston, 333 miles NE of New York City, and 17 miles NE of Portland

If **Freeport** were a mall (which is not all that far-fetched an analogy), L.L.Bean would be the anchor store. It's the business that launched this town to prominence, elevating its status from just another Maine fishing village near the interstate to one of the state's major tourist draws for the outlet centers that sprang up here in Bean's wake. Freeport still has the look of a classic Maine village, but it's a village that's been largely taken over by the national fashion industry; most of the old historic homes and stores have been converted into upscale factory shops purveying name-brand clothing and housewares at cut-rate prices. Banana Republic occupies an exceedingly handsome brick Federal-style home; a Carnegie library became an Abercrombie & Fitch pumping club music (oh, the inhumanity!); and even the McDonald's is inside a tasteful, understated Victorian farmhouse—you really have to look for the golden arches.

While some modern structures have also been built to accommodate the outlet boom, strict planning guidelines have managed to preserve most of the town's local charm, at least downtown. Huge parking lots are hidden from view off the main drag, and as a

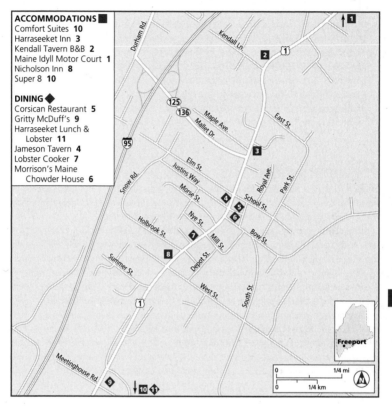

ACCOMMODATIONS ■
Comfort Suites 10
Harraseeket Inn 3
Kendall Tavern B&B 2
Maine Idyll Motor Court 1
Nicholson Inn 8
Super 8 10

DINING ◆
Corsican Restaurant 5
Gritty McDuff's 9
Harraseeket Lunch &
    Lobster 11
Jameson Tavern 4
Lobster Cooker 7
Morrison's Maine
    Chowder House 6

FREEPORT TO MONHEGAN ISLAND

7

FREEPORT

result Freeport is one of the more aesthetically pleasing places to shop in New England—though even with these large lots, parking can be scarce during the peak season. Expect crowds. Seeking the real Maine? Head at some point for **South Freeport,** which consists of a boat dock, general store, and lobster shack at the end of a finger of land reached via a numberless side road off U.S. Route 1.

ESSENTIALS
Getting There
Freeport is on U.S. Route 1, though the downtown is most easily reached via I-295 from either exit 20 or exit 22.

Visitor Information
The **Freeport Merchants Marketing Association,** P.O. Box 452, Freeport, ME 04032 (© **800/865-1994** [automated] or 207/865-1212; www.freeportusa.com), publishes a map and directory of businesses, restaurants, and overnight accommodations. The free map is widely available around town, or you can contact the association to have one sent to you.

(Finds) Mapping Your Next Stop

Right across the road from the state information center in Yarmouth is the **DeLorme Map Store** ((C) **800/642-0970**), open daily from 9:30am to 6pm. You'll find a wide selection of maps here, including the firm's trademark state atlases and a line of CD-ROM map products. The store's fun to browse even if you're not a map buff, but what makes the place really worth a detour off the interstate is Eartha, "the world's largest rotating and revolving globe." The 42-foot-diameter globe occupies the entire atrium lobby and is constructed on a scale of 1:1,000,000, the largest satellite image of the earth ever produced. Far-out.

EXPLORING FREEPORT

While Freeport is nationally known for its outlet shopping, that's not all it offers. Just outside of town you'll find a lovely pastoral landscape, picturesque picnicking spots, and scenic drives that make for a handy retreat from all that spending.

By car head east on Bow Street (down the hill from L.L.Bean's main entrance), and wind around for 1 mile to the sign for **Mast Landing Sanctuary** ★ ((C) **207/781-2330**). Turn left and then right about ¼ mile into the sanctuary parking lot. A network of trails totaling about 3 miles crisscrosses through a landscape of long-ago eroded hills and mixed woodlands; streams trickle down to the marshland estuary. The 140-acre property is owned by the Maine Audubon Society and is open to the public until dusk.

Back at the main road, turn left and continue eastward for 1½ miles; then turn right on Wolf Neck Road. Continue 1¾ miles and then turn left for ½ mile on a dirt farm road. **Wolfe's Neck Farm** ★ ((C) **207/865-4469** or 688-4808), owned and operated by a nonprofit trust, raises cattle without chemicals, and it sells its own line of organic meat. All this happens to take place at one of the most scenic coastal farms in Maine (especially beautiful near sunset). If you love pastoral scenes and cows, or your kids do, stop by and snap some photos; if you're also a proud carnivore, stop by the gray farmhouse and pick up some tasty frozen steaks or flavorful hamburger on the way out. The shop is open weekdays from 8am to 4pm.

Continue south on Wolfe's Neck Road, and you'll soon come to the 233-acre **Wolfe Neck Woods State Park** ((C) **207/865-4465**). This compact, attractive park has quiet woodland trails that run through forests of white pine and hemlock, past estuaries, and along the rocky shoreline of the bay. Googins Island, just offshore and reached by following the park's Casco Bay Trail, has an osprey nest on it. This is a good destination for enjoying a picnic brought from town or for letting the kids burn off some pent-up energy—there are guided nature walks at 2pm daily during the summer. The day-use fee for the park is $3 per adult, $1 for children ages 5 to 11.

SHOPPING

Freeport has more than 140 retail shops spaced out between exit 20 of I-295 (at the far lower end of Main St.) and Mallet Road, which connects to exit 22. Some shops have even begun to spread south of exit 20 toward Yarmouth. The bulk of them are "factory" or "outlet" stores. If you don't want to miss a single one, get off at exit 17 and head north on U.S. Route 1. The bargains can vary from extraordinary to "huh?" Plan on wearing out some shoe leather and taking at *least* a half-day if you're really intent on finding the best deals. The sometimes-changing rotation of national chains here has recently included Abercrombie & Fitch, Banana Republic, Gap, Calvin Klein, Patagonia, North Face, Nike, Chaudier ("the cookware of choice aboard Air Force One"), Mikasa, Nine West, Timberland, and Maidenform, among many others.

Stores in Freeport are typically open daily 9am to 9pm during the busy summer and close much earlier (at 5 or 6pm) in other seasons; between Thanksgiving and Christmas, they remain open late once more.

Cuddledown   Cuddledown started producing down comforters in 1973, and now makes a whole line of products much appreciated in northern climes and beyond. Some of the down pillows are made right in the outlet shop, which also carries a variety of European goose-down comforters in all sizes and weights. Look for linens, blankets, moccasins, and home furnishings, too. 475 U.S. Rte. 1 (btw. exits 17 and 20). © **207/865-1713** or 865-4993. www.cuddledown.com.

Freeport Knife Co. ★   This store sports a wide selection of knives for kitchen and camp alike, including blades from Germany, Switzerland, and Japan. Look for their custom line, or just bring in your dull blade for a sharpening. They also sell replacement parts and do repairs on all brands of knives. 181 Lower Main St. © **207/865-0779.** www.free portknife.com.

L.L.Bean ★★★   Monster outdoor retailer L.L.Bean traces its roots from the day Leon Leonwood Bean decided that what the world really needed was a good weatherproof hunting shoe. He joined a watertight gum shoe to a laced leather upper; hunters liked it; the store grew; an empire was born. Today, L.L.Bean sells millions of dollars' worth of clothing and outdoor goods nationwide through its well-respected catalogs, and it continues to draw hundreds of thousands of customers through its doors to a headquarters building and several offshoots around town. The modern, multilevel main store is about the size of a regional mall, but it's very tastefully done with its own indoor trout pond and lots of natural wood. Selections include Bean's own trademark clothing, along with home furnishings, books, shoes, and plenty of outdoor gear for camping, fishing, and hunting (a particularly good section). The staff is incredibly knowledgeable—Bean's encourages staff to take the gear home and try it out so as to better serve customers. A minute's walk away, behind the main store down a pathway, is the outlet store (see the "Need an Outlet?" box below). 95 Main St. (at Bow St.). © **800/559-0747.** www.llbean.com.

(Fun Facts   All Bean's, All the Time

One of the big reasons that L.L.Bean's flagship shop is such a tourist draw is that it's open 365 days a year, 7 days a week, 24 hours a day—note the lack of any locks or latches on the front doors. As such, it's a popular spot even in the dead of night, especially during summer or around holidays. Folks have been known to set out from New Hampshire at 1 or 2 in the morning to enjoy the best deals (and empty aisles) on their middle-of-the-night arrival.

Tale of the Tags: Freeport vs. Kittery

When visiting the Maine coast, many travelers only find time to shop once. Trouble is, there are *two* significant outlet centers on the southern coast. How to choose? Here's my quick take:

In **Kittery,** located at the southern edge of Maine, the malls are clumped along Route 1 just a couple of miles north of the New Hampshire border. Though the area appears at first glance to be a conglomerated, single huge mall, in fact there are five or six distinct areas with separate entrances. Choose carefully before you make your turn.

Generally speaking, Kittery is best for the name-brand shopper who wants to hit a large volume of places in a short time. It's easier to do Kittery more quickly than Freeport because of the side-by-side arrangement of the various stores and the malls. The trade-off is the blandness of the experience: Each of these side malls offers vast parking lots and boring architecture, and you cannot safely walk from one mall to another—you need wheels.

Among the best places to try among the various complexes are a **Gap** outlet, a **Samsonite** shop with knowledgeable sales help, a small but elegant **Coach** store, **Reebok** (I picked up swim trunks here for a fraction of the retail cost), **Stride-Rite** (excellent selection of cut-rate shoes), **J. Crew** (good prices on sweaters), **Seiko,** an **Orvis** sporting goods outlet, and a useful **Crate & Barrel** outlet. The Native American–themed **Kittery Trading Post** is not all it's hyped up to be, but at least prices are low.

There are also a couple of good places here for a snack: **Bob's Clam Hut,** with a long line of hungry patrons awaiting superlative fried clams, and **Ben & Jerry's** for ice cream. For a sit-down meal, I like the **Weathervane,** a small New England fish-house chain that delivers value at moderate prices and is an excellent choice for families.

Freeport is a different animal. The outlets here are crunched together and interspersed throughout Freeport's Main Street. That makes driving around town a headache, as pedestrians and cars cruising for parking bring things to a constant halt. My advice? Strap on your walking shoes, park anywhere you can find a spot—even in a distant satellite lot—and just resign yourself to a lot of hoofing it. Bring a portable dolly or luggage rack to carry packages if you're expecting to buy a lot.

Freeport's outlets generally offer a higher grade of product than Kittery, and the stores have a great deal more architectural (and corporate) personality, too. You will actually find local, small manufacturers here, not just the big guys, and inventive big brands that go beyond the usual.

Mangy Moose A souvenir shop with a twist: Virtually everything in this place is moose-related. Really. There are moose wineglasses, moose trivets, moose cookie cutters, and (of course) moose T-shirts. Somehow, this merchandise is a notch above what you'll find in most other souvenir shops around the state. 112 Main St. © **800/606-6517** or 207/865-6414. www.themangymoose.com.

You can troll **L.L.Bean**'s factory store (now tucked behind the flagship) for top-grade outdoors equipment and clothing, but even just sticking to Main Street you'll come across such finds as **Cuddledown of Maine**'s comfy pillows and comforters; the **Freeport Knife Co.**'s respected knife shop; **Abercrombie & Fitch**'s ever-young fashions (the girls will love this place), housed in a former Carnegie library; excellent bi-level **Gap** and **Banana Republic** outlets; and **Brooks Brothers, Burberry, Coach,** and **Patagonia** stores, among many other distinctive factory shops.

If you love shopping and you love quality, it's a genuinely enjoyable experience to stroll around here for a day, taking a snack of chowder or lobster (see "Where to Dine" in the Freeport section, p. 134); pausing to assess your finds; grabbing a soda, grilled hot dog, or ice cream from a vendor; then planning dinner somewhere. Parking and traffic are negatives to consider, however— you may cruise a half-hour before finding an open spot (if you ever do). You'll also probably spend more on a trip to Freeport, as price tags are generally higher.

The winner? It's close, but I'll take Freeport only for its walkability.

There's also a third option to consider, by the way. That's the big **Maine Mall,** which takes up a huge chunk of real estate near the Portland Jetport in South Portland (easily reached off the Maine Tpk. via its own exit). The options here are uniformly bland—this could be Anywheresville, America—and there are no outlet or factory stores; you'll pay full price, plus Maine state tax.

Still, if there's something reassuring about being able to bop among **Macy's, Bath & Body Works, Victoria's Secret, Pottery Barn,** the **Disney Store,** and **babyGAP,** then grabbing some chocolates from **Godiva** before settling down to coffee and a book or CD at **Borders** (in its own free-standing building), you might enjoy it. There's not much that's distinctive here, though the bookstore is very well stocked and the staff is helpful. Also check out the **Sports Authority** for low-priced sporting goods; watch for specials on exercise equipment, golf balls, camping gear, and the like, and hit **Williams-Sonoma** for a look at upscale cooking gear.

Needless to say, there's a food court here, though it isn't very good. Consider dining at a nearby restaurant instead; a number of them surround the moatlike ring road that surrounds the mall and its acres of parking lots. Good choices include the **Weathervane** for seafood, or even the Canadian chain **Tim Horton's** (rarely seen in the U.S. outside Michigan and upstate New York) for doughnuts.

Thos. Moser Cabinetmakers ★ Classic furniture reinterpreted in lustrous wood and leather is the focus at this shop, which—thanks to a steady parade of ads in the *New Yorker* and a Madison Avenue branch—has become nearly as representative of Maine as L.L.Bean has. Shaker, mission, and modern styles are wonderfully reinvented by Tom

(Tips) **Need an Outlet?**

In addition to its main store, L.L.Bean now maintains two **satellite shops** (© 800/ **559-0747,** ext. 37222) stocking inventories of specialized Bean goods. The **Bike, Boat & Ski Store** is right beside the mothership—just to the left, if you're standing on the sidewalk in front—and holds lots of canoes, kayaks, paddles, cycles, and helmets. It offers periodic, useful clinics on such topics as bike maintenance (learn to change a flat on the fly) and choosing the best kayak. There's also a bike repair shop on premises. The **Hunting & Fishing Store,** attached to the back of the main store, houses fly-fishing gear, archery gear, GPS units, hunting boots, and the like in hunting-lodge-like surrounds. Both of these shops are open 24-7-365, just like the flagship. Finally, the several-times-relocated **Outlet Store** appears to have found a final destination up behind the main campus, in a building that formerly housed L.L.Kids. It is *not* open all the time; figure 8am to 10pm daily.

Moser and his designers and woodworkers, who produce heirloom-quality signed pieces. Nationwide delivery is easy to arrange. There's a good selection of knotted rugs, too, made by an independent artisan, and a good gallery of Maine art on-site. 149 Main St. © **800/708-9041** or 207/865-4519. www.thomasmoser.com.

WHERE TO STAY

Freeport has more than 700 guest rooms, ranging from quiet B&Bs with just three rooms to chain motels with several dozen. Reservations are strongly recommended during the peak summer season; the recent opening of several new midrange chain hotels and motels south of town on Route 1 has helped accommodate the summer crush, and in a pinch you might try the **Comfort Suites,** 500 Rte. 1 (© **877/424-6423** or 207/865-9300), or the adjacent **Super 8** (© **800/800-8000** or 207/865-1408). Both are relatively new and good enough for a night's rest.

Harraseeket Inn ★★   The Harraseeket is a large, modern hotel 2 blocks north of L.L.Bean. Despite its size, a traveler could drive down Main Street and not notice it—and that's a good thing. A late-19th-century home is the soul of the hotel, though most of the rooms are in later additions built in 1989 and 1997. Guests can relax in the dining room, read the paper in a common room with the baby grand player piano, or sip a cocktail in the homey Broad Arrow Tavern (with its wood-fired oven and grill, it serves dinner as well as lunch). Guest rooms are large and tastefully furnished, with quarter-canopy beds and a mix of contemporary and antique furnishings; some have gas or wood-burning fireplaces, more than half now have whirlpools, and some are even done up with wet bars and refrigerators. This inn is especially pet-friendly, with doggy beds and treats for four-footed guests.

162 Main St., Freeport, ME 04032. © **800/342-6423** or 207/865-9377. www.harraseeketinn.com. 84 units. $125–$304 double and suite. All rates include full breakfast and afternoon tea. MAP rates available. Pets welcome ($25 per pet per night). AE, DC, DISC, MC, V. Take exit 22 off I-295 to Main St. **Amenities:** 2 restaurants; bar; indoor pool; concierge; business center; conference rooms; room service; laundry service; dry cleaning. *In room:* A/C, TV, dataport, coffeemaker, hair dryer (some units), safe, fridge (some units), Jacuzzi (some units), fireplace (some units).

> **(Tips)   Music to Shop By**
>
> Yet another of the many fine reasons to come to Freeport in summer is the abundant **free music performances** that take over the village's Discovery Park from mid-June through Labor Day. Underwritten by L.L.Bean (of course), the performers in this summer concert series are eclectic—and impressively famous: in 2008, they ranged from folkies Martin Sexton, Richie Havens, and John Hiatt to bluesman Keb Mo', bluegrass pioneer Jerry Douglas, 1980s pop heartthrob Darryl Hall, and country superstars Kathy Mattea and Lonestar. (Not to mention the Crickets and the Portland Symphony Orchestra thrown in, too, just for good measure.) The store sets up a shuttle bus running back and forth to and from satellite parking lots during performances by the biggest names. Get a concert schedule by picking up a brochure at Bean's information desk, or just check the company website.

Kendall Tavern Bed & Breakfast   If you want to avoid some of downtown's crowds without ever straying more than walking distance from the primo shopping, Kendall Tavern is your solution. This handsome B&B is in a cheerful yellow farmhouse on 3¹/₂ acres of land at a bend in the road a half-mile north of the center of Freeport. Rooms are simple, plushly carpeted, and comfortable. Everything is decorated in bright and airy style, with framed prints of New England scenes and Victorian ladies on the walls and mixes of antique and new furniture; some rooms have Vermont-style electric stoves. Rooms facing Main Street are a bit noisier due to traffic.

213 Main St., Freeport, ME 04032. © **800/341-9572** or 207/865-1338. Fax 207/865-3544. www.kendall tavern.com. 7 units. $140–$185 double; off-season and midweek discounts possible. Rates include full breakfast. AE, DISC, MC, V. Children age 9 and over welcome. **Amenities:** Jacuzzi. *In room:* A/C, no phone.

Maine Idyll Motor Court Ⓥⓐⓛⓤⓔ   Talk about a throwback to a happier time: This motel doesn't take any credit cards, but they will take your personal check. This 1932 "motor court" is a Maine classic—a cluster of 20 cottages scattered around a grove of oak and beech trees. Most cottages come with a tiny porch, wood-burning fireplace (birch logs are provided), television (yes, color), modest kitchen facilities (no ovens), and time-worn furniture. These cabins are not very big, but they're comfortable enough and kept clean; some have showers, some bathtubs. Kids might enjoy the swing set in the play area, dog-walkers the nature trails attached to the property, and picnickers the grill sets. The only interruption to the idyll here is the omnipresent drone of traffic: I-295 is just through the trees to one side, and U.S. 1 to the other side. Get past that, and you'll find good value for your money here. They even have Wi-Fi.

1411 U.S. Rte. 1, Freeport, ME 04032. © **207/865-4201.** www.maineidyll.com. 20 units. $59–$107 double; spring rates lower. Rates include continental breakfast. No credit cards. Closed Nov–Apr. Pets on leashes allowed. *In room:* Kitchenette, fireplace (most units), fridge, no phone.

Nicholson Inn   If your goal in Freeport is to hit as many outlets as humanly possible, there's no better choice than this simple B&B. Located right on Main Street (it's actually right in the central shopping district), this comfortable home was built in the mid-1920s; all units have private, shower-only bathrooms. Rooms have a pleasant floral motif.

Furnishings are country contemporary and oak Victorian, and a huge three-course break-fast is served daily. A front porch with wicker furniture is a good spot to rest up between forays, and there's plenty of parking for guests, who are allowed to leave their cars at the inn even after they check out—a big deal in this parking-challenged town.

25 Main St., Freeport, ME 04032. ℂ **800/344-6404** or 207/865-6404. www.nicholsoninn.com. 3 units. $110–$135 double. Rates include full breakfast. No credit cards (checks okay). *In room:* A/C, no phone.

WHERE TO DINE

Despite all the outlet glitz of Freeport, a couple of small-town restaurants have persisted. For a quick and simple meal, you might head down Mechanic Street (turn at the Mangy Moose, 112 Main St.) to the **Corsican Restaurant** ★, 9 Mechanic St. (ℂ **207/865-9421**), for a surprisingly healthful 10-inch pizza, calzone, or king-size sandwich. The **Lobster Cooker,** 39 Main St. (ℂ **207/865-4349**), serves daily seafood, sandwich, and chowder specials on an outdoor patio with views of the shopping hordes; go for salmon, lobster, or crab. Also nearby is **Morrison's Maine Chowder House,** 4 Mechanic St. (ℂ **207/865-3404**), with counter seating for about a dozen. It serves somewhat pricey fish, lobster, and clam chowder in paper bowls with plastic spoons. This is by no means a destination restaurant, but it is good for a quick bite because it's tucked right among the shops.

For yet another option, see the Harraseeket Inn, above, under "Where to Stay."

Gritty McDuff's BREWPUB   Spacious, informal, and air-conditioned in summer, Gritty's is an offshoot of Portland's first brewpub. It's a short drive south of the village center, and is best known for its varied selection of house-brewed beers such as the unfil-tered Black Fly Stout. The pub offers a wide-ranging bar menu of reliable salads, burgers, steaks, stone-oven pizzas, cheesesteak sandwiches, quesadillas, and pub classics including shepherd's pie and fish and chips. There's a kids' menu as well.

187 Rte. 1 (Main St.), Freeport. ℂ **207/865-4321.** Reservations not accepted. Main courses $10–$17. AE, DISC, MC, V. Daily 11:30am–11pm.

Harraseeket Lunch & Lobster ★ (Finds) LOBSTER   In a boatyard on the Harra-seeket River about a 10-minute drive away from Freeport's shopping district, this lobster pound gets crowded on sunny days—although, with its heated dining room, it's a worthy destination any time it's open. Point and order a lobster sized according to your hunger level, then take in river views from the dock as you wait for your number to be called. Come in late afternoon to avoid the lunch and dinner hordes. If you don't like lobster, you can also get fried fish, burgers, chowder, or an ice cream.

Main St., South Freeport. ℂ **207/865-4888.** Lobsters market price (typically $8–$15). No credit cards. Mid-June to Labor Day daily 11am–8:45pm; May to mid-June and early Sept to mid-Oct daily 11am–7:45pm. Closed mid-Oct to Apr. From Portland, take I-295 to exit 17 and head north on U.S. Rte. 1; turn right on S. Freeport Rd. at big Indian statue to South Freeport. Turn right and drive to waterfront. From downtown Freeport, take South St. (off Bow St.) to South Freeport and turn left at stop sign.

Jameson Tavern ★ AMERICAN/PUB FARE   In another historic farmhouse liter-ally in the shadow of L.L.Bean (on the north side), Jameson Tavern touts itself as the birthplace of Maine. And it is: In 1820, papers were signed here legally separating Maine from Massachusetts. Mainers still appreciate that pen stroke. Today, the tavern sports two restaurants under the same ownership; as you enter the door, the historic Tap Room is to your left, a compact and often crowded spot filled with the smell of fresh popcorn, draft beer, and pubby food. The other part of the house is the Dining Room, more formal in

Packing a Picnic in Freeport

South Freeport's **Winslow Park** offers camping but also day use. It's very scenic for this part of the coast, a great spot for picnics with a family. (There's a playground, too.) However, you've got to be sure to pick up food beforehand—perhaps a cup of chowder at nearby **Harraseeket Lunch & Lobster** (see above).

a country-colonial sort of way. Meals here are hearty fare, but healthier than they were in days of fore: filet mignon wrapped in bacon, yes, but also poached salmon, baked haddock, fresh pastas, and seafood salads.

115 Main St. ✆ **207/865-4196.** Reservations encouraged. Main courses: tap room and lunch $7–$18; dining room dinner $15–$26. AE, DC, DISC, MC, V. Tap room daily 11am–11pm. Dining room daily in summer 11am–10pm, winter 11:30am–9pm.

2 BRUNSWICK & BATH ★

10 miles NE of Freeport. Bath is 8 miles E of Brunswick

Brunswick and Bath are two handsome, historic towns that share a strong commercial past. Many travelers heading up Route 1 pass through both towns eager to reach areas with higher billing on the marquee. That's a shame, for both are well worth the detour to sample the sort of slower pace that's being lost elsewhere.

Brunswick was once home to several mills along the Androscoggin River. These have since been converted to offices and the like, but Brunswick's broad Maine Street still bustles with activity. (Idiosyncratic traffic patterns can lead to snarls of traffic in the late afternoon.) Brunswick is also home to **Bowdoin College ★**, one of the nation's most respected small colleges. The school was founded in 1794, offered its first classes 8 years later, and has since amassed an illustrious roster of prominent alumni, including Nathaniel Hawthorne, Henry Wadsworth Longfellow, President Franklin Pierce, and arctic explorer Robert E. Peary. Civil War hero Joshua Chamberlain served as president of the college after the war. The campus green is full of interesting buildings and museums (see below), and is well worth a short stroll.

Eight miles to the east of Brunswick, **Bath** is pleasantly situated on the broad Kennebec River and is a noted center of shipbuilding. The first U.S.-built ship was constructed downstream at the Popham Bay colony in the early 17th century. In the years since, shipbuilders have constructed more than 5,000 ships hereabout. Bath shipbuilding reached its heyday in the late 19th century, but the business of shipbuilding continues to this day. Bath Iron Works is one of the nation's preeminent boatyards, constructing and repairing ships for the U.S. Navy. The scaled-down military has left Bath shipbuilders in a somewhat tenuous state, but it's still common to see the steely gray ships in the dry dock (the best view is from the bridge over the Kennebec) and the towering red-and-white crane moving supplies and parts around the yard.

Bath is gaining attention from young professional émigrés attracted by its fine old houses, but it's still at heart a blue-collar town, with massive traffic tie-ups weekdays at

3pm when the shipyard changes shifts. Architecture buffs will find a detour here worthwhile. (Look for the free brochure *Architectural Tours: Walking and Driving in the Bath Area,* available at information centers listed below.) The Victorian era in particular is well represented. Washington Street, lined with maples and impressive homes, is one of the best-preserved displays in New England of late-19th-century residences. The compact downtown, on a rise overlooking the river, is also home to some pretty remarkable Victorian commercial architecture that even many Mainers don't realize is there.

Note that Christmas is a big time in Bath: For a full month, from Thanksgiving to the holiday, downtown features fun window displays, a parade, and other events. Contact the local tourist office for more details.

ESSENTIALS
Getting There
Brunswick and Bath are both on Route 1. Brunswick is accessible via exit 28 off I-95. If you're bypassing Brunswick and heading north up Route 1 to Bath or beyond, continue up I-95 and exit at the "coastal connector" exit in Topsham (exit 31), which avoids some of the slower traffic going through Brunswick.

For bus service from Portland or Boston, contact **Vermont Transit** (© 800/451-3292; www.vermonttransit.com) or **Concord Coach** (© 800/639-3317; www.concord trailways.com).

Visitor Information
The **Southern Midcoast Chamber of Commerce,** 2 Main St., Topsham, ME 04086 (© 877/725-8797, 207/725-8797, or 443-9751; www.midcoastmaine.com), offers information and lodging assistance Monday to Friday from 8:30am to 5pm from its offices in downtown Topsham.

FESTIVALS
In mid-August, look for posters for the ever-popular **Thomas Point Beach Bluegrass Festival ★** (© 877/TPB-4321 [827-4321] or 207/725-6009), now more than a quarter-century old. It takes place over Labor Day weekend at Thomas Point Beach between Brunswick and Bath. What started as a sort of counterculture celebration of folksy instruments has grown somewhat, but at its heart it's still just a bunch of like-minded folks collecting in song circles for some old-fashioned pickin' and grinnin'. Performers from throughout Maine gather at this pretty cove-side park (it's a private campground the rest of the summer) and put on shows from noon past dark. Admission varies, but generally it costs $3.50 per adult and $2 per child 11 and under; weekend "carload" and two-for-one specials can significantly reduce the cost of a group outing, however.

WHAT TO SEE & DO
Collectibles buffs and aficionados of antiques malls should schedule an hour or so for **Cabot Mill Antiques,** 14 Maine St., Brunswick (© 207/725-2855; www.cabotiques. com), located on the ground floor of a restored textile mill in downtown Brunswick. In the 15,000-square-foot showroom, more than 140 dealers purvey a wide variety of books, bottles, dolls, art, china, and porcelains. Quality is highly variable. The facility is open daily from 10am to 5pm.

In Brunswick

Bowdoin College Museum of Art ★★   This stern yet pleasing building on the Bowdoin campus (check out the dome) was designed by the prominent architectural firm of McKim, Mead & White. Its collections are small but superb, including a number of exceptionally fine paintings from Europe and America, plus early furniture and artifacts from classical antiquity—and it's free. Artists on show include Andrew and N. C. Wyeth, Marsden Hartley, Winslow Homer, John Singer Sargent, and other titans of the Maine landscape genre. The older upstairs galleries have soft, diffused lighting from skylights high above; the basement galleries, which feature rotating exhibits, are modern and spacious. A 2007 renovation improved the entryway and expanded the interior space a great deal, nearly doubling the number of galleries without taking away from the building's integrity.

Walker Art Building, Bowdoin College. ☎ **207/725-3275.** Free admission. Tues–Sat 10am–5pm (Thurs to 8:30pm); Sun 1–5pm.

Packing a Picnic

The campus of **Bowdoin College** (p. 135) in Brunswick is an attractive (though technically not public) place for a stroll and a bite on a bench. Better to eat in Brunswick's grassy public park (look for the gazebo), then walk it off around campus afterward. There's a big Hannaford's supermarket right downtown with a deli, but you may prefer the more natural fare of **Wild Oats Bakery and Café** (✆ **207/725-6287**) in the tiny Tontine Mall right on Maine Street.

Peary-MacMillan Arctic Museum ★★ (Finds)   While Admiral Robert E. Peary (Bowdoin class of 1887) is better known for his accomplishments (he "discovered" the North Pole at age 53 in 1909), Donald MacMillan (class of 1898) also racked up an impressive string of arctic achievements. You can learn about both men (and the wherefores of arctic exploration) in this tucked-away museum on the Bowdoin campus, just across the lawn from the college's fine museum of art (see above). The front room features mounted animals from the Arctic, including some impressive polar bears. A second room outlines Peary's historic 1909 expedition, complete with excerpts from his journal, and another room includes varied displays of Inuit arts and crafts, some historic and some modern. There are also perhaps 5,000 black-and-white photographs on archive for the truly interested. It's a compact museum that can be visited in about 20 minutes or so.

Hubbard Hall, Bowdoin College. ✆ **207/725-3416**. Free admission. Tues–Sat 10am–5pm; Sun 2–5pm. Closed holidays.

In Bath

Maine Maritime Museum & Shipyard ★ (Kids)   On the shores of the Kennebec River, this museum (just south of the big Bath Iron Works shipyard) features a wide array of displays and exhibits related to boat building. In fact, the museum is housed in the former Percy and Small shipyard, which built some 42 schooners in the late 19th and early 20th centuries. (The largest wooden ship built in the U.S.—the 329-foot *Wyoming*—was constructed here.) The centerpiece of the museum is the handsomely modern Maritime History Building, housing exhibits of maritime art and artifacts. There's also a gift shop with a good selection of books about ships. The remaining property houses a fleet of displays, including an intriguing exhibit on lobstering and a complete boat-building shop. Kids enjoy the play area (they can search for pirates from the crow's nest of a play boat, for instance), and there's always something interesting tied to the docks on the river.

243 Washington St. ✆ **207/443-1316**. www.bathmaine.com. Admission $10 adults, $9 seniors, $7 children 6–17. Daily 9:30am–5pm.

WHERE TO STAY

Brunswick Inn on Park Row ★   This handsome B&B in a rambling Federal-style house with a wraparound porch sits smack-dab in downtown Brunswick, facing the town green. It's run by enthusiastic and friendly owners, has been recently updated, and is positioned perfectly: within walking distance of Bowdoin College, a summer music theater, and restaurants lining Maine Street. Rooms are spacious, furnished in a country-modern style— some with wingback or wicker chairs, and all with attractive quilts; ask about the bright corner rooms and suites. The full breakfasts here are a highlight. Even better: A wine bar/ lounge serves up wine and microbrews before views of the park or a fireplace.

165 Park Row, Brunswick, ME 04011. (© **800/299-4914** or 207/729-4914. Fax 207/967-8451. www. brunswickbnb.com. 15 units. $125–$190 double and suite. Prices include full breakfast. MC, V. Closed Jan. No children 5 and under. **Amenities:** Lounge. In room: A/C, TV (9 units), hair dryer, iron/ironing board.

Galen C. Moses House ★   This 1874 inn is an extravagant, three-story Italianate home done up in exuberant colors by innkeepers Jim Haught and Larry Keift. The whole of the spacious first floor is open to guests and includes a TV room, lots of ticking clocks, and appropriately decorated Victorian double parlor. The old friezes and stained glass are original to the house. Guest rooms vary in decor and size, but all are quite welcoming. The Victorian occupies a corner and gets a lot of afternoon light; the Suite is ideal for families, with two sleeping rooms and a small kitchen; and the Safari is zanily done up (in zebra-stripe patterns), though it does share a bathroom with the '40s Room (yes, nicely decorated in home furnishings from the 1940s).

1009 Washington St., Bath, ME 04530. (© **888/442-8771** or 207/442-8771. www.galenmoses.com. 7 units (2 with shared bathroom). Mid-May to Oct $119–$259 double; Nov to mid-May $119–$129 double. Rates include breakfast. 2-night minimum stay on summer weekends. AE, DISC, MC, V. In room: A/C, hair dryer, iron, no phone.

Grey Havens ★   Located on Georgetown Island southeast of Bath, this gracefully aging 1904 shingled home with prominent turrets sits a high, rocky bluff overlooking the sea. Inside, you can relax in front of a cobblestone fireplace before checking in. Guest rooms are as simple as you'd expect, with plain bathrooms; oceanfront rooms command a premium but are worth it for the views—if you're looking to save a few bucks, ask about an oceanfront room with its bathroom located across the hall. Guests can use the inn's canoes or bikes to explore the area. (There's a little stairway down to a tiny dock on the water, from which guests have reportedly caught whopping fish.) A drawback? This inn has been lightly modernized, so its character remains authentic—and the walls thin. The wonderfully big and (half-screened) porch is worth sitting on for a while, and the lounge features a big picture window.

Seguinland Rd. (P.O. Box 308), Georgetown Island, ME 04548. (© **800/431-2316** or 207/371-2616. Fax 207/371-2613. www.greyhavens.com. 14 units (2 with private hall bathrooms). $160–$280 double. Rates include full breakfast. 2-night minimum stay weekends. MC, V. Closed Nov–May. From U.S. Rte. 1, go south on Rte. 127 and then follow signs for Reid State Park for 11 miles; just after turning onto Reid State Rd. (also known as Seguinland Rd.), watch for inn on left. No children 11 and under. In room: No phone.

WHERE TO DINE

Both downtown Brunswick and downtown Bath offer plenty of casual places to dine, ranging from burgers to barbecue and better. For informal fare, it's hard to go wrong at these cafes and restaurants.

For instance, Jessica Gorton has opened the **Sweet Leaves Teahouse** (© **207/725-1326;** www.sweetleaves.com), a welcome addition to Brunswick's downtown scene. Feast on cheese plates, panini, great salads, hanger steaks (dinnertime only), tea cakes, gourmet yogurt, upscale root beer floats, or cupcakes sided with chai ice cream. Of course, the selection of black, green, white, and herbal teas is extensive (and staff is knowledgeable about all of them); the establishment also serves beer and wine. It's located off the main street at 22 Lincoln St., open daily (except Mon) from lunch until 9pm.

Up in Bath, **Solo Bistro,** 128 Front St. (© **207/443-3373;** www.solobistro.com), is a great new addition to the area. Right on the city's main drag, this is a bistro/jazz club (live music Fri nights only, so far), with dinners of burgers, seared fish and seafood, lamb stews, and risotto among the possible offerings. Lunch runs more to upscale salads and sandwiches, and desserts are well thought out. The decor here is cooler than cool, including minimalist, brightly colored chairs; Scandinavian birch tabletops; and the space's native, rough-hewn stone walls. Interestingly, the husband-and-wife owners also own a Danish design shop right next door.

If you've just got to have lobster, head for Five Islands Lobster Co. (see below), or continue north across the Route 1 bridge a few miles to **Taste of Maine** (✆ **207/443-4554**), an over-large pit stop, which nevertheless delivers the goods with good marsh views.

Five Islands Lobster Co. (Finds) LOBSTER POUND   The drive alone makes this lobster pound a worthy destination. It's about 12 miles south of Route 1, down winding Route 127, past bogs and spruce forests with glimpses of the ocean. (Head south from Woolwich, just across the big bridge from downtown Bath.) Drive until you pass a cluster of clapboard homes, and then keep going until you can't go any farther. Wander out to the wharf (with great views) and place your order. This is a down-home affair, owned by local lobstermen and the proprietors of Grey Havens, a local inn (see above). The adjacent snack bar purveys soda and side dishes; gather all your grub and settle in at a picnic table or a grassy spot at the edge of the dirt parking lot. But don't expect to be alone: Despite its edge-of-the-world feel, this pound draws steady traffic and can actually get *crowded* on weekends.

1447 Five Islands Rd. (Rte. 127), Georgetown. ✆ 207/371-2990. Prices vary according to season. MC, V. Daily 11am–8pm July–Aug; shorter hours Mar–May and Sept to early Oct. Closed Columbus Day to Mother's Day.

Robinhood Free Meetinghouse ★★ FUSION   This place has attracted legions of dedicated local followers who appreciate the extraordinary attention paid to detail, such as foam baffles glued discreetly to the underside of the seats to dampen the echoes in the sparsely decorated, immaculately restored 1855 Greek Revival meetinghouse. Chef Michael Gagné features a raft of entrees, and they're wildly eclectic, with Asian accents (Szechuan-crusted seared tuna to salmon cooked in paper to two types of duck with honey butter and caramelized apples). Starters are equally fine, such as Thai crab soup or grilled shrimp adobo on homemade tortillas (served with banana salsa). Gagné almost always hits a high note—you can't go wrong on the careening menu. Even the sorbet served between courses is homemade. This is by no means a budget restaurant or waterside shack, but offers surprising skill given its out-of-the-way location.

210 Robinhood Rd., Georgetown. From Bath, cross the large bridge and turn south on Rte. 127, continue 6 miles, and turn left just after metal bridge, then continue 1 mile. ✆ 207/371-2188. www.robinhood-meetinghouse.com. Reservations encouraged. Main courses $22–$28. AE, DISC, MC, V. June to mid-Oct daily 5:30–9pm; rest of the year Thurs–Sun 5:30–9pm.

Sea Dog Brewing Co. PUB FARE   Relocated inside a historic old mill astride the Androscoggin River dividing Brunswick and Topsham, this brewpub makes a reasonable destination for grub such as nachos or hamburgers, plus a few more adventurous offerings that might run to a lobster bisque or a grilled-tuna sandwich. The eats won't necessarily set your taste buds on fire, but they do satisfy basic cravings. In any case, the beers here are consistently excellent, including the house hazelnut porter and India pale ale—and that's why you're here, right?

1 Main St., Topsham. ✆ 207/725-0162. Main courses $6–$18. AE, DISC, MC, V. Daily 11:30am–1am.

3 HARPSWELL PENINSULA ★★

Extending southwest from Brunswick and Bath is the picturesque Harpswell region. It's actually three peninsulas, like the tines of a pitchfork, if you include the islands of Orrs and Bailey, which are linked to the mainland by bridges. While close to some of Maine's larger towns (Portland is only 45 min. away), the Harpswell Peninsula has a remote, historical feel with sudden vistas across meadows to the blue waters of northern Casco Bay. No hiking trails, no garish attractions—just winding roads good for country drives. (Narrow shoulders and fast cars make for poor biking, however.) The islands are perfect for a beautiful drive back into an older Maine, and a good lobster dinner at the end of the peninsula (see "Where to Dine," below), on a good day. But if the weather's bad, skip it—you'll just find it monotonous. Note that, as in much of Maine, there is nothing at all to do on the peninsula at night besides enjoy the quiet.

The region is an amalgam—old houses with picturesque peeling paint next to manu-factured homes, and summer houses next to the homes of Brunswick commuters. Toward the southern tips of the peninsulas, the character changes as clusters of colorful Victorian-era summer cottages displace the farmhouses found farther inland. Some of these cottages rent by the week, but savvy families book up many of them years in advance. (If you're interested, drop by any local real estate agency.)

There's no set itinerary for exploring the area. Just drive south from Brunswick on Route 24 or Route 123 until you can't go any farther, and then backtrack for a bit and strike south again. Among the "attractions" worth looking for are the wonderful ocean and island views from **South Harpswell** at the tip of the westernmost peninsula (park and wander around for a bit), and the clever **Cobwork Bridge** ★★ connecting Bailey and Orrs islands. The hump-backed bridge was built in 1928 of granite blocks stacked in such a way that the strong tides could come and go and not drag the bridge out with it. No cement was used in its construction.

BEACHES

This part of Maine is better known for rocky cliffs and lobster pots than swimming beaches, with two notable exceptions.

Popham Beach State Park (© 207/389-1335 or 389-9125) is located at the tip of Route 209 (head south from Bath). This handsome park has a long and sandy strand, plus great views of knobby offshore islands such as Seguin Island, capped with a lone-some lighthouse. Parking and basic services, including changing rooms, are available. Admission is $4 for adults and $1 for children 5 to 11 in season; $1.50 for adults and free to children in the off season.

At the tip of the next peninsula to the east is **Reid State Park** (© 207/371-2303), an idyllic place to picnic on a summer day. Arrive early enough, and you can stake out a picnic table among the wind-blasted pines. The mile-and-half-long beach is great for strolling and splashing around. Services include changing rooms and a small snack bar. Admission is $4.50 for adults, $1 for children 5 to 11. To reach Reid State Park, follow Route 127 south from Bath and Route 1.

WHERE TO STAY

Driftwood Inn & Cottages The oceanside Driftwood Inn dates from 1910. This family-run retreat at the end of a dead-end road is just a compound of weathered, shingled buildings and a handful of cottages. The rooms of time-aged pine have a simple turn-of-the-last-century flavor that hasn't been gentrified in the least. Most rooms share bathrooms along the hallways, but some do have private sinks and toilets. (The inn also has seven rooms for solo travelers, a rarity these days.) Cottages on a small, private cove are furnished in budget style: Expect industrial carpeting and plastic shower stalls. Some beds could stand replacing, too, but where else in Maine can you sleep at water's edge this cheaply? The inn maintains an old saltwater pool and porches with wicker furniture to while away the afternoons, as well.

Washington Ave. (P.O. Box 16), Bailey Island, ME 04003. From Rte. 24 in Bailey Island, cross bridge and turn left onto Washington Ave. and proceed to end. ℭ **207/833-5461.** www.thedriftwoodinnmaine.com. 34 units (many units share hallway bathrooms). $75–$115 double; cottages $665–$700 per week peak season; some units $115–$125 per day off season. No credit cards. Closed mid-Oct to mid-May; dining room closed Labor Day to late June. **Amenities:** Saltwater pool. *In room:* No phone.

Sebasco Harbor Resort ★ (Kids)

Sebasco is a grand old seaside resort fighting a mostly successful battle against time; some guests have been returning for 60 years, and spacious grounds remain the star attraction. Expect sweeping ocean views, a lovely seaside pool, and great walks, plus children's activities (including a kids' camp), a brand-new spa, and pancake breakfasts on the lawn. Most guest rooms are adequate, not elegant, although the resort has poured a pile of money into renovation. Small decks on many of the inn rooms are a plus. Better are the quirky rooms in the octagonal Lighthouse Building; most have TVs. There are also interior-court and lakefront cottages of various sizes (with up to *10* bedrooms), though some are very expensive—figure $1,000 and up per night for lakeside digs.

Rte. 217 (P.O. Box 75), Sebasco Estates, ME 04565. South from Bath 11 miles on Rte. 209; look for Rte. 217, then signs to Sebasco. ℭ **800/225-3819** or 207/389-1161. Fax 207/389-2004. www.sebasco.com. 133 units (111 rooms, 22 cottages). Mid-June to Labor Day $199–$359 double, $459–$2,090 cottage; May to mid-June and Sept–Oct $139–$229 double, $319–$1,690 cottage. MAP rates also available. Rates do not include 10% resort service charge or state sales tax. 2-night minimum on weekends. AE, DISC, MC, V. Closed late Oct to early May. Pets allowed (some units). **Amenities:** Dining room; pool; golf course; tennis courts; health club; spa; sauna; hot tub; canoe and kayak rentals; sailing lessons; bike rentals; children's program; shuffleboard; bowling. *In room:* TV (some units), kitchenette (some units), fireplace (some units).

WHERE TO DINE

If a steamed lobster is what you want (and you do), several sprawling establishments specialize in delivering the crustaceans fresh from the sea. On the Bailey Island side, there's **Cook's Lobster House** (ℭ 207/833-2818; www.cookslobster.com), which has been serving up a choice of shore dinners since 1955 and is open daily from around 11:30am to 9pm in summer (call for off-season hours). The restaurant has two decks for outdoor dining. Past Harpswell down Route 123 at the *very end* of the point (great views) is the popular **Estes Lobster House** (ℭ 207/833-6340), which serves various lobster plates in relaxed, festive surroundings.

Dolphin Chowder House ★ (Finds)

TRADITIONAL NEW ENGLAND One of the premier places for chowder in the state is the down-home Dolphin Marina (now also known as the Dolphin Chowder House) at Basin Point. Wander inside the shingled building with small-paned windows adjacent to the boatyard, and you'll discover a tiny counter seating six and a handful of pine tables and booths with stunning views of Casco Bay. If it's crowded, you can get a meal to go—except the chowder. It's against Dolphin tradition to walk out with chowder; you have to sit down and enjoy it here. The chowders and lobster

stew are reasonably priced ($4.95–$12) and absolutely delicious, and the blueberry muffins **143**
are often warm and capped with a crispy crown. Note that the servers can sometimes seem
flummoxed at busy times, so bring your patience.

515 Basin Point, South Harpswell. (✆ **207/833-6000.** Breakfast items $1.25–$3; sandwiches $3.50–$7.95;
complete dinners $14–$17. MC, V. May–Oct daily 7:30am–8pm. Closed Nov–Apr. Drive 12 miles south of
Brunswick on Rte. 123, turn right at Ash Point Rd. near the West Harpswell School, and then take the next
right on Basin Point Rd. and continue to the end.

4 WISCASSET ★★ & THE BOOTHBAYS ★

11 miles NE of Bath; The Boothbays are 11 miles S of Wiscasset

Wiscasset ★★ is a cute riverside town just inland from the Atlantic (no views), and it's
not shy about letting you know: THE PRETTIEST VILLAGE IN MAINE boasts a sign at the
edge of town and on many brochures. Whether or not you agree with this self-assessment
(and not all locals do), the town is attractive, even if the persistent line of traffic snaking
through the center town through the summer diminishes its charm somewhat. Still, it
makes a good stop for stretching one's legs and grabbing a bite to eat en route to other
coastal destinations.

The **Boothbays** ★, 11 miles south of Route 1 on Route 27, are a string of several
small, scenic villages down a peninsula—East Boothbay, **Boothbay Harbor,** and Boothbay—close to the ocean that, in some cases, actually provide frontal views of it. Bland,
boxy motels hem in the harbor, where side-by-side boutiques hawk T-shirts emblazoned
with puffins; still, there's some charm to be found here among the clutter and cheese,
especially on days when foghorns bleat mournfully at the harbor's mouth.

ESSENTIALS
Getting There
Wiscasset is right on U.S. Route 1, between Bath and Damariscotta. Boothbay Harbor
is off Route 1, southeast down a peninsula on Route 27; coming from the south, turn
right shortly after crossing the bridge in Wiscasset.

Visitor Information
As befits a place where tourism is a major industry, the Boothbay region has *three* visitor
information centers in and around town. On U.S. Route 1, at the Route 27 turnoff,
there's an info center open seasonally, a good place to stock up on initial brochures. A
mile before you reach the villages is the also-seasonal **Boothbay Information Center**
(open June–Oct). If you zoom past that one or it's closed, don't fret: the year-round

---

(ⓘ Tips) **Get Your Kicks on Route 1? Umm . . . No.**

While there's a certain retro charm in the *idea* of traveling Maine on historic
Route 1, the reality is quite different. It can be congested and unattractive, and
you're not missing anything if you take alternative routes. For memorable explorations, be sure to leave enough time for forays both inland and down the lesser
roads along the coast.

Boothbay Harbor Region Chamber of Commerce, P.O. Box 356, Boothbay Harbor, ME 04538 (① **800/266-8422** or 207/633-2353; www.boothbayharbor.com), is at the intersection of routes 27 and 96.

EXPLORING WISCASSET

Aside from enjoying the town's handsome architecture and general quaintness, there are a few quirky, low-key attractions good for a break while traveling up along the coast. You'll also find a handful of worthwhile antiques shops and eateries.

Castle Tucker ★   This fascinating museum at the edge of town overlooking the river was first built in 1807 in the style of a Scottish mansion, then was radically added onto and altered in a more ostentatious style in 1858 (that's when the dramatic piazza was added). The home remains more or less in the same state it was in when reconfigured by cotton trader Capt. Richard Tucker. Tours of the lower floor are offered by the Society of New England Antiquities, which was given the house by its former owner, Richard's daughter Jane (ask about her story) in 1997. The detailing is exceptional and offers insight into the life of an affluent sea captain in the late 19th century. Be sure to note the extraordinary elliptical staircase and the painted plaster trim (which is not oak, though it looks like it).

Lee St. (at High St.). ① **207/882-7169.** Admission $5. Tours depart hourly Wed–Sun 11am–4pm from June to mid-Oct; closed the rest of the year.

Musical Wonder House ★ (Finds)   Danilo Konvalinka has been collecting music boxes for decades, and nothing seems to delight him more than playing them for awe-struck visitors; this offbeat museum, filling a 32-room sea captain's manse with some 5,000 of them (yes, *thousand*), is the happy result. The collection includes massive, ancient music boxes as resounding as orchestras (such as an 1870 Girard music box from Austria), as well as many smaller contraptions emitting tinnier, more tinkly sounds. The music boxes are displayed and played in four rooms of the 1852 home; admission is charged per room, and a tour can get quite pricey. If you're undecided about whether it's worth it, try this: Visit the free gift shop and sample some of the coin-operated 19th-century music boxes in the adjoining hallway first. Intrigued? Sign up for the next tour—there are three tiers of pricing.

18 High St. ① **207/882-7163.** www.musicalwonderhouse.com. 2-room tour $10, 3-room tour and quick upstairs walk-through $20, full tour $45; discounts for seniors. Late May to Oct daily 10am–5pm. Closed Nov to late May.

EXPLORING THE BOOTHBAY REGION

Boothbay Harbor ★ was just another fishing village until it was "discovered" by wealthy city folks who built imposing seaside homes here. Once it embraced the tourist dollar, the village never really looked back, and in recent years it has emerged as a premier destination for tourists in search of classic coastal Maine; the village is often a mandatory stop on bus tours, which have in turn attracted kitsch, but some of the outlying areas remain beautiful.

Summer parking in the town requires either great persistence or forking over a few dollars. A popular local attraction is the long, narrow **footbridge** across the harbor, built in 1901. It's more of a destination than a link—other than a few restaurants and motels, there's not much on the other side. The winding streets that weave through town are filled with souvenir shops purveying the usual trinkets.

(Tips) **Escaping the Crowds**

Boothbay Harbor is overrun with summer visitors, but at nearby Ocean Point, you can leave most of the crowds behind by following a picturesque lane that twists along the rocky shore past a colony of vintage summer homes. Follow Route 96 southward from just outside Boothbay Harbor, and you'll pass through the sleepy village of East Boothbay before continuing on to the point. The narrow road runs through piney forests before arriving at the rocky finger. It's one of a handful of Maine peninsulas with a road edging its perimeter, allowing you fine ocean views. Colorful Victorian-era summer cottages bloom along the roadside like wildflowers. Ocean Point makes for a good bike loop, too; mountain-bike rentals are available from the Tidal Transit folks (see below).

In good weather, stop by a Boothbay-region information center (see above) and request a free guide to the holdings of the **Boothbay Region Land Trust** (© 207/633-4818). More than a dozen of its properties dot the peninsula, most with quiet, lightly traveled trails good for a stroll or a picnic. Among the best: the **Linekin Preserve** ★, a 95-acre parcel en route to Ocean Point with 600 feet of riverfront. A hike around the loop trail (about 2 miles) occupies a pleasant hour. To find the preserve, drive south from Route 1 in Boothbay Harbor along Route 96 for about 3³/₄ miles, and look for the parking area on the left.

Coastal Maine Botanical Gardens ★ This expansive complex of waterside gardens is a work in progress, but it's well worth exploring. It's a natural habitat being gently coaxed into a more manicured state, with different pathways through the mossy forest featuring pocket gardens with different themes and flowers, plus an alley of more than 1,000 birch trees. Throughout, the walks are quiet and lush; one of the best trails runs along much of the tidal shoreline that's part of the property.

Barters Island Rd., Boothbay (near Hogdon Island). © **207/633-4333.** www.mainegardens.org. Admission $10 adults, $8 seniors, $5 children age 5–17, $25 family. Mon–Fri 9am–5pm; Sat–Sun 9am–6pm. From Rte. 27 in Boothbay Center, bear right at monument, then make the first right onto Barters Island Rd.; drive 1 mile to stone gate on the left.

Maine State Aquarium (Kids) Operated by the state's Department of Marine Resources, this compact aquarium offers a context for the marine life in the Atlantic. Kids can view rare albino and blue lobsters, or get their hands wet in a 20-foot touch tank—a sort of petting zoo of the slippery and slimy. The aquarium is located on a point across the water from Boothbay Harbor, and parking is tight; visitors are urged to take the free shuttle bus from downtown that runs daily until 5pm.

McKown Point Rd., West Boothbay Harbor. © **207/633-9542.** Admission $5 adults, $3 children 5–18 and seniors. Late May to Aug daily 10am–5pm; Sept Wed–Sun 10am–5pm. Closed Oct to Memorial Day.

BOAT TOURS

The best way to see the Maine coast around Boothbay is on a boat tour. Nearly two dozen tour boats berth at the harbor or nearby. **Balmy Days Cruises** (© **800/298-2284** or 207/633-2284; www.balmydayscruises.com), for instance, runs a half-dozen short trips daily ($12 for adults, $6 for children) around the harbor in summertime. If you'd rather be sailing, ask about the 90-minute cruises aboard the sloop *Friendship* ($20 per person; five cruises daily in summer). Schedules are reduced in spring and fall; call ahead for reservations.

The most personal way to see the harbor is via sea kayak. **Tidal Transit Kayak Co.** (*© 207/633-7140*; www.kayakboothbay.com) offers morning, afternoon, and sunset tours of the harbor for $35 (sunset's the best bet). Single kayaks can also be rented for $15 an hour or $50 per day; tandem kayaks costs more. The shop is open daily in summer (except when it rains heavily), and is actually located on a dock at 18 Granary Way.

WHERE TO STAY

One of the coast's best campgrounds, the **Chewonki Campground** ★ (*© 800/465-7747* or 207/882-7426; www.chewonkicampground.com) is located between Bath and Wiscasset. It occupies 50 acres overlooking a salt marsh and a confluence of lazy tidal streams. The 47 sites here are sizable and private; there's a nicely maintained pool with a sweeping view, and kayaks and canoes are available for rent. Campsites cost from $28 to $49 per night, which is at the high end of the camping price scale for Maine—but worth it. Drive 7 miles east of Bath on U.S. Route 1; turn right on Route 144, then take the next right past the airport and follow signs to the campground.

Five Gables Inn ★   East Boothbay was once home to a dozen summer hotels; now there's just one left. The handsome Five Gables was painstakingly restored in the late 1980s, and sits proudly amid a small colony of summer homes on a quiet road above a peaceful cove. It's nicely isolated from the confusion and hubbub of Boothbay Harbor. Rooms are pleasantly appointed, nearly all of them look out onto the water, and five have fireplaces burning manufactured logs; some also sport four-poster beds. Don't come expecting televisions or phones—it's a quiet place lacking both. Room no. 8 is a corner room with brilliant morning light and good coastal views; room no. 14 is the biggest and most frequently requested unit, with more views and a fireplace with a marble mantle. Some first-floor rooms open onto a common deck, which means little privacy. The inn's included breakfast buffet is very good.

Murray Hill Rd. (P.O. Box 335), East Boothbay, ME 04544. *© 800/451-5048* or 207/633-4551. www.five gablesinn.com. 16 units. $130–$225 double. Rates include breakfast. MC, V. Closed mid-Oct to mid-May. Drive through East Boothbay on Rte. 96; turn right at blinking light onto Murray Hill Rd. Children 12 and older are welcome. *In room:* Fireplace (some units), no phone.

The Lawnmere Inn   The Lawnmere, a short hop from Boothbay on the northern shore of Southport Island, offers easy access to town and a restful environment. It does indeed sit on a nice green lawn. The main inn was built as a guesthouse in the late 19th century, and has since been updated (with a slight loss of charm). Nearly two-thirds of the guest rooms, however, are housed in two motel-like annexes known as the "wings"; these rooms have private balconies with views of the quiet waterway separating South-port Island from the mainland. Good regional and global cuisine is served in a comfort-able, homey **dining room** ★ overlooking the water—some of the most reliable food in a town that has seen more than its share of restaurant turnover. Nonguests can also dine here; reservations are recommended.

Rte. 27 (P.O. Box 29), Southport, ME 04576. *© 800/633-7645* or 207/633-2544. www.lawnmereinn.com. 28 units. June to mid-Oct $89–$169 double; $169–$189 suite. 2-night minimum on holiday weekends. Packages available. MC, V. Closed mid-Oct to May. Pets accepted on limited basis; $10 per pet. Drive south through Boothbay Harbor on Rte. 27; cross bridge onto Southport Island. Inn is just past bridge, on the right. **Amenities:** Dining room; pub; free bikes. *In room:* A/C (some units).

Newagen Seaside Inn ★ Newagen is a good, small, low-key resort with stunning ocean views amid a fragrant spruce forest, and there's been a new push here to renovate everything from rooms to amenities; a spa is said to be on the way. The inn is housed in a low, white-shingled building with cruise ship–like hallways sporting pine wainscoting and a cozy lobby. The 30 guest rooms have polished wood floors, Amish-style quilts, and country-themed decor. Downstairs, adults can relax in a pub or shoot some pool while kids try out two candlepin lanes. (This may be the only inn in New England I've seen that has its own bowling alley.) The 85-acre grounds are filled with decks, gazebos, a handsome in-ground pool, and walkways bordering on the magical: Magnificent views are among the best of any inn in Maine. Five outlying cottages offer additional privacy and one to three bedrooms each.

Rte. 27 (P.O. Box 29), Newagen, ME 04576. (C) **800/654-5242** or 207/633-5242. www.newagenseasideinn. com. 35 units. $135–$235 double; $210–$285 suite; cottages $1,500–$3,000 weekly. Rates include breakfast (inn rooms only). Packages available. AE, MC, V. Closed mid-Oct to mid-May. Take Rte. 27 south from Boothbay Harbor across Southport Island bridge, continuing to the south tip of the island. **Amenities:** Dining room; pub; heated outdoor pool; saltwater pool; Jacuzzi; tennis courts; bowling alley; boat tours; free rowboats; bikes. *In room:* TV (1 unit), fridge (some units), coffeemaker (some units), kitchenette (some units).

Spruce Point Inn ★ On a rocky point facing west across the harbor, this inn was built as a hunting and fishing lodge in the 1890s and evolved into a summer resort soon thereafter; some find it a mixed-bag experience, but it has benefited greatly from a spiffing-up that's been ongoing since the late '80s, including the addition of 55 deluxe suites with modern amenities such as Jacuzzis, marble bathrooms, private decks, woodstoves, carpeting, and new furniture. Guests typically idle in Adirondack chairs admiring the 15 acres of grounds, or partake of croquet, shuffleboard, and tennis on clay courts. Although more of a couples' place, children's programs accommodate a growing number of kids here. The spa is a welcome addition, and the formal dining room (with average food) enjoys good sunset views across the mouth of the harbor.

88 Grandview Ave. (P.O. Box 237), Boothbay Harbor, ME 04538. (C) **800/553-0289** or 207/633-4152. www. sprucepointinn.com. 93 units. Late June to Aug $169–$359 double; spring and fall $139–$265 double; cottages and condos $255–$560. 3-night minimum stay in summer and some holidays. AE, DC, DISC, MC, V. Closed mid-Oct to Memorial Day. From Boothbay Harbor, turn seaward on Union St.; continue 2 miles to inn. **Amenities:** 2 restaurants; pub; 2 outdoor pools; 2 tennis courts; fitness center; spa; Jacuzzi; game room; concierge; conference rooms; massage; babysitting; laundry service; dry cleaning. *In room:* A/C, TV, kitchenette (some units), fridge, coffeemaker, iron/ironing board, safe, Jacuzzi (some units), fireplace (some units).

Topside This old gray house on the hilltop looming above dated motel buildings looks a bit spooky at first glance. Fear not; Topside has spectacular ocean views at a reasonable price from its quiet hilltop perch over downtown Boothbay Harbor. The inn—a former boardinghouse for shipyard workers—has simple, clean, comfortable rooms mostly done in whites and pastels, furnished with a mixture of antiques and contemporary furniture. At the edge of the lawn there are two outbuildings stocked with basic motel-style units; these are on the smallish side, with dated paneling and furniture, though two end units (room nos. 9 and 14) might have the best views on the whole property. Most units allow some glimpse of the water, in fact, and many have decks or patios. Topside updated about one-third of its rooms and unveiled the new decor in spring of 2008.

60 McKown St., Boothbay Harbor, ME 04538. (C) **888/633-5404** or 207/633-5404. Fax 207/633-2206. www.topsideinn.com. 21 units. $120–$185 double. Rates include full breakfast. 2-night minimum weekends, 3-night minimum holiday weekends. Children 6 and older welcome. DISC, MC, V. Closed Nov–Apr. *In room:* TV, fridge (some units).

In Wiscasset

Red's Eats ★ (Finds) LOBSTER/TAKEOUT   Red's is a tiny red shack next to Route 1 smack in downtown Wiscasset—right where the traffic maddeningly backs up at the bridge—that's received more than its fair share of national ink and TV attention for its famous lobster rolls. And they *are* good, consisting of big, moist, meaty chunks of chilled lobster in a toasted hot-dog roll with a little mayo on the side. (No skimpy pieces of celery here!) Be aware that they're pricey—you can find less expensive, less filling versions anywhere else—but these are the best-tasting in Maine. As a result, expect to stand in line for a while. The few tables behind the stand fill up quickly in summer; you can also walk downhill to the public riverfront dock a minute away. Beyond the lobster rolls, very cheap fare (hot dogs, sandwiches) dominates the rest of the menu. You can also get very good ice-cream cones here.

U.S. 1 at Water St. (just before bridge). ℂ **207/882-6128.** Sandwiches $2–$5; lobster rolls typically $13–$14. No credit cards. Mon–Thurs 11am–11pm; Fri–Sat 11am–2am; Sun noon–6pm. Closed Oct–Apr.

Sarah's Cafe ★ (Value) SANDWICHES/TRADITIONAL   Sarah's is a friendly Wiscasset family favorite that opened in 1987, then moved down the block to a place with a view of Sheepscot River a decade later. Expect personable service and filling, well-prepared food: lobster, pizzas, a changing menu of soups, stews, and more. It's usually crowded for lunch and early dinner, with items such as pita pockets, croissant sandwiches, and a cheesy local favorite called a whaleboat; the lobster rolls are uniformly excellent, and so are the dessert pies. Just want some takeout? They'll do a "bucket" of ravioli to go. This is a great choice for an informal lunch break when you're motoring up Route 1 and don't feel like standing in the long lines at Red's. The adjacent Twin Schooner Pub, also owned by Sarah's, is good for a beer.

Water St. and U.S. Rte. 1 (across street from Red's). ℂ **207/882-7504.** Sandwiches and meals mostly $5–$10; pizzas $5–$18. AE, DISC, MC, V. Daily 11am–8pm (until 9pm Fri–Sat).

In The Boothbays

More creative dining can be found in the dining rooms of both the Spruce Point Inn and the Lawnmere Inn (see "Where to Stay," above).

Boothbay Lobster Wharf SEAFOOD   Across the harbor from downtown Boothbay, this place offers no-frills lobster and seafood; it's the best pick from a cluster of lobster-in-the-rough places lining the waterfront nearby. Lobsters are priced to market, and there are the usual fried-food baskets and sandwiches for those who don't dig crustaceans. This is a fine place for a classic Maine outdoor meal on a sunny day, but it's probably uninteresting in rain or fog. There's now a new fish market here, open year-round, where you can pick up cooked or live lobsters and the day's fresh catch even after the restaurant closes down for the season.

97 Atlantic Ave., Boothbay Harbor. ℂ **207/633-4900.** Reservations not accepted. Fried and grilled foods $2–$10; dinner $7–$15. DISC, MC, V. Mid-May to mid-Oct daily 11:30am–9pm. By foot, cross footbridge and turn right; follow road for ¹/₃ mile to co-op.

Lobsterman's Wharf SEAFOOD   On the water in East Boothbay, the Lobsterman's Wharf has the comfortable, pubby feel of a popular neighborhood bar, complete with pool table. That makes it popular with locals, but the kitchen also serves better-than-standard meals and knows how to make out-of-towners feel at home. Specials have included a mixed-seafood grill, a barbecue shrimp-and-ribs platter, grilled swordfish with béarnaise sauce, seafood fettuccine, tuna sashimi, and lobsters served at least four different ways. Blueberry pie and chocolate cake make good finishers. At lunch, there are burgers, baked haddock, lobster rolls, and steamed lobsters.

224 Ocean Pt. Rd. (Rte. 96), East Boothbay. © **866/733-2057.** Reservations only accepted for parties of 6 or more. Lunch $5–$14; dinner $14–$25 (mostly $14–$16). AE, MC, V. Apr–Oct daily 11:30am–10pm. Closed Nov–Mar.

5 PEMAQUID PENINSULA ★★★

Pemaquid Peninsula ★★★ is an irregular, rocky wedge driven deep into the Gulf of Maine. Far less commercial than Boothbay Peninsula across the Damariscotta River, it's much more suited to relaxed exploration and nature appreciation than its cousin. Rugged and rocky Pemaquid Point, at the extreme southern tip of the peninsula, is one of the most dramatic destinations in Maine when the ocean surf pounds the shore.

ESSENTIALS
Getting There
The Pemaquid Peninsula is accessible from the south and west by taking U.S. Route 1 to Damariscotta, then turning south down Route 129/130. Coming from the north or northeast, take U.S. 1 through Waldoboro, then turn south down Route 32 just south of town.

Visitor Information
The **Damariscotta Region Chamber of Commerce,** P.O. Box 13, Damariscotta, ME 04543 (© **207/563-8340**), is a good source of local information and maintains a seasonal information booth just off U.S. Route 1 during the summer months. To get there, follow Route 27 south, leaving Route 1 just east (across the bridge) after Wiscasset.

EXPLORING THE PEMAQUID PENINSULA
The Pemaquid Peninsula invites slow driving and frequent stops. South on Route 129 toward Walpole is Damariscotta, a sleepy head-of-the-harbor village. On the left is the austerely handsome Walpole Meeting House, dating from 1772. Usually not open to the public, services are held here during the summer and the public is welcome.

Continue on Route 129 to picturesque **Christmas Cove,** so named because Capt. John Smith (of Pocahontas fame) anchored here on Christmas Day in 1614. While wandering about, look for the rustic **Coveside Bar and Restaurant** (© **207/644-8282**), a popular marina with a pennant-bedecked lounge and basic dining room. The food is okay, but the views are outstanding; you may catch a glimpse of the celebrity yachtsmen who tend to stop off here. Reservations are a good idea on summer weekends.

About 5 miles north of South Bristol, turn right on Pemaquid Road, which will take you to Route 130. Along the way, look for the **Harrington Meeting House** (the other 1772 structure), open to the public on occasional afternoons in July and August. It's an architectural gem inside, almost painfully austere, with a small museum of local artifacts on the second floor.

Continue south on Route 130 to the village of New Harbor, then look for signs to **Colonial Pemaquid** (© **207/677-2423**). Open daily from Memorial Day to Labor Day, this state historic site has exhibits on the original 1625 settlement here; archaeological digs take place in the summertime. The $2 admission charge (free for children 11 and under) includes a visit to stout **Fort William Henry,** a 1907 replica of a supposedly impregnable fortress. Nearby **Pemaquid Beach** is good for a (chilly) ocean dip or a picnic with the family.

But **Pemaquid Point ★★**, owned by the town of **Bristol,** should be your final destination; it's the place to while away an afternoon (© **207/677-2494**). Bring a picnic and a book, and find a spot on the dark, fractured rocks to settle in. The ocean views are superb, and the only distractions are the tenacious seagulls that might take a profound interest in your lunch.

From New Harbor, you can also get a great view of the coast from the sea by taking a boat trip. **Hardy Boat Cruises** (© **800/278-3346** or 207/677-2026; www.hardyboat. com) operates summertime tours aboard the 60-foot *Hardy III,* and excursions include a 1-hour sunset-and-lighthouse cruise ($13 for adults, $9 for children age 11 and under) and a 90-minute puffin tour out to Eastern Egg Rock ($21 for adults, $13 for children). Extra clothing for warmth is strongly recommended. The company operates from mid- or late May through Labor Day.

Route 32 strikes northwest out of New Harbor, and it's the most scenic way to leave the peninsula if you plan on continuing eastward on Route 1 to places such as Camden and Rockland. Along the way, look for the sign pointing to the **Rachel Carson Salt Pond Preserve ★★**, a Nature Conservancy property. The noted naturalist Rachel Carson studied these roadside tidepools extensively while researching her 1956 bestseller *The Edge of the Sea,* and it's still a good spot for budding naturalists and experts alike. At low tide, you can see starfish, green crabs, periwinkles, and other creatures in the tidal pools and among the rocks.

WHERE TO STAY

Bradley Inn ★   The Bradley Inn is within easy hiking or biking distance to the point, but there are plenty of reasons to lag behind at the inn, too. Wander the nicely land-scaped grounds or settle in for a game of cards at the pub. The rooms are tastefully appointed with four-poster cherry beds (though no televisions). The third-floor rooms are the best despite the hike up to them, thanks to distant glimpses of John's Bay, and a high-ceilinged second-floor suite occupying the entire floor is equipped with a full kitchen and dining room. The inn is popular for summer weekend weddings, so ask in advance if you're seeking solitude and quiet. A seaside spa, opened in 2007, offers a menu of wellness services.

(Tips) **Lobster Pricing**

Travelers may be in for a rude surprise when they get the bill for a meal at a casual wharfside lobster restaurant. Prices posted for lobsters are per *pound,* not per *lobster.* This can be inadvertently misleading, as a range of prices is often posted—for example, $6.99 FOR 1¼-LB. LOBSTERS, $7.99 FOR 1½-LB. LOBSTERS, and so on. That's the price per pound, not the total price, so you'll need to do a little math to figure out the final price of your lobster.

Rte. 130, 3063 Bristol Rd., New Harbor, ME 04554. © **800/942-5560** or 207/677-2105. Fax 207/677-3367. www.bradleyinn.com. 17 units. $160–$235 double; $225–$325 suite and cottage. Rates include full breakfast and afternoon tea. Packages available. AE, MC, V. Closed Nov–Mar. **Amenities:** Dining room; pub; spa; free bikes; room service. *In room:* Fireplace (some units), kitchen (1 unit).

Hotel Pemaquid (Value) This 1889 coastal classic isn't directly on the water—it's about a 1- or 2-minute walk from Pemaquid Point—but the main inn has the flavor of an old-time boardinghouse. Outbuildings are a bit more modern. Though most rooms now have a private bathroom, the inn is still old-fashioned at heart, with a no-credit cards policy, narrow hallways, and antiques, including a great collection of old radios and phonographs. The two- and three-bedroom suites—one with a sun porch and one with a kitchen—are good for families, and there are cottages and a carriage house rented by the week.

Rte. 130, Pemaquid Point (mailing address: 3098 Bristol Rd., New Harbor, ME 04554). © **207/677-2312.** www.hotelpemaquid.com. 23 units (4 with shared bathrooms). $80–$100 double with private bathroom; $65–$75 double with shared bathroom; $125–$240 suite; cottages $775–$825 weekly. 2-night minimum stay on weekends. No credit cards. Closed mid-Oct to mid-Apr. *In room:* TV (some units), no phone.

WHERE TO DINE

Shaw's Fish and Lobster Wharf ★ LOBSTER   Shaw's attracts hordes of tourists, but it's no trick to figure out why: It's one of the best-situated lobster pounds, with postcard-perfect views of the working harbor. You can stake out a seat on either the open deck or the indoor dining room (go for the deck), or order up some appetizers from the raw bar. This is one of the few lobster joints in Maine with a full liquor license.

On the water, New Harbor. © **207/677-2200.** Lobster priced to market (typically $7 per pound). MC, V. Mid-May to mid-Oct daily 11am–8pm (until 9pm July–Aug). Closed mid-Oct to mid-May.

6 MONHEGAN ISLAND ★★★

Monhegan Island ★★★ is Maine's premier island destination. Visited by Europeans as early as 1497, the wild, remote island was settled by fishermen attracted to the sea's bounty in offshore waters. In the 1870s, artists discovered the island and stayed for a spell, including Rockwell Kent (the artist most closely associated with the island), George Bellows, Edward Hopper, and Robert Henri.

It's not hard to figure out why artists have been attracted to this place, with its almost-mystical sense of tranquillity. It's also a superb destination for hikers, since most of the island is undeveloped and laced with footpaths.

Just be aware that this is not Martha's Vineyard. There's one ATM on Monhegan, and few pay phones—heck, even electricity is scarce. That's what most visitors seem to like about it, and an overnight at one of the island's very simple inns is strongly recommended if you've got time; the island's true character doesn't emerge until the last day boat sails back to the mainland. If you just can't stomach the complete quiet and the lack of phones, TVs, and late-night takeout, day trips are also easy to arrange.

ESSENTIALS
Getting There
Access to Monhegan Island is via boat from New Harbor, Boothbay Harbor, or Port Clyde. The picturesque trip from Port Clyde is the favorite route of longtime visitors; the

boat passes the Marshall Point Lighthouse and a series of spruce-clad islands before reaching the open sea and plying its way island-ward.

Two boats make the run to Monhegan from little Port Clyde. The *Laura B* is a doughty workboat (building supplies and boxes of food are loaded on first; passengers fill in the available niches on the deck and in the small cabin), and makes the run in about 70 minutes. A newer boat—the slightly faster, passenger-oriented *Elizabeth Ann*—also makes the run, offering a large heated cabin and more seating, in about 50 minutes. You'll need to leave your car behind, so pack light and wear sturdy shoes. The fare is $30 round-trip for adults, $16 for children ages 2 to 12, and $5 for pets. They do take credit cards, but reservations are advised. Contact **Monhegan Boat Line,** P.O. Box 238, Port Clyde, ME 04855 (© **207/372-8848;** www.monheganboat.com). Parking is available just off the Port Clyde dock for $4 per day.

Visitor Information

Monhegan Island has no formal visitor center, but it's small and friendly enough that you can make inquiries of just about anyone you meet on the island pathways. Clerks at the ferry dock in Port Clyde may also be helpful. Be sure to pick up the inexpensive map of the island's hiking trails at the ticket office or various shops around the island. Also, a good website maintained by an island resident dispenses good info to first-time visitors (www.monheganwelcome.com).

EXPLORING PORT CLYDE

Port Clyde is located at the tip of a long finger of land about 15 miles south of Route 1. Its charm derives from the fact that it's still just a fishing village. While some small-scale tourist enterprises have made their mark here, it caters primarily to working fishermen and the ferrymen who keep Monhegan supplied.

Head to the **Port Clyde General Store** ★ on the waterfront and soak up the cracker-barrel ambience (there's actually a decent selection of wine here, attesting to encroaching upscalism). Order a sandwich to go, and then drive to the **Marshall Point Lighthouse Museum** (© 207/372-6450; www.marshallpoint.org)—to find it, follow the road along the harbor east and bear right to reach the point. The museum opens weekends only during May, then daily from Memorial Day until Columbus Day. This small lighthouse received a few moments of fame when Forrest Gump turned around here and headed back west during his cross-country walks in the movie, but it also happens to be one of the most peaceful and scenic lighthouses in the state.

EXPLORING MONHEGAN

Walking is the chief activity on the island; it's genuinely surprising how much distance you can cover on these 700 acres (about $1^1/_2$ miles long and $^1/_2$ mile wide). The village clusters tightly around the harbor; the rest of the island is mostly wild land, laced with 17 miles of trails. Much of the island is ringed with high, open bluffs atop fissured cliffs; pack a picnic lunch and hike the **perimeter trail** ★★★, spending much the day sitting, reading, and enjoying the surf rolling in against the cliffs.

The inland trails are appealing in a far different way. Deep, dark **Cathedral Woods** ★★ is mossy and fragrant; sunlight only dimly filters through the evergreens to the forest floor. **Birding** is also a popular spring and fall activity. The island is right on the Atlantic flyway, and a wide variety of birds stop here during annual migrations.

The sole attraction on the island is the good **Monhegan Museum** ★ (www.monhegan museum.org), next to the 1824 lighthouse on a high point above the village. The museum, open for a few hours in the middle of each day from late June through September, has a quirky collection of historical artifacts and provides context for this rugged island's history. Nearby is a small and select art museum that opened in 1998 and features changing exhibits showcasing the works of illustrious island artists, including Rockwell Kent.

The spectacular **view** ★★ from the grassy slope in front of the lighthouse is the real prize, though. The vista sweeps across a marsh, past one of the island's most historic hotels, past Manana Island, and across the sea beyond. Get here early if you want a good seat for the sunset; folks often congregate here after dinner for the view.

Artists are still attracted to this island in great numbers, and many open their **studios** to visitors during posted hours in summer. Some of the artwork runs along the lines of predictable seascapes and sunsets, but much of it rises above the banal. Look for the bulletin board along the main pathway in the village for a listing of the days and hours the studios are open.

WHERE TO STAY & DINE ON MONHEGAN

Things have changed—a little—since the day when you had zero options for sleeping or dining overnight on Monhegan, and had to retreat to the mainland. There are a handful of cottages, simple inns, and plain restaurants on the island. In a pinch, hit the **North End Market** (✆ **207/594-5546**) for picnic supplies.

Monhegan House ★   The handsome Monhegan House has been accommodating guests since 1870, and it has the comfortable, worn patina of a venerable lodging house. The accommodations at this four-story walk-up are austere but comfortable, more so after recent renovations; there are no closets, and everyone uses clean dormitory-style bathrooms except denizens who rent the new two-bedroom suite (with a queen-size bed and a double sofa). The downstairs lobby with fireplace is a welcome spot to sit and take the fog-induced chill out of your bones, since it can get cool on the island even in August. A dining room serves dinner nightly during the short summer season, and Monhegan's first public Wi-Fi hotspot (never thought I'd be writing *that* sentence) and ATM are in the casual eatery the Novelty behind the inn.

Monhegan Island, ME 04852. ✆ **207/594-7983**. www.monheganhouse.com. 31 units (most with shared bathroom). $109–$140 double, $165–$185 suite. Rates include breakfast. MC, V. Closed Oct to late May. **Amenities:** 2 restaurants. *In room:* No phone. Located across road from island's church.

Trailing Yew   At the end of long summer afternoons, guests congregate near the flagpole in front of the main building of this simple, rustic hillside compound. They're waiting for the ringing of the bell that signals the start of the included-with-the-price dinner, just like at summer camp. Inside, guests sit around long tables, introduce themselves to their neighbors, and wait for the family-style repast. This is a friendly, informal place popular with hikers and birders. Guest rooms are simply furnished in a pleasantly dated, summer-home style. Only one of the four guest buildings has electricity, however—guests in rooms without electricity are provided kerosene lamps and instructions for their use. Also, all rooms are unheated. Rates here are charged per person: $90 for adult in 2007, less for children (pro-rated according to age).

Lobster Cove Rd., Monhegan Island, ME 04852. ✆ **207/596-0440**. 37 units (36 with shared bathrooms). $180 double (2 adults); children rates differ according to age. Rates include breakfast, dinner, taxes, and tips. No credit cards. Closed early Oct to mid-May. **Amenities:** Dining room. *In room:* No phone.

Midcoast Maine

Let's say you're traveling east on the Maine coast along Route 1, and you're the sort of person who travels with one eye on the compass or GPS heading. Somewhere around **Rockland,** you suddenly notice something strange: you're pointed almost due *north.* Huh? Yet it's true. The culprit behind this geographic quirk is **Penobscot Bay,** a sizable bite out of the coast that forces a lengthy northerly detour to cross the head of the bay where the Penobscot River flows into it at Bucksport.

Fear not; you'll find some of Maine's most distinctive coastal scenery in this little region, which is dotted with offshore islands and hills rising above the shore. Although the mouth of Penobscot Bay is occupied by two large islands, its waters still churn when the winds and tides are right.

Thanks to both its natural beauty and architectural cuteness, the bay's western shore sees a steady stream of tourist traffic in summer, especially along the stretch of U.S. Route 1 passing through Rockland and **Camden.** You'll need a small miracle to find a weekend bed without a reservation in

summer or early fall. Nevertheless, this is a great area to get a taste of the real Maine coast. Services for travelers are everywhere.

Forming the eastern boundary of Penobscot Bay—though you must drive north and then back *south* to get there— the lovely Blue Hill Peninsula is a sort of back-roads paradise. If you came to Maine to get lost on country lanes that dead-end at the sea or loop back on themselves, this is the place. In contrast to the western shores of Penobscot Bay, this peninsula attracts far fewer tourists and has much more of a lost-in-time, Maine-as-it-was character. The roads here are hilly, winding, and narrow, passing through forests, past old-time saltwater farms, and ticking the edge of a blue inlet here or there. The local radio station's a hoot, too.

By and large, the peninsula is overlooked by the majority of Maine's tourists, especially those who like their itineraries well structured and their destinations clear. In my book, that makes it doubly worth considering for a day or two's visit.

1 ENJOYING THE GREAT OUTDOORS ★

BEACHGOING **Pemaquid Beach Park,** about 15 miles from Damariscotta (follow Rte. 130 to New Harbor, then turn right on Snowball Hill Rd.), and **Swan Lake State Park** (© 207/525-4404), 6 miles north of Belfast, are both worthy beaches, albeit small ones, open June through Columbus Day. Small (figure $1–$4 per person) admission fees are charged at both.

BICYCLING **Vinalhaven** and **North Haven** in Penobscot Bay and **Swan's Island** in Blue Hill Bay are popular with bikers.

GOLFING With 6 of its holes bordering Penobscot Bay, the golf course at the **Samoset Resort** in Rockport (© 800/341-1650 or 207/594-2511) is easily the state's most dramatically scenic and challenging. It's also among the priciest, with greens fees running $105 during peak season—if you can get a reservation.

HIKING   A good destination for hilly coastal hiking is **Camden Hills State Park,** on the west shore of Penobscot Bay. *Fifty Hikes in Southern and Coastal Maine,* by John Gibson (The Countryman Press, 2003), is a reliable directory to trails in the Camden Hills area.

For a coastal walking vacation with all the details taken care of, contact **New England Hiking Holidays,** P.O. Box 1648, North Conway, NH 03860 (© **800/869-0949** or 603/356-9696; www.nehikingholidays.com), which offers guided excursions to Mount Desert Island each summer. The typically 4-night trips involve moderate days of hiking, coupled with nights at comfortable local inns; a lobster feast is included 1 night, as well, to provide calories to burn.

SAILING   An ideal way to combine time in the outdoors with relative luxury and an easy-to-digest education in maritime history is aboard a windjammer cruise on the coast. Maine boasts a sizable fleet of sailing ships both vintage and modern that offer private cabins, meals, entertainment, and adventure. The ships range in size from 53 to 132 feet, and most are berthed in the region between Boothbay Harbor and Belfast. You choose your adventure: An array of excursions is available, from simple overnights to weeklong expeditions gunkholing among Maine's thousands of scenic islands and coves.

> ## (Tips) Summer Camp for Families
>
> If you're looking for an active summer destination with the family in these parts, the summer camp/retreat known as **Medomak** ((C) **207/845-6001;** www.medomakcamp.com) offers an interesting lakeside set of options (as it has been doing since 1904), from archery and tennis to yoga and beer or cheese tastings. You sleep in pine cabins, and the emphasis is on the idea of living lightly on the earth—the director has a background in environmental education, and there are regular programs and workshops. Only catch? This is a half-hour inland from the prime coastal towns such as Camden, Rockland, and Rockport. Also bear in mind that the camp season only runs from late June through mid-August.

Several windjammer festivals and races are held along the Maine coast throughout the summer; these are perfect events to shop for a ship on which to spend a few days. Among the more notable events are **Windjammer Days** in Boothbay Harbor (late June) and the **Camden Windjammer Weekend** in early September. For information on windjammer vacations, contact **Maine Windjammer Association** at (C) **800/807-WIND** (9463) or online at www.sailmainecoast.com.

SKIING   The only downhill peak of any significance along the coast would be the **Camden Snow Bowl** (p. 164), and even it's not terribly lofty. If you'd like to detour inland a bit and ski while visiting the coast, get a pamphlet with basic information about Maine skiing from the **Ski Maine Association,** P.O. Box 7566, Portland, ME 04112 ((C) **207/773-7669;** www.skimaine.com). The association's website also offers up-to-date reports on ski conditions during the winter.

2 ROCKLAND & ENVIRONS ★

185 miles NE of Boston and 78 miles NE of Portland

Located on the southwestern edge of Penobscot Bay, Rockland has long been proud of its blue-collar waterfront roots. Built around the fishing industry, the city long historically dabbled in tourism but never really waded. With the recent decline of local fisheries and the rise of Maine's tourist economy, though, that balance has shifted. Rockland is swiftly being colonized by restaurateurs, innkeepers, artisans, and other folks who are transforming the place from fish-processing center to arts-and-crafts mecca.

The waterfront has a small park from which windjammers come and go, but even more appealing is Rockland's downtown—basically, one long street lined with historic brick architecture. If you're seeking picturesque harbor towns, head instead for Camden, Rockport, Port Clyde, or Stonington. Rockland is best as a local base for exploring a beautiful coastal region, especially if you like your towns to be a bit rough and salty around the edges.

Getting There

By car, U.S. Route 1 passes directly through the center of Rockland. **Concord Coach** (© **800/639-3317;** www.concordtrailways.com) runs two to three daily buses from Portland and Boston.

Surprisingly, Rockland's tiny **airport** (Knox County Regional Airport, airport code RKD) is served by daily direct flights from Boston on **US Airways Express** (© **800/428-4322;** www.usairways.com). There's a local taxi on call, and a single rental car kiosk at the terminal. The airport itself is actually in Owls Head, off Route 73.

From spring through fall (and again in Dec), the **Maine Eastern Railroad** (© **866/637-2457;** www.maineeasternrailroad.com) runs excursion trains between Brunswick (p. 135) and Rockland. Round-trip fares are $40 per adult, $35 for seniors, and $20 for children ages 5 to 15.

Visitor Information

The **Penobscot Bay Regional Chamber of Commerce,** P.O. Box 508, Rockland, ME 04841 (© **800/562-2529** or 207/596-0376; www.therealmaine.com), staffs an information desk at Harbor Park. It's open daily 9am to 5pm Memorial Day to Labor Day, and on weekdays the rest of the year.

EVENTS

The **Maine Lobster Festival** (© **800/562-2529** or 207/596-0376) takes place at Harbor Park the first weekend in August (plus the preceding Thurs and Fri). Entertainers and vendors of all sorts of Maine products—especially, of course, the famous Maine crustaceans—fill the waterfront parking lot for thousands of festivalgoers who enjoy the pleasantly buttery atmosphere. The event includes the Maine Sea Goddess Coronation Pageant. Admission is $7 to $10 per day; food, of course, costs extra.

Rockland celebrates the changing of colors during the last 2 weeks of October—though with a unique twist: a scarecrow-making contest. It's part of the city's Festival of Scarecrows and Harvest Day celebration. Find the 'crows on the lawn of the Farnsworth Art Museum downtown.

Later, in late November, Rockland's Festival of Lights kicks off with Santa arriving not by reindeer but by Coast Guard boat—make of that what you will—then moves on to a program of caroling, horse-drawn carriage rides, a parade, and interesting tours of some of the area's most historic inns. Call © **207/596-0376** for more information.

MUSEUMS

Farnsworth Museum ★★★ Rockland, for all its rough edges, has long and historic ties to the arts. The noted sculptor Louise Nevelson grew up in Rockland, and in 1935 philanthropist Lucy Farnsworth bequeathed a fortune to establish the Farnsworth Museum, which has since become one of the most respected little art museums in New England. Located right downtown, the Farnsworth has a superb collection of paintings and sculptures by renowned American artists with connections to Maine—not only Nevelson but three generations of Wyeths (N. C., Andrew, and Jamie), plus Rockwell Kent, Childe Hassam, and Maurice Prendergast. The exhibit halls are modern, spacious, and well designed, and shows are professionally prepared. In 1998, the museum expanded with the opening of the **Farnsworth Center for the Wyeth Family,** housed in a former Methodist church. The Farnsworth also owns two other buildings open to the public. One is the Farnsworth Homestead, behind the museum, offering a glimpse into the life of prosperous coastal Victorians. Even more interesting is the **Olson House ★**, a 25-minute drive away in the village of Cushing; it's perhaps Maine's most well-known home, immortalized in Andrew Wyeth's famous painting *Christina's World.*

356 Main St., Rockland. (℃ **207/596-6457.** www.farnsworthmuseum.org. Museum $10 adults, $8 seniors and students 18 and older, free for children 17 and under (includes admission to Olson House and Farnsworth Victorian Homestead); Olson House only $4 per person. MC, V. Memorial Day to Columbus Day daily 10am–5pm; rest of the year Tues–Sun 10am–5pm.

Owls Head Transportation Museum ★ (Finds)   You don't need to be a car or plane buff to enjoy this museum, 3 miles south of Rockland on Route 73, though it helps. Founded in 1974, the museum has an extraordinary collection of cars, motorcycles, bicycles, and planes, nicely displayed in a tidy, hangar-like building at the edge of the Knox County Airport. Look for the beautiful early Harley Davidson and a sleek Rolls-Royce Phantom dating from 1929.

Rte. 73, Owls Head. (℃ **207/594-4418.** www.ohtm.org. $8 adults, $7 seniors, $5 children 5–17, $20 families. Apr–Oct daily 10am–5pm; Nov–Mar daily 10am–4pm.

WINDJAMMER TOURS ★★★

During the transition from sail to steam, captains of fancy new steamships belittled old-fashioned sailing ships as "windjammers." The term stuck; through a curious metamorphosis, the name evolved into one of adventure and romance.

Today, windjammer vacations combine adventure with limited creature comforts—such as lodging at a backcountry cabin floating on the water. Guests typically bunk in small two-person cabins with cold running water, a porthole to let in fresh air, and not much else. (You know it's not like a fancy inn when one ship's brochure boasts that all cabins "are at least 6 feet by 8 feet.")

Maine is the windjammer cruising capital of the U.S., and the two most active Maine harbors are **Rockland** and **Camden** on Penobscot Bay. Cruises last from 3 days to a week, during which these handsome, creaky vessels poke around tidal inlets and small coves that ring the beautiful bay. It's a superb way to explore the coast the way it's historically always been explored—from out on the water, looking in. Rates run between about $110 and $150 per day per person (which is $300–$1,000 per person for an entire trip); the best rates are offered early and late in the season.

Cruise schedules and amenities vary widely from ship to ship, even from week to week, depending on the inclinations of captains and the vagaries of Maine weather. A "standard" cruise often features a stop at one or more of the myriad spruce-studded Maine islands (perhaps with a lobster bake on shore), breakfasts served at tables below decks (or perched cross-legged on the deck), and a palpable sense of maritime history as the ships scud through frothy waters. More than a dozen windjammers cruise the Penobscot Bay region during summer (some migrate south to the Caribbean for the winter); the ships vary widely in size and vintage, and accommodations range from cramped and rustic to reasonably spacious and well appointed.

Ideally, you'll have a chance to look at a couple of ships to find one that suits you before signing up. If you can't do that, contact the **Maine Windjammer Association** (℃ **800/807-9463;** www.sailmainecoast.com) for a packet of brochures or simply check its good website of member ships and comparison-shop. If you're trying to book a *last-minute* windjammer cruise on a whim, stop by the chamber of commerce office on the Rockland waterfront (see above) and inquire about open berths.

Captain Lindsey House Inn ★   The three-story, brick Captain Lindsey House is a couple minutes' walk from the Farnsworth Museum. It was originally erected as a hotel in 1835, then went through several subsequent incarnations, including one as headquarters of the Rockland Water Co. Guests enter through a doorway a few steps off Rockland's Main Street into an opulent first-floor common area done up in rich tones, dark-wood paneling, and a mix of antique and contemporary furniture. The upstairs rooms are decorated in simple country style with back-in-time beds, coffee tables, rocking chairs, and desks; even smaller rooms are well done, and rooms on the third floor have attractive exposed pine floors and Oriental carpets. All of the beds are covered with feather duvets, though only two rooms have tubs. This isn't the most luxurious option in town, but it does have plenty of throwback-Maine character.

5 Lindsey St., Rockland, ME 04841. ℂ **800/523-2145** or 207/596-7950. Fax 207/596-2758. www.lindsey house.com. 9 units. $120–$211 double. Rates include breakfast. AE, DISC, MC, V. **Amenities:** Fax service. *In room:* A/C, TV, hair dryer.

East Wind Inn ★   Here's how *you* become the "tenants" in Tenants Harbor: head for the East Wind, acclaimed in places including *Architectural Digest*. It's a former sail loft converted to lodgings, perfectly situated beside the harbor with water views from all rooms and a long wraparound porch. This is your classic seaside hostelry of simple beds with white bedspreads, busy wallpaper, simple colonial reproduction furniture, and tidy rooms; some units have twin beds, though room no. 1 is a good corner suite with a queen-size bed and a sofa. (There are more rooms across the way at a former sea captain's house.) The atmosphere is relaxed almost to the point of ennui, and the service is good. Traditional New England fare is served in an Edwardian-era dining room from spring through fall.

P.O. Box 149, Tenants Harbor, ME 04860. ℂ **800/241-8439** or 207/372-6366. Fax 207/372-6320. www. eastwindinn.com. 22 units (6 with shared bathroom). $66–$109 double (shared bathroom); $126–$149 double (private bathroom); $156–$201 suite; $176–$201 apt. Rates include full breakfast. 2-night minimum stay weekends. AE, DISC, MC, V. Drive south on Rte. 131 from Thomaston to Tenants Harbor; turn left at post office. Pets allowed with advance notice ($15 per pet per night), but not in public rooms of inn. **Amenities:** Dining room.

LimeRock Inn ★★   This beautiful Queen Anne–style inn is on a quiet side street 2 blocks off Rockland's Main Street. Its latest owners have done a commendable job keeping this one of the area's very best choices for B&B. Attention has been paid to detail throughout, from the kingly choices of country Victorian furniture to the Egyptian cotton bedsheets. All guest rooms are welcoming; among the best choices is the Island Cottage Room, a bright and airy south-of-France-like chamber wonderfully converted from an old shed (it has a private deck and a Jacuzzi); the Turret Room, with a lovely canopy bed, cherry daybed, and French doors leading into a bathroom with a claw-foot tub and shower; and the elegant Grand Manan Room, with a big four-poster mahogany king-size bed, fireplace, and double Jacuzzi that puts one in mind of a Southern plantation home.

96 Limerock St. Rockland, ME 04841. ℂ **800/546-3762.** www.limerockinn.com. 8 units. $110–$229 double. Rates include full breakfast. DISC, MC, V. *In room:* Hair dryer, Jacuzzi (some units), fireplace (some units).

Samoset Resort ★★   The Samoset is something of a Maine coast rarity—a modern, self-contained resort with contemporary styling, ocean views, and lots of golf. Both the hotel and town houses here are surrounded by the handsome golf course, with expansive

(Tips) **Boat & Breakfast**

A growing trend in Maine is the "boat-and-breakfast," a working fishing or tour boat that takes overnight lodgers and often serves a meal or does a cruise. You wake up in the morning and disembark. Many (though not all) of Maine's BO-&-B's are berthed in Penobscot. Try one if you're looking for a different way to experience the coast (and pack Dramamine if you tend to become nauseous at sea). A few of the best current options include:

Morning in Maine (℃ **207/594-1844** or 691-SAIL [7245]; www.amorningin maine.com), 4 Beach St., Owls Head, ME 04854. Captain Bob Pratt runs a 55-foot ketch around Penobscot Bay, serving lobster dinners on board and making time for fishing or stargazing. Continental breakfast is also served in the morning. Cost is $500 for two, plus $150 for each addition person up to a maximum of six.

The *Rachel B. Jackson* (℃ **888/405-SAIL** [7245] or 207/288-2216; www. downeastsail.com), P.O. Box 901, Bar Harbor, ME 04609. A 67-foot topsail schooner based in Bar Harbor, the *Rachel B. Jackson* is a handsome reproduction ship of oak, pine, and brass. (It was built in Maine.) The overnight cruise begins at 6:30pm, discharges day travelers, then continues to anchorage somewhere in Acadia; cost, including breakfast but not dinner, is $500 per couple or $750 for a party of four.

The *Symbion* (℃ **207/725-0979**), 252 Pinkham Point Rd., Harpswell, ME 04079. A 38-foot sloop captained by Ken Brigham, the *Symbion* ties up at Card Cove in Harpswell and circumnavigates Casco Bay, allowing guests to take the wheel from time to time (with a bit of instruction). There's a private restroom for overnight guests, and the itinerary may take in local sights such as Eagle Island, Christmas Cove, a series of lighthouses, or Monhegan Island. There's usually a 2-night minimum; a single night costs $500 per couple, if available. Longer cruises of up to 5 days are also possible; overnight rates vary by length of trip.

views of it (and the ocean beyond) from almost every window on the property. The lobby is constructed of massive timbers recovered from an old grain silo in Portland, and guest rooms all have balconies or terraces, plus newly installed flatscreen TVs and improved vanities, makeup mirrors, and fixtures. Bathrooms are extra-big, many with soaker tubs. Golfers like the place for its scenic 18-hole course with several waterside holes, and there's a new golf school. Families can always find plenty of activities for kids here (including a summer camp during high season and babysitting year-round). The health club, with three separate areas, is excellent.

220 Warrenton St., Rockport, ME 04856. ℃ **800/341-1650** or 207/594-2511. www.samoset.com. 178 units. Early July to late Aug $259–$289 double, $369 suite; mid-Apr to early July and late Aug to early Oct $179–$289 double, $259–$289 suite; winter starting at $129 double, $209 suite. Cottage $539–$769. MAP rates available. AE, DC, DISC, MC, V. **Amenities:** 3 restaurants; indoor pool; heated outdoor pool; golf course; golf school; 4 tennis courts; health club; Jacuzzi; sauna; children's programs; concierge; courtesy car; business center; room service; shopping arcade; massage; babysitting; laundry service; dry cleaning. *In room:* A/C, TV, coffeemaker, hair dryer, iron/ironing board, safe.

Another good choice for the family in downtown Rockland is the Italian eatery **Rustica Cucina** (📞 **207/594-0015**), serving standard Italian favorites. It's open for lunch and dinner Monday through Saturday in high season; call for off-season hours.

Cafe Miranda ★★ (Finds) WORLD CUISINE   Hidden on a side street, this tiny restaurant has a huge menu with big flavors and a hip attitude. "We do not serve the food of cowards," owner-chef Kerry Altiero has said. The fare draws from cuisines around the globe. (Altiero again: "It's comfort food for whatever planet you're from.") Given these wide-ranging aspirations, it's surprising how good everything is. Previous items have included chargrilled pork-and-shrimp cakes with a ginger-lime-coconut sauce; pork ribs in smoked jalapeño sauce; Indian almond chicken; Ducks of Spanish Pleasure (a kind of duck curry, perhaps in homage to Bob Dylan?); and small plates such as gazpacho, roasted corn with pickled banana peppers, grilled rare beef with wasabi, and fried oysters with buttermilk sherry vinegar. Sunday brunches feature eggs, hot dogs, salads, and smoked haddock cakes. This place provides some of the best value (and wine and beer lists) of any cafe in Maine.

15 Oak St., Rockland. 📞 **207/594-2034.** www.cafemiranda.com. Reservations strongly encouraged. Small plates and main courses $9–$22. DISC, MC, V. Mon–Sat 5:30–9:30pm; Sun 10:30am–2:30pm and 5:30–9:30pm.

Cod End Cookhouse ★ (Kids) LOBSTER POUND   Part of the allure of Cod End is its hidden and scenic location—it seems as though you've stumbled upon a secret spot. Situated between the Town Landing and the East Wind Inn in little Tenants Harbor, it's a classic lobster joint with fine views of said harbor. You walk through a fish market (where you can buy fish or lobster to go, along with various lobster-related souvenirs) and place your order at an outdoor shack. Lobsters are the main draw here, naturally, but there's plenty more to eat including chowders, stews, linguini with seafood, clam and haddock rolls, and a simple kids' menu of burgers, dogs, and sandwiches (including peanut butter and jelly) for the youngsters.

Commercial St. (next to the town dock), Tenants Harbor. 📞 **207/372-6782.** www.codend.com. Lunch entrees $5–$10; dinner $8–$15. DISC, MC, V. Memorial Day to Sept daily 11am–8:30pm; closed Oct to mid-May.

Primo ★★★ MEDITERRANEAN/NEW AMERICAN   Primo opened in 2000 and quickly developed massive buzz. The restaurant, owned by chef Melissa Kelly and pastry chef Price Kushner, occupies two floors of a century-old home just south of Rockland. The Italian-inflected menu reflects the seasons and draws from local products: Start with a truffle-y mushroom pie, steak salad with Vidalia onions, ale-battered crab, or a cream of (local) asparagus soup. Entrees might include saffron tagliolini with steamed mussels, lobster with peas, grilled leg of lamb with ricotta gnocchi, rhubarb-glazed duck, or seared halibut with Maine fiddleheads. Finish with an inventive dessert: warmed Belgian chocolate cake, an espresso float, a rhubarb-strawberry tartlet with vanilla gelato and strawberry sauce, homemade cannoli, a bowl of Italian doughnuts in cinnamon and sugar, or a *crostata* of local apples. The wine list is outstanding. It's challenging to get a table here during summer, but you can also eat at the upstairs bar.

2 S. Main St. (Rte. 173), Rockland. 📞 **207/596-0770.** www.primorestaurant.com. Reservations strongly suggested. Main courses $23–$38. AE, DC, DISC, MC, V. Summer daily 5:30–9pm; call for dates/hours in off season.

MIDCOAST MAINE

8

ROCKLAND & ENVIRONS

The Waterworks PUB FARE   Set half a block off Rockland's Main Street in the brick garage of the town's former waterworks (of course), this pub has the informal, comfortable feel of a brewpub—except there's no actual brewery. The restaurant is divided into two sections, with lots of sun streaming through tall windows on one side; on the pub side, which is also open and airy, tramp across wooden floors and plunk yourself down at one of the long oak tables for a pint. The dining room to the right is carpeted and quieter. Expect pub fare and comfort food such as roast turkey, pork loin, meatloaf, and fish. New owners took over in 2008 and seem to be upgrading the place gradually.

7 Lindsey St., Rockland. (C) 207/596-2753. Reservations for parties of 6 or more only. Lunch $4–$8.95; dinner $8–$15. DISC, MC, V. Mon–Sat 11am–9pm. Closed Mon in winter.

---

3 CAMDEN ★★

---

8 miles N of Rockland

A quintessential coastal Maine town at the foot of wooded Camden Hills, the affluent village of Camden sits on a picturesque harbor that no Hollywood movie set could improve on. It has been attracting the gentry of the eastern seaboard for more than a century. The mansions of the moneyed set still dominate the town's shady side streets (many have been converted into bed-and-breakfasts), and Camden is possessed of a grace and sophistication that eludes many other coastal towns.

The best way to enjoy Camden is to park your car—which may require driving a block or two off U.S. Route 1, which unfortunately runs right up through the center of town. The village is of a perfect scale to explore on foot, with plenty of boutiques and galleries. Don't miss the hidden town park (look behind the library), either: It was designed by none other than the firm of Frederick Law Olmsted, the famed landscape architect who designed New York City's Central Park.

On the downside, some longtime visitors say that all this attention (and Camden's growing appeal to bus tours) is having a deleterious impact on the atmosphere; yes, there are T-shirt shops here. And there are occasional cries raised about the increasing snootiness of the place. As long as you don't expect a pristine, undiscovered fishing village, you'll be in good shape to enjoy the place.

ESSENTIALS
Getting There
By car, Camden is right on U.S. Route 1. Coming from the south, you can shave a few minutes off the trip here by turning left onto state Route 90 about 6 miles past Waldoboro, bypassing the downtown streets of the city of Rockland. **Concord Coach** ((C) **800/639-3317;** www.concordtrailways.com) runs bus service (two–three trips daily) to Camden from Boston and Portland.

Visitor Information
The **Camden-Rockport-Lincolnville Chamber of Commerce,** P.O. Box 919, Camden, ME 04843 ((C) **800/223-5459** or 207/236-4404; www.camdenme.org), dispenses helpful information from its center at the Public Landing in Camden, where there's also free parking (although spaces are scarce in summer). The chamber is open year-round weekdays and Saturdays. In summer, it's also open Sundays from about 10am to 4pm.

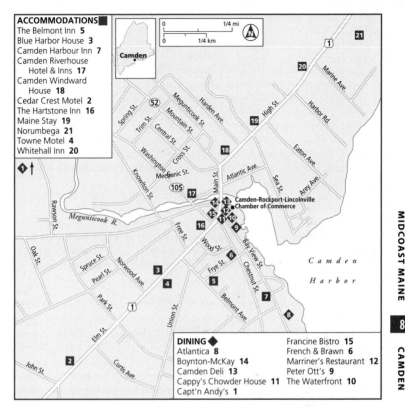

ACCOMMODATIONS ■
The Belmont Inn **5**
Blue Harbor House **3**
Camden Harbour Inn **7**
Camden Riverhouse
   Hotel & Inns **17**
Camden Windward
   House **18**
Cedar Crest Motel **2**
The Hartstone Inn **16**
Maine Stay **19**
Norumbega **21**
Towne Motel **4**
Whitehall Inn **20**

Camden-Rockport-Lincolnville
Chamber of Commerce

Megunticook R.

Camden
Harbor

DINING ◆
Atlantica **8**
Boynton-McKay **14**
Camden Deli **13**
Cappy's Chowder House **11**
Capt'n Andy's **1**

Francine Bistro **15**
French & Brawn **6**
Marriner's Restaurant **12**
Peter Ott's **9**
The Waterfront **10**

MIDCOAST MAINE

8

CAMDEN

EXPLORING CAMDEN

Camden Hills State Park ★★ (© 207/236-3109) is about a mile north of the village center on Route 1. This 6,500-acre park has an oceanside picnic area, camping at 107 sites, a winding toll road up 800-foot Mount Battie with spectacular views from the summit, and a variety of well-marked hiking trails. The day-use fee is $3 for adults and $1 for children ages 5 to 11. It's open from mid-May to mid-October.

If hikes and mild heights don't bother you, I definitely recommend an ascent to the ledges of **Mount Megunticook ★★**, preferably early in the morning before the crowds have amassed (and while mists still linger in the valleys). Leave from near the state park's campground—the trail head is clearly marked—and follow the well-maintained path to open ledges. The hike takes only 30 to 45 minutes; spectacular views of the harbor await, plus glimpses of smaller hills and valleys. Depending on your stamina level, you can keep walking on the park's trail network to Mount Battie, or into lesser-traveled woodlands on the east side of the Camden Hills.

The Camden area is also great for exploring by bike. A nice loop several miles long takes you from Camden into the cute little village of **Rockport ★**, which has an equally scenic harbor and fewer tourists. There's a boat landing, small park, cafe, one of the state's

(**Moments**) **Rocking It in Rockport**

Rockport ★ is absolutely worth a few hours during any trip to Camden. Try this route, either by bike or by car: Take Bayview Street from the center of Camden out along the bay, passing by opulent seaside estates. The road soon narrows and becomes quiet and pastoral, overarched by leafy trees. At the stop sign just past the cemetery, turn left and continue into Rockport. (Along the way, you might pass happily grazing cows.) In Rockport, snoop around the historic harbor and stop by the **Center for Maine Contemporary Art** ★★, 162 Russell Ave. ((℗ **207/236-2875;** www.artsmaine.org), a stately gallery with rotating exhibits of local painters, sculptors, and craftspeople. Admission is $5 per adult (free for children); the gallery is open Tuesday to Saturday from 10am until 5pm and Sundays from 1 to 5pm.

Also visit the **Prism Glass Studio & Gallery** ((℗ **207/230-0061;** www.prism glassgallery.com). This combination glass-blowing gallery and cafe is at 297 Commercial St. in the heart of the village; it's open Wednesdays through Sundays. Patti Kissinger and Lisa Sojka own the 6,500-square-foot facility, which showcases glass blown by top blowers, maintain a studio for stained glass (Tiffany lamp reproductions and the like), and serve impressive cuisine in the Gallery Café.

best art galleries, and a very highly regarded school of photography in Rockport, as well (see the "Rocking It In Rockport" box above).

The Camden-Rockport Historical Society has prepared a 9-mile bike (or car) tour with brief descriptions of some of the historic properties along the way. The brochure describing the tour is free; check for it at the chamber of commerce at the town's Public Landing (see above), or ask for one at the Whitehall Inn (see below). The brochure also includes a 2-mile walking tour of downtown Camden. Bike rentals, repairs, maps, and local riding advice are available in town at **Ragged Mountain Sports,** 46 Elm St. ((℗ **207/236-6664**).

Come winter, there's skiing at the **Camden Snow Bowl** ★ ((℗ **207/236-3438;** www. camdensnowbowl.com), just outside of town on Hosmer's Pond Road. This small, family-oriented ski area has a handful of trails and a modest vertical drop of 950 feet (full-day lift tickets cost $18–$30), but it also has good views of the open ocean and—maybe best of all—an exhilarating **toboggan run** ★★, open weekends only. Toboggans are available for rent, or you can bring your own; either way, it's $5 per person per hour to zip down the slopes.

ON THE WATER

Several sailing ships make Camden their home base, and it's a rare treat to come and go from this harbor, which is considered by many to be the most beautiful in the state.

The 57-foot windjammer *Surprise* was launched in 1918 and has been based in Camden Harbor for a quarter-century now. Captain Jack Moore and his wife Barbara take a maximum of 18 passengers on 2-hour, nonsmoking cruises from the town's Public

Landing (Jack's son Joshua sometimes fills in as captain). Fruit juices and cookies are served on board; children 12 and older are permitted. Four excursions ($30 adults, discount for seniors) are offered daily from July to mid-September, and three are run daily in late May, June, and from mid-September through late October. Reservations are helpful, though you must e-mail (surprise@midcoast.com) to make them; if you can't book ahead, show up at the ticket table on the waterfront and hope for a seat.

The *Schooner Lazy Jack* (© 866/970-2628 or 207/633-3444) has been plying the waters since 1947 and is modeled after the Gloucester fishing schooners of the late 19th century. They run four cruises per day (though only on weekends during the spring and fall) from May through mid-October. There's a maximum of 13 passengers; children must be 10 or older. The 2-hour tours are $28 per person; snacks are available on board, and you can BYOB.

For a more intimate view of the harbor, **Maine Sport Outfitters** (© 800/722-0826 or 207/236-8797) offers sea-kayaking tours of Camden's scenic harbor. The standard tour lasts 2 hours, costs $35 for adults ($30 for children ages 10–15), and takes paddlers out to Curtis Island at the outer edge of the harbor. This beginner's tour is offered three times daily and is an easy, delightful way to get a taste of the area's maritime culture. Longer trips and instruction are also available. The outfitter's main shop, located on Route 1 in Rockport (a few minutes' drive south of Camden), has a good selection of outdoor gear and is worth a stop for outdoor enthusiasts gearing up for local adventures or heading on to Acadia. Sign up for the tours either at the store or at the boathouse, which is located at the head of the harbor (near the town park).

EVENTS

Fall travelers will enjoy Camden's annual Fall Festival Arts & Crafts Show, a weekend of local artworks displayed against the stunningly scenic backdrop of the Camden Hills' changing colors. Rockport has its own October crafts show, the annual Work of the Hand art show, featuring an opening bash and 9 days of impressive contemporary crafts for sale. There's a small admission charge. Call © 207/236-2875 for details.

Packing a Picnic

Harbor Park, on the upper part of Camden's main street, is all you could want in a park: grassy, ideal for people-watching, and possessed of outstanding bay views.

Just north of town, **Camden Hills State Park** (p. 163) is ideal for a picnic, too, whether you're on the bottom section (sea views) or drive to the top of the toll road (great bay views). I'd pick up my picnic at **Boynton-McKay,** a superlative sandwich shop just across Main Street from Harbor Park, or **French & Brawn,** an upscale provisions shop on a corner just down the block; see "Where to Dine," later in this chapter, for more details.

A little hard to find, tiny **Rockport** (p. 164) has its own scenic public park by the boat landing—small, with only a tiny sitting area, but there's a great view of the boats in the harbor. Snag it if you can. Failing that, **Walker Park** and **Mary Lea Park,** just uphill, offer grassy expanses and nice views.

Crafting a Vacation

The Maine coast has been a haven for visual artists, jewelers, sculptors, photographers, potters, and other creative types for as long as I can remember. Studios, galleries, arts centers, and museums of surprising quality crop up nearly everywhere, even in the tiniest coastal villages.

While cruising the coast, you'd do well to drop in to some of these crafts studios—and the best way to find them quickly is to contact the **Maine Crafts Association** (© 207/564-0041; www.mainecrafts.org), which publishes a comprehensive annual guidebook to its member artists, the *Maine Guide to Craft Artists and Culture* (the list is also available online). It contains everything from the big Portland Museum of Art to tiny places such as Handworks Gallery (in Blue Hill) or Isleford Pottery. The guide also includes small black-and-white photographs of member work, so you can get a handle on a particular style before you barrel 30 miles down a peninsula to find it.

Speaking of that, you may wish to call ahead to get studio hours before making the trek to an out-of-the-way crafts studio or gallery. They *are* artists, after all—hours are likely to be a little whimsical.

WHERE TO STAY

Camden vies with Kennebunkport, Maine, and Manchester, Vermont, for the title of "bed-and-breakfast capital of New England." They're everywhere. The stretch of Route 1 just north of the village center—called High Street here—is a virtual bed-and-breakfast alley, with many handsome homes converted to lodgings. Others are tucked away on side streets.

Despite the preponderance of B&Bs, though, the total number of guest rooms in town is still too small to accommodate the crush of peak-season visitors, and during summer or fall, the lodging is tight. It's best to reserve well in advance. You might also try **Camden Accommodations and Reservations** (© 800/344-4830 or 207/236-6090; www.camdenac.com), which provides assistance with everything from booking rooms at local B&Bs to finding cottages for seasonal rentals.

If the inns and B&Bs listed below are unavailable or out of your budget, a handful of area motels and hotels might be able to accommodate you. South of the village center is the **Cedar Crest Motel,** 115 Elm St. (© 800/422-4964 or 207/236-4839), a handsome compound with a coffee shop and a shuttle-bus connection downtown (closed winter; peak-season rates $124–$139), and the longtime mainstay **Towne Motel,** 68 Elm St. (© 800/656-4999 or 207/236-3377), within walking distance of the village (open year-round; peak season, $106–$130 double). Also right in town, just across the footbridge, is the modern, if generic, **Camden Riverhouse Hotel and Inns,** 11 Tannery Lane (© 800/755-7483 or 207/236-0500; www.camdenmaine.com), with an indoor pool, fitness center, and new Wi-Fi and high-speed Internet access (open year-round; peak season $179–$250).

Also, there's camping at seasonally open **Camden Hills State Park** (see "Exploring Camden," above). Sites cost $15 to $30 per night for non-Maine residents in summer, depending on whether you snag one of the new water-and-electrical hookup sites or not. There's a discount from mid-September until the park closes.

The Belmont Inn ★ The Belmont is in a handsome, shingle-style 1890s home with a wraparound porch set in a quiet residential neighborhood of unpretentious homes away from Route 1. The inn has an understated, Victorian sort of theme throughout, featuring numerous floral prints by Maine artist Jo Spiller for instance (there's also a guest room with great morning light named after Spiller). All units have polished wood floors and are furnished simply with eclectic antiques and country touches such as cast-iron stoves, sleigh beds, writing desks, and wingback chairs. Downstairs, there's an elegant common room with a fireplace alcove and built-in benches.

6 Belmont Ave., Camden, ME 04843. ⓒ **800/238-8053** or 207/236-8053. Fax 207/236-9872. www.the belmontinn.com. 6 units. $100–$175 double. Rates include full breakfast. AE, MC, V. From south on Rte. 1: Turn right at 1st stop sign in Camden. Continue straight for 1 block; inn is on your left. From north: After passing through town on Rte. 1, turn left at blinking yellow light. Continue straight for 1 block; inn is on your left. No children 11 and under. *In room:* A/C.

Blue Harbor House ★ On busy Route 1 just south of town, this pale-blue 1810 farmhouse has been an inn since 1978, decorated throughout with a feminine country look. Rooms and suites vary in size; some are smallish, but all include touches such as four-poster beds, claw-foot tubs, wicker furniture, Jacuzzis, triptych mirrors, writing desks, or slipper chairs. The best rooms are the carriage house suites, with their private entrances and extra amenities. The dining room serves nice candlelit prix-fixe dinners and lobster feeds to guests.

67 Elm St., Camden, ME 04843. ⓒ **800/248-3196** or 207/236-3196. Fax 207/236-6523. www.blueharbor house.com. 11 units. $95–$155 double; $145–$185 suite. Rates include breakfast. AE, DISC, MC, V. Closed mid-Oct to mid-May. Pets allowed in some units with prior permission. **Amenities:** Dining room. *In room:* A/C, TV, hair dryer, Jacuzzi (some units), fireplace (some units).

Camden Harbour Inn ★★ (Finds) The 1871 Camden Harbour Inn sits in a quiet neighborhood on a rise with a view of the sea and mountains beyond. It *had* been just another fusty, Victorian-era hotel . . . until 2007, when it got a complete makeover from two Dutchmen (the new owners). No longer a creaky, classic-Maine place of floral wallpaper and simple antiques, it's now a luxury inn with a spa, gourmet restaurant, and even a wine refrigerator in every room. The place is all about modern design. All rooms have private bathrooms and flatscreen TVs, of course, but most also sport views, fireplaces, and/or terraces. The New Amsterdam Suite is one of the poshest in town with its king-size featherbed and two private decks; other suites are designed in Taiwanese, Thai, and Mauritian themes. The inn's within walking distance of downtown, and there's a French restaurant (Natalie's) and bar, as well.

83 Bayview St., Camden, ME 04843. ⓒ **800/236-4266** or 207/236-4200. Fax 207/236-7063. www. camdenharbourinn.com. 22 units. Mid-June to mid-Oct $175–$450 double; $225–$700 suite. Rates include full breakfast. 2-night minimum in peak season. AE, DISC, MC, V. Closed Dec–Apr. Pets allowed on ground floor only. No children 11 and under. **Amenities:** Restaurant; bar; spa. *In room:* A/C, TV, dataport, coffeemaker, hair dryer, iron/ironing board, fireplace (some units).

Camden Windward House ★★ One of the big complaints from travelers staying on Camden's High Street is the noise from passing traffic. The Windward's owners solved that problem by installing double windows on their historic 1854 home; as a result, when you close the door behind you, the village feels miles away. Welcoming common rooms are decorated with a light Victorian hand and cranberry glass; in the library, you'll find a refrigerator, icemaker, and afternoon libations for fixing. Rooms vary in size, but all have flatscreen televisions, phones, and air-conditioning; some suites have gas fireplaces, Jacuzzis, claw-foot tubs, or private decks, as well. Even the simpler Brass Room is elegant with a private deck. Guests choose from lots of hot breakfast entrees, served in a pleasant dining room of maple tables. This place is better and friendlier than it needs to be.

6 High St., Camden, ME 04843. © **877/492-9656** or 207/236-9656. www.windwardhouse.com. 8 units. Peak season $190–$280 double; off season $110–$240 double. Rates include full breakfast and afternoon tea. AE, MC, V. No children 11 and under. **Amenities:** Library; bar. In room: A/C, TV, dataport, hair dryer, Jacuzzi (some units).

Cedarholm Garden Bay Inn ★ This is literally a homegrown operation (the six cottages were built by the owners). The four cottages nearest to the water date from 2001, although they look newer than that; two (Loon and Puffin) are gabled and sport double tiled Jacuzzis, handmade cobblestone fireplaces, and staircases up to second levels, while the other two are simpler, but just as dramatically sited. Two more units farther from the water feature exposed beamwork. All cottages have private decks. The property's 16 acres include gardens that bloom at timed intervals through the season and 460 feet of shoreline (Loon, Tern, Osprey, and Puffin sit right on it) where guests can take a dip or kayak (rentals are two doors down). Lincolnville Beach's tiny harbor is only a mile away.

2159 Atlantic Hwy. (Mailing address: P.O. Box 345, Camden, ME 04843), Lincolnville Beach, ME 04849. © **800/540-3886** or 207/236-3886. www.cedarholm.com. 6 units. $195–$525 double and cottage. Rates include continental breakfast. 2-night minimum stay. DISC, MC, V. Closed Dec–Apr. Children age 16 and over welcome. In room: TV, coffeemaker, hair dryer, iron, fridge, Jacuzzi (some units), no phone (in some).

The Hartstone Inn ★★ (Finds) Chef/innkeeper Michael Salmon draws raves for his cooking at this downtown Camden inn, but the accommodations in the early-19th-century Victorian home are fine, too. He and his wife previously operated a resort in Aruba; you'll be glad they traded down in weather. Now expanded to 21 units, the Hartstone's rooms are studded with antiques and some of the most beautiful decor on the entire Midcoast; suites invariably include Jacuzzis. The full breakfasts are a major reason to come, and **five-course dinners ★** marry local Maine seafood with Caribbean chilies, spices, and cooking techniques (lobster with vanilla beurre blanc). This is definitely a unique dining experience on a coastline full of B&Bs, and one worth traveling to find. There's a cooking school on the premises, too.

41 Elm St., Camden, ME 04843. © **800/788-4823** or 207/236-4259. www.hartstoneinn.com. 21 units, 1 with bathroom across hall. $105–$190 double; $150–$265 suite. MC, V. Closed late Nov to late Apr. **Amenities:** Restaurant. In room: A/C, TV, dataport, Jacuzzi (some units), fireplace (some units).

Inn at Ocean's Edge ★★★ On 22 gorgeous acres, this former one-building inn has committed to a far-reaching concept, remaking itself into one of Maine's premier ocean-front properties. The inn is in the process of adding new buildings, rooms, and spa services, and the inn's restaurant, the Edge, is sure to draw foodies. The grounds feature new gardens, an in-ground vanishing-edge pool, and an inlaid hot tub overlooking the sea. Units in the main inn and the hilltop annex are nearly identical: Jacuzzi tubs, four-poster beds, ocean views, TVs, VCRs, and tasteful wallpaper prints and art. Hilltop units add fridges, coffeemakers, and balconies (but sacrifice distance from the common room), while the new poolhouse suites are most luxe of all. The full breakfasts are a real highlight, too. This is as personable and well-kept a place as you'll find along this stretch of coast, and word is spreading.

Rte. 1, Lincolnville Beach (P.O. Box 74), Camden, ME 04843. (C) **207/236-0945.** Fax 207/236-0609. www.
innatoceansedge.com. 33 units. Peak season $195–$350 double and suite; rest of the year $260–$425.
Rates include full breakfast. AE, DISC, MC, V. **Amenities:** Restaurant; pub; fitness room. *In room:* A/C, TV/
VCR, coffeemaker (some), fridge (some).

Inn at Sunrise Point ★★   This peaceful, private sanctuary 4 miles north of Camden
Harbor seems a world apart from the bustling town. Service is crisp and helpful, and the
setting can't be beat: the edge of Penobscot Bay, down a long, tree-lined gravel road. The
property is a cluster of contemporary, yet classic, shingled buildings; a granite bench and
Adirondack chairs on the lawn allow guests to enjoy the views. Guest rooms and suites—
all named for Maine writers and artists—are spacious, comfortable, and packed with
amenities such as fireplaces, TVs with VCRs, individual heat controls, and stunning
views from the plentiful windows. Breakfasts are served in a sunny conservatory. The
inn's four cottages are even more luxe and private, featuring double Jacuzzis, fireplaces,
wet bars, and private decks; the Fitz Hugh Lane cottage almost feels like it's *in* the bay.

U.S. Rte. 1 (P.O. Box 1344), Camden, ME 04843. (C) **207/236-7716.** Fax 207/236-0820. www.sunrisepoint.
com. 10 units. $300–$445 double and suite; $340–$595 cottage. Rates include full breakfast. Rates do
not include 5% inn service charge or 7% state sales tax. 2-night minimum stay Memorial Day through
Columbus Day. AE, MC, V. Closed Jan–Apr. No children 11 and under. *In room:* TV/VCR, dataport, minibar
(some units), fridge (some units), coffeemaker, hair dryer, iron.

Maine Stay ★★   The Maine Stay is one of Camden's premier bed-and-breakfasts. In
a home dating from 1802 (expanded in Greek Revival style in 1840), it's a classic slate-
roofed New England home set in a shady yard within walking distance of both downtown and Camden Hills State Park. The guest rooms, spaced out over three floors, have
ceiling fans (and a few have televisions); each is distinctively furnished in antiques, and
the lovely wooden floors are often exposed. Top-floor rooms have foreshortened ceilings
with interesting angles. One favorite unit is the downstairs Carriage House Room, away
from the buzz of Route 1, with French doors leading to its own stone patio and a Vermont Castings stove to keep warm.

22 High St., Camden, ME 04843. (C) **207/236-9636.** Fax 207/236-0621. www.mainestay.com. 8 units.
$110–$250 double and suite. Rates include full breakfast. Packages available. AE, MC, V. Children 11 and
over welcome. *In room:* TV (some units), kitchenette (1 unit), fireplace (some units).

Norumbega ★★★ (Finds)   You'll have no problem finding Norumbega; head north
out of town and look for the castle on the right. This 1886 stone mansion, built by
telegraph system inventor Joseph Stearns, is wonderfully eccentric, full of wondrous
curves, angles, and materials; it's on the National Historic Registry. There's extravagant
carved-oak woodwork in the lobby, a stunning oak-and-mahogany-inlaid floor, and a
kingly downstairs billiards room. Guest rooms have been meticulously restored and furnished with antiques; some have fireplaces, three ground-level units sport private decks,
and most now have televisions. Two suites rank among the finest in northern New England: the amazingly bright and airy Library Suite, in the original two-story library (it has
an interior balcony) and the sprawling Penthouse with its superlative bay views, king-size
bed, and huge oval tub. Don't miss Norumbega's "Murder Mystery" weekends; solve the
mystery first, and you win a free stay.

63 High St., Camden, ME 04843. (C) **877/363-4646** or 207/236-4646. www.norumbegainn.com. 12 units.
July to mid-Oct $285–$475 double and suite; mid-May to June and late Oct $125–$275 double and suite;
Nov to mid-May $225–$375 double and suite. All rates include full breakfast and evening snacks and
refreshments. 2-night minimum in summer, weekends, and holidays. AE, DISC, MC, V. Children age 7 and
older welcome. **Amenities:** Billiards room. *In room:* TV (most units), fireplace (some units).

8

CAMDEN

Whitehall Inn ★ The Whitehall is a venerable Camden establishment, thanks (but only partly) to local poetess Edna St. Vincent Millay, who was "discovered" in a room here while still a teen; the room where it happened still has the 1904 Steinway she played. Set at the edge of town on busy Route 1, the three-story inn has a striking architectural integrity of columns, gables, a long roofline, and atmospherically winding staircases. The antique furnishings—including a handsome Seth Thomas clock, Oriental carpets, and cane-seated rockers on the front porch—are cared for impeccably. Guest rooms are simple, yet appealing; many lack phones and TVs, and a few double up on shared bathrooms, but even these "economy" rooms have sturdy Maine charm. The only drawback? That traffic; try to get a room in back.

52 High St., Camden, ME 04843. ☎ **800/789-6565** or 207/236-3391. www.whitehall-inn.com. 50 units (8 with shared bathroom). July to mid-Oct $149–$199 double; mid-May to June $99–$159 double. Rates include full breakfast and afternoon tea. AE, MC, V. Closed mid-Oct to mid-May. **Amenities:** 2 restaurants; tennis court; tour desk; conference rooms; babysitting. *In room:* TV (some units), no phone (some units).

WHERE TO DINE

In addition to its fine-dining options, downtown Camden has a wealth of places to nosh, snack, lunch, and brunch. Some great doughnuts, for instance, are fried up at **Boynton-McKay,** 30 Main St. (☎ **207/236-2465**), a former pharmacy that's now a great spot for lunch, coffee, a sandwich, or blue-plate special such as grilled meatloaf. It's closed Mondays. Just up the street, pick up a bag of gourmet groceries at **French & Brawn** (☎ **207/236-3361**) on Main Street at the corner of Elm. Other local favorites include **Capt'n Andy's,** 156 Washington St. (☎ **207/236-2312**), for its chowder and seafood; and the **Camden Deli,** 37 Main St. (☎ **207/236-8343**), serving gourmet sandwiches, beer, and wine.

Atlantica ★★ SEAFOOD/ECLECTIC Atlantica gets high marks for its seafood menu, always well prepared under the management of executive chef Ken Paquin, a graduate of the Culinary Institute of America (and former top dog at a number of other establishments, including the Equinox in Vermont). On the waterfront with a small indoor seating area and an equally small deck, Paquin cooks subtly creative fare such as seared dayboat scallops over lemon risotto with a steamed lobster; roasted breast of duck with a sweet-corn béarnaise sauce; butter-poached lobster in a mushroom fondue; porcini-dusted bass; chipotle-rubbed pork; creamy chowders; Pemaquid oysters; and the catch of the day, perhaps plated with a pistachio "crumble," a red-beet purée, or a polenta cake.

1 Bayview Landing. ☎ **888/507-8514** or 207/236-6011. www.atlanticarestaurant.com. Reservations suggested. Main courses $26–$36. AE, MC, V. Wed–Mon 5–9pm. Closed Nov–Mar.

Cappy's Chowder House Kids SEAFOOD/AMERICAN "People always remember their meals here," say local fans of Cappy's, a local institution smack in the middle of Camden for close to 3 decades. Well, maybe. Travelers—especially families—do drift in here to drink up the atom and fill up on the famous thick clam chowder (it's even been noted in *Gourmet* magazine). There's also seafood stew, rotating special chowders, burgers, club sandwiches, fried fish, lobster and lobster rolls in summer, and . . . a wine list? Why, yes. It's all well worth a quick stop if you're looking for a reasonably priced and filling meal for the family late at night. By the way, who's Cappy? An old salt who worked the local docks for years; he's not with us any longer—but his name lives on. There's also a little bakery around the side.

1 Main St. ☎ **207/236-2254.** www.cappyschowder.com. Main courses $8–$20. MC, V. Daily 11:30am–9pm.

Chez Michel ★ (Kids) FRENCH/SEAFOOD   This French-and-seafood restaurant, right across the road from the Islesboro ferry, has had a great local following since 1992 when chef Jean Michel Hetuin opened it. That's because it offers good value amid a sea of higher-priced area options, though inside it's not nearly as fancy you as might expect from the name. Instead, the menu blends elements of French, Maine, and American cooking. You might begin with mussels steamed in wine or locally smoked salmon, then move on to duck au poivre, steak Oscar, or haddock in meunière sauce . . . or you might get plunked down next to a local family enjoying a feed of lobsters, scallops, pasta, or fried oysters, and decide to join in the fun. Specials could be anything from salmon Béarnaise to pan-fried haddock or tenderloin brochette—or could be a simple chicken parm.

Rte. 1, Lincolnville Beach. ℂ **207/789-5600.** Entrees $13–$18. AE, DC, DISC, MC, V. Tues–Sat 4–9:30pm; Sun 11:30am–9pm.

Francine Bistro ★★ FRENCH BISTRO   This place feels more like a French brasserie in Manhattan's Meatpacking District than a coastal seafood joint—and that's a good thing. A meal from chef/owner Brian Hill (long-ago of the seminal Boston alternative-rock band Heretix, but I digress) might begin with fish, onion, or lentil soup; a seviche of halibut, serrano chilies, and red onions; mussels in bordeaux and shallots; or skewers of grilled lamb with white pesto, orange, and endive—nice to see in a state dominated by fried fish and lobster. Entrees might run to roast chicken with a chèvre gratin or a cauliflower-cheese hash; duck a l'orange; a crispy skate wing with Jerusalem artichokes; a roasted sea bass in caramelized garlic sauce; seared halibut with shrimp; a haddock stuffed with scallops; or some reliable steak frites. Hill cut his teeth in some truly great kitchens around the country, and it shows.

55 Chestnut St., Camden. ℂ **207/230-0083.** www.francinebistro.com. Reservations recommended. Entrees $17–$25. MC, V. Tues–Sat 5:30–10pm.

The Lobster Pound ★ LOBSTER POUND   Among the many lobster shacks up and down the Midcoast, this one holds its own by offering not only steamed lobsters and lobster stew but a variety of surf-and-turf combos and shore dinners (read: fried fish sided with fries). But, surprisingly, they also serve "regular" meals leaning toward the home-cooking end of things: grilled steaks, roast turkey dinners with the trimmings, grilled swordfish, and combinations thereof. The baked scallops are good, too. There's also a takeout shack for those who don't want to stick around for a sit-down meal.

U.S. Rte. 1, Lincolnville Beach. ℂ **207/789-5550.** Sandwiches $5.95–$7.20; lunch portions $9.95–$15; dinner entrees $12–$37. AE, DISC, MC, V. Daily 11:30am–8pm.

Marriner's Restaurant DINER   "The last local luncheonette" is how Marriner's sums itself up, and has used a sign with the legend DOWN HOME, DOWN EAST, NO FERNS, NO QUICHE to also get its message across: namely, that this is a small and no-frills affair, totally Maine, so don't expect snootiness or pretense. The space is done up in a not-too-subtle nautical theme of pine booths and vinyl seats, some of which are sometimes held together with duct tape. These folks have been dishing up filling breakfasts and lunches for the locals since 1942; it's a great place for early risers to get a quick start on the day and check out the local characters. Lunches are basic and good, too, especially the chowders and lobster and crab rolls—and don't miss the homemade pies.

35 Main St., Camden. ℂ **207/236-4949.** Most breakfast items $4–$6; lunch items $4–$12 (mostly under $7). MC, V. Daily 6am–2pm.

Peter Ott's AMERICAN   Peter Ott's has attracted a steady stream of satisfied local customers and repeat-visitor yachtsmen since it opened in the middle of Camden in 1974. While it poses as a steakhouse with simple wooden tables and chairs and meat dishes (charbroiled Black Angus with mushrooms and onions, sirloin steak Dijonaise), it's also said by some locals to serve some of the best seafood in town, such as pan-blackened fish and grilled salmon in a lemon-caper sauce. And the salad bar continues to draw local raves. Be sure to leave room for specialty coffees and desserts. One caution: it's pricier than most family restaurants in Maine.

16 Bayview St., Camden. (*C* 207/236-4032. Main courses $17–$26. MC, V. Daily 5:30–9pm.

The Waterfront SEAFOOD   The Waterfront disproves the restaurant rule of thumb that "the better the view, the worse the food." Here you can watch multimillion-dollar yachts and windjammers come and go (angle for a harborside seat on the deck), yet still be pleasantly surprised by the food. The house specialty is fresh seafood. Lunch and dinner menus are an enterprising mix of old favorites and creative originals; expect fried clams, crab cakes, boiled lobster, and a fisherman's platter of fried seafood, but also more adventurous offerings. Those might run to a warm duck breast salad with spinach, kalamata olives, roasted red peppers, and feta cheese; sautéed Gulf shrimp primavera with olive oil; or some Chablis-tossed linguine with vegetables and Parmesan cheese. More earthbound fare includes burgers, pitas, and strip steaks. A lighter, pub-style menu is served between 2:30 and 5pm.

40 Bayview St. on Camden Harbor. (*C* 207/236-3747. Main courses lunch $7–$15, dinner $16–$18; lobsters market price. AE, MC, V. Daily 11:30am–9:30pm.

4 BELFAST TO BUCKSPORT ★

Belfast is 18 miles N of Camden; Bucksport is 19 miles NE of Belfast.

The northerly stretch of Penobscot Bay is rich in history, especially maritime history. In the mid–19th century, Belfast and Searsport produced more than their share of ships, along with the captains to pilot them on trading ventures around the globe. In 1856 alone, 24 ships of more than 1,000 tons were launched from Belfast. The now-sleepy village of Searsport once had 17 active shipyards, which turned out some 200 ships over the years.

When shipbuilding died out, the Belfast area was sustained by a thriving poultry industry. Alas, that too declined as the industry moved south. In recent decades the area has attracted artisans of various stripes who sell their wares at various shops. Tourists tend to pass through the region quickly, en route from the tourist enclave of Camden to the tourist enclave of Bar Harbor. It's worth slowing down for.

ESSENTIALS

Getting There
Route 1 connects Belfast, Searsport, and Bucksport.

Visitor Information
The **Belfast Area Chamber of Commerce,** P.O. Box 58, Belfast, ME 04915 (*C* **207/ 338-5900;** www.belfastmaine.org), staffs an information booth at 17 Main St., near the waterfront park, that's open May to November daily from 10am to 6pm. Farther north, try the **Bucksport Bay Area Chamber of Commerce,** 52 Main St. (P.O. Box 1676),

Bucksport, ME 04416 (✆ **207/469-6818** or 888/678-6746; www.bucksportchamber. **173**
org).

EXPLORING THE REGION

When approaching the area from the south, some splendid historic homes may be viewed by veering off Route 1 and entering downtown Belfast via High Street (look for the first DOWNTOWN BELFAST sign). The **Primrose Hill District** along High Street was the most fashionable place for prosperous merchants to settle during the early and mid–19th century, and their stately homes reflect an era when stature was equal to both the size of one's home and the care one took in designing and embellishing it. Downtown Belfast also has some superb examples of historic brick commercial architecture, including the elaborate High Victorian Gothic–style building on Main Street that formerly housed the Belfast National Bank.

If you'd like to explore the area by water, call Harvey Schiller at **Belfast Kayak Tours** (✆ **207/382-6204**), or just show up at the Belfast City Pier boat ramp. With a great deal of charm and even more enthusiasm, Harvey will provide paddle instruction and take you out for a guided tour—the perfect way to get up close and personal with both the river and Penobscot Bay. (His handmade uniform is a kick, too.) Trips last about 2 hours. They also rent kayaks to kayakers intent on constructing their own itineraries.

At the northern tip of the bay, the Penobscot River squeezes through a dramatic gorge near Verona Island, which Route 1 spans on an attractive suspension bridge. The new **Penobscot Narrows Observatory** ★ (www.maine.gov/observatory) sits high on this bridge. However, there is an addition to the Midcoast: **a new observatory on the lovely Verona Island bridge** (U.S. Route 1, just outside Bucksport). It's said to be the world's *highest* public bridge observatory, some 437 feet above the river, with panoramic views of the mountains, lakes, and even Penobscot Bay. The elevator ride to the glassed-in viewing area takes just 1 minute, and placards help you interpret the landscape features you're looking at. It's open from mid-May through the end of October.

You must enter and pay admission to the adjacent **Fort Knox State Park** (✆ **207/469-7719**) first to enjoy the views; this easily defended pinch in the river was perceived

---

ⓜ **Moments** **A Quirky Museum**

If you enjoy kitsch and uniquely American things, on a rainy day in Belfast, you could do worse than making the 30-minute detour inland through the hills to lit-tle Thorndike and experience the **Bryant Stove Museum** (✆ **207/568-3665;** www.bryantstove.com), a nothing-if-not-entertaining experience. Joe and Bea Bryant exhibit, refurbish, and sell gorgeous cast-iron woodstoves. But looking these over is only part of the fun: The premises also house a huge selection of vintage dolls, toys, antique cars, player pianos, calliopes, concertinas, and oodles of other musical instruments and mechanical contraptions. Entering the rooms where the goodies are stored is like opening a door into an alternate universe— one presided over by suspender-wearing Joe, who sings lustily along with the pianos while puppets (rigged to the instruments) bob along in time. Get there by taking Waldo Avenue (Rte. 137) west out of Belfast for about 15 miles, then turn-ing right onto Route 200 and continuing a bit farther. The shop attached to the museum is open 8am to 4:30pm Monday to Saturday. Admission is free.

to be of strategic importance in the 1840s, when the solid and imposing fort was constructed. While it was never attacked, the fort was manned during the Civil War and Spanish-American War. It's an impressive edifice to explore, with graceful granite staircases and subterranean chambers that produce wonderful echoes. Admission to the park only is $3 for adults and $1 for children 11 and under; there's a $2 per person (all ages) surcharge to ascend the observatory. The park is open from 9am until sunset daily from May through October, though the tower closes at 5pm each day during the season.

Across the river from Fort Knox in the paper-mill town of Bucksport is **Northeast Historic Film** (📞 **800/639-1636** or 207/469-0924; www.oldfilm.org), an organization founded in 1986 and dedicated to preserving and showing early films related to New England. In 1992 the group bought Bucksport's Alamo Theatre, which was built in 1916 and closed (after a showing of *Godzilla*) in 1956. Films are shown weekends in the renovated theater; call or check the group's website to see what's coming up. Visitors can also stop by the museum at the front of the theater (open Mon–Fri 9am–4pm) to browse videos and other items.

THE SEAFARING LIFE

Penobscot Marine Museum ★★★ The Penobscot Marine Museum is one of the best small museums in New England. Housed in a cluster of eight historic buildings atop a gentle rise in tiny downtown Searsport, the museum does a deft job of educating visitors about the vitality of the local shipbuilding industry, the essential role of international trade to daily life in the 19th century, and the hazards of life at sea. Exhibits (such as "The Art of Lobstering") are uncommonly well organized, and wandering from building to building induces a keen sense of wonderment at the vast enterprise that was Maine's maritime trade, and there's also the landscape art of Thomas and James Buttersworth and Robert Salmon. Among the most intriguing exhibits are a wide selection of dramatic marine paintings, black-and-white photographs of many of the 286 weathered sea captains who once called Searsport home, exceptional photographs of a 1902 voyage to Argentina, and an early home decorated in the style of a sea captain, complete with lacquered furniture and accessories hauled back from trade missions to the Orient. Throughout, the curators do a fine job of both educating and entertaining visitors. It's well worth the price if you're the least bit interested in Maine's rich culture of the sea.

5 Church St. (at corner of U.S. Rte. 1), Searsport. 📞 **207/548-2529.** www.penobscotmarinemuseum.org. $8 adults, $3 children 7–15, $18 families. Memorial Day to mid-Oct Mon–Sat 10am–5pm; Sun noon–5pm. Last tickets sold at 4pm.

WHERE TO STAY

If you're stuck for a bed along this stretch of the coast and don't mind the chain-hotel ambience for a night, the **Comfort Inn,** 159 Searsport Ave. (U.S. Rte. 1) (📞 **207/338-2090**), is a good backup option. Some rooms have kitchenettes and/or whirlpools; there's a pool; a small breakfast is served; and some rooms come with sublime views of the bay (if there's no fog, that is). However, check as soon as possible—the place sometimes fills up early. High season double rooms run from $109 to $209 per night; suites are more expensive.

The White House ★★ This architecturally stunning Greek Revival home is just a 10-minute walk from downtown Belfast and offers a lot more B&B than you might expect for the rates, which are somewhat low for this part of the coast. Originally built as a sea captain's home in the 1840s and topped with a striking eight-sided cupola, the home has been exquisitely refurnished (mainly in four-poster beds), painted, and

Packing a Picnic

Searsport has an outstanding little pocket park just off the hustle of busy Route 1; look for the post office, then walk downhill. It makes for a great quick picnic. Pick up rudimentary foods at **Tozier's Market,** on Route 1 just south of the Maritime Museum; you can't miss it.

wallpapered. Downstairs, guests have the run of a library, an elegant parlor area, and a dining room where the hearty breakfasts are served. All of the guest rooms (some with TVs) have private bathrooms stocked with soft Egyptian cotton towels and robes. The Belfast Bay unit is an over-the-top Louis XVI–style room with a fireplace, crystal chandelier, Jacuzzi, and water views; the less fancy Copperbeech suite, at the back of the house, is also appealing: it features a sitting room and classic pumpkin pine floors.

1 Church St., Belfast, ME 04915. ✆ **888/290-1901** or 207/338-1901. Fax 207/338-5161. www.mainebb. com. 6 units (1 with private hall bathroom). $125–$185 double. Rates include full breakfast. DISC, MC, V. **Amenities:** Library; laundry service. *In room:* TV (some units), hair dryer.

Wildflower Inn ★ (**Value**)   This former sail-maker's home is elegant yet comfortable. A bright, open sitting room and dining area are good introductions for travelers looking for something more personal than a hotel; it's less fusty—and less expensive—than expected. They don't put on airs here, yet rooms are spacious, spotlessly clean, and filled with welcome extras: bottles of water, chocolates, wineglasses, corkscrews. The Delphinium Room is the most luxurious, with its bay view, Jacuzzi, and king-size bed; the Sage and Viola rooms feature antique sink fittings, while the Buttercup Room is furnished with a smallish double bed and lacks a TV. Breakfasts might include blueberry pancakes, bacon, or quiche. (Light sleepers should note that the inn sits right on busy Rte. 1.) The basement is a comfy retreat room where guests escape to play backgammon, watch films, or snooze on the couch; and the gardens host an abundance of, yes, wildflowers.

2 Black Rd. (U.S. Rte. 1), Searsport, ME 04974. ✆ **888/546-2112** or 207/548-2112. www.wildflowerinnme. com. 4 units. $89–$145 double. Rates include full breakfast. MC, V. *In room:* TV (most units), coffeemaker, no phone.

WHERE TO DINE

Just south of Belfast on Route 1, **Seng Thai** ★ (✆ **207/338-0010**)—one of many Thai restaurants you'll be surprised to find as you cruise up and down the Maine coast—serves up well-spiced classic dishes such as pad Thai and various curries, but also a uniquely creative take on more upscale fare such as lobster and fish. Top off your meal with a potent Thai tea or coffee. It's open daily from 11am until 10pm in summer, until 8 or 8:30pm in winter.

A surprisingly hip new spot in downtown Belfast is **three tides,** 3 Pinchy Lane (next to the waterfront; ✆ **207/338-1707;** www.3tides.com); it's got a more contemporary, urban feel than Belfast's workaday bars and pubs. They serve fancy sandwiches, salads, panini, local oysters and mussels, and a selection of beers. Jazz shows and dance parties have been known to break out. The outdoor deck is a good spot to relax while the sun goes down. It's open Tuesday to Saturday from 4pm onward.

Finally, if you're packing a picnic, one of Maine's oldest, biggest, and best natural-foods stores, the **Belfast Co-op** ★ (© **207/338-2532**), is at 123 High St. Not every-thing here is for the virtuous: The selection of imported beers and the cuts of organic beef are surprisingly good; the co-op also features a deli. It's open from 7:30am to 8pm daily.

Chase's Daily Restaurant ★ VEGETARIAN   A vegetarian restaurant that doesn't make a point of being too politically correct, Chase's maintains a good balance between simple, hearty food and more sophisticated offerings. Breakfast ranges from oatmeal to breakfast burritos to healthy fruit smoothies; lunch segues nicely into a menu of pizzas, sandwiches, soups, and salads with an emphasis on Asian, Latin American, and European themes. There's also a daily pasta dish. Coffee drinks here are high quality: The restaurant serves fair-trade beans roasted at a New York coffeehouse. The whole room is inviting and light-filled, with wooden floorboards and a pressed-tin ceiling; Sunday brunches and Friday-night-only dinners are very highly regarded around town, so call ahead about table availability if you're interested.

96 Main St., Belfast. © **207/338-0555.** Main courses $3.50–$14. DISC, MC, V. Tues–Sat 7am–5pm (Fri to 9pm); Sun 8am–2pm.

Darby's AMERICAN/ECLECTIC   Located in a Civil War–era pub with attractive stamped tin ceilings and a beautiful back bar with Corinthian columns, Darby's is a popular local hangout that boasts a comfortable, neighborhoody feel. Order a Maine microbrew or a single-malt whiskey while you read the menu, which is more creative than you might expect given the surroundings. Darby's serves up not only basic bar favorites (burgers on a bulky roll), but also more inventive dishes such as mahogany duck, pad Thai, and big salads. The food is nothing out of this world, but the convivial pubby atmosphere at the bar is. Desserts here are homemade and tend toward the basic, with cheesecake, pies, and an interesting "Russian cream." If you like the artwork on the wall, ask about it—it was probably painted by a local artist, and it's probably for sale.

155 High St., Belfast. © **207/338-2339.** Reservations suggested after 7pm. Main courses $5.95–$9.95 lunch, $11–$20 dinner. AE, DC, DISC, MC, V. Mon–Sat 11:30am–3:30pm and 5–9pm; Sun noon–3:30pm and 5–8:30pm.

MacLeod's ECLECTIC HOME-STYLE   In Bucksport, George MacLeod is the man. MacLeod's pub is the comfortable, everybody-knows-your-name sort of spot that every small town needs; and in downtown Bucksport, this is it. MacLeod's teems on weekends with local residents, from workers at the big pulp mill nearby to businessmen to the blow-in tourist. With its simple wood tables, Windsor chairs, and upbeat music, this won't be confused with a place for fancy dining, but it does offer good meals, sizable portions, and consistent quality. For dinner, entrees might include lamb shish kabobs, raspberry-flavored chicken, baked scallops, or a unique "lasagna al pescatore" made with shrimp, scallops, crabmeat, and lobster sauce.

Main St., Bucksport. © **207/469-3963.** Reservations recommended on weekends and in summer. Main courses $5–$11 lunch, $9–$15 dinner. AE, DC, MC, V. Mon–Fri 11:30am–9pm; Sat–Sun 5–9pm (to 8pm in off season).

The Rhumb Line NEW AMERICAN   The Rhumb Line doesn't look like anything special from the outside, but it actually serves pretty good meals. The chef features locally grown ingredients where possible—tomatoes in the salad might have been picked out back, the tender horseradish-crusted salmon (served with a rémoulade) farmed in nearby

Ellsworth, the salmon in the salmon salad smoked in Belfast. Start with a fresh salad, escargot, shrimp wrapped in prosciutto, or some crostini with hot crab dip. As for the entrees, stick with favorites such as grilled rack of lamb with mint-fig balsamic vinegar, or the sautéed filet of haddock with roasted garlic, basil oil, and olives.

200 E. Main St. (Rte. 1), Searsport. ✆ **207/548-2600.** Reservations suggested. Main courses $21–$28. MC, V. Summer daily 5:30–8pm; winter Sat only 5:30–8pm.

Young's Lobster Pound ★ Finds LOBSTER This is one of my favorite lobster shacks in all of Maine—though calling it a "shack" might be a euphemism. Beyond the driveway you'll find a hangar-size door; fear not, for behind it sits a counter of friendly locals taking your order. Guys in slickers and boots do all the dirty work, plucking lobsters from long lobster tanks gurgling seawater. Eat upstairs, where picnic tables are arrayed in an open, barn-like area, or out on the deck with views across the river to Belfast. Remember: Don't wear your finest threads, and get *lots* of napkins. The lobsters, served on paper plates with butter and corn on the cob, are tasty and fairly inexpensive.

4 Mitchell St., E. Belfast. ✆ **207/338-1160.** Reservations not accepted. Lobster prices seasonal. MC, V. Daily 7:30am–7pm. Closed Dec–Mar. From Belfast, follow U.S. Rte. 1 north across bridge; just after bridge, look for signs to pound on right. Turn right and follow road to the water.

---

5 CASTINE & ENVIRONS ★★

Quiet little Castine, off the beaten track, must be one of the most gracious villages in Maine. It's not so much the handsome, meticulously maintained mid-19th-century homes that fill the side streets. Nor is it the location on a quiet peninsula, 16 miles south of tourist-clotted Route 1. No, what lends Castine most of its charm are the splendid, towering elm trees that still overarch many of the village's streets. Before Dutch elm disease ravaged the nation's elms, much of America once looked like this. Through perseverance and a measure of good luck, Castine has managed to keep several hundred of its elms alive, and it's worth the drive here to see them.

But Castine offers more than trees. It's enduringly quiet, which is probably what you're seeking in your Maine vacation. And it's full of history. This outpost served as a strategic town during various battles among the British, Dutch, French, and colonists in the centuries following its settlement in 1613 (yes, 7 years before Plymouth Rock). Castine was occupied by each of those groups at some point; and historical personages such as Miles Standish and Paul Revere passed through town. It was a very important place—strange, because now it seems almost thoroughly forgotten, except for the maritime academy at one end of the village, which still trains young sailors and cadets. Castine still looks and feels like it has not changed much since the locals welcomed British soldiers with open arms during the American Revolution.

You'll have to work (which means drive significant distances) to find nightlife and dining, but if you like your towns quiet, you'll love it here.

ESSENTIALS
Getting There
Castine is 16 miles south of U.S. Route 1. Turn south on Route 175 in Orland (east of Bucksport) and follow it to Route 166, which winds its way to Castine. Route 166A offers another, alternate route along Penobscot Bay.

Castine lacks a formal information center, though the clerks at the **town office** (✆ 207/
326-4502) are often helpful with local information. (Don't abuse this privilege, though,
since they have actual work to do running the town.) The town office is open weekdays
from 11am to 3pm. The **Blue Hill Peninsula Chamber of Commerce** (see later in this
chapter) handles tourist inquiries in a more formal manner.

EXPLORING CASTINE

One of the town's more intriguing attractions is the **Wilson Museum** ★ (✆ 207/326-
9247; www.wilsonmuseum.org) on Perkins Street, an appealing and quirky anthropo-
logical museum constructed in 1921. This small museum contains the collections of
John Howard Wilson, an archaeologist and collector of prehistoric artifacts from around
the globe. His gleanings are neatly arranged in a staid, classical arrangement of the sort
that proliferated in the late 19th and early 20th centuries. The museum is open from the
end of May to the end of September, Tuesday to Sunday from 2 to 5pm; admission is
free.

Next door is the affiliated **John Perkins House** (same phone number as the museum),
Castine's oldest home. It was occupied by the British during the Revolution and the War
of 1812, and a tour features demonstrations of old-fashioned cooking techniques. This
house is only open in July and August, and only Wednesdays and Sundays (from
2–5pm). There is a fee for guided tours of the home. Two additional attractions in the
Wilson-Perkins complex (it's almost like a little historical campus, really) include a **black-
smith shop** and the **Hearse House,** both free to tour; both of these outbuildings have
the same limited hours as the Perkins House.

Castine is also home to the **Maine Maritime Academy** (✆ 207/326-4311), which
trains sailors for the rigors of life at sea with the merchant marine. The campus is on the
western edge of the village, and the 500-foot T.S. (for Training Ship) *State of Maine* ★,
a hulking black-and-white vessel, is often docked here—all but overwhelming the village.
(It's off cruising to places such as Odessa, Germany, and Gibraltar when it's not here.) Free
half-hour tours of the ship are offered in summer when the ship is in port.

ON THE WATER

This is a lovely open harbor, with open land and forest edging the watery expanse. A
couple of options exist for cruising on the water:

Castine Kayak Adventures (✆ 207/866-3506; www.castinekayak.com) offers full-
($110) and half-day ($60) sea kayak tours departing from Dennett's Wharf restaurant.
Both trips are appropriate for those without experience; a brief intro will get you started
with this graceful and often meditative sport. You'll often spot wildlife, such as bald
eagles, harbor seals, and ospreys.

A TOUR OF CAPE ROSIER ★★

Across the Bagaduce River from Castine is Cape Rosier, one of Maine's best-kept secrets.
The bad news is, to reach the cape you need to backtrack to Route 175, head south
toward Deer Isle, and then follow Route 176 to the turnoff for Cape Rosier—about 18
miles of driving to cross 1 mile of water. As a dead-end peninsula, there's no through
traffic and roads suddenly turn to dirt in sections. The cape still has a wild, unkempt
flavor with salty views of Penobscot Bay; it's not hard to imagine that you're back in
1940s Maine.

A loop of 15 miles or so around the cape starting on Goose Falls Road—begin by following Route 176 to Brooksville, then taking Cape Rosier Road—is suitable for travel by mountain bike or as a leisurely car trip. The views are uncommonly beautiful, with a mix of blueberry barrens, boreal forest, farmsteads, summer estate houses, and coves dotted with yachts and lobster boats. There's virtually no commercial development of any sort. It's no accident that Helen and Scott Nearing, the late back-to-the-land gurus and authors of *Living the Good Life,* chose to settle here when Vermont became too developed for their tastes. A number of Nearing acolytes continue to live on Cape Rosier.

If the weather's agreeable, stop for a walk on the state-owned **Holbrook Island Wildlife Sanctuary,** a 1,200-acre preserve laced with trails and abandoned roads. The sanctuary is located at the northern end of the cape (look for signs). Among the choices: The Backshore Trail passes along open meadows to the shoreline, and the Summit Trail is all mossy, mushroom-y, and medieval, with teasing glimpses of the water from the top.

WHERE TO STAY

Castine Harbor Lodge ★ (Kids)   Housed in a red-roofed 1893 mansion, this is a good place for families to hole up for a night or two. The only inn actually on the water in Castine, it's run with a good cheer that allows kids to feel at home amid the regal architecture. The main parlor is good for a game of pool, while the spacious rooms are eclectically furnished with a mix of antiques and modern furniture. Two of the guest rooms share an adjoining bathroom, but that's almost okay—the bathrooms at this hotel have some of best "loo" views in the state.

147 Perkins St. (P.O. Box 215), Castine, ME 04421. ⓒ 207/326-4335. www.castinemaine.com. 16 units (2 with shared bathrooms), 1 cottage. $85–$245 double; cottage $1,250 weekly. Rates include continental breakfast. MC, V. Pets allowed ($10 per pet per night). **Amenities:** Dining room; bar; pool table.

Castine Inn ★   The Castine Inn is a Maine Coast rarity: a hotel that was originally built as a hotel, not a residence, in 1898. This handsome, cream-colored inn, designed in an eclectic Georgian Federal Revival style, has a great wraparound porch and attractive gardens. The lobby takes its cue from the '40s, with wingback chairs and love seats and a fireplace in the parlor. Guest rooms on the two upper floors are attractively (sometimes unevenly) furnished in Early American style with graceful prints, pastel walls, pencil-poster beds, and sofas; three suites have recently been added, consolidating formerly smaller rooms and upping the amenities a bit. The elegant dining room (see "Where to Dine," below) serves some of the coast's best dinners.

Main St. (P.O. Box 41), Castine, ME 04421. ⓒ **207/326-4365.** Fax 207/326-4570. www.castineinn.com. 17 units. Peak season $90–$245 double; off-season rates lower. Rates include full breakfast. 2-night minimum July–Aug. MC, V. Closed early Oct to late Apr. Children 8 and older are welcome. **Amenities:** Dining room; sauna.

Pentagöet Inn ★★   At the Pentagöet, "activities" consist of sitting on the wraparound front porch on cane-seated rockers watching the hum (though I hesitate to call it that) of Main Street. This quirky, yellow-and-green (ca. 1894) inn with the prominent turret is tastefully, sturdily built. The lobby features hardwood floors, oval braided rugs, and a woodstove; it's all comfortable without being prissy, professional without being chilly. Most units sport king-size beds with ornate headboards and lacy white coverlets—some have claw-foot bathtubs and/or fireplaces, and one even includes a balcony with flowers. Rooms on the upper two floors of the main house are furnished eclectically in a mix of antiques and collectibles, while five units in the adjacent Perkins Street building (an austere, Federal-era house) are furnished more simply and show off painted wooden floors. The amazingly character-filled **pub** ★ and delicious fare in the **dining room** ★ are both excellent.

26 Main St. (P.O. Box 4), Castine, ME 04421. ✆ **800/845-1701** or 207/326-8616. www.pentagoet.com. 16 units (2 with private hallway bathrooms). Peak season $115–$245 double; off-season rates lower. Rates include full breakfast. MC, V. Closed Nov–Apr. Pets by reservation only. Suitable for older children only. **Amenities:** Dining room; pub; bikes. *In room:* Fireplace (some units).

WHERE TO DINE

Castine Inn ★★ NEW AMERICAN   Castine Inn chef/owner Tom Gutow served stints at acclaimed places such as Bouley and (now-shuttered) Verbena in the brutal restaurant climate of New York City, so he isn't timid about experimenting with local meats and produce here in Midcoast Maine. The menu changes too regularly to be pinned down, but expect permutations riffing on some of the same notes as dinner entrees such as lobster with vanilla butter, mango mayonnaise, and a tropical-fruit salsa or lamb loin with eggplant, green lentils, tomatoes, and a rosemary *jus*. There's also an attached wine bar.

Main St. ✆ **207/326-4365.** Reservations recommended. Main courses $26–$33. MC, V. Daily 6–9pm. Closed early Oct to late Apr.

Dennett's Wharf Restaurant & Oyster Bar PUB FARE   In a soaring waterfront sail loft with dollar bills tacked all over the high ceiling, Dennett's Wharf serves upscale bar food in a lively setting leavened by a good selection of microbrews. When the weather is decent, there's outside dining beneath a bright yellow awning with superb harbor views. Look for sandwiches, salads, and fried clams at lunch; dinner includes local lobsters, baby back ribs, pad Thai, and hanger steak. The newish oyster bar serves, obviously, oysters on the half-shell. But how did all those bills get on the ceiling? Ask your server; it will cost you exactly $1 to find out.

15 Sea St. (next to the town dock). ✆ **207/326-9045.** Reservations recommended in summer and for parties of 6 or more. Lunch items $5–$13; dinner items $9–$27. AE, DISC, MC, V. Daily 11am–midnight. Closed mid-Oct to Apr.

6 DEER ISLE ★★

The island known as **Deer Isle** ★★ is well off the beaten path, yet worth the long detour from Route 1. Looping, winding roads cross through forest and farmland, and travelers are rewarded with sudden glimpses of hidden coves. An occasional settlement even crops up now and again. This island doesn't cater exclusively to tourists the way many coastal towns and islands do; it's still largely occupied by fifth- or sixth-generation fishermen, farmers, second-home owners, and artists who prize their seclusion here.

The main village—**Stonington,** on the island's southern tip—is still a rough-hewn sea town. Despite serious incursions over the past 10 years by galleries and enterprises partly or wholly dependent on tourism, it remains dominated in spirit by fishermen and the occasional quarryworker. This village does now have a handful of inns and galleries, but its primary focus is to serve locals and summer residents, not travelers. *Outside* magazine once named this one of America's 10 best towns to live in if you're an extreme/outdoorsy type. Um . . . sure, if you don't mind living several hours removed from the nearest significant population centers and airports in Maine (which are not all that significant anyway). I've yet to see a lobsterman kayaking on his downtime, either—they're too busy working—though I suppose it does happen.

Be that as it may, this is a great island on which to simply relax and smell the salt air **181** and watch the changing landscapes.

ESSENTIALS
Getting There
Deer Isle is accessible via several winding country roads that split off of U.S. Route 1. Coming from the south or west (Portland or Camden), turn onto Route 175 in Orland, then connect to Route 15 and continue to Deer Isle. From the east (that is, Bar Harbor), head south on Route 172 to Blue Hill, where you can also pick up Route 15. Deer Isle is connected to the mainland via a high, narrow, and graceful **suspension bridge** built in 1938—still a bit harrowing to cross in high winds.

Visitor Information
The **Deer Isle–Stonington Chamber of Commerce,** P.O. Box 490, Deer Isle, ME 04627 (© **207/348-6124;** www.deerislemaine.com) staffs a seasonal information booth just beyond the bridge on Little Deer Isle. The booth is normally open daily in summer, its opening hours dependant on volunteer availability.

EXPLORING DEER ISLE
Deer Isle, with its network of narrow roads to nowhere, is ideal for rambling. It's a pleasure to explore by car and is also inviting to travel by bike, although hasty and careening fishermen in pickups can make this unnerving at times. Especially tranquil is **Deer Isle.** Especially tranquil is the narrow road between Deer Isle and **Sunshine** to the east. Plan to stop and explore coves and inlets along the way. To get here, follow Route 15; south of Deer Isle, turn east toward **Stinson Neck,** continuing on this **scenic byway** ★ for about 10 miles over bridges and causeways.

Stonington ★, at the southern end of Deer Isle, consists of one commercial street that wraps along the harbor's edge. While B&Bs and boutiques have made inroads here in recent years, it's still a slightly rough-and-tumble waterfront town. You can learn about the town's stone industry at the **Deer Isle Granite Museum,** 51 Main St. (© **207/367-6331**). The museum features some historical artifacts from the local quarry's golden years, but the real draw is a working diorama (8×15 ft.) of Crotch Island as it would have appeared around 1900, complete with miniature railroad, boats, and cranes moving stones around. Kids find it endlessly fascinating. The museum is open daily from late May to August; donations are requested.

The town opera house is home to a summer-stock theater company; log on to **www.operahousearts.org** for a schedule and other details. Stonington is also another of Maine's fishing villages to feature some big-time **lobster-boat racing;** this town's event occurs in late July. You'll be amazed at how quickly one of these workhorses can get going when the captain's going full throttle.

WHERE TO STAY
Goose Cove Lodge ★★ **Kids**   A 22-acre compound beside a nature preserve on a remote point, Goose Cove Lodge is a great destination for families and lovers of the outdoors. Exploring the grounds is a different adventure every day; you can hike at low tide to Barred Island, take a guided walk on the trails, mess around in the cove (there are kayaks and canoes for guests), or borrow a bike and set out for a ride. There's a mix of different cottages and inn rooms, some with great bay views. Most units have fireplaces or Franklin stoves; cottages add private decks with Adirondack chairs and lovely touches

such as the stonework inside Bayberry. Most romantic? Elm and Linnea are tucked into the woods on a rise overlooking the beach, while newbies Bayberry and Thistle are luxed out with French doors and huge fireplaces. The kids' programs are worthy of praise, and dinners are an event.

Goose Cove Rd. (P.O. Box 40), Sunset, ME 04683. ✆ **800/728-1963** or 207/348-2508. Fax 207/348-2624. www.goosecovelodge.com. 21 units. Mid-June to Aug $180–$295 double, $230–$550 cottage; mid-May to mid-June and Sept to mid-Oct $80–$195 double, $95–$295 cottage. Rates include full breakfast. MAP rates available in summer. Packages available in off season. 2-night minimum stay in inn rooms and 1-week minimum stay in cottages July–Aug; 3-person minimum in high season (some units). MC, V. Closed mid-Oct to mid-May. **Amenities:** Dining room; bar. *In room:* Kitchenette (some units), fireplace (some units).

Inn on the Harbor ★ (Value)

This appealingly quirky waterfront inn has the best location in town—perched over the harbor and right on the main street. After a major makeover, the guest rooms (more than half of which overlook the harbor) are now nicely appointed with antiques and carpets. The more inexpensive rooms are a bargain, in or out of season: This is a great spot for resting up before or after a kayak expedition, or as a base for day trips out to Isle au Haut. All units except the two-bedroom suite across town in the innkeeper's home have in-room phones; the newly updated American Eagle Suite has a glass-fronted woodstove, private kitchen, and private deck.

45 Main St. (P.O. Box 69), Stonington, ME 04681. ✆ **800/942-2420** or 207/367-2420. Fax 207/367-5165. www.innontheharbor.com. 14 units. Mid-May to mid-Oct $130–$215 double; mid-Oct to mid-May $65–$130 double. Rates include continental breakfast mid-May to mid-Oct. AE, DISC, MC, V. Children 12 and older welcome. **Amenities:** Spa services. *In room:* TV, dataport (most units), kitchenette (1 unit), no phone (1 unit).

Oakland House Seaside Resort/Shore Oaks ★★ (Kids)

It doesn't get much more Maine than this: Innkeeper Jim Littlefield is a great-grandson of the original owner, a sea captain who opened the inn in 1889 on land acquired from King George. (The original inn sign remains.) On the mainland just north of the bridge to Deer Isle, it's a classic summer resort; the main house, known as Shore Oaks, consists of 10 classic Arts and Crafts–style rooms, 7 with private bathrooms. None have televisions or phones. The main drawing cards, however, are the simple but wonderfully relaxing cottages dotting the property. Tucked among 50 acres of shoreline with extraordinary views of Eggemoggin Reach, they have one to five bedrooms each and are of varying vintages—most have fireplaces (wood is delivered); televisions or phones; and a variety of other amenities, from kitchenettes to claw-foot tubs. The dining room is quite good.

435 Herrick Rd., Brooksville, ME 04617. ✆ **800/359-7352** or 207/359-8521. www.oaklandhouse.com. 25 units (3 with private bathroom). $185–$265 double with private bathroom; $99–$175 double with shared bathroom; $475–$2,750 weekly cottage. Inn rates include full breakfast; cottage rates include breakfast and dinner mid-June to early Sept, but include no meals in spring and fall. Inn MAP rates also available. 2-night minimum for inn on weekends, 7-night minimum for cottages in summer. MC, V. Inn closed mid-Oct to early May, some cottages available year-round. Children age 14 and up welcome in main inn; all children welcome in cottages. **Amenities:** Dining room; boats; fax service. *In room:* TV (some units), kitchenette (some units), fireplace (some units), no phone (some units).

Pilgrim's Inn ★★

Set just off a town road and between an open bay and a mill pond, this is a historic, handsomely renovated inn. The inn was built in 1793 by Ignatius Haskell, a prosperous sawmill owner. His granddaughter opened the home to boarders, and it has housed summer guests ever since. The interior is tastefully decorated in a style that's informed by Early Americana but not beholden to it. The guest rooms are well appointed with antiques and painted in muted colonial colors; especially intriguing are rooms on the top floor, showing off some impressive diagonal beams. Other accents **183** include private staircases, cherry beds, antique tubs, woodstoves, and fireplaces. Two nearby cottages are also rented by the inn and allow pets.

20 Main St. (P.O. Box 69), Deer Isle, ME 04627. ℂ **888/778-7505** or 207/348-6615. Fax 207/348-7769. www.pilgrimsinn.com. 15 units. $99–$209 double; $179–$249 cottage. Rates include full breakfast. MC, V. Closed mid-Oct to mid-May (1 cottage available year-round). Packages available. Pets allowed in cottages only ($50 fee). Children 10 and older welcome in inn, all children welcome in cottages. **Amenities:** Restaurant; pub; bikes. *In room:* Kitchenette (1 room), fireplace (some units).

WHERE TO DINE

For fine dining, try the dining rooms at Goose Cove Lodge and the Pilgrim's Inn (see "Where to Stay," above); be aware, however, that both often require dinner reservations in high season.

Fisherman's Friend (Value) SEAFOOD This is a local-eats place, lively and boisterous, usually as crowded as it is unpretentious. The menu features basic home-cooked meals, typically including a range of fresh fish cooked in a variety of styles, including charbroiled. Order a bowl of the lobster stew, brimming with meaty lobster chunks; travelers have been known to find reasons to linger in Stonington longer just to indulge in a second bowl. Dessert selections, which include such local specialties as berry pie and shortcake, are extensive and traditional New England.

School St., Stonington. ℂ **207/367-2442.** Reservations recommended peak season and weekends. Sandwiches $2.50–$6.50; dinner entrees $5–$20. DISC, MC, V. May–Oct daily 11am–10pm; Apr and Nov–Jan daily Thurs–Sun 11am–9pm. Closed Feb–Mar. Located up the hill from the harbor past the Opera House.

A DAY TRIP TO ISLE AU HAUT ★★

Rocky and remote Isle au Haut offers one of the most unusual hiking and camping experiences in northern New England. This 6×3-mile island, located 6 miles south of Stonington, was originally named Isle Haut (or High Island) in 1604 by French explorer Samuel de Champlain. The name and its pronunciation evolved—today it's generally pronounced "aisle-a-*ho*"—but the island itself has remained steadfastly unchanged over the centuries.

About half of the island is owned by the National Park Service and maintained as an outpost of Acadia National Park (see chapter 9). A 60-passenger ferry run by the Isle au Haut Boat Company (see below) makes a stop in the morning and late afternoon at Duck Harbor, allowing for a solid day of hiking while still returning to Stonington by nightfall.

Note: The ferry stops at two different landings. Most of the time, they stop at the "town landing"—convenient for groceries, but a 4-mile, 2-hour hike through the island's woods along the Duck Harbor Trail to the only campsite (see below). During summer, usually twice a day, special boats run directly to the Duck Harbor landing, an easy few minutes' walk to the sites. I cannot stress enough: *Check first* where your ferry is going if you are not ready or able to walk 4 miles twice. The small harborside village, which has a few old homes, a handsome church, and a tiny schoolhouse, post office, and store, is interesting, but campers and most day-trippers are better served ferrying straight to Duck Harbor.

At Duck Harbor, the NPS maintains its cluster of five Adirondack-style lean-tos, which are available for overnight **camping ★**; cost is $25 per site, and they can be used up to 3 nights in a row (5 outside high season). A maximum of six campers can use each site, and there are no showers or electricity; there's a water pump about ¹/₃ mile away. These sites fill up fast, and advance reservations are essential (due by Apr 1 of the year you want to visit, though occasional cancellations merit checking afterward anyway). Contact **Acadia National Park,** Eagle Lake Road (P.O. Box 177), Bar Harbor, ME 04609, call © **207/288-3338,** or download a reservation form at www.nps.gov/acad/pdf/iahreserve.pdf. Other than for camping, the park doesn't charge a fee to explore its island holdings.

Who lives here? The island is partly inhabited by some fishermen who can trace their island ancestry back 3 centuries, and partly by summer visitors whose forebears discovered the bucolic splendor of Isle au Haut in the 1880s. The summer population of the island is about 300, with about 50 die-hards remaining year-round. (One resident is writer Linda Greenlaw, the former fishing-boat captain profiled in the book and movie *The Perfect Storm* and author of *The Lobster Chronicles* as well as a cookbook of recipes from the island.)

You can stroll the often-unpaved main road that circles the island, but many hardy visitors choose to explore the excellent **island trails** ★★ that penetrate and encircle the isle. Some of the more scenic ones include Western Head Trail (requiring perhaps 1¹/₄ hr. one-way) and Cliff Trail (about 45 min. one-way), with expansive cliff and sea views. The NPS can furnish you with a trail map at the campground, and rangers sometimes ride the ferries. Be careful, however: Some of these trails are rough on the feet, and they can get wet from the sea, fog, or rain; rain, in fact, may render a few (such as Goat Trail) impassable at times.

The **Isle au Haut Boat Company** (© **207/367-5193;** www.isleauhaut.com) operates the ferry run, leaving from the pier at the end of Sea Breeze Avenue in Stonington. In summer (roughly mid-June to mid-Sept), there are about 10 daily runs to the island, with four to six runs in spring and fall; call or check the website for exact schedules. The round-trip boat fare to either the town landing or Duck Harbor is $32 for adults and $16 for children 11 and under. (There's also a small extra surcharge if you pay by credit card.) Bikes cost $16 round-trip, kayaks $30. The crossing takes about 45 minutes to the village landing, or 1 hour and 15 minutes to Duck Harbor. Reservations are not accepted; it's best to arrive at least a half-hour before departure.

SEA KAYAKING

Peer southward from Stonington, and you'll see dozens of spruce-studded islands between the mainland and the dark, distant ridges of Isle au Haut. These islands, ringed with salmon-pink granite, are collectively called Merchant's Row, and they're invariably ranked by experienced coastal boaters as among the most beautiful in the state. Thanks to these exceptional islands, Stonington is among Maine's most popular destinations for sea kayaking. Many of the islands are open to day visitors and overnight camping, and one of the Nature Conservancy islands even hosts a flock of sheep. Experienced kayakers should contact the **Maine Island Trail Association** (© **207/761-8225;** www.mita.org) for more information about paddling here; several of the islands are open only to association members.

Old Quarry Charters (© **207/367-8977;** www.oldquarry.com), just outside the village of Stonington, offers guided kayak tours as well as kayaks for rent. (Old Quarry will rent only to those with prior experience, so it's best to call ahead to discuss your needs.) Tours range from a half-day tour ($55) to a full-day 7-hour tour that weaves out through the islands and includes a stop for a swim or a picnic at an abandoned quarry. Overnight camping trips are also offered. Other services: parking and a launch site for those who've brought their own boats, sailboat tours and lessons, charter tours aboard a 38-foot lobster boat, and camping ($24–$50 per tent site, more for RVs). For more information, visit the company's website.

Outfitters based outside the region that offer guided overnight kayak trips around Merchant's Row include **Maine Island Kayak Co.** (© **207/766-2373;** www.maine islandkayak.com) on Peaks Island near Portland or **Maine Sport Outfitters** (© **800/722-0826** or 207/236-8797; www.mainesport.com).

7 BLUE HILL ★★

Blue Hill ★★, population 2,400, is easy to find—just look for the dome of Blue Hill itself, which lords over the northern end of (of course) Blue Hill Bay. Set between the mountain and the bay is the quiet and historic town, clustering along the bay's shore and a little stream. There's never much going on here, which seems to be exactly what attracts repeat summer visitors; it might also explain why two excellent bookstores are located in this dot of a town. Many old-money families maintain lovely retreats along the water or in the hills around here, but the village center offers a couple choices for lodging even if you don't have local connections. It's a good place for a quiet break.

ESSENTIALS
Getting There
Blue Hill is southeast of Ellsworth, at the juncture of routes 15 and 172. From Bar Harbor, follow Route 3 through Ellsworth, cross the bridge, then follow Route 172 about 14 miles to Blue Hill. Coming from the south (Rockland or Belfast) on Route 1/Route 3, turn south onto Route 15 about 5 miles east of Bucksport, and drive about 12 miles.

Visitor Information
Blue Hill does not maintain a true staffed visitor information booth. Look for the "Blue Hill, Maine" brochure and map at state information centers, or write to the **Blue Hill Peninsula Chamber of Commerce** (© **207/374-3242;** www.bluehillpeninsula.org), 28 Water St., Blue Hill, ME 04614. Locals are usually able to answer any questions you may have.

SPECIAL EVENTS
The **Blue Hill Fair** ★★ (© **207/374-3701;** www.bluehillfair.com) is a traditional country fair with livestock competitions, vegetable displays, and carnival rides. The fair takes place at the fairgrounds northwest of the village on Route 172 on Labor Day weekend. Admission costs $5 to $7 per person each day; rides are individually priced. Parking is free on the fairgrounds.

EXPLORING BLUE HILL
A good way to start your exploration is to ascend the open summit of **Blue Hill** ★★, from which you'll gain superb views of the bay and the bald mountaintops on nearby Mount Desert Island. To reach the trail head from the center of the village, drive north on Route 172 about 1¹/₂ miles, then turn west (left) on Mountain Road at the Blue Hill Fairgrounds. Drive another ³/₄ mile and look for the well-marked trail; park on the

MIDCOAST MAINE **8** **BLUE HILL**

(Tips) Community Radio

When in the Blue Hill area, tune to the local community radio station, WERU at 89.9 FM. Started by Noel Paul Stookey (Paul in the folk trio Peter, Paul, and Mary) in a former chicken coop, the idea was to spread good music and encourage provocative thinking. It's become slicker and more professional in recent years but still retains a pleasantly homespun flavor at times, with an eclectic range of music and commentary.

shoulder of the road. The fairly easy ascent is about a mile, and takes about 45 minutes. Bring a picnic lunch.

Blue Hill has traditionally attracted more than its fair share of artists, especially potters. On Union Street, stop by **Rowantrees Pottery** (© 207/374-5535), which has been a Blue Hill institution for more than half a century. Another inventive shop, the family-run **Rackliffe Pottery** (© 888/631-3321 or 207/374-2297) on Route 172 (Ellsworth Rd.), uses native clay and lead-free glazes. Visitors are welcome to watch the potters at work. Both shops are open year-round.

Even if you're not given to swooning over historic homes, you owe yourself a visit to the intriguing **Parson Fisher House ★** (© 207/374-2459; www.jonathanfisherhouse. org), on routes 176 and 15, a half-mile west of the village. Fisher, Blue Hill's first permanent minister, was a small-town-Maine version of a Renaissance man when he settled here in 1796. Educated at Harvard, Fisher not only delivered sermons in six different languages (including Aramaic), but was also a writer, painter, and inventor of boundless energy. On a tour of his home, which he built himself in 1814, you can see a clock with wooden works he fashioned, as well as books he wrote, published, and bound by hand. The house is open from July to mid-September, Thursdays through Saturdays, from 1 to 4pm. Admission is by donation; $5 per person is suggested.

If you're an ardent antiques hunter or bibliophile, it's worth your while to detour to the **Big Chicken Barn** (© 207/667-7308), on Route 1 between Ellsworth and Bucksport (it's 9 miles west of Ellsworth and 11 miles east of Bucksport). This sprawling antiques mall and bookstore is of nearly shopping-mall proportions—more than 21,000 square feet of stuff in an old poultry barn. It's open daily from 9am to 6pm during summer, 10am to 4pm in the off season.

WHERE TO STAY

Blue Hill Farm Country Inn   Comfortably situated on 48 acres about 2 miles north of the Blue Hill's village center, the Country Inn (not to be confused with its neighbor; see below) has some of the most relaxing and comfortable common areas you'll find; the first floor of a big barn was converted into a spacious living room, with sitting areas arrayed so that you can opt either for the privacy or the company of others. Guest rooms are smallish and lightly furnished, though—none have anything larger than a double-size bed. The more modern rooms are upstairs in the barn loft and are nicely decorated in a country-farmhouse style, though they're a bit motel-like. The seven older rooms in the farmhouse have more character and share a single bathroom with a small tub and hand-held shower.

Rte. 15 (P.O. Box 437), Blue Hill, ME 04614. ℂ **207/374-5126.** www.bluehillfarminn.com. 14 units (7 with shared bathroom). $90–$110 double with private bathroom; $80–$90 double with shared bathroom. Rates include continental breakfast. AE, MC, V. *In room:* No phone.

Blue Hill Inn ★★   The Blue Hill Inn has been hosting travelers since 1840. On one of the village's main streets, and within walking distance of almost everything, this Federal-style lodging house displays a convincing Colonial American motif, its authenticity enhanced by creaky floors. Friendly innkeepers have furnished all of the rooms pleasantly with antiques and down comforters; four units in the main house have wood-burning fireplaces, although these rooms are open only from mid-May through the end of October. A large contemporary suite in an adjacent, free-standing building has a cathedral ceiling, fireplace, full kitchen, living room, and deck; this Cape House Suite is available to guests year-round. Ask about packages that include kayaking, hiking, or sailing.

40 Union St. (P.O. Box 403), Blue Hill, ME 04614. ℂ **800/826-7415** or 207/374-2844. Fax 207/374-2829. www.bluehillinn.com. 12 units. $138–$195 double; $165–$285 suite. Rates include full breakfast and afternoon tea. 2-night minimum in summer. DISC, MC, V. Main inn closed Dec to mid-May, 1 cottage open year-round. Children 13 and older are welcome. **Amenities:** Dining room. *In room:* A/C, kitchenette (1 unit), fireplace (some units).

WHERE TO DINE

The **Fish Net,** at the north end of Main Street (near the junction of routes 172 and 177; ℂ **207/374-5240**), is a longtime local favorite for its lobster rolls, fried clam baskets, ice-cream cones, and the like; it has all the atmosphere of a carhop place. It's open seasonally.

There's also a new dining spot in town called the **Wescott Forge,** 66 Main St. (the barn-red building at the bridge; ℂ **207/374-9909**). The lunch menu is mostly sandwiches, salads, and pizzas, while duck, steaks, and seafood are served for dinner. This building has held a number of restaurants over the years, but none of them has succeeded for long; let's see what happens this time.

Arborvine ★★ SEAFOOD/FUSION   In recent years, Blue Hill saw the closing of two of its longtime favorite dining spots (Firepond and the Left Bank Cafe). Fortunately, the Arborvine stepped in to fill the gap, once again giving this sleepy town a top-flight eatery. In a beautifully renovated Cape Cod–style house, the restaurant's interior is warm and inviting—think rough-hewn timbers, polished wooden floors, and a cozy bar area. The owners are careful to use locally procured ingredients, such as Bagaduce River oysters on the half-shell as an appetizer. The intriguing nightly main courses change but might run to haddock Nicoise, broiled Stonington halibut with grilled polenta, coriander-crusted *aki* with seaweed and Japanese flavorings, *gallettes* of Maine crab and shrimp, or seared local scallops in a garlicky saffron broth. The non-seafood choices are equally exciting: a rack of lamb in pine nuts and basil, beef medallions over a dollop of Vermont chèvre, crispy roast duckling glazed with kumquat with an apple-ginger chutney, or just a simple boneless rib-eye with duxelle sauce. Yummy desserts could include a Grand Marnier–spiked chocolate mousse; a gingery vanilla crème brûlée; or a Bartlett pear in puff pastry sided with macadamia nut–flavored cream, pomegranate sauce, and a bit of cinnamon ice cream.

Main St., Blue Hill, ME 04614. ℂ **207/374-2119.** www.arborvine.com. Dinner $27–$30. MC, V. Summer daily 5:30–8:30pm; off season Fri–Sun 5:30–8:30pm.

MIDCOAST MAINE

8

BLUE HILL

8 BANGOR, ORONO & OLD TOWN

The towns of Bangor (pronounced *bayn*-gore, please—not "banger"), Orono, and Old Town lie along the western banks of the Penobscot River—not far inland from Ellsworth and Belfast on the coast—and serve as gateways to the North Woods. They may be worth a day or a half-day if you're interested in sampling an inland slice of the real Maine.

Bangor is Maine's third-largest city (after Portland and Lewiston), the last major urban outpost with a full-fledged mall. It's a good destination for history buffs curious about the early North Woods economy. Bangor was once a thriving lumber port, shipping millions of board feet cut from the woods to the north and floated down the Penobscot River. While much of the town burned in 1911 and has since suffered from ill-considered urban-renewal schemes, visitors can still discern a robust history just below the surface. Orono and Old Town, two smaller towns to the north, offer an afternoon's diversion on rainy days.

This is a major transportation hub and the commercial center for much of eastern and northern Maine. But, quite frankly, it's not much of a tourist destination. The downtown has a handful of buildings of interest to those intrigued by late Victorian architecture, and a new and fun children's museum, but overall the city has little of the charm or urbanity of Portland. Travelers may not wish to budget a significant amount of time for exploring Bangor.

ESSENTIALS

Getting There

Bangor is located just off the Maine Turnpike. Take I-395 east, exit at Main Street (Rte. 1A), and follow signs for downtown.

As with many smaller regional airports, **Bangor International Airport (BGR)** (© 207/992-4600; www.flybangor.com) has had a tough time persuading airlines to keep a schedule of full-service flights; thus, many flights begin or end via commuter planes to or from Boston. Due in part to recent airline turnovers, many travelers have reported problems with delays and lost luggage at Bangor.

Airlines serving Bangor currently include **US Airways Express** (© 800/428-4322; www.usair.com), from New York City's LaGuardia Airport (seasonally) and Philadelphia (year-round); and **Northwest** (© 800/225-2525; www.nwa.com), from Detroit and (in summer) Minneapolis.

Concord Coach (© 800/639-3317; www.concordtrailways.com) and **Vermont Transit** (© 800/451-3292; www.vermonttransit.com) offer bus service to Bangor from Portland.

Visitor Information

The **Bangor Visitors Information Office** is staffed in summer near the big, scary statue of Paul Bunyan at the convention center on Main Street near I-395. Contact the **Bangor Region Chamber of Commerce,** 519 Main St., Bangor, ME 04401 (© 207/947-0307; www.bangorregion.com), open year-round from 8am to 5pm Monday through Friday.

EXPLORING BANGOR, ORONO & OLD TOWN

IN BANGOR The **Bangor Museum and Center for History** (© 207/942-5766; www.bangormuseum.com) offers a glimpse of life in Bangor during the golden days of the late 19th century. The museum is on Broad Street, but it's temporarily closed for

(Fun Facts)   I Left My Heart in Bangor, Maine

One of Bangor's claims to tourist fame is that in 1977 an addled German tourist, Erwin Kreuz, accidentally disembarked here during a transatlantic refueling stop. He spent a few days wandering the city, believing the whole time he was in San Francisco. This would be an urban legend except for the fact that it's true. It's a wonder that a statue hasn't been erected of this man.

renovations; no matter, because the Thomas Hill House—a handsome brick home built in 1836 for a prominent businessman—is also worth touring. It features displays of furniture and historical artifacts at 159 Union St. (just off High St.). Guided tours cost $5 for adults, $4 for seniors, and are free for 12 and under. The museum is open April through December, Tuesday through Friday from noon to 4pm (last tour at 3pm); June through September, it's also open Saturday from noon to 4pm (last tour at 3pm).

Vintage-car and early transportation buffs will enjoy a detour to the **Cole Land Transportation Museum** ★ (© 207/990-3600; www.colemuseum.org), 405 Perry Rd., off exit 45B of I-95 near the intersection with I-395 (left at the first light, then left onto Perry Rd.). The museum features old automobiles lined up in a warehouse-size display space, along with quirky machinery such as snow rollers, cement mixers, power shovels, and tractors. Especially well represented are early trucks, appropriate given its connection with Cole Express, a Maine trucking company founded in 1917. The museum is open daily from May to mid-November from 9am to 5pm; admission is $6 for adults, $4 for seniors, and free for those 17 and under.

Despite the city's rich history and the distinguished architecture of the commercial district, Bangor is probably best known as home to horror novelist and one-man Maine industry **Stephen King.** King's sprawling Victorian home seems a fitting place for the Maine native author; it's got an *Addams Family*–like creepiness, which is only enhanced by the wrought-iron fence with bats on it. His home isn't open to the public, but it's worth a drive by. To find the house, take the Union Street exit off I-95, head toward town for 6 blocks, then turn right on West Broadway. I trust you'll figure out which one it is.

IN ORONO & OLD TOWN   Orono is home to the University of Maine, which was founded in 1868. The campus is spread out on a plain and features a pleasing mix of historic and contemporary buildings. (The campus was originally designed by noted landscape architect Frederick Law Olmsted, but its early look has been obscured by later additions.) On campus, the modern and spacious **Hudson Museum** ★ (© 207/581-1901) features exhibits on anthropology and native culture. The museum displays crafts and artwork from native cultures around the world and is especially well represented with North American displays. It's open Tuesday to Friday from 9am to 4pm and Saturday from 11am to 4pm. Admission is free. (Note that this museum was closed at press time for renovations; call to inquire about its status.)

A few minutes north on Route 178 is riverside Old Town, famous for the classic canoes made by hand here since the turn of the 20th century. The offices of **Old Town Canoe** (© 207/827-5514; www.oldtowncanoe.com), now owned by Johnson Outdoors of Wisconsin but still cranking out top-quality watercraft, are located at 35 Middle St. (Mon–Sat 9am–5pm).

MIDCOAST MAINE

8

BANGOR, ORONO & OLD TOWN

Bangor has plenty of guest rooms, many along charmless strips near the airport and the mall. If you're not choosy or if you're arriving late at night, these are fine. Be aware that even these can fill up during the peak summer season, so reservations are advised. Try the **Comfort Inn,** 750 Hogan Rd. (© **877/424-6423** or 207/942-7899); **Howard Johnson Inn,** 336 Odlin Rd. (© **800/446-4656** or 207/942-5251); or the **Fairfield Inn by Marriott,** 300 Odlin Rd. (© **888/236-2427** or 207/990-0001).

Other options: Connected to Bangor's airport is a **Four Points by Sheraton,** 308 Godfrey Blvd. (© **800/368-7764** or 207/947-6721; www.sheraton.com); near the Bangor Mall and other chain stores is the **Country Inn at the Mall,** 936 Stillwater Ave. (© **800/244-3961** or 207/941-0200; www.countryinnatthemall.net); and downtown by the Civic Center is the **Holiday Inn,** 500 Main St. (© **888/465-4329** or 207/947-8651; www.holiday-inn.com).

Mount Desert Island

Mount Desert Island is home to spectacular Acadia National Park, and for many visitors, the two places are one and the same. Yet the park's holdings are only part of the appeal of this popular island, which is connected to the mainland by a short causeway. Besides the parklands, there are scenic harborside villages and remote backcountry roads aplenty, lovely B&Bs and fine restaurants, oversize 19th-century summer "cottages," and the historic tourist town of Bar Harbor.

The island is split in two by an inlet (see the "Fjord Tough" box below). Most of the park's land is on the eastern side of the island, though there are some vast holdings in the west, too. The eastern side is much more heavily developed. **Bar Harbor** is the island's center of commerce and entertainment, a once-charming resort

now in danger of being swallowed up by T-shirt and trinket shops. The western side has a quieter, more settled air and teems with more wildlife than tourists; here, the villages are mostly filled with fishermen and second-homers rather than actual commerce.

The island isn't huge—it's only about 15 miles from the causeway to the southernmost tip at Bass Harbor Head—yet you can do an awful lot of adventuring in such a compact space and see many different kinds of towns and landscapes. The best plan is to take it slowly, exploring if possible by foot, bicycle, canoe, and/or kayak, giving yourself a week to do it. You'll be glad you did.

To help orient you, I've placed a color map of Mount Desert Island inside the front cover of this guidebook.

1 ENJOYING THE GREAT OUTDOORS

Acadia is a fine, even world-class, destination for those who like their coastal vacations seasoned with adventure. While southern Maine has classic beach towns where the smell of salt air mixes with coconut oil and taffy, much of the rest of the Maine coast is unruly and wild. In parts it seems to share more in common with Alaska—you can see bald eagles soaring above and whales breaching below. In between these two archetypes, you'll find remote coves perfect for a rowboat jaunt and isolated offshore islands accessible only by sea kayak.

The best places for coastal adventure are often not the most obvious places—those tend to be crowded and more developed. You'll need to do a bit of homework to find the real treasures. A growing number of specialized guidebooks and outfitters can help point visitors in the right direction; some of the best are mentioned below.

Keep in mind that no other New England state offers as much outdoor recreational diversity as Maine. Bring your mountain bike, hiking boots, sea kayak, canoe, fishing rod, and/or snowmobile—there'll be plenty for you to do here.

If your outdoor skills are rusty or nonexistent, you can brush up at **L.L.Bean Outdoor Discovery Schools** (© **888/552-3261**), which offers a series of lectures and workshops

Tips **See It, Say It**

There is some debate about how to correctly pronounce the island to which I'm referring throughout this chapter. The name is of French origin; technically, it should be "Mount days-AIRT," but nobody says it that way anymore. Some locals say "Mount Des-SERT," like what you have after dinner, which is pretty close to the French way of saying things. (Notice the accent on the last syllable.) However, plenty of tourists, transplants, and locals *also* say DEZ-ert (like the Sahara), and that's not wrong . . . after all, that's how it's *spelled*. As for me, I go with "dessert."

that run anywhere from 2 hours to 3 days. Classes are offered at various locations around the state, covering a whole range of subjects, including fly-fishing, outdoor photography, and first aid in the wilderness. L.L.Bean also hosts periodic (and popular) canoeing, sea-kayaking, and skiing festivals that bring together instructors, lecturers, and equipment vendors for 2 or 3 days of learning and outdoor diversion. Call for a brochure, or check the L.L.Bean website (www.llbean.com/outdoorsonline/odp) for a schedule.

BEACHGOING The average ocean temperature at Bar Harbor in summer is 54°F (12°C); farther east in Passamaquoddy Bay it's 51°F (11°C). Cold. But small, crescent-shaped **Sand Beach** in Acadia National Park makes for a wonderfully scenic day outing—and the water's good for wading (but not exactly for swimming).

BICYCLING **Mount Desert Island** and **Acadia National Park** are the premier coastal destinations for bikers, especially mountain bikers who prefer easy-riding terrain—the cycling here may be some of the most pleasant in America. Its 57 miles of well-maintained national-park carriage roads offer superb cruising through thick forests and to ocean views atop rocky knolls. No cars are permitted on these grass and gravel lanes; bikers and walkers have them all to themselves. You can rent mountain bikes in Bar Harbor, which has several bike shops from which to choose. The Park Loop Road, while often crowded with slow-moving cars, offers one of the more memorable road-biking experiences in the state. The rest of Mount Desert Island is also good for highway biking, especially on the quieter western half of the island, where traffic is almost never a problem.

CAMPING Car campers traveling the Maine coast have plenty of choices, from well-developed private campgrounds to more basic state parks. **Acadia National Park** tends to be the biggest draw, but there's no shortage of other options on and near the coast.

Among the coastal state parks worthy of an overnight are **Lamoine State Park** (© 207/667-4778), which is convenient to Acadia National Park yet away from the thickest of the crowds (check here if you're stuck for a place to stay on Mount Desert Island), and remote **Cobscook Bay State Park** (© 207/726-4412). Most campsites in this nearly 900-acre park are right on the water, offering a great view of the massive 28-foot tides that slosh in and out. See chapter 10 for more details on Cobscook Bay State Park.

CANOEING For many outdoors enthusiasts in the Northeast, Maine is very alluring to serious paddlers. In fact, you can't travel very far in Maine without stumbling upon a great canoe trip. The state's best canoeing tends to be far inland and deep in the woods, true, but day paddlers can still find good trips at several lakes along the coast or in some of the protected bays.

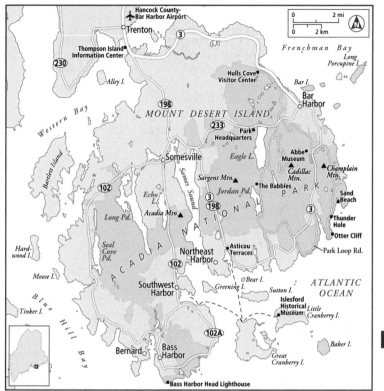

Mount Desert's ponds offer scenic if limited canoeing; most have public boat access. Canoe rentals are available at the north end of **Long Pond** (the largest pond on the island, at 3 miles long) in Somesville from **National Park Canoe & Kayak Rental (© 207/ 244-5854)**. The cost is about $25 for 4 hours, or $40 per day. Much of the west shore and southern tip are within park boundaries. Jet skis are banned in the park, and swimming is prohibited in ponds that serve as public water reservoirs (including Bubble, Jordan, Eagle, and the south end of Long Pond).

Two excellent sources of detailed canoeing information are the *AMC River Guide: Maine* and *Quiet Water Canoe Guide: Maine,* both published by the Appalachian Mountain Club, 5 Joy St., Boston, MA 02108.

CARRIAGE RIDES ★★ Several types of carriage rides are offered by the park-managed **Wildwood Stables (© 207/276-3622;** www.acadia.net/wildwood), about a half-mile south of the Jordan Pond House. The tours depart daily in season and take in sweeping ocean views from a local mountaintop, ramble over the Rockefeller bridges, or drop by the Jordan Pond House for (optional) tea and popovers (extra charge). The tours cost from $16 to $22 per adult, or $4.50 to $9 per child ages 2 to 12. There's a special carriage designed for passengers with disabilities, and you can even charter your own carriage for a private group. Reservations are recommended.

FISHING   For freshwater fishing not too far from the Downeast coast, **Grand Lake Stream** is a popular and historic destination. Located deep in the woods of Washington County, close to the border with Canada, the area has a rich heritage as a fisherman's settlement, and a number of camps and outfitters cater to the serious angler, especially those in search of landlocked salmon, smallmouth bass, and brook trout. Among the classic fishing lodges in this area are **Weatherby's** (℃ **207/796-5558**) and **Indian Rock Camps** (℃ **800/498-2821** or 207/796-2822).

GOLF   There are two good golf courses on Mount Desert Island. The **Kebo Valley Golf Club** (℃ **207/288-3000**) is one of the oldest in America, open since 1888; it's a beauty. (*Golf Digest* awarded it four stars.) Greens fees are $50 to $85 per person for 18 holes (highest in summer), and it can get very busy in summertime—try to reserve ahead. The **Northeast Harbor Golf Club** (℃ **207/276-5335**) is another good choice. Greens fees at both range from about $40 to $80 per person for 18 holes in season.

SEA KAYAKING ★★   Sea kayaking has boomed around Mount Desert Island during the past decade. Experienced kayakers arrive in droves with their own boats. Novices sign up for guided tours that are offered by several outfitters. Many new paddlers have found their inaugural experiences gratifying; others have complained that the quantity of paddlers on quick tours in peak season makes the experience a little too much like a cattle drive to truly enjoy. A variety of options can be found on the island, ranging from a 2½-hour harbor tour to a 7-hour excursion; there are plenty of outfitters in Bar Harbor and the other towns offering guided excursions.

Details are available from **Coastal Kayaking Tours,** 48 Cottage St. (℃ **800/526-8615** or 207/288-9605), and **National Park Sea Kayak Tours,** 39 Cottage St. (℃ **800/347-0940**). Rates range from approximately $40 to $50 per person for a 2- to 3-hour harbor or sunset tour, up to $75 for a 1-day excursion.

Sea-kayak rentals are available from **Loon Bay Kayak,** which is located on Shore in Lamoine, just off Mount Desert Island (℃ **888/786-0676**), and which will deliver a boat to you; and from **Aquaterra Adventures,** 1 West St., Bar Harbor (℃ **877/386-4124** or 207/288-0007). With unpredictable weather and squirrelly tides, kayakers are advised to have some prior experience before attempting to set out on their own. They do tons of guided tours if you have any doubt about your abilities.

SKIING   Cross-country skiers have a glorious mix of terrain to choose from, especially within **Acadia National Park,** where skiing is allowed for free on park grounds throughout the winter. For more about cross-country ski areas in Maine, visit the Nordic skiing website of the trade association **Ski Maine** (www.skimaine.com).

2 ACADIA NATIONAL PARK ★★★

It's not hard to understand why Acadia is one of the crown jewels of the U.S. national park system. (It draws the second-most visitors annually of any national park.) The landscape here is a rich tapestry of rugged cliffs, pounding ocean surf, fishing and leisure boats lolling in harbors, and quiet forest paths.

> **Fun Facts**   **Fjord Tough**
>
> Mount Desert Island is divided deeply right down the middle into two lobes (almost like a brain) by **Somes Sound,** a tidal inlet that is also the only true fjord—that is, a valley carved out by a glacier and then subsequently filled in with rising ocean water—in the entire lower 48 states of the U.S. No, it's not nearly as scenic as the ones in Norway and Alaska, but when you drive over that little bridge from one side to the other, you can truthfully report to friends back home that you crossed a fjord this morning. Pretty cool.

Acadia's terrain, like so much of the rest of northern New England, was shaped by the cutting action of the last great glaciers moving into and then out of the region about 18,000 years ago. A mile-high ice sheet rumbled slowly over the land, scouring valleys into deep U shapes, rounding many once-jagged peaks, and depositing boulders at odd places in the landscape—including the famous 10-foot-tall Bubble Rock, which appears perched precariously on the side of South Bubble Mountain.

In the 1840s, Hudson River School painter Thomas Cole brought his sketchbooks and easels to remote Mount Desert Island, which was then home to a small number of fishermen and boat builders. His stunning renditions of the coast were displayed in New York City, triggering a tourism boom as urbanites flocked to the island to "rusticate." By 1872, national magazines were touting Eden (Bar Harbor's name until 1919) as a desirable summer getaway. It attracted the attention of wealthy industrialists, and soon became the de rigeur summer home of Carnegies, Rockefellers, Astors, and Vanderbilts, who built massive "cottages" with dozens of rooms.

By the early 1900s, the island's popularity and growing development began to concern its most ardent supporters. Boston textile heir George Dorr and Harvard president Charles Eliot, aided by the largesse of John D. Rockefeller, Jr., began acquiring and protecting large tracts of the island for the public to enjoy. These parcels were eventually donated to the U.S. government, and in 1919, the land was originally designated as Lafayette National Park—the first national park east of the Mississippi—after the French general who assisted colonists in the American Revolution.

Rockefeller alone purchased and donated some 11,000 acres—about $\frac{1}{3}$ of the park— and was responsible for its extraordinary **carriage roads.** Around 1905, a dispute erupted over whether to allow noisy new motorcars onto the island at all. Resident islanders wanted these new conveniences to aid their mobility; yet Rockefeller, whose fortune had been made in the oil industry, strenuously objected, preferring the tranquillity of a car-free island. He went down to defeat on this issue, and the island was opened to cars in 1913; in response, the multimillionaire set about building an elaborate 57-mile system of private carriage roads on his holdings in the park, complete with a dozen gracefully handcrafted stone bridges. These roads, open today to pedestrians, bicyclists, and equestrians, are concentrated most densely around Jordan Pond, but they also wind through wooded valleys and ascend some of the park's most scenic open peaks.

Renamed as "Acadia National Park" in 1929, the park has now grown to encompass nearly half the island, its holdings scattered piecemeal. It is a fine, even world-class, destination for those who like coastal vacations salted with adventure. Southern Maine is full of classic beach towns where the smell of sea air mixes with coconut oil, taffy, and fried dough, but the eastern Maine coast is mostly unruly and wild, and never more so than here. In between, you'll find remote coves perfect for beach picnics, lovely offshore islands accessible only by sea kayak, clear ponds and lakes with nary a boat, and uncrowded mountaintops (reached by car or foot) with views of it all.

Try to allow 3 or 4 days, at a minimum, for visiting the park. If you're passing through just briefly, try to work in at least two of the big three activities (hiking, biking, driving) I've described below.

And when you set out to explore the park, bring a picnic. (See "Packing a Picnic" later in this chapter.)

ESSENTIALS

Getting There

Acadia National Park is near Ellsworth, reached via Route 3. Normally travelers take U.S. Route 1 to Ellsworth from southern Maine, but you can avoid coastal congestion by taking the Maine Turnpike to Bangor, then picking up I-395 to Route 1A and continuing south into Ellsworth. Though this is longer in terms of miles, it's the quicker route in summer.

Year-round, there are several flights daily from Boston on small planes to the **Hancock County-Bar Harbor airport** (airport code BHB; www.bhbairport.com) in Trenton, just across the causeway from Mount Desert Island. Contact **US Airways Express** (© 800/ 428-4322; www.usairaways.com). From here, call a taxi, rent a car, or ride the free shuttle bus (late June through mid-Oct only) to downtown Bar Harbor.

It's difficult to get here by bus. In summer only, **Vermont Transit** (© 800/552-8737; www.vermonttransit.com), affiliated with Greyhound, runs buses from Boston's South Station to Bangor, continuing onward once daily to Bar Harbor. **Concord Coach** (© 800/639-3317; www.concordtrailways.com) also runs a few buses daily to Bangor from Boston, but does not continue onto the island; you'll need to change to a taxi (a long, expensive ride) or Vermont Transit.

Getting Around

A free **summer shuttle bus service** ★★ known as the *Island Explorer* (www.explore acadia.com) was inaugurated in 1999 as part of an effort to reduce the number of cars on the island's roads. It's working; the propane-powered buses—equipped with racks for bikes—serve multiple routes covering nearly the entire island, and will stop anywhere you request outside the village centers, including trail heads, ferries, small villages, and campgrounds. Bring a book; there are lots of stops. All routes begin or end at the Village

---

ⓉTips Cost-Effective Acadia

No daily pass to Acadia is available, so if you'll be here more than 2 weeks, purchase a $40 annual Acadia pass for your car instead of several $20 weekly passes. Or consider buying a $80 National Parks Pass, which allows you and your vehicle entry to *all* national parks during a calendar year.

> ⓣ **Tips   Avoiding Crowds in the Park**
>
> Early fall is the best time to miss the mobs yet still enjoy the weather here. If you come midsummer, try to venture out in early morning or early evening to the most popular spots, such as Thunder Hole or the summit of Cadillac Mountain. Setting off into the woods at every opportunity is also a good strategy. Some four out of five visitors restrict their tours to the loop road and a handful of other major attractions, leaving most of the gorgeous backcountry to the more adventurous.
>
> The best guarantee of solitude is to head to the most remote outposts managed by Acadia, such as **Isle au Haut** and **Schoodic Peninsula,** across the bay to the east. Ask for more information about these areas at the visitor centers.

Green in Bar Harbor, but you can and should pick up the bus almost anywhere else to avoid parking hassles in town. Route no. 3 runs from Bar Harbor along much of the Park Loop, offering easy free access to some of the park's best hiking trails. The buses operate from late June through mid-October (with fewer, but still enough, buses running from Sept to mid-Oct); ask for a schedule at island information centers, in shops, or at your hotel or campground.

GUIDED TOURS

Acadia National Park Tours (ⓒ **207/288-0300;** www.acadiatours.com) offers 2¹/₂-hour park tours departing twice daily (10am and 2pm) from downtown Bar Harbor. The bus tour includes three stops (Sieur De Monts Springs, Thunder Hole, and Cadillac Mountain) and plenty of park trivia, courtesy of the driver. This is an easy way for first-time visitors to get a quick introduction to the park before setting out on their own side trips. Tickets are available at Testa's Restaurant, 53 Main St., in Bar Harbor; the cost is $25 for adults, $10 for children 11 and under.

ENTRY POINTS & FEES

Entrance fees to the park are collected at several gates and points from May through October; the rest of the year, entrance is free—one of this nation's great outdoor bargains either way. A 1-week pass, which includes unlimited trips on the Park Loop Road (closed in winter), costs $20 per car from late June through early October and $10 per car in spring and fall; there's no additional charge per passenger once you've bought the pass. Hikers, cyclists, and anyone else traveling without a vehicle (that is, motorcyclists or boaters) must pay a $5 per person fee.

You can enter the park at several points in the interwoven network of park and town roads—a glance at a park map, available free at the visitor center, will make these access points self-evident. The main point of entry to Park Loop Road, the park's most scenic byway, is near the official park visitor center at **Hulls Cove** (on Rte. 3 just north of Bar Harbor); the entry fee is collected at a tollbooth on the loop road, a half-mile north of Sand Beach.

Acadia staffs two visitor centers. The **Thompson Island Information Center** (📞 207/ **288-3411**) on Route 3 is the first you'll pass as you enter Mount Desert Island. This center is maintained by the local chambers of commerce, but park personnel are often on hand to answer inquiries. It's open daily from May to mid-October, 6am until 10pm, and is a good first stop for general lodging and restaurant information.

If you're interested primarily in information about the park itself, continue on Route 3 to the National Park Service's **Hulls Cove Visitor Center,** about 7¹/₂ miles beyond Thompson Island. This attractive, stone-walled center has professionally pre- pared park service displays, such as a large relief map of the island, natural history exhib- its, and a short introductory film. You can also request free brochures about hiking trails and the carriage roads, or purchase postcards and more detailed guidebooks. The center is open daily mid-April through October from 8am to 4:30pm (to 6pm in July and Aug, to 5pm in Sept and Oct). Information is available year-round, by phone or in person, from the park's **headquarters** (📞 **207/288-3338**) on Route 233 between Bar Harbor and Somesville, open 8am to 4:30pm daily. You can also ask questions online at the website **www.nps.gov/acad**.

SEASONS

Spring is forgettable in Acadia, but summer is the peak season. The weather in July and August is perfect for just about any outdoor activity. Most days are warm (in the 70s or 80s/low to mid-20s Celsius), with afternoons frequently cooler than mornings owing to the sea breezes. (Fogs occasionally roll in from the southeast on a hot day, which gives a magical quality to the landscape.) While sun seems to be the norm, come prepared for rain; it's not uncommon at all. Once or twice each summer, a heat wave somehow settles onto the island, producing temperatures in the 90s (30s Celsius), dense haze, and stifling humidity, but this rarely lasts more than a few days. Enjoy summer: Soon enough (some- times even during late Aug), a brisk north wind will blow in from the Canadian Arctic, forcing visitors into sweaters at night. You'll smell the approach of autumn, with winter not far behind.

Tips **Packing a Picnic for Acadia**

Before you set out to explore, pack a lunch and keep it handy. Once you get inside it, the park has very few places (other than the Jordan Pond House, see later in this chapter) to stop for lunch or snacks. Having drinks and snacks at hand will prevent you from having to backtrack into Bar Harbor or elsewhere to fend off starvation midday. The more food you bring, the more your options for a day expand, so hit up one of the charming general stores in any of the island's villages first and stock up on sandwiches, sweets, camera batteries, and hydration.

Acadia National Park is full of picnic opportunities at every turn. **Sand Beach** is gloriously scenic (bring a blanket, plus a sweater for sea winds). A hike up any of the smaller mountains such as **Day Mountain** or **Flying Mountain** is rewarded with ocean views and cooling winds (or, in fall, a blaze of colors). If you're too tired to hike, truck over to **Jordan Pond** or to **The Bubbles** for good views.

Regulations

The usual national park rules apply. Guns may not be used in the park; if you have a gun, it must be "cased, broken down, or otherwise packaged against use." Fires and camping are allowed only at designated areas. Pets must be on leashes at all times. Seat belts must be worn in the national park (this is a federal law). Don't remove anything from the park, either man-made or natural; this includes cobblestones from the shore.

Fall here is wonderful. Between Labor Day and the foliage season in early October, days are often warm and clear, nights have a crisp tang, and you can avoid the congestion, crowds, and pesky insects of summer. It's not that the park is empty in September; bus tours seem to proliferate at this time, which can mean periodic crowds and backups at the most popular sites (such as Thunder Hole). Not to worry: If you walk a minute or two off the road, you can find solitude and an agreeably peaceful walk or perch. Hikers and bikers will have the trails and carriage roads to themselves.

Winter is an increasingly popular time to travel to Acadia, especially among those who enjoy cross-country skiing the carriage roads. Be aware, though, that snow along the coast is inconsistent, and services—including most restaurants and many inns—are often closed down outright in winter. Expect to stay in either a really cheap motel or an expensive resort, and to often eat what locals do: pizza, burgers, and sandwiches.

RANGER PROGRAMS

Frequent ranger programs are offered throughout the year at Acadia. These include talks at campground amphitheaters and tours of various island locales and attractions. Examples include an Otter Point nature hike, walks across the carriage roads' stone bridges, cruises on Frenchman Bay (rangers provide commentary on many trips), and discussions of the changes in Acadia's landscape—there was even a small *earthquake* here in October 2006, causing rock slides that still keep a few trails closed. Ask for a schedule of park events and more information at any visitor center or campground.

DRIVING TOUR   **DRIVING THE PARK LOOP ROAD**

The 20-mile **Park Loop Road** ★★ is to Acadia what Half Dome is to Yosemite—the park's premier attraction, and a magnet for the largest crowds. This remarkable roadway starts near the Hulls Cove Visitor Center and follows the high ridges above Bar Harbor before dropping down along the rocky coast. Here, spires of spruce and fir cap dark granite ledges, making a sharp contrast with the white surf and steel-blue sea. After following the picturesque coast and touching on several coves, the road loops back inland along Jordan Pond and Eagle Lake, with a detour to the summit of the island's highest peak, Cadillac Mountain.

Ideally, visitors should try to make two circuits of the loop road. The first time, go for the sheer exhilaration of it and to get the lay of the land. On the second time around, plan to stop frequently and poke around on foot, setting off on trails or scrambling along the coastline. Scenic pull-offs are staggered at frequent intervals. The two-lane road is one-way along its coastal sections; the right-hand lane is set aside for parking, so you can stop wherever you'd like, admire the vistas, and click away.

From about 10am until 4pm in July and August, anticipate big crowds along the loop road, at least on days when the sun is shining. Parking lots often fill up and close at some of the most popular destinations, including Sand Beach, Thunder Hole, and the Cadillac Mountain summit, so try to visit these spots early or late in a day. Alternatively, make the best of cloudy or drizzly days by letting the weather work to your advantage; you'll sometimes discover that you have the place nearly to yourself.

From the Hulls Cove Visitor Center, the Park Loop initially runs atop:

❶ Paradise Hill

The tour starts with sweeping views eastward over Frenchman Bay. You'll see the town of Bar Harbor far below, and just beyond it the Porcupines, a cluster of islands that look like, well, just what you'd expect from the name.

Following the Park Loop Road clockwise, you'll dip into a wooded valley and come to:

❷ Sieur de Monts Spring

Here you'll find a rather uninteresting natural spring, unnaturally encased, along with a botanical garden with some 300 species showcased in 12 habitats. The original **Abbe Museum** (✆ 207/288-3519) is here, featuring a small but select collection of Native American artifacts. It's open daily from late May to early October, 9am to 4pm; admission is $2 for adults, $1 for children ages 6 to 15. (A larger and more modern branch of the museum in Bar Harbor features more and better-curated displays; a ticket here gets you a $2 discount there. See "Exploring Bar Harbor," later in this chapter, for details.)

The **Tarn** is the chief reason to stop here; a few hundred yards south of the springs via a footpath, it's a slightly medieval-looking and forsaken pond sandwiched between steep hills. Departing from the south end of the Tarn is the fine **Dorr Ladder Trail** (see "Hiking in the Park," below).

Continue the clockwise trip on the loop road; views eastward over the bay soon resume, almost uninterruptedly, until you get to:

❸ The Precipice Trail

The park's most dramatic trail, this ascends sheer rock faces on the east side of Champlain Mountain. Only about ³/₄ of a mile to the summit, it's rigorous and involves scrambling up iron rungs and ladders in exposed places (those with a fear of heights and those under 5 ft. tall should avoid this trail). The trail is often closed midsummer to protect nesting peregrine falcons. Rangers are often on hand in the trail-head parking lot to point out the birds and suggest alternative hikes.

Between the Precipice Trail and Sand Beach is a tollbooth where visitors have to pay the park entrance fee.

Picturesquely set between the arms of a rocky cove is:

❹ Sand Beach

Sand Beach ★ is virtually the only sand beach on the island, although swimming these cold waters (about 50°F/10°C) is best enjoyed on extremely hot days or by those with a freakishly robust metabolism. When it's sunny out, the sandy strand is crowded midday with picnickers. (The water at the far end of the beach—where a gentle stream enters the cove—is often a few degrees warmer than the part beside the access stairway.)

Two worthwhile hikes start near this beach. The **Beehive Trail** overlooks Sand Beach (see "Hiking in the Park," below); it starts from a trail head across the loop road. From the east end of Sand Beach, look for the start of the **Great Head Trail,** a loop of about 2 miles that follows on the bluff overlooking the beach, then circles back along the shimmering bay before cutting through the woods back to Sand Beach.

About a mile south of Sand Beach is:

➎ Thunder Hole

Thunder Hole ★ is a shallow oceanside cavern into which surf surges, compresses, and bursts out. (A walking trail on the road allows you to leave your car parked at the beach). When the sea is as quiet as a pond—and it can be, on some midsummer days—just drive right on past without stopping.

However, on days when the seas are rough and large swells roll in all the way from the Bay of Fundy, this is a must-see, three-star attraction; you can feel the ocean's power and force resonating under your sternum. The best viewing time is 3 hours before high tide; check tide tables, obtainable at local hotels, restaurants, and info kiosks.

Just before the road curves around Otter Point, you'll be driving atop:

➏ Otter Cliffs

This set of 100-foot-high precipices is capped with dense stands of spruce trees. From the top, look for spouting whales in summer. In early fall, thousands of eider ducks can sometimes be seen floating in big, raft-like flocks just offshore. A footpath traces the edge of the crags.

➐ Jordan Pond

Jordan Pond ★★ is a small but beautiful body of water encased by gentle, forested hills. A 3-mile hiking loop follows the pond's shoreline (see "Hiking in the Park," below), and a network of splendid carriage roads converges at the pond. After a hike or mountain-bike excursion, spend some time at a table on the lawn of the Jordan Pond House restaurant (see "Where to Dine," below).

Shortly before the loop road ends, you'll pass the entrance to:

➑ Cadillac Mountain

Reach this **mountain** ★ by car, ascending an early carriage road. At 1,528 feet, it's the highest peak on the Atlantic between Canada and Brazil. (Really.) During much of the year, it's also the first place on U.S. soil touched by the rays of sunrise. But because Cadillac Mountain is the only mountaintop in the park accessible by car, and because it's also the island's highest point, the parking lot at the summit can get jammed. Views are undeniably great, though the shopping-mall-at-Christmas atmosphere can put a serious crimp in your enjoyment of the place if it's *too* packed. Some lower peaks accessible only by foot—such as Acadia and Champlain mountains—have equally excellent views and far fewer crowds.

BIKING THE CARRIAGE ROADS ★★

The 57 miles of **carriage roads** built by John D. Rockefeller, Jr., are among the park's most extraordinary hidden treasures. Though built for horse and carriage, they are ideal for cruising by mountain bike and offer some of the most scenic, relaxing biking found anywhere in the United States. Park your car near Jordan Pond, then plumb the tree-shrouded lanes that lace the area, taking time to admire the stonework on the uncommonly fine bridges. Afterward, stop for tea and popovers at the **Jordan Pond House** (see "Where to Dine," below), which has been a popular island destination for over a century, although it's unlikely as much Lycra was in evidence 100 years ago.

The carriage roads were maintained by Rockefeller until his death in 1960, after which they became shaggy and overgrown. A major restoration effort was launched in 1990, and today the roads are superbly restored and maintained. With their wide hard-packed surfaces, gentle grades, and extensive directional signs, they make for very smooth biking. Note that bikes are also allowed on the island's free shuttle buses (see "Getting Around," earlier in this chapter).

A useful map of the roads is available free at visitor centers; more-detailed guides may be purchased at area bookshops but aren't necessary. Where carriage roads cross private land (generally btw. Seal Harbor and Northeast Harbor), they're closed to mountain bikes, which are also banned from hiking trails.

Mountain bikes can be rented along Cottage Street in Bar Harbor, with rates generally ranging from around $20 for a full day, $15 for a half-day (which is only 4 hr. in the bike-rental universe). High-performance and tandem bikes cost a bit more than that, children's bikes a bit less. Most bike shops include locks and helmets as basic equipment, but ask what's included before you rent. Also ask about closing times, since you'll be able to get in a couple of extra hours with a late-closing shop. The **Bar Harbor Bicycle Shop,** 141 Cottage St. (© **207/288-3886;** www.barharborbike.com), gets many people's vote for the most convenient and friendliest. You could also try **Acadia Bike & Canoe,** 48 Cottage St. (© **800/526-8615;** www.acadiabike.com).

HIKING IN THE PARK

Hiking is the quintessential Acadia experience, and it should be experienced by everyone at least once. The park has 120 miles of hiking trails in all, plus 57 miles of carriage roads, which are great for easier walking. Some traverse the sides or faces of low "mountains" (which would be called hills anywhere else), and almost all summits have superb views of the Atlantic. Many of these pathways were crafted by stonemasons or others with aesthetic intent, so the routes aren't always the most direct—but they're often incredibly scenic, taking advantage of natural fractures in the rocks, picturesque ledges, and sudden, sweeping vistas.

The Hulls Cove Visitor Center has a brief chart summarizing area hikes; combined with the park map, this is all you need to find one of the well-maintained, well-marked trails and start exploring. Cobble together different loop hikes to make your trips more varied, and be sure to coordinate your hiking with the weather; if it's damp or foggy, you'll stay drier and warmer strolling the carriage roads. If it's clear and dry, head for the highest peaks (Cadillac, The Bubbles) with the best views.

One of the best trails is the **Dorr Ladder Trail ★**, which departs from Route 3 near the Tarn just south of the Sieur de Monts entrance to the Loop Road. This trail begins with a series of massive stone steps ascending along the base of a vast slab of granite and then passes through crevasses (not for the wide of girth) and up ladders affixed to the granite. The views east and south are superb.

An easy lowland hike is around **Jordan Pond,** with the northward leg along the pond's east shore on a hiking trail and the return via carriage road. It's mostly level, with the total loop measuring just more than 3 miles. At the north end of Jordan Pond, consider heading up the prominent, oddly symmetrical mounds called **The Bubbles ★**. These detours shouldn't take much more than 20 minutes each; look for signs off the Jordan Pond Shore Trail.

On the western side of the island, an ascent of **Acadia Mountain** and return takes about 1¹/₂ hours, but hikers should schedule in some time for lingering while they enjoy the view of Somes Sound and the smaller islands off Mount Desert's southern shores. This 2¹/₂-mile loop hike begins off Route 102 at a trail head 3 miles south of Somesville. Head eastward through rolling mixed forest, then begin an ascent over ledge-y terrain. Be sure to visit both the east and west peaks (the east peak has the better views), and look for hidden clearings in the summit forest that open up to unexpected vistas.

Many of the ocean-side rock faces attract experienced rock climbers, as much for the beauty of the climbing areas as the challenge of the climbs and the high-grade quality of the rock. For novices or experienced climbers, **Acadia Mountain Guides** (℃ **888/232-9559** or 207/288-8186; www.acadiamountainguides.com) offers rock-climbing lessons and guide services, ranging from a half-day introduction to rock climbing to intensive workshops on self-rescue and instruction on how to lead climbs. The Bar Harbor shop, open during summer only, is located at 198 Main St., at the corner of Mount Desert Street.

CAMPING IN & NEAR THE PARK

The National Park Service maintains two campgrounds within Acadia National Park. Both are extremely popular; during July and August, expect both of them to fill up by early to mid-morning.

The more popular of the two is **Blackwoods** ★★ (℃ **207/288-3274**), on the island's eastern side, with about 300 sites. To get there, follow Route 3 about 5 miles south out of Bar Harbor; bikers and pedestrians have easy access to the loop road from the campground via a short trail, and the Island Explorer bus stops here as well. This campground has no public showers or electrical hookups, but an enterprising business just outside the campground entrance provides clean showers for a modest fee. Camping fees at Blackwoods are $20 per night from May through October, $10 per site in April and November. Advance **reservations** can be made to Blackwoods by calling ℃ **877/444-6777** between 10am and midnight (only until 10pm in winter), or by using a new reservations system online at **www.recreation.gov**. An Acadia pass (see earlier in this chapter) is also required for campground entry.

The **Seawall** ★ (℃ **207/244-3600**) campground is located over on the quieter western half of the island, near the tiny fishing village of Bass Harbor (one of the Island Explorer bus routes also has a stop here). Seawall has about 215 sites, and it's a good base for cyclists or those wishing to explore several short coastal hikes within easy striking distance. However, it's quite a way from Bar Harbor and Sand Beach on the other side of the island; for families, it might not be the best choice. The campground is open mid-May through the end of September, but they *do not take reservations.* It's first-come, first-served all the way—and the lines form early. In general, if you get here by 9 or 10am you're pretty much assured of a campsite, especially if you want a walk-in site.

Camping fees at Seawall are $14 to $20 per night, depending on whether you want to drive directly to your site or can pack a tent in for a distance of up to 150 yards. There are also no electrical or water hookups here, and (as it is with Blackwoods) prior acquisition of an Acadia entrance pass is required to stay at the campground.

Private campgrounds handle the overflow. The region from Ellsworth south boasts 14 private campgrounds, which offer varying amenities. The **Thompson Island**

Information Center (☎ 207/288-3411), open 6am to 10pm daily from May through mid-October, posts up-to-the-minute information on which campgrounds still have vacancies; it's a good first stop for those arriving without camping reservations.

Two private campgrounds stand above the rest. **Bar Harbor Campground,** Route 3, Salisbury Cove (☎ **207/288-5185**), on the main route between the causeway and Bar Harbor, doesn't take reservations, and you can often find a good selection of sites if you arrive before noon, even during the peak season. Some of its 300 sites are set in piney woods; others are on an open hillside edged with blueberry barrens. The wooded sites are quite private. There's a pool for campers and uncommonly clean bathhouses, and campers always get to pick their own sites rather than be arbitrarily assigned one. Rates range from around $26 for a basic, no-services site to around $30 for those with hookups.

At the head of Somes Sound is **Mount Desert Campground,** Route 198 (☎ **207/ 244-3710**), which is especially well suited for campers (RVs to a maximum of 20 ft. only). This heavily wooded campground has very few undesirable sites and a great many desirable ones, including some walk-in sites right at the water's edge. The rate ranges from $36 to $49 per night in high season, $29 to $38 per site in the off season. It's open from mid-June to about mid-September. (***Note:*** This campground should not be confused with the Mount Desert Narrows Campground, which is more RV-oriented and located closer to the causeway.)

Another option is **Lamoine State Park** (☎ 207/667-4778), which faces Mount Desert from the mainland across the cold waters of northernmost Frenchman Bay. This is an exceptionally pleasant, quiet park with private sites, a shower house, and a small beach about a half-hour's drive from the action at Bar Harbor. The campground has been belatedly discovered by travelers in the last half-dozen years, but still rarely fills to capacity. It's open from mid-May to early September, and sites cost $20 per night for nonresidents of Maine.

Should all these options be full, don't despair: You can find a room, especially in Bar Harbor, which is teeming with motels and inns. The rest of the island also has a good, if scattered, selection of places to spend the night. See the "Where to Stay" sections for Bar Harbor and the rest of Mount Desert Island later in this chapter. Still desperate? Head off-island to Trenton (a clutch of motels along Rte. 3) and then Ellsworth.

WHERE TO DINE

Jordan Pond House ★★ (Finds) AMERICAN   The secret to the Jordan Pond House? Location, location, location. The restaurant traces its roots from 1847, when a farm was established on this picturesque property at the southern tip of Jordan Pond looking north toward The Bubbles, a picturesque pair of glacially sculpted mounds. In 1979, the original structure and its birch-bark dining room were destroyed by fire. A more modern, two-level dining room was built in its place—it has less charm, but it still has the island's best dining location, on a nice lawn. Afternoon tea with popovers and jam is a hallowed tradition here. The lobster stew is expensive but very good. Dinners include classic entrees such as prime rib, steamed lobster, and baked scallops.

Park Loop Rd. (near Seal Harbor), Acadia National Park. ☎ **207/276-3316.** www.jordanpond.com. Advance reservations not accepted; call before arriving to hold a table. Main courses lunch $8.50–$18; dinner $17–$20. AE, DISC, MC, V. Mid-May to late Oct daily 11:30am–8pm (until 9pm July–Aug).

Landscape Is Not Just Scenery

The places you'll be traveling are not just scenery. They are the home to millennia of natural history (volcanoes, icebergs, polar bears, whales, and caribou, oh my!), as well as a deep human history (Vikings, native Canadians fishing and hunting long before Europeans showed up, lobstermen). And the great part is, this story continues today: These layers overlap in fascinating ways to create the "place" that is now coastal Maine. Understand these creatures and landscapes you'll be interacting with *before* you get there, and you'll have a better trip—and become a more ecologically aware traveler with a deeper respect for what you're experiencing.

Pick up the books of Canadian author Farley Mowat; a locally written book on eastern Canadian geography, geology, natural history, or native Canadian culture (library book sales and local gifts shops are two great sources); or a novel by E. Annie Proulx. For information about the whales you'll be glimpsing (and how to respect them), visit the **Whale and Dolphin Conservation Society** (www.wdcs.org). For info on traveling lightly in general, see **Tread Lightly** (www.treadlightly.org) online.

3 A NATURE GUIDE TO ACADIA NATIONAL PARK

The human history of Acadia National Park is usually thought of as beginning in the early 20th century, when preservationists banded together with wealthy philanthropists to set aside and create the park we know today. In fact, its clock winds much farther back than that—beginning thousands of years ago, when local Native American tribes fished its shores and hunted its hills. But even *that* is just a flake off the deep, deep time that has been required to create Acadia. The rocks upon which you climb, sun yourself, and picnic are old—staggeringly old.

Before arriving, then, one would do well to acquaint oneself with the natural history of the place. Armed with a respect and appreciation for the landscape before you, you just might treat it a bit more reverently while you're here and help ensure it remains for future generations to behold for many years.

THE LANDSCAPE

The beginnings of Acadia National Park as we see it today are perhaps a half *billion* years old. At that time, deep wells of liquid rock known as magma were moving upward, exploding in underground volcanoes, then hardening—still underground, mind you—into granite-like rocks. Later, as natural forces such as wind and water wore away the upper layers of rock above these rocks, the rocks began to be exposed. Their journey was only beginning, however; soon enough (geologically speaking, that is), what is now eastern North America and most of Europe began to shove up against each other, slowly but inexorably. This "collision" (which was more like an extremely slow-motion car wreck), heated, squeezed, transformed, and thrust up the rocks that now form the backbone of Mount Desert Island. Now in place, the rocks were once again changed by everything around them. Ice ages came and went, but the rocks remained; the successive waves of great glaciation and retreat scratched up the rocks like old vinyl records, and the thick tongues of pressing ice cut deep notches out of the rock. Near Somesville it nearly divided the island in two, creating the only natural fjord in the United States; farther "inland," the slowly flowing ice pushed forward and scooped out several more narrow, parallel valleys that would later be filled by rainwater to form Jordan Pond and Eagle Lake. Huge boulders were swept up and deposited by the ice in odd places, such as the tops of mountains (Bubble Rock is one).

When the glaciers finally retreated for the last time, tens of thousands of years ago, the water melting from the huge ice sheet covering North America swelled the level of the Atlantic high enough to submerge formerly free-flowing river valleys and give Mount Desert Island the distinctive, knuckled-fist shape we know it for today.

Onto the bones of this landscape came plants and then animals. After each ice age, conifers such as spruce and fir trees—alongside countless grasses and weeds—began to reform, decompose, and form soils. It was tough work: Acadia is a rocky, acidic place. Yet they persevered, and soon the spruces, firs, and hemlocks formed an impenetrable thicket covering the bedrock. Land animals came here, too, some of them now extinct from the island—the caribou, elk, eastern timber wolf, and sea mink among those extirpated by human presence. Many others survived, however, and there's plenty of wildlife here today; while the lynx and eastern cougar may no longer roam the woods, hills, and fields of Acadia, plenty of other creatures do.

The park, though it appears to be fixed in time now, is actually in constant flux. Islanders got a lesson in nature's restorative powers in 1947, when a huge forest fire swept across the park and island, devastating most of it; in the ashes soon grew not more spruces and firs, but rather an entire new set of flowers, weeds, and trees better adapted to grow in bright, sunny, nutrient-poor meadows. Fireweeds, wildflowers, aspens, birch, oak, pine, and maple trees began to slowly fill in the denuded landscape and today help create the mixture of plants (and the fall foliage, and the deer, mice, and other animals that favor this mixture) in the park today. The spruces and firs may, eventually, take over again—but it will take generations to happen.

Acadia's unique position—it is very near the warm Gulf Stream, yet possesses very cold waters; it is not far from the high, shallow undersea plateau known as Georges Bank—has also brought an astonishing variety of marine life to its doorstep. Migrating whales make for a wonderful spectacle twice each year (and whale-watching tours out of Bar Harbor bring the lives of whales closer to the visitor). Seabirds make similar passages, lighting upon the rocks and lakes of the park coming and going. And the waters teem—though not as they once did—with fish large and small, lobsters, crabs, dolphins, and a great deal more (each creature with its particular habits, habitats, diets, life cycles, and seasonal migration patterns).

This is to say almost nothing of Acadia's tide pools, in that precarious zone where land and rock meet crashing ocean; a closer look at these pools reveals an ever-changing world of seaweed, snails, barnacles, darting water bugs, clams, shellfish, mud-burrowing worms, and other creatures. Interestingly, the type of life you'll find changes in well-marked "bands" as you get closer to water; rocks that are always submerged contain one mixture of seaweeds and marine organism, rocks that are exposed and then resubmerged each day by the tides contain another. Mostly dry surfaces of the shore rocks contain yet another mixture of living things. It's fascinating to note how each particular organism has found its niche, maintained it, and continues to live hardily and well—within its particular band. Move it up or down a foot, and it would perish.

What follows is only the barest sketch of the natural world in Acadia. For a real look at it, go and see it yourself—preferably by as many means as possible. Whether you choose to explore Acadia on foot, bicycle, horse-drawn carriage, kayak, charter boat, or some other way, you're almost certain to see something here you've never seen before. If you're attentive, you'll come away with a deeper respect for things natural—here, and everywhere.

THE FLORA

BALSAM FIR   The best-smelling tree in the park must be the mighty balsam fir, whose tips are harvested elsewhere to fabricate aromatic Christmas-tree wreaths. It's sometimes hard to tell a fir from a spruce or hemlock, though the balsam's flat, paddle-like needles (white underneath) are nearly unique—only a hemlock's are similar. Pull one off the twig to be sure; a fir's needle comes off clean, a hemlock's ragged. Still not sure you've got a fir tree on your hands? The long, glossy, almost purplish cones are absolutely distinctive.

Balsam Fir

RED, WHITE, AND PITCH PINE   The pines grow in Acadia's sandy soils and normally like some sunlight. **White pine** is the familiar "King's pine" prevalent throughout Maine; its trunk was prized for the masts of British ships of war, and countless huge pines were floated down Maine rivers by logger men. Sadly, very few virgin pine trees remain in Maine today. The white pine's extremely long, strong needles come five to a bunch. The **red pine,** not so common, can be distinguished by its pairs of needles and pitchy trunk. The presence of a **pitch pine** indicates poor, acidic soils, and this is one of the first trees to successfully rush in and take root in the wake of a fire. It can grow in the oddest places—along a cliff, on a lip of crumbling stone, in waste soil. The shorter, scrubby clumps of needles (arranged three to a group) don't look attractive but belie the tree's toughness.

Red Pine   *White Pine*

RED AND SUGAR MAPLE   These two maple trees look vaguely alike when turning color in fall, but they're actually quite different—from the shapes of their leaves to the habitats they prefer. **Red maples** have skinny, gray trunks and like a swampy or wet area; often, several of the slim trunks grow together into a clump, and in fall the red maples' pointy leaves turn a brilliant scarlet color almost at once. **Sugar maples,** on the other hand, are stout-trunked trees with lovely, substantial leaves (marked with distinctive U-shaped notches), which autumn slowly changes to red and flame-orange. Sugar maples grow in or at the edges of mixed forests, often in combination with birch trees, oak trees, beech trees, hemlocks, and the like. Their sap, of course, can be collected and boiled down to make delicious maple syrup.

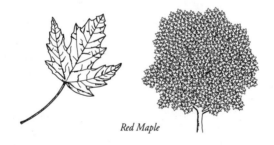

Red Maple

LOWBUSH BLUEBERRY   The lowbush blueberry, with its shrubby, tealike leaves and hardy, thick twigging, lies low to exposed rocks on sunny hillsides or sometimes crops up in shady woods; most of the year, it's inconspicuous as anything, trailing harmlessly underfoot. Come late summer, however, and it's suddenly the island's most popular plant—among bears as well as humans. The wild blueberries ripen slowly in the sun (look behind and beneath the leaves for the best bunches), and make for fine eating, pancake baking, and jam.

THE FAUNA
Mammals
Land Mammals
BEAVER   Reintroduced to Acadia in the 1920s (it had earlier nearly gone extinct from brisk world trade in beaver pelts), the beaver's lodge-building, stick-chewing, and hibernating habits are well known. You'll find it in streams, lakes, and ponds around Mount Desert Island.

Beaver

BLACK BEAR Black bears do occur in Acadia, though in small numbers (still, you may want to keep a cover on that campfire food). The bears are mostly—emphasis on mostly—plant-eaters and docile. Though they'll eat just about anything, black bears prefer easily reached foods on the woodland floor such as berries, mushrooms, and nuts. They need them for a long winter hibernation that averages 6 months.

Black Bear

MOOSE Nothing says Maine like a moose, and the huge, skinny-legged, vegetarian moose is occasionally seen in Acadia National Park; not very often, however. It far prefers the deep woods, lakes, ponds, and uninhabited areas of Maine's Great North Woods. You can't miss it if you see it, though—the rack of antlers (on the male), the broad, lineman shoulder, the spindly (but quick) legs, and the sheer bulk of the thing—big as a truck— ensure you won't mistake it for anything else on the planet. Hope you don't run into one late at night, on a highway: Each year cars and moose meet up in Maine. Everybody loses, but the car gets a lot more banged up than the moose.

Moose

AMERICAN LOBSTER   Everyone knows the lobster by sight and taste; what few know is that not so long ago it was considered ugly, tasteless, and unfit to eat. In fact, there was a time when mainly prisoners in Maine were served lobster and lobster stew—three meals a day! Today, of course, the situation is very different. Lobsters, which are related to crabs and shrimp (and more generally to spiders and insects), slowly scour the ocean bottom in shallow, dark waters, locating food by smell. They actually see very poorly. The hard shell, which they periodically shed in order to grow, is the lobster's skeleton: a greenish-black color in life, bright red only after having been cooked.

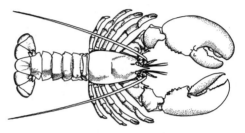

American Lobster

Whales, Dolphins, Porpoises & Seals

FINBACK WHALE   A seasonal visitor to Maine's waters twice a year when migrating between polar and equatorial waters, the finback is one of the biggest whales, and also one of the most collegial. It often travels in pairs or groups of a half-dozen or more (most whales are relatively solitary), though it does not travel close to shore or in shallow waters; you'll need a whale-watch boat to spot it. Find it by its rather triangular head and a fin that sweeps backward (like a dolphin's) rather than standing straight up like many other whales'.

Finback Whale

HUMPBACK WHALE   Though this whale's Latin name roughly translates as "large-winged New England resident," the gentle, gigantic humpback actually isn't so often seen off the coast of Acadia. (That's mostly because they were easy targets in the heyday of whaling.) But if you do see it, you'll know it: It's huge, dark black, blows tremendous amounts of water when surfacing, and does some amazingly playful acrobatics above water. The males also sing haunting songs, sometimes for as long as 2 days at a time. The world population has shrunk to perhaps 20,000 individuals.

MINKE WHALE   The smallest (and most human-friendly) of the whales, the minke swims off Acadia's coast, usually moving in groups of two or three whales—but much larger groups collect in feeding areas and seasons. It has a unique habit of approaching and congregating around boats and ships, making this a whale you're quite likely to see while on a whale-watching tour. The minke is dark gray on top; the throat has grooves; and each black flipper fin is marked with a conspicuous white band.

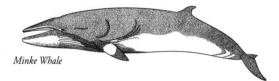

Minke Whale

NORTHERN RIGHT WHALE   If you see a right whale, you've really seen something: It's the most endangered of all the living whales—there are probably fewer than a thousand left in all the oceans of the world, and the northern right is even scarcer—yet one has occasionally been seen off the coast of Acadia. Experts predict it will become extinct within a few more human generations, if not sooner. Huge and active as the humpback, the right is known for doing headstands (so to speak) underwater, poking its tail fins above. It can be spotted by its light color—often blue, brown, or even off-white—and the whitish calcium growths that often appear on its head.

Northern Right Whale

PILOT WHALE   A small whale, the pilot is very rarely seen off Acadia, and very poorly understood. Its habits, world population, and diet are nearly unknown. It is known to congregate in large groups, sometimes consisting of up to several hundred, and even to swim with other species of whale at sea. Nearly unique among the whales that pass Maine, it has teeth, and the roundish fin is swept back like a dolphin's or shark's. Sightings are possible and should be cherished.

Pilot Whale

DOLPHINS   Two very similar-looking species of dolphin—the **Atlantic white-sided dolphin** and the **white-beaked dolphin**—rarely come to the coast of Maine. Cute and athletic, these dolphins sometimes also occasionally turn up on southern New England's beaches, for a more tragic reason: Large groups are occasionally stranded by the tide, then perish when they cannot get back to sea in time.

White-Beaked Dolphin

Atlantic White-Sided Dolphin

HARBOR PORPOISE Quiet in behavior and habit, the porpoise is not the same thing as a dolphin; in fact, it's darker, much less athletic, and with a blunter, triangular fin. (The dolphin jumps out of the water, and has a pointier fin that sweeps backward.)

Harbor Porpoise

HARBOR SEAL Related to sea lions, the whiskered harbor seal is best seen by using one of the charter boat services that leaves from Bar Harbor and other local harbors. You can also sometimes see it basking in the sun or on the rocks of an offshore island. You'll easily recognize it: The seal's flippers have five claws, almost like a human hand; its neck is stocky and strong (as are its teeth); and then there are those whiskers and that fur.

Birds
Waterfowl

DUCKS Between one and two dozen species of ducks and ducklike geese, brant, and teal seasonally visit the lakes, ponds, and tidal coves of Acadia every year, including—though hardly limited to—the **red-breasted merganser, common eider,** and the **bufflehead.** Mergansers, characterized by very white sides and very red bills (males) or reddish crests (females), occur year-round in the park but are more common in winter months. So is the eider, which inhabits offshore islands and coastal waters rather than Mount Desert Island's freshwater lakes; Maine is actually the southernmost tip of its breeding range—in winter, it forms huge rafts of birds. Males are marked with a sharp black-and-white pattern. The chubby, squat bufflehead is also distinctively black and white, with a glossy green-and-purple head; it is entirely absent from the park in summer, but passes through in spring and fall, sometimes lingering for the winter. It flies much more quickly than one might imagine from its appearance.

Red-Breasted Merganser

Common Eider

GREATBLUE HERON Everyone recognizes a great blue at once by its prehistoric flapping wings, comb of feathers, and spindly legs. These magnificent hunters wade tidal
rivers, fishing with lightning strikes beneath the surface, from May through around
October. The smaller, stealthier green heron occurs less commonly, and occasional sightings of black-crowned and yellow-crowned night herons have also been recorded within
the park's boundaries.

Great Blue Heron

LOONS Two species of loon visit the island's lakes and tidal inlets, fishing for dinner.
The **red-throated loon,** grayish with a red neck, is mostly a spring visitor and barely
present at all in the heat of summer. The **common loon** is, indeed, more common—it
can be distinguished by a black band around the neck, as well as black-and-white stripes
and dots—and can be found in Acadia year-round, though it's most easily spotted in late
spring and late fall. It gives the distinctive mournful, almost laughing cry for which the
birds are famous. Both have been decimated by human environmental changes such as
oil spills, acid rain, and airborne mercury.

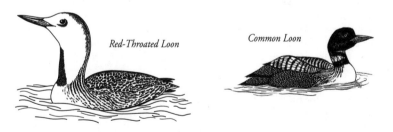

Red-Throated Loon

Common Loon

PLOVERS Plovers inhabit and breed in Acadia's muddy tidal flats, and their habitat is
understandably precarious; a single human step could crush an entire generation of eggs.
Only two species of plover visit the park, and they're here in significant numbers for only
a relatively short time. The **black-bellied plover**—marked with a snowy black-and-white
pattern—arrives in May, breeds in August and September, and is gone by Thanksgiving.
The **semipalmated plover,** with its quite different brownish body and white breast, has
a similar life cycle.

Black-Bellied Plover

Semipalmated Plover

SEAGULLS   No bird is so closely associated with Maine as the seagull. But, in fact, there's more than one kind of gull here; three or four distinct gulls are commonly found here year-round, a few more visit seasonally, and a few more pop up occasionally. Most common is the grayish **herring gull,** which is also the gull least afraid of humans. It's found in prevalence every month of the year. The aggressive **great black-backed gull** is similarly common, and is nearly all white (except for that black back and wings); it will even eat the eggs of another gull, but in general avoids humans. Less common are the glaucous, **ring-billed gull,** and even the **laughing and Bonaparte's gulls** (in summer only), not to mention the related **black-legged kittiwake.** Each has a distinctive look; consult a bird guide if you're interested in telling them apart.

Herring Gull

Black-Backed Gull

Bonaparte's Gull

STORM PETRELS The tiny storm petrel is a fascinating creature. These plucky little birds fly astonishing distances in winter, eating insects on the wing, only to return to Acadia each spring like clockwork, usually in May. They spend an amazing 4 months in the nest incubating, hatching, and tending to their single, white eggs. **Wilson's storm petrel** is here for a shorter time than the **Leach's storm petrel,** which restricts its visits and nests solely to offshore rocks and islands. Both breed in the height of summer, then pack up and head south again by fall.

Wilson's Storm Petrel

Land Birds

BALD EAGLE Yes, they're here—year-round—and even breed in Acadia, though they're difficult to find and hardly conspicuous. (Their endangered status means you shouldn't really try to seek them out.) The bald eagle's black body, white head, and yellow bill make it almost impossible to confuse with any other bird. It was nearly wiped out by the 1970s, mainly due to environmental poisons such as DDT-based pesticides, which caused female eagles to lay eggs that were too weak to sustain growing baby chicks. However, the bird has begun to come back.

Bald Eagle

COMMON RAVEN   The park holds jays and crows aplenty, but the raven is a breed apart—tougher, more reclusive, more ragged, more interesting. Look (or listen) for it on cliff tops, mountains, and in deep woods.

Common Raven

SONGBIRDS   There are literally dozens of species of songbirds coming to roost in Acadia's open fields, forests, and dead snags—even in the rafters and bird boxes of houses. They are not so common on this rocky, shady island as in Maine's suburbia (Greater Portland, for instance) or in the farmlands of central and western Maine, but they are here. One thing is for certain: Songbirds love human company, thus look for them near the settled areas. The park hosts perhaps 15 or more distinct types of chirpy little **warblers,** each with unique and often liquid songs; a half-dozen **thrushes** occurring in significant numbers; winter **wrens, swallows, sparrows, vireos, finches, creepers,** and **thrashers;** the whimsical black-capped **chickadee;** and occasional (and lovely) sightings of **bluebirds, cardinals,** and **tanagers,** among many other species.

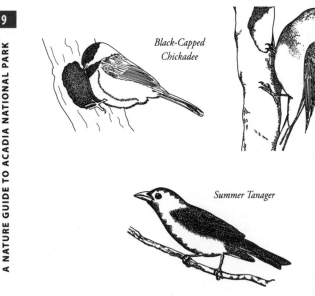

Black-Capped Chickadee

Eastern Bluebird

Summer Tanager

4 BAR HARBOR ★

Bar Harbor provides most of the meals and beds to travelers coming to the island, as it has done since the grand resort era of the late 19th century, when wealthy vacationers first discovered the Acadia region. Later, sprawling hotels and boardinghouses cluttered the shores and hillsides as a newly affluent middle class flocked here by the steamboat and rail car from the city.

The tourist business continued to boom through the early 1900s, then all but collapsed when the Depression and the growing popularity of car travel doomed the era of steamship travel and extended vacations. Bar Harbor was dealt another blow in 1947, when an accidental fire spread rapidly and leveled many of the opulent cottages and a large portion of the island. Some 17,000 acres burned in all, though downtown Bar Harbor and some in-town mansions on the oceanfront were spared.

In recent years, though, Bar Harbor has bounced back hard, revived and rediscovered by visitors and entrepreneurs alike. Some see Bar Harbor as a tacky tourist mecca, replete with T-shirt vendors, ice-cream shops, and souvenir palaces, crowds spilling off the sidewalks into the street, and appalling traffic for such a small town. That is all somewhat true. Yet the town's history, distinguished architecture, and beautiful location on French-man Bay *still* make it a desirable base for exploring the island anyway, and it has by far the best selection of lodging, meals, supplies, and services. If you want to shop, fine-dine, or go out at night, you've pretty much got to stay here. Otherwise, consider elsewhere on the island (see later in this chapter).

ESSENTIALS

Getting There

Bar Harbor is on Route 3, about 10 miles southeast of the causeway leading onto Mount Desert Island. For plane and bus access, see "Getting There," in the Acadia National Park section earlier in this chapter.

Visitor Information

The **Bar Harbor Chamber of Commerce,** P.O. Box 158, Bar Harbor, ME 04609 (© 207/288-5103; www.barharborinfo.com), stockpiles a huge arsenal of information about local attractions both at its offices on 1 West St. (at the pier) and in a welcome center on Route 3 in Trenton, just before the bridge onto the island. Write, call, or e-mail in advance for a directory of area lodging and attractions. The chamber's website is chock-full of information and helpful links.

EXPLORING BAR HARBOR

The best water views in town are from the foot of Main Street at grassy **Agamont Park,** which overlooks the town pier and Frenchman Bay. From here, set off past the Bar Harbor Inn on the **Shore Path ★★,** a wide, winding trail that follows the shoreline for half a mile along a public right of way. The pathway passes in front of many elegant summer homes (some converted to inns), offering a superb vantage point to view the area's architecture.

The **Abbe Museum ★,** 26 Mount Desert St. (© 207/288-3519; www.abbemuseum. org), opened in 2001 as an in-town extension of the smaller, simpler museum at the Sieur de Monts spring in the national park (see above), showcasing a top-rate collection of

Tips   **Parking in Bar Harbor**

If parking spaces are scarce downtown, head to the end of Albert Meadow (a side street across from the Village Green). At the end of the road is a small waterfront park with free parking, great views of the bay, and foot access to Shore Path. It's not well marked or publicized, so you can often find a place to park when much of the rest of town is filled up.

Native American artifacts. A 17,000-square-foot gallery, this downtown branch has an orientation center and a glass-walled lab where visitors can see archaeologists at work preserving recently recovered artifacts, along with changing exhibits and videos that focus largely on Maine and other New England tribes. From late May through October, it opens daily from 10am to 6pm; then, from November through late April, it's open Thursdays to Saturdays (same hours). In late April and most of May, it's open Friday to Sunday only. Admission is $6 for adults, $2 for children ages 6 to 15.

A short stroll around the corner from the new Abbe Museum is the **Bar Harbor Historical Society,** 33 Ledgelawn Ave. (© **207/288-0000** or 288-3807). The society moved into this handsome 1918 former convent in 1997, where it has showcased artifacts of life in the old days—dishware and photos from the grand old hotels, and exhibits on noted landscape architect Beatrix Farrand. Leave enough time to spend a few minutes thumbing through the scrapbooks about the devastating 1947 fire. The museum is open from June to October, Monday to Saturday from 1 to 4pm; admission is free. Even during the off season, entrance can sometimes be arranged.

At the north edge of town on Route 3 is the **College of the Atlantic** (© **207/288-5015**), a school founded in 1969 with a strong emphasis on environmental education. The campus, with its old and new buildings, features the **George B. Dorr Museum of Natural History** (© **207/288-5395;** www.coamuseum.org) at 105 Eden St. It features exhibits that focus on interactions among island residents, from the two-legged to the four-legged, finny, and furry. From mid-June to Thanksgiving, the museum is Monday through Saturday from 10am to 5pm; the rest of the year, it's open by appointment only. Admission is $3.50 for adults, $2.50 for seniors, $1.50 for teens, and $1 for children ages 3 to 12.

One of downtown's less obvious attractions is the **Criterion Theatre,** 35 Cottage St. (© **207/288-3441**), a movie house built in 1932 in a classic Art Deco style and that so far has avoided the degradation of multiplexification. The 900-seat theater, located on Cottage Street, shows first-run movies in summer and is worth the price of admission for the fantastic, if somewhat faded, interiors; the movie is secondary. As once was the case at most movie palaces, it still costs extra to sit in the more exclusive loges upstairs.

WHALE-WATCHING

Bar Harbor is a base for several ocean endeavors, including whale-watching tours. Operators offer excursions in search of humpbacks, finbacks, minkes, and the infrequently seen endangered right whale. The sleekest is the Bar Harbor Whale Watch Company's *Friendship V* (© **888/942-5374** or 207/288-2386; www.whalesrus.com), which operates from the municipal pier at 1 West St. in downtown Bar Harbor. Tours

ACCOMMODATIONS ■
Acadia Hotel **23**
Balance Rock Inn **26**
Bar Harbor
    Grand Hotel **29**
Bar Harbor Hotel-
    Bluenose Inn **1**
Bar Harbor Inn **8**
Bass Cottage Inn **10**
Black Friar Inn **13**
Harborside Hotel &
    Marina **6**
Highbrook Motel **1**
Ivy Manor Inn **27**
Ledgelawn Inn **20**
Maples Inn **19**
Mira Monte Inn **17**
Primrose Inn **16**
Rockhurst Motel **18**
The Tides **4**
Villager Motel **28**

DINING ◆
Ben & Bill's Chocolate
    Emporium **9**
Café This Way **24**
Eden Vegetarian Café **5**
Galyn's **7**
Havana **30**
Jordan's Restaurant **14**
Lompoc Café &
    Brewpub **11**
Mâche Bistro **15**
Maggie's Restaurant **12**
Michelle's Fine Dining **27**
Mt. Desert Ice Cream **25**
The Rose Garden
    Restaurant **2**

ATTRACTIONS ●
Abbe Museum **22**
Bar Harbor Historical
    Society **21**
George B. Dorr Museum
    of Natural History **3**

Frenchman Bay

Town Pier

Shore Path

are on a fast, twin-hulled three-level excursion boat that can hold 200 passengers in two heated cabins. The tours run 3 hours plus; the cost is $49 per adult, $26 per child age 6 to 14, and $8 per child age 5 and under. A puffin- and whale-watching tour is also offered for the same price, and there are shorter seal-watching tours for about half the price. There's free on-site parking and a money-back guarantee that you'll see whales. The daily tours begin each season in late May and run through fall; call ahead for dates.

WHERE TO STAY

Bar Harbor is the bedroom community for Mount Desert Island, with hundreds of hotel, motel, and inn rooms. They're invariably filled during the busy days of summer, and even the most basic of rooms can be quite expensive in July and August. It's essential to reserve as early in advance as possible.

Reputable motels in or near town that have some rooms under $100 in peak season include the conveniently located **Villager Motel,** 207 Main St. (© **888/383-3211** or 207/ 288-3211); the in-town, pet-friendly **Rockhurst Motel,** 68 Mount Desert St. (© **207/ 288-3140**); and the **Highbrook Motel,** 94 Eden St. (© **800/338-9688** or 207/288-3591).

Packing a Picnic in Bar Harbor

Even in downtown Bar Harbor, you can have a nice picnic experience simply by settling onto a bench on the **Village Green**—that's the green, rectangular space tucked behind and between Mount Desert and Kennebec streets (beside from which island buses depart; it's a block off Cottage St.). People-watching abounds, and art shows and festivals sometimes come to the green.

Closer to the water, at the tip of the land (at the end of West and Main sts.), the pocket **Agamont Park** is superlative for its picnic spot and a view of boats and islands. There's also the quiet campus of earthy **College of the Atlantic,** back on Route 3; they surely won't mind if you plunk down a basket and graze—in the interest of researching the college for future enrollment, of course. You're surrounded by food in downtown Bar Harbor; the natural-foods store **Alternative Market,** 16 Mount Desert St. (℃ **207/288-8225**), is probably your best choice for prepared foods, drinks, and natural snacks. It's open daily from 10am to 6pm.

About 4 miles west of Bar Harbor on Route 3 is **Hanscom's Motel and Cottages** (℃ 207/ 288-3744; www.hanscomsmotel.com), an old-fashioned motor court with 12 units (some two-bedroom) that have been well maintained. Its rates range from $92 to $120 in summer; from $62 off season.

Very Expensive

Balance Rock Inn ★★★   Tucked down a quiet side alley just off Bar Harbor's main drag, the Balance Rock (built in 1903 for a Scottish railroad magnate) reaches for and achieves a gracefully upscale Long Island beach house feel. The entrance alone is nearly worth the steep rack rates: You enter a sitting room, which looks out onto the sort of azure outdoor swimming pool you'd expect to find in a Tuscan villa, and just beyond looms the Atlantic. Rooms are as elegant as any on the island, with a variety of layouts, some with sea views; some have whirlpools and saunas, while the penthouse suite adds a full kitchen. The comfortable king-size beds are adjustable using controls and have been fitted with feather beds and quality linens. A poolside bar, piano room, gracious staff, and fragrant flowers lining the driveway complete the romance of the experience.

21 Albert Meadow, Bar Harbor, ME 04609. ℃ **800/753-0494** or 207/288-2610. www.barharborvacations. com. 17 units. July to mid-Oct and holidays $275–$625 double and suite; May–June and mid- to late Oct $115–$625 double and suite. Rates include full breakfast. AE, DISC, MC, V. Closed Nov to early May. Well-behaved pets welcome, $30 per pet per night. **Amenities:** Poolside bar; outdoor pool; fitness room. *In room:* A/C, hair dryer, iron.

Expensive

Bar Harbor Grand Hotel ★   This big hotel fills a lodging gap between quaint, expensive inns and B&Bs and the island's family-owned motels, hotels, and cottages. The hotel's blocky, two-towered design faithfully copies the style of the Rodick House, a now-defunct 19th-century lodging in Bar Harbor that could once boast of being Maine's

largest hotel; the Grand, however, does the former one better with spacious rooms and
bathrooms and, of course, modern fixtures. Rooms and suites are decked out in the same
floral bedspreads and curtains you'd expect in any upscale business hotel, and the access
to downtown Bar Harbor and the nearby ocean are big pluses. Concessions to business
and tourist travelers include a guest laundry facility, gift shop, and high-speed Internet
access. Not surprisingly, they're getting a lot of tour groups here. Expect comfort rather
than island character.

269 Main St., Bar Harbor, ME 04609. *✆* **888/766-2529** or 207/288-5226. www.barharborgrand.com. 70
units. Mid-June to mid-Nov $145–$205 double; mid-Apr to mid-June $79–$129 double. Suites more
expensive. Rates include continental breakfast. Packages available. DISC, MC, V. Closed mid-Nov to mid-
Apr. **Amenities:** Heated outdoor pool; Jacuzzi; fitness room; coin-op laundry. *In room:* A/C, TV, fridge,
coffeemaker.

Bar Harbor Hotel–Bluenose Inn ★★ This resort-style complex—situated in two
buildings topping a small rise—offers stunning views of the surrounding terrain. Facilities here are more modern, too: Expect spacious carpeted rooms with huge bathrooms,
small refrigerators, and balconies; a good fitness center; indoor and outdoor pools (the
indoor pool is fairly palatial); and one of the island's best dining rooms, the Rose Garden
(see "Where to Dine," below). The two buildings are slightly different in character, but
in either case upper-floor rooms with sea views are worth the extra cost, especially if the
weather is good. Staff here is professional and friendly.

90 Eden St., Bar Harbor, ME 04609. *✆* **800/445-4077** or 207/288-3348. www.bluenoseinn.com. 97 units.
Mid-June to mid-Oct $145–$405 double; spring and late fall $75–$299 double. AE, DC, DISC, MC, V.
Closed Nov–Apr. **Amenities:** Restaurant; indoor pool; outdoor pool; fitness center; spa; Jacuzzi. *In room:*
A/C, TV, fridge, coffeemaker, hair dryer, iron/ironing board, fireplace (some units).

The Bar Harbor Inn ★★ The Bar Harbor Inn, just off Agamont Park, nicely mixes
traditional and contemporary. On shady grounds just a minute's stroll from downtown,
the inn offers convenience and gracious charm. The shingled main inn, which dates from
the turn of the 19th century, has a settled, old-money feel, with its semicircular dining
room and a buttoned-down lobby; guest rooms, located in the main inn and two additional structures, are decidedly more contemporary. Units in the Oceanfront Lodge and
Main Inn both offer spectacular bay views, and many have private balconies; the less
expensive Newport Building lacks views but is comfortable and up-to-date. In 2006 the
inn added a new spa with Vichy showers, aromatherapy, heated-stone treatments, and
facials. The semiformal Reading Room serves resort meals before the best dining-room
views in town.

Newport Dr. (P.O. Box 7), Bar Harbor, ME 04609. *✆* **800/248-3351** or 207/288-3351. www.barharborinn.
com. 153 units. Late May to late Oct $119–$379 double; late Mar to late May and late Oct to late Nov
$79–$215 double. Rates include continental breakfast. AE, DISC, MC, V. Closed Dec to late Mar. **Amenities:** Dining room; heated outdoor pool; fitness room; spa; Jacuzzi; conference room; limited room service. *In room:* A/C, TV, hair dryer.

Bass Cottage Inn ★★ This tucked-away inn gets very high marks for friendliness,
service, and proximity to the water. The 10 rooms here are decked out in cast-iron beds,
silk canopies, love seats, armoires, writing desks, and the like. The gentle color schemes
range from ivory to sky blue to taupe, reflecting the soft light of the island, and many are
decorated with nautical prints; several have Jacuzzis and/or views, as well (and the entire-
top-floor suite has both). This is just a 2-minute walk from downtown, yet breakfast

feasts are worthy of a gourmet restaurant: They might include cornmeal griddle cakes with blueberries, French toast with vanilla sauce, scrambled eggs with smoked salmon. Innkeepers Teri and Jeff Anderholm are unfailingly helpful and generous with extra flourishes such as a piano, a DVD library for anytime use, and a 24-hour guest pantry stocked with snacks.

14 The Field (P.O. Box 242), Bar Harbor, ME 04609. ℂ **866/782-9224** or 207/288-1234. www.basscottage. com. 10 units. $175–$360 double and suite. Rates include full breakfast. 2-night stay minimum weekends, 3-day minimum stay holiday weekends. AE, MC, V. Closed late Oct to mid-May. Children age 12 and over welcome. **Amenities:** Concierge. *In room:* A/C, TV, Jacuzzi (some units), fireplace (some units).

Harborside Hotel & Marina ★★   Formerly an inexpensive, family-style motel, the Harborside has transformed itself into upscale digs. It offers a range of studios and two- and three-bedroom suites sporting fancier bathrooms, more business-hotel amenities, and bigger televisions than before. The priciest suites are similar to condominium units, with various combinations of Jacuzzis, fireplaces, balconies, water views, and even some full kitchens and dining rooms. For dining and nightlife, this property covers all the bases: there's a bar at the outdoor pool, another chandeliered-and-tapestried bar (as well as a formal dining room) in the adjacent Bar Harbor Club, and a homey Italian trattoria—not to mention a lobster shack next door.

55 West St., Bar Harbor, ME 04609. ℂ **800/328-5033** or 207/288-5033. www.theharborsidehotel.com. 187 units. $139–$259 double; $225–$850 suite. Off-season rates sometimes lower. DISC, MC, V. Closed Nov–Apr. **Amenities:** 2 restaurants; 2 bars; outdoor pool; fitness center; spa; Jacuzzi; conference room. *In room:* A/C, TV, dataport, kitchenette (some units), Jacuzzi (some units), fireplace (some units).

Ivy Manor Inn ★   The Ivy Manor quickly proved a welcome addition to Bar Harbor's upscale lodging pool when it opened in 1997. Located in a 1940s-era Tudor-style house, the inn has been thoroughly done over in an understated French Victorian style, mostly in rich colors such as burgundy. The rooms here are larger than average; most are carpeted and furnished with attractive, tasteful antiques from the innkeeper's collection. Some have antique claw-foot tubs; others have small outdoor sitting decks. Among the best units: no. 6, a small suite with a private sitting room and small fireplace; and no. 1, the king-size-bedded Honeymoon Room, with an imposing walnut headboard and matching armoire. The restaurant, Michelle's, is one of the town's best (see "Where to Dine," below).

194 Main St., Bar Harbor, ME 04609. ℂ **888/670-1997** or 207/288-2138. www.ivymanor.com. 8 units. Mid-June to Oct $200–$325 double; Apr to mid-June $185–$275 double. Rates include full breakfast. Closed Nov–Mar. 2-night minimum on holiday weekends. AE, DISC, MC, V. Children 11 and over welcome. **Amenities:** Restaurant; lounge. *In room:* A/C, TV, fireplace (some units).

The Tides ★   The Tides consists of just four guest rooms (three of which are suites) in a sprawling yellow mansion built in 1887. It's at the head of a long, lush lawn that descends to water's edge, on 1 1/2 acres in a neighborhood of imposing homes within easy walking distance of the center of town. Guests unwind in one of two spacious living rooms (one on each floor) and on the veranda, which has a unique outdoor fireplace. Breakfast is served on this porch in good weather; otherwise, it's enjoyed in a regal dining room, with polished wood floors and views out to Bar Island. There's a 2-night minimum stay at all times of the week and year here.

119 West St., Bar Harbor, ME 04609. ℂ **207/288-4968.** www.barharbortides.com. 4 units. Peak season $275 double, $375–$395 suite; off-season rates lower. Rates include full breakfast. 2-night minimum stay year-round. AE, DISC, MC, V. *In room:* TV, dataport, fireplace (most units).

Moderate

Acadia Hotel ★ (Value)   The Acadia Hotel is nicely situated overlooking Bar Harbor's village green, easily accessible to in-town activities and the free shuttles dispersing throughout the island; all things considered, it's an amazing value (prices have actually gone *down* in the last couple years). A handsome, simple home dating from the late 19th century, it has a wraparound porch and guest rooms decorated in nice floral motifs. Rooms vary widely in size and amenities; some units have whirlpool tubs, phones, and/ or king-size beds. One has a kitchenette, and about half have small refrigerators. It's a simple place, sure, but quite clean and well run.

20 Mt. Desert St., Bar Harbor, ME 04609. *C* **888/876-2463** or 207/288-5721. www.acadiahotel.com. 11 units. July to mid-Oct $119–$149 double; Apr–June and mid-Oct to mid-Nov $59–$99 double. Packages available. AE, MC, V. *In room:* A/C, TV, fridge (some units), no phone (some units).

Black Friar Inn ★   The Black Friar Inn, tucked on a side street overlooking a parking lot, is a yellow-shingled structure with quirky pediments and a somewhat eccentric air. It offers decent value. A former owner "collected" interiors and installed them throughout the home, among them a replica of a namesake pub in London with elaborate carved-wood paneling (now a common room), stamped-tin walls (now in the breakfast room), and a doctor's office (now a guest room). Rooms are carpeted and furnished in a mix of antiques; most are small, though the big suite features nice paneling, a sofa, wingback chair, and gas fireplace. Other rooms sport such touches as rose-tinted stained-glass windows, brass beds, and a mini–spiral staircase. The least expensive units are two garret rooms on the third floor, each of which has a detached private bathroom down the hall.

10 Summer St., Bar Harbor, ME 04609. *C* **207/288-5091.** Fax 207/288-4197. www.blackfriar.com. 7 units (2 with private hallway bathrooms). Peak season $110–$160 double; off-season rates lower. Rates include full breakfast. 2-night minimum mid-June to mid-Oct. DISC, MC, V. Closed Dec–Apr. Children 12 and older welcome. *In room:* A/C, fireplace (1 unit).

Coach Stop Inn ★ (Value)   Built in 1804, this claims to be Acadia's oldest inn. Surprisingly low-priced for such a well-run place, it's one of the island's best values—though it comes with the caveat of being located about as far from most of the prime attractions as you can get on Acadia. The shingled home sits on the main highway, close to the bridge to the mainland. (It's about 5 easy miles to downtown Bar Harbor, or 12 miles to Southwest Harbor.) Guests effuse about the owners' hospitality, the five simple but prettily decorated rooms; expect queen-size beds, fireplaces with mantles, claw-foot tubs, tasteful floral prints and wallpapers, sitting rooms in the suites, and (in one case) a small private porch. Breakfast might include pistachio-stuffed French toast, blueberry fritters, or eggs Napoleon. The grounds here include a meadow and apple trees, viewable from the patio if you're too full to walk.

715 Acadia Hwy. (Rte. 3; from bridge, turn left on Rte. 3 and continue 4 miles to inn on right), Bar Harbor, ME 04609. *C* **800/927-3097** or 207/288-9886. www.coachstopinn.com. 5 units. $125–$155 double. Rates include full breakfast. MC, V. Not recommended for children 9 and under. *In room:* A/C, fridge, no phone.

Maples Inn ★   A modest home tucked away on a side street among other Bar Harbor B&Bs, the Maples is an easy walk downtown to a movie or dinner. It's a popular destination for those attracted to outdoor activities, and you'll often find guests swapping stories about the day's adventures on the handsome front porch, or lingering over breakfast to compare notes about hiking trails. The innkeeper, an interior designer, has a way of making guests comfortable; rooms are small to medium-size, but you're not likely to feel cramped—they have private bathrooms, wicker furniture, pencil poster beds, and handsome antique wooden writing desks. The two-room White Birch has a fireplace, a lacy canopy bed with a down comforter, and a bright blue-and-white decor; Red Oak has a private deck with plastic lounge chairs. Gourmet breakfasts are served in a sunny dining room.

16 Roberts Ave., Bar Harbor, ME 04609. ✆ **207/288-3443.** www.maplesinn.com. 6 units. Mid-June to mid-Oct $85–$120 double; May to mid-June and mid-Oct to mid-Nov $125–$170 double. Memorial Day weekend $20 higher. Rates include full breakfast. 2-night minimum stay, 3-night minimum on holiday weekends. DISC, MC, V. Closed mid-Nov to Apr. Not appropriate for children. *In room:* Fireplace (1 unit), no phone.

Mira Monte Inn   A stay at this Italianate home (built in 1864) a few minutes' walk from Bar Harbor's restaurants and attractions feels a bit like a trip to your grandmother's house. Common rooms are furnished in a pleasant country Victorian style; 2 acres of grounds are nicely landscaped. There's a nice brick terrace away from the street, a good place to enjoy breakfast on warm summer mornings. Most of the guest rooms have a balcony, fireplace, or both, though the room styles vary widely—some are pretty heavy on the Victorian, while others have the feel of a country farmhouse. All are adequate, rather than elegant or spectacular, for the price. If you're a light sleeper, avoid rooms facing Mount Desert Street; those facing the gardens in the rear are much quieter. Families should inquire about suites in an adjacent outbuilding.

69 Mount Desert St., Bar Harbor, ME 04609. ✆ **800/553-5109.** www.miramonte.com. 12 units. Late June to mid-Oct $169–$219 double, $220–$290 suite; mid-May to late June and mid- to late Oct $99–$170 double, $130–$204 suite. Winter discount suite rates lower. Rates include breakfast. 2-night minimum stay in midsummer. AE, DISC, MC, V. Most units closed late Oct to mid-May. *In room:* A/C, fireplace (some units).

Primrose Inn ★   This handsome Victorian stick–style inn, originally built in 1878, is one of the most notable properties on the "mansion row" along Mount Desert Street. Its distinctive architecture has been preserved, and was perhaps even enhanced during a 1987 addition of rooms, private bathrooms, and balconies to the mix. This inn is comfortable, furnished with "functional antiques" and modern reproductions; many rooms have a floral theme, thick carpets, and adjacent sitting or reading rooms. Two newer, "premium" rooms have private entrances and are stocked with king-size beds, gas fireplaces, and such other amenities as a porch or whirlpool tub. Remember that a 2-night minimum stay is required, and that pets are not allowed.

73 Mount Desert St., Bar Harbor, ME 04609. ✆ **877/846-3424** or 207/288-4031. www.primroseinn.com. 13 units. Late June to Aug $145–$245 double; late May to late June and Sept–Oct $95–$195 double. Daily rates include full breakfast and afternoon tea. 2-night minimum stay. AE, DISC, MC, V. Closed late Nov to late May. *In room:* A/C, TV, hair dryer, iron/ironing board, Jacuzzi (1 unit), fireplace (some units).

Inexpensive

The Colony (Value   Owned by the same family since 1950, Colony is a vintage motor court consisting of a handful of motel rooms plus a battery of cottages arrayed around a long green. It's best appreciated by those with a taste for things retro; others might decide to look for something fancier. But the price is right. Rooms are furnished in a simple '70s style that won't win any awards for decor, but they're adequate; there are two classes of motel room, regular and luxury—the difference being better views and bigger beds (queens and kings instead of paired doubles). Some of the cottages have phones and kitchenettes, some don't, but all have TVs. This complex is just across Route 3 from a cobblestone beach, and about a 10-minute drive into Bar Harbor.

Rte. 3 (P.O. Box 56), Hulls Cove, ME 04644. © 207/288-3383. www.acadia.net/thecolony. 55 units. Peak season $65–$125 double; off-season rates lower. AE, DC, DISC, MC, V. *In room:* A/C (some units), TV, kitchenette (some units), fridge (some units), no phone (some units).

WHERE TO DINE

If you're craving something sweet, head over to **Ben & Bill's Chocolate Emporium,** 66 Main St. (© **800/806-3281** or 207/288-3281), for a big ice-cream cone. In the evenings, you may have to join the line spilling out the door. Visitors are often tempted to try the house novelty, lobster ice cream. Resist.

Or if you enjoy experimenting with *other* ice cream flavors, **Mt. Desert Ice Cream ★**, 7 Firefly Lane (© **207/460-5515**), beside the tourist office is the place for you. It gives all the appearances of being just another ho-hum scoop shop of the vanilla-chocolate-strawberry ilk, but it's not: there's little conventional about a place featuring gourmet concoctions spiked with tarragon, chili, and wasabi, among other flavors. There's another branch at 325 Main St. Both serve coffee, tea, and yerba mate, as well.

Very Expensive

The Rose Garden Restaurant ★★★ NEW AMERICAN   One of only a handful of fine-dining establishments in Bar Harbor that delivers a big-league dining experience, this unassuming room—in the Bluenose Inn (see "Where to Stay," above)—turns out wonderful meals. The a la carte and prix-fixe menus aren't cheap, but they're very good. Appetizers might include smoked salmon, foie gras, crab cakes, strudel filled with asparagus and Gruyère, or lobster bisque with sweet brandy cream. Main courses could include seared tenderloin steaks; grilled salmon with mustard sauce and a potato cake; fresh lobster meat over pasta; a roasted rack of lamb; or peppery venison with squash purée and cranberry sauce. When they're on the menu, the chocolate mousse cake, crème brûlée, apple tart, or mascarpone cheesecake are good dessert choices.

90 Eden St. © **800/445-4077** or 207/288-3348. Reservations recommended. Breakfast $10–$17; dinner prix-fixe menu $63, a la carte entrees $40. MC, V. May to late Oct breakfast 6–10:30am; dinner 5:30–9:30pm. Closed late Oct to Apr.

Expensive

Havana ★★ LATINO/FUSION   Havana set a high bar when it opened in 1999 in what was then a town of fried fish and stuffed haddock. The spare, sparkling decor in an old storefront is as classy as anything you'll find in Boston, and the menu can hold its own in any big city, too. Chef/owner Michael Boland says his menu is inspired by Latino fare, melded nicely with New American ideas. While the offerings change weekly, expect appetizers such as kuje monkfish seviche, Cuban-style beef tenderloin-and-pineapple brochettes, or Thai tofu with a plantain crust. Entrees could include choices such as spicy Chilean black-bean stew, tuna seasoned with *guajillo* chilies, grilled pork chops rubbed with maple sugar and chilies, and filet mignon rubbed with Cuban coffee and black pepper. Finish with desserts such as pistachio-mousse popovers with chocolate Cointreau sauce, a pecan tart sided with cinnamon gelato, or a *tres leches* (three-milk) cake.

318 Main St. © **207/288-2822.** www.havanamaine.com. Reservations recommended. Main courses $16–$33. AE, DC, DISC, MC, V. Daily 5–10pm.

Mâche Bistro ★★ BISTRO   Little Mâche Bistro has developed a devoted local following among those who know good food; its soothing yet plain decor conceals a sophisticated kitchen—you wouldn't expect an imported cheese course offered in a place with plywood floors, but there is one. The menu here changes monthly; appetizers could include a salad of Maytag blue cheese, apples, and truffle vinaigrette; garlic-seared shrimp; or a cheese plate. Main courses might include coq au vin, sirloin steaks roasted in a mushroom jus, good duck breast braised in an orange-ginger sauce, braised lamb shank, pan-fried tempeh and vegetables with a ponzu sauce, sole meunière, and a smoky seafood stew.

135 Cottage St. 🄲 **207/288-0447**. www.machebistro.com. Reservations recommended. Main courses $12–$21. AE, MC, V. Tues–Sun 5–9pm.

Maggie's Restaurant ★★ SEAFOOD   The slogan for Maggie's is "Notably fresh seafood," and the place invariably delivers on that understated promise. (Only locally caught fish is used.) It's a casually elegant spot, good for a romantic evening enjoying the soothing music, attentive service, and excellent seafood. Appetizers could include grilled cherrystone clams in white-wine sauce or lobster stew; main courses on a given night might be bronzed cod with a lime-tartar sauce, lobster crepes, Gulf shrimp with feta and olives over rice, pan-seared scallops, or salmon seared in Indian spices and served with cucumber-mint salsa. They also do nice steaks and chicken, but that's not why you dine here. Desserts are homemade and it's worth leaving room for them: blueberry pie, lemon curd and dark chocolate pudding cakes, and a delicious menu of sundaes—the island's best.

6 Summer St. 🄲 **207/288-9007**. www.maggiesbarharbor.com. Reservations recommended July–Aug. Main courses $16–$24. MC, V. Mon–Sat 5–9:30pm.

Michelle's Fine Dining ★★ FRENCH/SEAFOOD   Michelle's is located in the graceful Ivy Manor Inn (see "Where to Stay," above), and it's one of the island's best dinner experiences. The three dining rooms are elegant, and there's outside seating when the weather's good. The extensive menu elaborates on traditional French cuisine with New England twists; as you'd expect, the seafood selection is extensive. Nightly appetizers might include smoked salmon layered with a chervil mousse, or foie gras with black truffles. Main courses are even more elaborate, with dishes such as chateaubriand for two (carved tableside), roasted lobster in a basil-cream sauce, rack of lamb, and a bouillabaisse of lobster, mussels, clams, and scallops. Finish with the house's unique "bag of chocolate," which comes with berries and is served in an edible chocolate bag, or one of several excellent soufflés.

194 Main St. 🄲 **888/670-1997** or 207/288-0038. www.michellesfinedining.com. Reservations required during peak season. Main courses $26–$40. AE, DISC, MC, V. Daily 6–9pm. Closed late Oct to early May.

Moderate
Cafe This Way ★★ ECLECTIC   Cafe This Way has the feel of a hip coffeehouse, yet it's more airy and creative than that. Bookshelves line one wall, and there's a small bar tucked into a nook; oddly, they serve breakfast and dinner but no lunch. Breakfasts are excellent but sinful—more like brunch. Go for the burritos, corned beef hash with eggs, a range of omelets, or the calorific Café Monte Cristo: a French toast sandwich stuffed with fried eggs, ham, and cheddar cheese served with fries and syrup. Yikes. Dinner could start with Maine crab cakes in tequila-lime sauce, grilled chunks of Cyprus cheese, or

lobster spring rolls. The main-course offerings of the night could include lobster stewed in spinach and Gruyère cheese, sea scallops in vinaigrette, steaks, grilled lamb, peachy pork chops, or the filling Korean stir-fry dish known as *bibimbap*.

14¹/₂ Mount Desert St. ℭ **207/288-4483.** www.cafethisway.com. Reservations recommended for dinner. Breakfast items $5–$8; dinner main courses $7–$24. MC, V. Mid-Apr to Oct Mon–Sat 7–11am; Sun 8am–1pm; dinner daily 5:30–9pm.

Eden Vegetarian Café ★★ ⒻⓘⓃⒹⓈ VEGETARIAN   Right across from the harbor, chef Mark Rampacek operates Bar Harbor's only vegetarian eatery, bringing culinary flair to his cause. Most dishes here use organic and/or locally grown ingredients, and all are inventive. Depending on time of year, he might offer starters of pumpkin soup, shiitake crepes, or a beet carpaccio. Main courses could include a bento box of grilled tofu, edamame, and Japanese rolls and salads; Korean-style hot pots; Thai drunken noodles in a sweet-and-sour broth; or a lovely carbonara pasta subbing in smoked-dulse cream for the bacon. For dessert, you might find chocolate fondue, dairy-free ice creams, or sponge cake with lemon curd. There's also a full range of coffees and teas and a full bar.

78 West St. ℭ **207/288-4422.** www.barharborvegetarian.com. Reservations strongly recommended. Main courses $9–$17. MC, V. Summer daily 5–9pm, spring and fall closed Sun; call for exact hours.

Galyn's ★★ ⒻⓘⓃⒹⓈ SEAFOOD   Normally I avoid midpriced bistros in tourist towns like the plague, because they're generally pretty much all the same and almost never as special as their precious signs proclaim they are. But charming, unassuming Galyn's is the exception; Galyn's gets it right. From perfectly blackened and grilled Cajun shrimp, hand-cut steaks, and daily fish specials to seafood stews and penne tossed with oil, garlic, bits of feta, and all the right vegetables, everything's on point here. Finish with real Indian pudding (worth trying, and very hard to find) or the cappuccino sundae served in a cappuccino glass, which packs two helpful shots of espresso to fuel your sightseeing. There are nice dining rooms both upstairs and down, with art on the walls, but try to snag one of the tables out on the little street-side deck if you can: All face Agamont Park and stunning bay views beyond.

17 Main St. ℭ **207/288-9706.** www.galynsbarharbor.com. Reservations recommended. Main courses lunch $7–$17, dinner $14–$31. AE, MC, V. Daily 11:30am–10pm.

Inexpensive

Jordan's Restaurant ⓋⓐⓁⓤⒺ DINER   This unpretentious breakfast-and-lunch joint has been dishing up filling fare since 1976, and offers a glimpse of the old Bar Harbor. It's a popular haunt of local working folks and retirees, but staff is also genuinely friendly to tourists. Diners can settle into one of the pine booths or at a laminated table and order off the place-mat menu, choosing from basic fare such as grilled cheese with tomato and a slight but serviceable hamburger. The soups and chowders are all homemade. Breakfast is the specialty here, with a broad selection of three-egg omelets, along with muffins and locally famous pancakes made with wild Maine blueberries. With its atmosphere of seniors at kaffeeklatsch and its rock-bottom prices, this is not a gourmet experience, but fans of Americana and diner-like places might enjoy it.

80 Cottage St. ℭ **207/288-3586.** Breakfast $2.95–$6.75; lunch $2.25–$8.25. MC, V. Daily 4:30am–2pm. Closed Feb–Mar.

Lompoc Cafe and Brewpub ★ AMERICAN/ECLECTIC   The Lompoc Cafe has a neighborhood-bar feel to it—little wonder, since waiters and other workers from around Bar Harbor congregate here after hours. The cafe consists of three sections—there's the original bar, a tidy beer garden just outside (try your hand at bocce), and a small and open barnlike structure at the garden's edge to handle the overflow. The brewery next door produces several unique beers, including a blueberry ale (ask for a sample before ordering a full glass) and a smooth porter. Bar menus are usually yawn-inducing, but this one actually has some pleasant surprises, such as Caesar salads; lobster quesadillas; local mussels in white wine, Dijon mustard, and cream; grilled miso tofu; chicken-and-green chili burritos; bourbony barbecue pork sandwiches; and grilled portobello slices over soba noodles in a spicy peanut sauce. The outdoor tables are appealing, and live music acts frequently play here.

36 Rodick St. ☎ 207/288-9392. www.lompoccafe.com. Reservations not accepted. Lunch and dinner items $4–$13. MC, V. May–Nov daily 11:30am–1am. Closed Dec–Apr.

SHOPPING

Bar Harbor is full of boutiques and souvenir shops along two intersecting commercial streets, Main Street and Cottage Street. Most sell the usual tourist tack, but look a little harder and you can find some original items for sale at places like these.

Bar Harbor Hemporium   The Hemporium is dedicated to promoting products made from hemp such as paper, clothing, and more. Surprisingly, there's some interesting stuff here. 116 Main St. ☎ 207/288-3014. www.barharborhemp.com.

Cadillac Mountain Sports   Sleeping bags, backpacks, outdoor clothing, and hiking boots are found at this shop, which caters to the ragged-wool and fleece set. There's a good selection of hiking and travel guides to the island, too. 26 Cottage St. ☎ 207/288-4532. www.cadillacmountain.com.

Island Artisans   This is the place to browse for products made by local craftspeople, such as tiles, sweetgrass baskets, pottery, jewelry, and soaps. 99 Main St. ☎ 207/288-4214. www.islandartisans.com.

RainWise   This Bar Harbor–based company manufactures weather stations for companies, agencies, and serious Weather Channel–heads; its factory store, off Cottage Street, sells these stations plus a variety of thermometers and barometers. 25 Federal St. ☎ 800/762-5723 or 207/288-5169. www.rainwise.com.

5 ELSEWHERE ON MOUNT DESERT ISLAND ★★

You'll find plenty to explore outside of Acadia National Park and Bar Harbor. Quiet fishing villages, deep woodlands, and unexpected ocean views are among the jewels you can turn up once you get beyond Bar Harbor town limits.

ESSENTIALS
Getting Around

The eastern half of the island is best navigated using Route 3, which forms a rough loop from Bar Harbor through Seal Harbor and past Northeast Harbor, then runs up along the eastern shore of Somes Sound. Route 102 and Route 102A provide access to the island's western half. Without a car, use the free Island Explorer shuttle. (See "Getting Around" in the Acadia National Park section, earlier in this chapter.)

Visitor Information

The **Thompson Island Information Center** as you enter the island is a great info source. Locally, the **Southwest Harbor-Tremont Chamber of Commerce,** P.O. Box 1143, Southwest Harbor, ME 04679 (© **800/423-9264** or 207/244-9264), and the **Mount Desert Chamber of Commerce,** P.O. Box 675, Northeast Harbor, ME 04662 (© **207/ 276-5040**), can also help.

EXPLORING THE REST OF THE ISLAND

On the tip of the eastern lobe of Mount Desert Island is the staid, prosperous little village of **Northeast Harbor** ★, long a favorite retreat of well-heeled folks up and down the Eastern Seaboard. You can see their shingled palaces poking out of the forest and along the shore, but the village itself (which consists of one short main street and a marina) is also worth investigating.

One of the best, least publicized places for enjoying views of the harbor is from the understatedly spectacular **Asticou Terraces** ★★. Finding the parking lot can be tricky: Head ¹/₂ mile east (toward Seal Harbor) on Route 3 from the junction with Route 198, and look for the small gravel lot on the water side of the road with a sign reading ASTICOU TER-RACES. Park here, cross the road on foot, and set off up a magnificent path made of local rock that ascends the sheer hillside, with expanding views of the harbor and the town.

When leaving Northeast Harbor, plan to drive out via **Sargent Drive.** This one-way route runs through Acadia National Park along the shore of Somes Sound, affording superb views of this glacially carved inlet. On the far side of Somes Sound, there's good hiking (see earlier in this chapter) and the towns of **Southwest Harbor** ★ and Bass Harbor. These are both home to fishermen and boat builders, and though the character of these towns is changing, they're both still far more humble than Northeast and Seal harbors.

Continue on the trail at the top of the hillside, and you'll soon arrive at Curtis's cabin (open to the public daily in summer), behind which lies the formal **Thuya Garden,** which is as manicured as the terraces are natural. This wonderfully maintained garden, designed by noted landscape architect Charles K. Savage, attracts flower enthusiasts, students of landscape architecture, and local folks looking for a quiet place to rest. It's well worth the trip. A small donation is requested of visitors to the garden; admission to the terraces is free.

From the harbor, visitors can depart on a seaward trip to the beguilingly remote **Cranberry Islands** ★. You have a couple of options: Either travel with a national park guide to Baker Island, the most distant of this small cluster of low islands, and explore the natural terrain; or hop one of the ferries to either Great or Little Cranberry Island and explore on your own. On Little Cranberry there's a small historical **museum** ★ run by the National Park Service that's worth a few minutes. Both islands feature a sense of being well away from it all, but neither offers much in the way of shelter or tourist amenities, so travelers should head out prepared for the possibility of shifting weather.

Cranberry Cove Boating Co. (© **207/244-5882** or 207/460-1981) runs a regular ferry schedule from Southwest Harbor and Manset to the islands, for $22 round-trip per adult or $14 per child. **Beal & Bunker** (© **207/244-3575**) also runs mail boats to the islands from Northeast Harbor. Fares are $20 round-trip per adult, $10 for children age 3 to 11, and $7 per bicycle. However you get there, be sure to check schedules to ensure that you don't miss the last ferry back to Mount Desert.

In Southwest Harbor look for the intriguing **Wendell Gilley Museum of Bird Carving** (© **207/244-7555;** www.wendellgilleymuseum.org), on Route 102 just north of town. Housed in a new building constructed specifically to display the woodcarvings, the museum contains the masterwork of Wendell Gilley, a plumber who took up carving birds as a hobby in 1930. His creations, ranging from regal bald eagles to delicate chickadees, are startlingly lifelike and beautiful. The museum offers woodcarving classes for those inspired by the displays, and a gift shop sells fine woodcarvings. It's open Tuesday to Sunday from 10am to 4pm June to October, Friday to Sunday from 10am to 4pm in May, November, and December. The museum is closed January to April. Admission is $5 adults, $2 children 5 to 12.

WHERE TO STAY

In addition to the choices listed below, a good budget choice is the **Otter Creek Inn** (© **800/845-5852** or 207/288-5151; www.ottercreekme.com), attached to a food market in a village center (near Day Mountain) purveying lobsters, firewood, pie, and other essentials. An assortment of motel rooms, simple cabins, and apartments cost $105 to $175 double in summer, $85 to $125 in spring and fall. Pets are allowed; it's closed from November through the end of April.

Asticou Inn ★ The once-grand Asticou Inn, which dates from 1883, still occupies a prime location at the head of Northeast Harbor and is desirable for many even as it shows signs of tiring. The weathered gray shingles and profusion of overhanging eaves give it a stern demeanor, but it also has elements of eccentricity; despite some incipient shabbiness, a cozy old-world gentility seems to arise from the creaking floorboards and through the thin guest-room walls. Rooms are furnished in a simple summer-home style; some rooms have claw-foot tubs, and a few have fireplaces or kitchenettes, but none have phones or TVs. Dinner in the airy, wooden-floored main dining room focuses, as expected, on seafood entrees served with class.

Rte. 3 (P.O. Box 337), Northeast Harbor, ME 04662. © **800/258-3373** or 207/276-3344. www.asticou.com. 44 units. July–Aug $230–$340 double; May and Sept–Oct $135–$245 double. Rates include breakfast. MAP plans available July–Aug only. DISC, MC, V. Valet parking. Closed Nov–Apr. No children 5 and under. **Amenities:** Dining room; outdoor pool; tennis court; concierge; business center; limited room service; babysitting; laundry service. *In room:* Kitchenette (few units), fireplace (few units), no phone.

The Claremont ★ Early prints of the Claremont show an austere, four-story wooden building overlooking Somes Sound from a grassy rise; it hasn't changed much since. The place offers nothing fancy or elaborate, just classic New England grace. It's somehow appropriate that the state's largest croquet tournament (yes, really) is held here for a week each August. Common areas and dining rooms are pleasantly appointed in country style; there are a library, fireplace, and puzzles aplenty. Most of the guest rooms are bright and airy, outfitted with antiques, old furniture, and modern bathrooms. Guests opting for meal plans get dibs on rooms overlooking the water, which are nice (though the fare is middling). There's also a set of cottages of varied vintages and styles in the woods and on the water, all with fireplaces and kitchenettes.

P.O. Box 137, Southwest Harbor, ME 04679. © **800/244-5036.** www.theclaremonthotel.com. 44 units. Inn rooms July–Aug $184–$245 double; mid-June to late June and Sept to mid-Oct $115–$175 double. Cottages July–Aug $203–$291 double; late May to June and Sept to mid-Oct $150–$218 double. Rates include breakfast. MAP rates available for inn rooms only. 3-night minimum in cottages. MC, V. Closed mid-Oct to late May; inn rooms closed until mid-June. **Amenities:** 2 restaurants; lounge; tennis court; croquet; free bikes; rowboats; babysitting. *In room:* Kitchenette (some units).

Inn at Southwest ★ There's a decidedly late-19th-century air to this mansard-
roofed Victorian home, but it holds back on overdoing the frills. All guest rooms are
named for Maine lighthouses and are furnished in both contemporary and antique furniture. All rooms have ceiling fans and down comforters. Among the most pleasant
rooms is Blue Hill Bay on the third floor, with its yellow-and-blue color scheme, large
bathroom, sturdy oak bed and bureau, and glimpses of the scenic harbor; Pumpkin
Island, featuring a sleigh bed and a rosewood sofa; and the Winter Harbor Suite has a
pencil-poster canopy bed, French doors, and a gas-log fireplace. Breakfasts here give lodgers good incentive to rise and shine, with changing specialties such as Belgian waffles with
raspberry sauce, poached pears, and blueberry-stuffed French toast.

371 Main St. (P.O. Box 593), Southwest Harbor, ME 04679. ℂ **207/244-3835.** www.innatsouthwest.com.
7 units. $105–$185 double. Rates include full breakfast. DISC, MC, V. Closed Nov to late Apr. *In room:* No
phone.

Kingsleigh Inn ★ In a 1904 Queen Anne–style home right on Southwest Harbor's
main street, the Kingsleigh has long been a reliable stop. Its living room features a wood-
burning fireplace and fine art, while sitting and breakfast rooms offer further refuge. All
rooms are outfitted with sound machines to drown out ambient noise, wineglasses, and
robes; some also have air conditioners. The huge third-floor suite has outstanding views
(with a telescope to see them better), DVR and VCR players, a fireplace, and a king-size
bed, though other rooms are only small to moderately sized. The three-course breakfasts
are filling and artistic, with choices such as asparagus frittata, fruit crepes, Belgian waffles,
and stuffed French toast. Other nice touches include walking sticks for guest use and
all-day, self-service espresso.

373 Main St. (P.O. Box 1426), Southwest Harbor, ME 04679. ℂ **207/244-5302.** Fax 207/244-7691. www.
kingsleighinn.com. 8 units. $130–$195 double; $245–$305 suite. Closed Nov–Mar. Rates include full
breakfast. Children 13 and older welcome. AE, MC, V. *In room:* A/C (some units), hair dryer, no phone.

Lindenwood Inn ★★ Australian innkeeper Jim King gave up cabinetmaking to
open a string of successful B&Bs in Southwest Harbor, and his latest is his best; it feels
like renting a home with friends. In a handsome Queen Anne–style captain's home built
in 1904 over harbor's edge, King has modernized the rooms in simple, bold colors and
accented them with items from his collections of African and aboriginal art—a strikingly
unique interior and feel you can't find anywhere else in New England. Most units have
balconies and plenty of windows, some have fireplaces or French doors, and all possess
comfy beds. The public areas remain funky and appealing, and the heated in-ground
pool and Jacuzzi are wonderful. There's a small honor bar for fixing a late-night cocktail,
plus (as of 2008) a private club/lounge in the basement. The biggest draws, however,
remain the outstanding hospitality and laid-back vibe.

118 Clark Point Rd. (P.O. Box 1328), Southwest Harbor, ME 04679. ℂ **800/307-5335** or 207/244-5335.
www.lindenwoodinn.com. 8 units. July–Oct $125–$195 double; $225–$325 suite. Nov–June $85–$175
double; $165–$295 suite. Rates include full breakfast. AE, MC, V. **Amenities:** Bar; heated outdoor pool;
Jacuzzi. *In room:* TV, kitchenette (1 unit), fridge (2 units), no phone.

WHERE TO DINE

Ten years ago, there were virtually no serious dining options anywhere on the quiet side
of Mount Desert Island. Things have definitely changed with the times. In addition to
the choices listed below, you can find plenty of good restaurants in **Southwest Harbor**
and several in **Northeast Harbor.** There are even decent options in tiny, one-dock fishing

> (Fun Facts) **Cracking the Lobster Conundrum**
>
> While you struggle to crack that lobster claw (and avoid spilling juice and butter all over your nappies), here are a few more fascinating lobster facts to chew on:
>
> - Lobster prices in most Maine shacks vary, sometimes by a lot; it depends almost exclusively on the current year's take. (In a down year, you'll pay more.)
> - There are two kinds of lobster, soft-shell and hard-shell. Many lobsters still have soft shells in the summer, 'cause they've slipped off old ones and are still growing new ones back. People vary in their preferences. I'm a hard-shell man.
> - In fall and early winter, hard-shell lobsters become more numerous in the sea—and their price drops. If you're in Maine from September onward, fill 'er up.
> - The worst time to eat a lobster has got be spring, when the crustaceans—both kinds—are scarce, shrimpy, and overpriced. Put off that May feast.

villages such as **Manset** and **Bernard.** Or just pack a picnic at either of the excellent local markets in Southwest Harbor and Northeast Harbor.

The current big hitters include Red Sky and Fiddlers' Green (see below for details). There's also the **Café Drydock,** 357 Main St. (© **207/244-5842**), with an extensive seafood menu, landlubber-friendly lunch and dinner options such as pasta, burgers, and salads, and a Sunday brunch.

Should you tire of eating both gourmet fare and seafood, fear not. Instead, head for one of several cafes lining the town's main street. **Quietside,** 360 Main St. (© **207/244-9444**), serves inexpensive club sandwiches and ice-cream cones. The **Little Notch Pizzeria,** 340 Main St. (© **207/244-3357**), an offshoot of a nearby bakery, makes decent pizzas, plus gourmet sandwiches on its own bread in the vein of grilled chicken in focaccia with onions and aioli, prosciutto with Asiago and roasted peppers on an onion roll, and grilled flank steak on a baguette. It gets crowded and convivial on summer weekend evenings. **Eat-A-Pita,** 326 Main St. (© **207/244-4344**), serves pitas, salads, and egg dishes.

Find Bernard, a few miles south of Southwest Harbor, for some of Maine's outstanding lobsters at **Thurston's** (see below).

For a quick bite or a picnic lunch to go in Northeast Harbor, don't overlook the informal **Docksider Restaurant,** hidden a block off the main commercial drag at 14 Sea St. (© **207/276-3965**). The crab rolls and lobster rolls are outstanding, made simply and perfectly. The small restaurant also features a host of other fare, including lobster dinners, sandwiches, chowder, fried seafood, and grilled salmon.

Finally, there's an offbeat option: **XYZ ★** (© **207/244-5221**) at Bennett Lane in Southwest Harbor (head south down Main St., then bear left onto Rte. 102A toward Manset) serves very authentic Mexican cuisine—the acronym means Xalapa, Yucatan, and Zacatecas (provinces). Expect mole sauces, spicy meals, and sweet desserts. It's open nightly from 5:30 to 9pm in summer; call ahead for opening days and hours in the off season.

Beal's Lobster Pound ★ LOBSTER POUND   Purists claim this is among the best lobster shacks in Maine. Don't know about that (I prefer Thurston's; see below), but this place has certainly got the right atmosphere: Creaky picnic tables on a plain concrete pier, overlooking a working-class harbor, next to a Coast Guard base. Translation: Don't wear a jacket and tie. You go inside to pick out lobster from a tank (pay by the pound), then choose side dishes (corn on the cob, slaw, steamed clams) and wait for your number to be called. Your meal will arrive on Styrofoam or paper plates, but you won't care. There's also a takeout window across the deck serving fries, fried clams, and fried fish (sensing a theme?), all of it frankly pretty mediocre, but they'll also dish you up an ice-cream cone.

182 Clark Point Rd., Southwest Harbor. ☎ **207/244-7178** or 244-3202. www.bealslobster.com. Lobsters market price. AE, DISC, MC, V. Summer daily 9am–8pm; after Labor Day daily 9am–5pm. Closed Columbus Day to Memorial Day.

The Burning Tree ★★ (Finds) REGIONAL/SEAFOOD   Located on a busy straightaway of Route 3 between Bar Harbor and Otter Creek, the Burning Tree is an easy restaurant to speed right past; that would be a mistake. This low-key place, with its bright, open (and vibrant) dining room serves up some of the best and freshest dinners on the island. Much of the produce and herbs comes from its own gardens (which some diners can look onto while eating), and the remainders of the ingredients are supplied locally whenever possible. Seafood is the specialty here, and it's consistently prepared with imagination and skill—expect unusual spicings (such as New Orleans–style lobster) and combinations. The crab cakes and halibut, when they're on the menu, come highly recommended.

Rte. 3, Otter Creek. ☎ **207/288-9331.** Reservations recommended. Main courses $18–$23. DISC, MC, V. Mid-June to Columbus Day Wed–Mon 5–10pm. Closed Columbus Day to late May.

Fiddlers' Green ★★ (Kids) ECLECTIC/NEW AMERICAN   Island native chef Derek Wilbur's bistro is a big hit in these seafaring parts. Begin with something from the cold seafood bar: smoked salmon wrapped in gravlax and horseradished chèvre, oysters on the half shell, or Wilbur's sashimi martini—a cup of smoked mussels, scallop seviche, and raw tuna in a pear-tahini marinade. Or start with small plates such as Thai-curried shrimp with coconut milk, fried catfish filet with a Cajun rémoulade, or smoked baby back ribs. There are always lots of steaks and a few excellent pasta dishes on the menu, such as lobster strozzapretti with a *vinho verde* cream sauce; meatier main dishes could

---

(Kids) **Netting a Net Cafe on the Island**

Mount Desert isn't really a need-to-be-online-every-second type of place—in fact, that's the primary charm of it—but the neighborhood's changing. And **Harbor Treats,** in a small plaza just off the main drag at 19 Clark Point Rd. (☎ **207/244-0313**), fills that niche in Southwest Harbor: It serves the traveler (or traveler's teenager) who just can't live without gourmet coffee *and* high-speed Internet access. Even the technology-challenged can enjoy gourmet baked goods, customized ice-cream sundaes, and Asian snacks purveyed from the small shop. Best of all, there's a small outdoor patio with wooden tables.

include Asian hot pots, Creole-spiced roasted half chickens, pork Cubano, tempura-fried scallops, lobster potpie, or a good old steamed lobster. There's quite an extensive wine list, and martini drinkers should take note: Wilbur's bar serves a long list of classic and obscure versions. There's even a kids' menu.

411 Main St., Southwest Harbor. ☎ **207/244-9416.** www.fiddlersgreenrestaurant.com. Reservations recommended. Main courses $16–$32. AE, DISC, MC, V. Tues–Sun 11:30am–3pm and 5:30–9pm. Closed Columbus Day to Memorial Day.

Redbird Provisions ★★ ITALIAN/SEAFOOD   Redbird opened in 2007 in a renovated cottage on Northeast Harbor's main street, and it's a winner. The kitchen cooks up local seafood and other good stuff using Asian, French, and Italian accents in a no-pretense room. Lunches run to smoked trout Niçoise, seared yellowfin tuna, crab sushi rolls, poached lobster tails, chicken burgers on brioche buns, and seared sea scallops, while dinners might feature Cape Neddick oysters on the half shell, risotto with clams or wild mushrooms, cuts of organic salmon with white-bean ragout and roasted figs, steamed halibut with Asian spices and vegetables, pork loin with spring onions and polenta, or strip steaks with Yukon gold potatoes. A spa menu offers lighter fare (Vietnamese spring rolls, shrimp seviche over cumin crackers, a fruit-and-cheese plate), while the simple outdoor terrace is another splendid surprise; they also cook, package, and deliver lovely picnic meals on request. This is one to watch.

11 Sea St., Northeast Harbor. ☎ **207/276-3006.** www.redbirdprovisions.com. Reservations recommended. Entrees $10–$26. DISC, MC, V. Wed–Sat 11:30am–2pm and 6–9pm. Closed late Oct to late May.

Red Sky ★★ CONTINENTAL/NEW AMERICAN   Despite a change in ownership and chefs, Red Sky continues to bring big-city dining sensibilities to its little village. Meals take New England ingredients to creative heights, using French and other Continental techniques and accents. Begin with intriguing starters such as organic chicken liver pâté, baked oysters stuffed with crab and bacon, duck-pork sausage, or a crispy, layered polenta. Salads here are excellent, and main courses include a New York strip steak grilled and topped with Maytag blue cheese, Dijon-baked salmon, spicy molasses-flavored grilled scallops, pan-roasted breast of duck with blueberry-Chambord sauce, and maple-glazed baby back ribs. Finish with a *very* lemony lemon cake, bittersweet Belgian chocolate pudding, toasted gingerbread with caramel sauce and brandied whipped cream, or one of the sorbets or ice creams.

14 Clark Point Rd., Southwest Harbor. ☎ **207/244-0476.** www.redskyrestaurant.com. Entrees $19–$30. AE, DISC, MC, V. July–Sept Wed–Sun 5:30–9pm; rest of the year closed Sun. Closed Jan.

Thurston's Lobster Pound ★ (Finds) LOBSTER POUND   Right off the end of a dock (the same place where they load the lobsters up), Thurston's possesses all three key requirements of a great Maine lobster shack: one, a great view of Bass Harbor and its fishing boats; two, great lobster and side dishes at reasonable prices; and three, an unpretentious vibe blended with a dash of friendly sass. It's like a place out of the movies. The lobsters come quickly, their claws precracked for easier access; the corn on the cob is perfectly cooked; scallop chowder, crunchy crab cakes, and bags of steamed mussels and clams all provide toothsome sides; and the "plain dinner" option ($5 extra) finishes with a wonderfully eggy cinnamon-blueberry cake. There are two decks, upstairs and down, and a convivial atmosphere pervades at both, as perfect strangers break the ice over crustaceans. This place is a true Maine classic.

Steamboat Wharf Rd. (at the docks), Bernard. ☎ **207/244-7600.** Lobsters market price. MC, V. Memorial Day to Columbus Day daily 11am–8:30pm.

The Downeast Coast

The term Downeast, as in "Downeast Maine," comes from the days when ships were still powered by sail. East Coast ships heading north and east along this coastline had strong prevailing winds at their backs—making it an easy "downhill" run to the farthest eastern ports. (Returning took more skill and determination.)

Today it's a rare traveler who gets downeast to explore the rugged coastline of Washington County. Very few tourists venture beyond the turnoff to Mount Desert Isle, discouraged by a lack of services and high-marquee attractions. Yet Downeast Maine does have appeal—so long as you're not looking for luxury. There's an authenticity here that's been lost in much of the rest of Maine. Many longtime visitors say *this* is how all of Maine used to look in the 1940s and 1950s, when writers like E. B. White first arrived. Thai food, the *New York Times,* and designer coffee have yet to make serious inroads into Washington County, where a rugged, hardscrabble way of life and tough interdependence among neighbors still predominates.

Many residents here still get by as their forebears did—scratching a living from the land. Scalloping, lobstering, and fishing remain the major sources of income, as do blueberrying, logging, and other forest work. Grubbing for bloodworms in spring, picking berries in the barrens in late summer, climbing fir trees to get the fragrant tips for Christmas wreaths in the fall—that's not a vacation around here, that's what people do to make ends meet. In recent years aquaculture has also become an important part of the economy around Passamaquoddy and Cobscook bays; travelers can sometimes see vast floating pens, especially around Eastport and Lubec, where salmon are farmed for gourmet diners worldwide.

The geographical isolation of this region ensures that you'll have these back roads and tiny towns to yourself—most of your fellow travelers have long since been waylaid by the charms of Kennebunkport, Portland, Camden, or Acadia. But if you're hoping to get a peek at the *real* Maine, the one that never shows up on the tourist brochures, you'd be wise to make a trip here for a day or two. You might never see Maine the same way again.

1 ESSENTIALS

GETTING THERE

Downeast Maine is usually reached via U.S. Route 1, coming north from Ellsworth. You can also take a more direct, less congested route via Route 9 from Brewer (across the river from Bangor), connecting to Route 1 via Route 193 or Route 192.

VISITOR INFORMATION

For information on the Machias area and other parts of Downeast Maine, contact the **Machias Bay Area Chamber of Commerce,** 12 E. Main St. (P.O. Box 606), Machias,

ME 04654 (© **207/255-4402;** www.machiaschamber.org), on U.S. Route 1. It's open from 10am to 3pm weekdays.

EVENTS

Eastport celebrates the **Fourth of July** in extravagant fashion each year, a tradition that began in 1820 after the British gave up possession of the city (they captured it during the War of 1812). Some 15,000 New Englanders pour into this little city of 1,900 for the 4-day event, which includes vendors, games, boat races, contests, and food, culminating with a grand parade on the Fourth.

The popular **Machias Wild Blueberry Festival ★**, operated by the local Congregation Church, celebrates the local cash crop each summer. Washington County claims to produce an astonishing 85% of the world's wild blueberry harvest, so there's bound to be some for the tasting when you show up. The festivities typically begin with a children's parade and fish fry, continue with a Saturday blueberry pancake breakfast (of course) and road race, then move on to lobster feeds, the raffling of a blueberry quilt, a book sale, and a blueberry-pie-eating contest. There are also performances and the sales of blueberry-theme gift items. Stamp collectors should plan to drop by the local post office for special-issue cancellation stamps, uniquely themed to blueberries each year.

Check the festival website (www.machiasblueberry.com) or contact the local chamber of commerce (© **207/255-4402**) for the exact dates of the festival; it usually takes place in mid- to late August.

2 ENJOYING THE GREAT OUTDOORS

There are several good tour outfitters and boat-tour operators in these parts, offering everything from kayak day trips to whale-watches.

Bold Coast Charter Company ★ (© **207/259-4484;** www.boldcoast.com) operates cruises out of little Cutler harbor to Machias Seal Island from May through August, and to Cross Island from May through October. Captain Andrew Patterson's 40-foot *Barbara Frost* tour boat sometimes lands ashore and sometimes doesn't, but either way viewing of puffins and razorbills on Machias Seal Island (which is claimed by both Canada and the U.S. as territory; stay tuned) is almost guaranteed. You might see arctic terns, petrels, seals, eagles, or porpoises in the vicinity of Cross Island, a noted bird-and-wildlife refuge. Patterson also makes occasional trips past Libby Island and its lighthouse. The 5-hour bird-watching tours leave around 7 or 8am and cost $80 per person, $45 for children (there's no children's discount if the boat stops and lands on the island). Remember that many birds have already packed up and headed south by Labor Day (first week of Sept) and won't be there for the watching; come earlier than that, if you can. You board the boat at Cutler's little boat ramp on the harbor.

3 EXPLORING DOWNEAST MAINE

Ellsworth is 27 miles SE of Bangor

The best way to see this area—the only way, really—is to simply drive along U.S. Route 1 and a few associated back roads and shortcuts north from Ellsworth all the way to the Canadian border . . . and beyond, if you brought your passport.

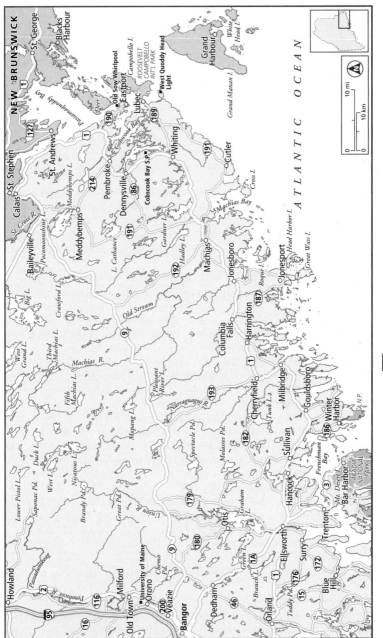

Ellsworth doesn't get much due from travelers hell-bent on making it to Mount Desert Island before dinner, but those in the know are increasingly stopping to sample a town that has significantly expanded its cultural offerings. In fact, though it seems pedestrian and overcommercialized—the town's Main Street was long ago usurped by Route 1, lending it a chaotic air out of step with Ellsworth's actual character—the community gives Bar Harbor a serious run for the title of Downeast arts capital.

The town was first settled by Passamaquoddy and Penobscot tribes; later, French woodsmen explored the area, and the British inevitably followed with bridges, sawmills, and ships on the Union River. By the late 19th century, Ellsworth had become both a significant port of departure for lumber cut from the big Maine woods and an important shipbuilding center. Those industries soon faded away, but Ellsworth swiftly reinvented itself as a tourist jumping-off point—playing off its proximity to Mount Desert Island—and arts center, capitalizing on the concentration of artists and musicians attracted to its services.

Traveling north from Ellsworth, it's about 13 miles from Ellsworth to **Sullivan,** nicely situated on a rise overlooking Frenchman Bay. This town was briefly home to a mini–gold rush, but today it's little more than a quiet fishing village consisting primarily of a general store and an intriguing combination smokehouse/rental cottage operation where you can buy smoked fish for picnics (see "Where to Stay & Dine," later in this chapter).

It's 8 miles farther along Route 1 to **Gouldsboro,** which is actually a series of five villages. The area contains a handful of accommodations. For a look at some real fishing villages, turn south off Route 1 down Route 186 and drive through Winter Harbor, Prospect Harbor, and Corea—don't expect anything fancy here. And do not miss **Schoodic Point,** at the end of this road (see later in this chapter); it's another bonus sliver of Acadia National Park, overlooked by almost all travelers, a fine spot for dramatic photographs of surf crashing over the big rocks.

Continue north 10 more miles to **Milbridge,** a former shipbuilding town, where the little **Milbridge Historical Museum** (see later in this chapter) captures some of the local history; as recently as 1983 a boat was built and launched here.

From here, it's shorter to cut north along Route 1A, but if you do so, you'll miss quaint Cherryfield. The **Cherryfield-Narraguargus Historical Society** (© **207/546-7979**), housed right on Main Street in Cherryfield, maintains its own small museum of tools, photographs, and other 19th-century items. However, it's only open in July and August, from 1 to 4pm Wednesday through Friday. (If you're really interested, they might let you come another time by appointment.)

Five miles north, the center of tiny **Columbia Falls** retains its longtime charm thanks to the good fortune of having been bypassed by Route 1; if you're stopping here to visit the historic **Ruggles House** (see later in this chapter), also check out April Adams's excellent **Columbia Falls Pottery** shop (© **800/235-2512** or 207/483-4075; www.columbia fallspottery.com) in the restored schoolhouse next door, where you can look over nature-inspired designs such as Lupine, Blueberry, Flag Iris, and Lady's-Slipper. They take credit cards.

Just north of Columbia Falls, detour south along Route 187 (which makes a complete loop of its peninsula) to the end of the point. You will come to **Jonesport,** a photogenic, lost-in-time fishing village dominated by lobstermen and boat work. Beyond the pretty village and the dramatic local tides, you'll also find—should you venture offshore—some of the biggest puffin colonies in the world. July 4th is a surprisingly big deal here, featuring an impressive little parade, games, food, fireworks, and lobster boats racing in the harbor.

Jonesport is the jumping-off point for the nature preserve on **Great Wass Island** too, as well as some puffin-tour operators. **John Norton** runs boat tours to Machias Seal Island (and its colony of 3,000-plus puffins) out of Jonesport from June through mid-August aboard the *Chief;* call © **207/497-2560** or 497-5933 for details of the tours, which leave quite early, take about 5 hours in total (up to 2 hr. maximum on the island) and cost $100 per person.

Rejoin Route 1 at **Jonesboro,** from where you can head east again—down empty highways—to scenic Roque Bluffs State Park (see later in this chapter), a good place to go swimming in either saltwater or freshwater pools.

MACHIAS
90 miles E of Bangor and 64 miles E of Ellsworth

The trim market town of **Machias** (ma-*CHAI*-us) is the county seat of, and by far the biggest community in, Washington County—though it's not very big at all. Its year-round population of 2,400 seems positively Manhattan-esque in these parts by comparison to the rest of the towns, and a University of Maine satellite campus has attracted a welcome clutch of coffee shops, galleries, and other trappings of culture. The town's name is a native word translating approximately to "Bad Little Falls," a tribute to the rough rapids and waterfalls formed where river and coast meet here; the town was originally settled by Native Americans, who used it as a fishing camp.

Early explorers used the same river mouth as a trade port, although true colonial settlement of the town waited until the mid–18th century. This river even became the site of the Revolutionary War's first naval battle on June 12, 1775, when locals turned back the British gunboat the *Margaretta,* a story that's told and re-told for visitors at the Burnham Tavern (see below).

Downtown Machias still possesses a surprising number of historic structures. The **George Foster House** and Andrew Gilson House on North Street both display distinctive mansards, while Court Street is packed with historic structures: Machias's town offices are housed inside an Italianate former schoolhouse, the **Clark Perry House** has peaked lintels, and the granite **Porter Memorial Library** incorporates ballast and andirons from the *Margaretta* (talk about taking a war trophy). The **Carrie Albee House** at the corner of West and Court streets is a Victorian home dating from 1900.

Ⓣ**ips** **You Light Up My Life**

While in the Machias area, try to get a look at the historic **Libby Island Light,** a 42-foot-tall, solar-powered lighthouse in an extremely foggy spot 4 miles out to sea. Its granite tower was built in 1884, and the light—though visible from the local beach—is best seen by boat with a tour operator such as Bold Coast Charter Company (p. 236).

Just outside town, on Route 92 in **Machiasport,** the **Gates House Museum** (© **207/255-8461**)—the riverside home of the Machiasport Historical Society—functions as a small local museum. It's open June to August, Tuesday to Sunday from 12:30 to 4:30pm.

MACHIAS TO EASTPORT

North of Machias, be sure to detour south and east along Route 191 to find **Cutler** (pop. 400 on a good day), an attractive small village once actively devoted to shipbuilding but now a sleepy place of lobster boats and enormous salmon farms. The coastal scenery north of Cutler, known here as the **Bold Coast**—and it is—makes for an impressive drive or hike. In addition to being the home of a former navy base, Cutler is also a great place to shove off on a **whale-watching cruise;** some routes also take in rare seabirds and/or basking seals on the way to the whale grounds.

Back on Route 1, you pass through nondescript **Whiting,** an entry point to the easternmost national wildlife refuge on the Atlantic migration corridor: **Moosehorn National Wildlife Refuge.** The refuge was created back in 1934 with proceeds from President Franklin D. Roosevelt's Duck Stamp program; it's one of America's oldest such refuges, and still home to eagles, osprey, and the unusual woodcock (check out its remarkable courtship flights). Cycling, skiing, hiking, and leashed pets are allowed on the refuge roads, though not in the wildlife areas; there are more than 50 miles of trails, plus observation decks for watching some of the many birds here. Tours are often given in summer. Note that the refuge consists of two disjoined chunks of land—one here along Cobscook Bay on Route 1 between Dennysville and Whiting, the other to the southwest of Calais.

If you continue north along Route 1, north of Dennysville you cross Cobscook Bay at **Pembroke** (once the site of an ironworks) and an unusual reversing falls; the direction of the river—actually a tidal inlet—and the falls reverses twice each day, depending on the prevailing tides. From here to French-inflected **Calais** (pronounced just like *callous,* unfortunately), there are more tiny towns along Cobscook Bay and the St. Croix River. Calais is connected by bridge to St. Stephen, New Brunswick, which has a chocolate factory and museum worth checking out; go that way if you're planning to visit lovely St. Andrews or seafaring Grand Manan island, both described in chapter 11—and don't forget a passport.

If you plan to confine your explorations to American soil, split off Route 1 at Route 189 or 190, where you'll discover charming **Lubec** and **Eastport** as well as the gateways to Campobello Island (described below) and Deer Island, two lovely slices of New Brunswick. **Lubec** is the end of the line, literally: the northeasternmost community in the United States and one connected by a bridge to Canada. (Locals joke that although this isn't the end of the earth, at least you can *see* the ends of it from here.) The tidal mixing of two bays at this point has long proven to be a popular hangout for massive schools of fish, and fish canning and packing plants once filled the town. Today Lubec is notable chiefly for its vistas of the ocean and offshore lighthouses; set a course for Quoddy Head if you crave high tides, early sunrises, and a view that would stretch all the way to Europe and Africa if not for the curve of the earth.

If Lubec doesn't grab you, get back on Route 1 and continue north to Perry; a turn down Route 190 takes you to Eastport. First, however, you must pass through the **Pleasant Point Passamaquoddy Indian Reservation,** one of a handful of Maine's native

Ⓜ **Moments** **Radar Love**

Cutler is more than a fishing village: It was once an important Navy communications outpost, its proximity to Europe and northerly location making it ideal for communicating with submarines plying European waters.

Those two dozen or so big antennas poking up above the coast? They're said to make up the most powerful VLF transmitter in the world, and this quiet headland was for years considered a very high-risk target in the event of war. If you're an aficionado of things military, be sure to have a look. However, you should also know that the base's usefulness has greatly diminished in modern times, and the equipment is now operated by civilian personnel; most of the Navy property, located on a scenic peninsula, is now in the process of being redeveloped.

American reservations. (*Don't* speed.) The Passamaquoddy tribe here won a landmark settlement in 1981 and received a huge land-and-cash award; in exchange, the tribe agreed to drop a series of land claims that might have succeeded in court—and, some believe, bankrupted the state if they had. (The tribe would have received more than half the state of Maine had they won). There are few tourist facilities here save a few souvenir shops and the tribal Waponahki Museum, 59 Passamaquoddy Rd. (Ⓒ **207/853-4001**), upstairs in the Sipayik Youth Center, with photographs, baskets, art, and cultural exhibits. Call ahead if you're intent on visiting.

EASTPORT

Eastport, situated on a small island across a causeway at the tip of America, was once among the busiest ports on the entire East Coast; later, it became a major center for sardine tinning. Today it's a sleepy fishing village rather than a shipping destination, but the historic downtown has lately begun to make itself over as an artsy place of writers, musicians, and other creative types attracted to the slow pace of life and closeness to the sea. (The fishing industry has also reinvented itself: Salmon farm pens now fill the near-shore waters.)

The most interesting things here are the growing arts scene, the local historic district (see below), and an honest-to-goodness mustard mill (see below).

Eastport is also well known for its **Fourth of July** celebrations, which run several days and include pie-eating competitions, a flotilla of boats and ships in the harbor, a huge torch-lit parade (Maine's largest), parachutes, pipe bands, and the like. They go over-the-top, culminating in impressive (for the town's size) fireworks.

The **Eastport Salmon Festival** ★ takes over town each year during the first weekend after Labor Day, with a very full weekend of arts, crafts, a road race, a sailboat race, a walking tour, and plenty of seafood. Call Ⓒ **207/853-4644** for more details, or check the festival website (www.eastportme.net).

Although Eastport is pretty quiet, the 90-acre peninsula of **Shackford Head State Park** ★ is even quieter; get there by following Route 190 almost into town, turn right at the gas station, and continue almost 1 mile along Deep Cove Road. There's a hiking trail here with nice views. Interestingly, you can see remains of several Civil War–era ships here at low tide. They were brought here for salvage in the early 20th century. The park is open from sunrise to sunset and is, unlike many of Maine's state parks, free to enter. No campfires or all-terrain vehicles are allowed.

Finally, if you're into whirlpools, you've come to the right place. Just north of Eastport is the **Old Sow,** said to be the largest whirlpool in the Western Hemisphere. It's a bit finicky and is impressive only during the highest tides; the best way to see it is to take a seasonal **ferry** to Deer Island in New Brunswick, Canada (see chapter 11), and back. The ferry departs from behind the Eastport Fish and Lobster House at 167 Water St.

For more information on the Eastport area, contact the **Eastport Chamber of Commerce,** P.O. Box 254, Eastport, ME 04631 (✆ **207/853-4644;** www.eastport.net).

4 WHAT TO SEE & DO

Below are some of the highlights of the region. The driving time direct from Ellsworth to Lubec via routes 1 and 189 is about 2 hours with no stops. Allow considerably more time for visiting the sites mentioned below and just plain snooping around.

Burnham Tavern   Gambrel-roofed Burnham Tavern was built on a rise overlooking the Machias River in 1770, and it's said to be the oldest existing building in eastern Maine. It also occupies a unique place in local history: In June 1775, a month after the Battle of Lexington, a group of locals hatched a plan here that led to the first naval battle of the Revolutionary War. The armed schooner *Margaretta* was in Machias harbor to stock up on wood for the British barracks. Locals didn't think much of that plan, and attacked the ship with smaller boats, muskets, swords, axes, pitchforks—whatever they could grab. The Mainers prevailed, killing the captain of the *Margaretta* in the process; visitors can learn all about the episode during a tour of the tavern. On display is booty taken from the British ship, along with the original tap table and other historic furniture and ephemera. The tours last around 1 hour.

Main St. (Rte. 192), Machias. ✆ **207/255-6930.** www.burnhamtavern.com. Admission $2 adults, 25¢ children. Mid-June to early Sept Mon–Fri 9am–5pm. Closed early Sept to mid-June.

Cobscook Bay State Park ★★★   One of Maine's hidden jewels, this state park is an outstanding camping or day-trip destination for the family. Tides flow back and forth across cribworked rocks, exposing deep tidal pools, rocks, and clam-rich mudflats; bird life is also prodigious. There are some 900 acres of trails (cross-country skiable in winter) and tidal exposure in all, and the hundred-plus campsites here include a number of waterside sites.

U.S. Rte. 1 (RR #1, Box 127, Dennysville ME 04628), 4 miles south of Dennysville. ✆ **207/726-4412.** Open mid-May to mid-Oct. High season admission $3 adults, $1 children 5–11; off season $1.50 per adult.

Cutler Coastal Trail ★   Marked by a sign in a small parking lot, this dramatic loop trail passes through diverse ecosystems, including bogs, barrens, and dark and tangled spruce forests. But the highlight of the trail, which traverses state-owned land, is a mile-long segment along rocky headlands high above the Atlantic. Some of the most dramatic coastal views in the state are located along this isolated stretch, which overlooks dark-gray-to-black rocks and the tumultuous sea. Visible on the horizon across the Bay of

Fundy are the west-facing cliffs of the Canadian island of Grand Manan. Plan on at least 2 or 3 hours for the whole loop. If it's damp or foggy, rain pants are advised to fend off the moisture from the low brush along the trail.

Rte. 191, Cutler. Contact Maine Bureau of Park and Recreation (C) **207/827-1818.** Free admission. Always open. From the village of Cutler, head northeast on Rte. 191; approx. 4¹/₂ miles outside of town, look for parking lot and signs on right.

Eastport Historic District ★   In the late 19th century, Eastport (3 miles from Lubec by water, but 50 min. by car) was home to nearly 5,000 residents and 18 sardine plants. The census now counts less than 2,000, and the sardine plants are gone, but much of the handsome brick architecture remains on Water Street—a compact thoroughfare that also affords lovely views of Campobello Island and Passamaquoddy Bay. The majority of the buildings between the post office and the library are on the National Register of Historic Places.

Water St., Eastport. From Rte. 1 in Perry, take Rte. 190 south for 7 miles.

Great Wass Island Preserve ★   This exceptional 1,524-acre island, acquired by the Nature Conservancy in 1978, contains an excellent 5¹/₂-mile loop hike covering a wide cross section of native terrain, including bogs, heath, rocky coastline, and forests of twisted jack pines. Maps and a birding checklist can be found in a stand at the parking lot. Follow one fork of the trail to the shoreline; work your way along boulders to the other fork, then back to your car. Though mostly flat, the hike is rocky and slow in places—it's no pushover. Yet it's worth doing if you're up for the challenge. If a heavy fog has settled in, it's even more beautiful; just make sure you stay on the trail. Afterward, consider making a donation to the Nature Conservancy (www.tnc.org), a great organization whose active local chapter carefully maintains this preserve as well as many other important ones in the state.

Black Duck Cove Rd., Great Wass Island, Jonesport. Contact the Nature Conservancy (C) **207/729-5181.** Free admission. Open daylight hours. From Jonesport, cross bridge to Beals Island (signs); continue across causeway to Great Wass Island. Bear right at next fork; pavement ends. Continue past lobster pound to a small parking lot on the left marked by Nature Conservancy logo (oak leaf).

Maine Coastal Islands National Wildlife Refuge ★★   This refuge strings together a collection of uninhabited islands and parcels of land, protecting them as habitat for nesting seabirds and birds of prey. The entire refuge now includes about 50 islands, three onshore areas, and more than 8,000 acres in all. It's home to terns, plovers, bald eagles, puffins, razorbills, storm petrels, and eiders, among other birds; hiking trails run through forests, marshes, and mudflats; there's even a loop along stony beaches (the Hollingsworth Trail, 6 miles off Rte. 1 in Steuben) and another passing through a blueberry field (Birch Point Trail). Note that some parts of the refuge are open to the public (Cross, Scotch, Halifax, and Bois Bubert islands); some are always closed (Seal Island); the rest are closed to public egress from April through August. Check ahead with administrators. To get to the refuge, you'll need your own boat—or someone else's (see the "Getting Out to Sea" box below).

P.O. Box 279, Milbridge. (C) **207/546-2124.** http://petitmanan.fws.gov.

Milbridge Historical Museum   This low-key museum focuses mostly on shipbuilding and fishing as a local way of life, with exhibits such as *Getting Through the Long Winter*, *Old Ways of Fishing*, and *Rusticators* (about summer tourists seeking to escape to

Getting Out to Sea

To see the Maine Coastal Islands National Refuge, or whales, seals, or light-houses, you'll usually need to arrange for a personalized tour from a local charter boat operator. One of the best in these parts is captain Winston Shaw's **Sea Venture** (© 207/288-3355; www.svboattours.com)—he charges about $85 to $105 per hour, which covers a group of up to six travelers—if you want to view these islands. Captain Shaw ties up at the Atlantic Oakes Motel, on Route 3 just north of downtown Bar Harbor.

The **Bar Harbor Whale Watch Co.** (© 888/WHALES4 [942-5374] or 207/288-2386; www.whalesrus.com) will also run you through some of these islands on its lighthouse tour; see "Whale-Watching" in chapter 9 for more details on their operations. If you set foot on those islands that are open to public for walking, please respect the rules that protect these delicate ecosystems. Tread lightly, and light no open fires or unleash any dogs.

a more basic way of life here). The displays include vintage photos, shipbuilding tools, and a time capsule filled with items from Downeast Maine.

Main St. (Rte. 1), Milbridge. © 207/546-4471. Free admission. July–Aug Tues and Sat–Sun 1–4pm; June and Sept Sat–Sun 1–4pm. Oct–Feb by appointment only. Closed Mar–May.

Raye's Mustard Mill (Finds)
Foodies may feel they've gone to heaven after stumbling across Raye's artisanal mustard factory here in downtown Eastport, powered by one of the last stone mills in America. The Raye family has been cold-grinding mustard seeds and bottling various mustard concoctions here since 1903, when J. W. "Wes" Raye built the place to create mustards for a booming local sardine-tinning trade. Now he supplies sardine plants as far away as Norway, too. Free hourly tours of the factory are given, where new flavors are sometimes in the offing; in the gift shop, pick up gifts for the mustard-crazed back home.

P.O. Box 2, Eastport, ME 04631. © 800/853-1903 or 207/853-4451. www.rayesmustard.com. Tours Mon–Fri 8:30am–5pm on the hour, also sometimes weekends 10am–5pm.

Roque Bluffs State Park (Kids)
A day-use-only park, Roque Bluffs features impressive coastal scenery plus the added attraction of both freshwater and saltwater swimming areas. Jasper Beach is particularly noteworthy for the uniformly smooth jasper stones that make it up. There are family-friendly amenities here such as grills, changing areas, a playground, and a lifeguard.

145 Schoppee Point Rd. (6 miles off U.S. Rte. 1), Roque Bluffs. © 207/255-3475. $3 adults, $1 children ages 5–11, free for children 4 and under. Open mid-May to Sept.

Ruggles House
This Federal home dates from 1818 and was built for Thomas Ruggles, a local timber merchant and civic leader. The house is grand and opulent, but in a curiously miniature sort of way. There's a flying staircase in the central hallway, pine doors hand-painted to resemble mahogany, and detailed woodcarvings in the main parlor

done over the course of 3 years by an English craftsman equipped, legend has it, with just
a penknife. Tours last 20 minutes to a half-hour.

Main St., Columbia Falls. © **207/483-4637.** www.ruggleshouse.org. Tours $5 adults, $2 children ages 6–12. June to mid-Oct Mon–Sat 9:30am–4:30pm; Sun 11am–4:30pm. Closed mid-Oct to Apr.

Schoodic Point ★★   This remote, scenic, and free unit of Acadia National Park is just 7 miles from Mount Desert Island across Frenchman Bay, but it's a 50-mile drive to get here. A pleasing one-way loop road hooks around the point (no park entry pass or fee required) and winds along the water and through forests of spruce and fir. Good views of the mountains of Acadia open up across Frenchman Bay; you can also see part of a historic naval station housed on the point. Park near the tip and explore salmon-colored rocks that plunge into the ocean, especially dramatic when the seas are agitated.

Acadia National Park, Winter Harbor. © **207/288-3338.** Free admission. Drive east from Ellsworth on Rte. 1 for 17 miles to W. Gouldsboro; then turn south on Rte. 186 to Winter Harbor and look for the brown-and-white national park signs.

The Telephone Museum   It's not exactly comprehensive, but the tiny telephone museum here, in a barn about 10 miles outside Ellsworth, makes for a rainy-day diversion as you explore the ins and outs of the hand-crank system that first made it possible to reach out and touch someone. Talk to a switchboard operator—the early heroines of the system (my mom was one)—and learn about telephone poles, line, linesmen, switching stations, and how they kept it all running smoothly back in a day when cellphones were just science fiction. Tours are available.

166 Winkumpaugh Rd. (P.O. Box 1377), Ellsworth. © **207/667-9491.** www.thetelephonemuseum.org. Admission $5 adults, $2.50 children. July–Sept Thurs–Sun 1–4pm; May–June and Oct by appointment only. Closed Nov–Apr. From Rte. 1 in Ellsworth, go 7 miles south on Rte. 1 to Happytown Rd., turn right, and continue 6 miles to crossroads. Turn right onto Winkumpaugh Rd. Museum is on left.

West Quoddy Head Light & Quoddy Head State Park ★★   This red-and-white lighthouse, which has been likened to a barbershop pole or a candy cane, marks the easternmost point of the United States and helps guide boats into the Lubec Channel. (Interestingly, it's also the nearest geographical point in the U.S. to Africa.) The light, operated by the Coast Guard, isn't open to the public, but visitors can walk the grounds near the light and along headlands at an adjacent state park. A visitor center inside the light-keeper's house overlooks rocky shoals, pounding waves, and some of the most powerful tides on the

(Moments)   **Touring Eastport Via the "Woody"**

One of the most distinctive ways to see the town of Eastport is to take Jim Blankman's "woody" (wood-paneled station bus) tour. Blankman, who works as a coffin maker/woodworker/luthier/salmon smoker when he's not giving tours—people tend to double up around here—bought and restored a 1947 1-ton Dodge bus from a local family and now runs it around town. The tour includes a picnic lunch of salmon and chicken, and seats a maximum of 11. Contact Blankman's **Moose Island Tour Bus** outfit at © **207/853-4831** for schedule and fee details.

planet. Watch for fishing boats straining against the currents and seals playing in the waves or sunning on offshore rocks. The park also includes 480 acres of coastline and bogs, with several trails winding through the forest and atop rocky cliffs; some of the most dramatic views can be found just a short walk down the path at the far end of the parking lot.

W. Quoddy Head Rd., Lubec. ✆ **207/733-0911** (state park) or 207/733-2180 (lighthouse). www.west-quoddy.com. Lighthouse grounds: free admission. State park admission: $2 adults, $1 children 5–11. State park grounds mid-May to mid-Oct daily 9am–sunset; lighthouse visitor center late May to mid-Oct daily 10am–4pm. Closed mid-Oct to mid-May.

5 PASSAMAQUODDY BAY

Once in Lubec or Eastport, it's only a short drive to Canada, where you'll find Campobello Island, a quiet jewel once favored by president Franklin D. Roosevelt.

From Campobello, you can catch a ferry to quiet Deer Island, then onward to New Brunswick's Passamaquoddy Bay region, which adjoins the Maine coast and is easily reached via a boat ride from Campobello. Or take a 1-minute drive across a bridge in Calais, Maine (assuming the border checks go smoothly), to St. Stephen, New Brunswick, for a look at a French town with a yummy chocolate museum.

You might also push a bit farther into New Brunswick and check out the lovely seaside town of St. Andrews. For more information about this scenic town, see chapter 11. It's a worthwhile day or overnight trip.

CAMPOBELLO ISLAND ★

Campobello is a compact island (about 10 miles long and 3 miles wide) at the mouth of Passamaquoddy Bay. Among its other distinctions, it's connected by a graceful modern bridge to Lubec, Maine, and is thus easier to get to from the United States than from Canada. Getting here from the Canadian mainland without driving through the United States requires two ferries, one of which operates only during the summer.

Campobello has been home to both humble fishermen and wealthy families over the years, and both have coexisted quite nicely. (Locals approved when summer folks built golf courses because it gave them a place to graze their sheep.) Today the island is a mix of elegant summer homes and less interesting tract homes of a more recent vintage.

The island offers excellent shoreline **walks** ★ at both Roosevelt Campobello International Park (see below for more) and **Herring Cove Provincial Park** (✆ **506/752-7010**), which is open year-round and maintains both a golf course (open late Apr to Oct) and campsites (open late May to late Sept). The landscapes are extraordinarily diverse. On some trails you'll enjoy a Currier and Ives tableau of white houses and church spires across the channel in Lubec and Eastport; 10 minutes later you'll be walking along a wild, rocky coast pummeled by surging waves. Herring Cove has a mile-long beach that's perfect for a slow stroll in the fog. Camping and very scenic golf are also offered at the provincial park.

Nature lovers should note that Campobello's mixed terrain also attracts a good mix of birds, including sharp-shinned hawk, common eider, and black guillemot. Ask for a checklist and map at the visitor center.

(Tips) Like Bikes? You'll Love Campobello.

If you like bikes, the islands and peninsulas of Passamaquoddy Bay lend themselves nicely to cruising in the slow lane—especially pretty Campobello, which has plenty of good dirt roads perfect for mountain biking. But you'll need a guidebook to show you the way. Fortunately, Kent Thompson has written a handy one, called *Biking to Blissville*. It covers 35 lovely rides in the Maritimes, including some on the island, and costs C$15 (about US$11). Unfortunately, it was published in 1993. Try to order it through the publisher, Goose Lane Editions, 500 Beaverbrook Court, Ste. 330, Fredericton, NB E3B 5X4 (*C* **888/926-8377** or 506/450-4251; www.gooselane.com), or, failing that, through an online retailer such as **Amazon** (www.amazon.ca).

Essentials

GETTING THERE   Campobello Island is accessible year-round from the United States. From Route 1 in Whiting, Maine, take Route 189 to Lubec, where a bridge links Lubec with Campobello. In the summer, there's another option. From the Canadian mainland, take the free ferry to Deer Island, drive the length of the island, and then board the small seasonal ferry to Campobello. The ferry is operated by **East Coast Ferries** (*C* **506/747-2159**) and runs from late June to September. The fare is C$14 (US$13/£7) for car and driver, C$3 (US$2.70/£1.50) for each additional passenger.

VISITOR INFORMATION   The **Campobello Welcome Center,** 44 Rte. 774, Welshpool, NB E5E 1A3 (*C* **506/752-7043**), is on the right side just after you cross the bridge from Lubec. It's open daily mid-May to early September from 9am to 7pm, and daily from 10am to 6pm until mid-October.

Roosevelt Campobello International Park ★★   Take a brief excursion out of the country and across the time zone. The U.S. and Canada maintain a joint national park here, celebrating the life of Franklin D. Roosevelt, who summered here with his family in the early 1900s. Like other affluent Americans, the Roosevelt family made an annual trek to the prosperous colony at Campobello Island. The island lured folks from the sultry cities with a promise of cool air and a salubrious effect on the circulatory system. ("The extensive forests of balsamic firs seem to affect the atmosphere of this region, causing a quiet of the nervous system and inviting sleep," read an 1890 real-estate brochure.) The future U.S. president came to this island every summer between 1883—the year after he was born—and 1921, when he was suddenly stricken with polio. Franklin and his siblings spent those summers exploring the coves and sailing around the bay, and he always recalled his time here fondly. (It was his "beloved island," he said, coining a phrase that gets no rest in local promotional brochures.)

You can view a brief film at the visitor center and take a self-guided tour of the elaborate mansion, which is covered in cranberry-colored shingles, to learn about Roosevelt and his early life. For a "cottage" this huge, it is surprisingly comfortable and intimate. The park is truly an international park, run by a commission with representatives from both the U.S. and Canada, making it like none other in the world. Because of Homeland Security measures currently in place, I suggest you bring with you either a passport or birth certificate, although checks are rarely enforced.

> **(Tips) Time Has Come Today**
>
> Remember that New Brunswick is in the *Atlantic* Standard Time (AST) zone, also known as ADT (Atlantic Daylight Time) during the summer, and that it's 1 hour *ahead* of Maine, Boston, and New York time (Eastern Standard Time). Let's just call it New Brunswick time, for now. That means if it's 9am in Eastport, Maine, when you cross the border, it's 10:01am in New Brunswick when you get across. And if you step right back across, it's 9:02am. You get the idea: reset your watch—or at least make a mental note—when crossing the border, and again when coming back. I have expressed all opening and closings times for New Brunswick attractions and restaurants in AST; in other words, in New Brunswick time.

Leave some time to explore farther afield in the 2,800-acre park, which offers scenic coastline and 8.5 miles of walking trails. Maps and walk suggestions are available at the visitor center.

459 Rte. 774, Welshpool NB (in Canada). ☎ **506/752-2922.** www.fdr.net. Free admission. Daily 10am–6pm (last tour at 5:45pm). Visitor center closed mid-Oct to mid-May; grounds open year-round. Reached via U.S. 1 to Whiting and then Rte. 189 to Lubec; follow signs to bridge.

ST. STEPHEN

St. Stephen is the gateway to Canada for many travelers arriving from the United States. It's directly across the tidal St. Croix River from Calais, Maine, and the two towns share a symbiotic relationship—it's a local call across the international border from one town to the other, fire engines from one country will respond to fires in the other, and during an annual summer parade, bands and floats have sometimes marched right through Customs. Though downtown St. Stephen is hardly a destination in and of itself, it is a handy pit stop—and the smell of chocolate (as you'll read below) does sneakily attempt to entice you into a longer stay.

Essentials

VISITOR INFORMATION The **Provincial Visitor Information Centre** (☎ **506/466-7390**) is open daily from 9am to 8pm mid-June to August and 9am to 6pm in the shoulder seasons (May, June, Sept, and early Oct). It's in the old train station at Milltown Boulevard and King Street, about a mile from Canadian Customs; turn right after crossing the border (following signs for St. Andrews and Saint John), and watch for the information center at the light where the road turns left.

Exploring St. Stephen

St. Stephen is a town in transition. The lumber industry and wood trade that were responsible for those handsome brick-and-stone buildings that line the main street have mostly dried up. The town now depends on its paper mill, the large Ganong chocolate factory, and pass-through tourists like yourself for its economic mainstays. (For the truly cocoa bean–obsessed, there's also a small Chocolate Festival in summer.) As a regional commercial center, it has a gritty, lived-in feel to it, though not much in the way of stylish shopping or restaurants to keep you more than a moment.

> ## (Tips) The Sweet Truth About St. Stephen's Sweet Tooth
>
> St. Stephen's claim to fame is that it's purported the home of the chocolate bar—the first place where somebody thought to wrap chocolate pieces in foil and sell them individually. In 1910, they claim. At least that's according to local lore. Chocolate is big around here—not as big as in Hershey, Pennsylvania, but still a big part of the local psyche and economy. The Ganong brothers began selling chocolate from their general store here in 1873, and from that an empire was built, employing some 700 people by the 1930s. Ganong was also the first place to package chocolates in heart-shaped boxes for Valentine's Day, and still holds 30% of the Canadian market for heart-box chocolates. The modern new plant on the outskirts of town isn't open to the public, but there's a museum in one of the company's early factories, a large brick structure on the main street.

Want even more? **Ganong's Chocolatier,** an old-fashioned candy shop, is located in the storefront adjacent to the museum. Don't miss the budget bags of factory seconds. There's also a Heritage Chocolate Walk offered, which combines a factory tour with a walk through the downtown's historic areas.

Still, you can learn about the region's history with a brief stop at the **Charlotte County Museum,** 443 Milltown Blvd. (✆ **506/466-3295**), open June through September only; it's quite close to the tourist office described above.

The Chocolate Museum (Kids)   Chocolate is integral to this town's history (see "The Sweet Truth about St. Stephen's Sweet Tooth," above), so of course there's a museum to the cacao bean. Here you can view an 11-minute video about the history of local chocolates. Displays and exhibits explain 19th-century chocolate boxes, and there are interactive multimedia displays about the making of candy and games for young children (such as "Guess the Centers"). One highlight is watching the expert hand-dippers make chocolates the old-fashioned way; samples, of course, are available afterward. Want more? Ganong's Chocolatier, the company's candy shop, is located in the storefront adjacent to the museum. (Don't miss the budget bags of factory seconds.) There's also a "Heritage Chocolate Walk" offered, which combines a factory tour with a walk through the downtown's historic areas. Plan to spend about an hour here altogether.

73 Milltown Blvd. ✆ **506/466-7848.** www.chocolatemuseum.ca. Admission C$5 (US$4.50/£2.50) adults, C$4 (US$3.60/£2) students and seniors, C$3 (US$2.70/£1.50) children under 6, C$15 (US$14/£7.50) families. Downtown tour plus museum C$10 (US$9/£5) adults, C$8 (US$7.20/£4) seniors and students, C$6 (US$5.50/£3) children 5 and under, C$25 (US$23/£13) family. Mid-June to Aug Mon–Sat 9:30am–6:30pm, Sun 11am–3pm; mid-Mar to June and Sept–Nov Mon–Fri 10am–4pm (Sept also open Sat). Closed Dec to mid-Mar.

6 WHERE TO STAY & DINE

IN MAINE

Small motels, inns, and B&Bs abound along this part of the Maine coast; resorts, on the other hand, are almost nonexistent. The message: Prepare to rusticate.

The upside of this situation is that budget travelers seeking to minimize costs can do well here. Low-end offerings include the Machias Motor Inn, with 35 air-conditioned riverside rooms at 26 E. Main St. (Rte. 1) in Machias (© **207/255-4861** or 255-4862); the Margaretta Motel (© **207/255-6500**), with swimming pool and air-conditioning, and the Bluebird Motel (© **207/255-3332**), with 40 air-conditioned units, both also on U.S. 1 in Machias; the Blueberry Patch Motel & Cabins (© **207/434-5411**), on Route 1 in Jonesboro; the Eastland Motel, with 20 rooms on Route 189 in Lubec (© **207/733-5501**); or the Motel East, overlooking the bay at 23A Water St. in Eastport (© **207/853-4747**). These establishments are mostly family-run, and usually most rooms cost no more than $80 per night for a double room, though summer can bring price spikes. Most are closed in winter.

Those with RVs can camp out at Pleasant River RV Park at 11 W. Side Rd. in Addison (© **207/483-4083**). It's open May through October, though it only has a half-dozen sites from which to choose.

In addition to gleaning the listings below, you might also think about renting a cottage or farmhouse by the week or month; there are plenty to choose from along this stretch of coast in summer, though digging them up can take some doing. Among the offerings, check out the unique **Quoddy Head Station** (© **877/535-4714** or 860/535-4714; www.quoddyvacation.com), on W. Quoddy Head Road in Lubec, a former Coast Guard lifesaving station built in 1918. You can rent the five-bedroom station house or one of five other units, all with terrific coastal views, in July and August for $750 to $1,500 per week (lower off season) or from $75 and up per night in the off season only.

Eats are likewise thin on the ground up here. If you're simply looking to fuel up on fast food or family-style fare, Ellsworth is your main (and, actually, only) supply depot; expect the usual franchise chains along Route 1, especially near the point where routes 1 and 3 diverge.

On the town's main drag, you can also fuel up with standard Mexican fare at the **Mex,** 191 Main St. (© **207/667-4494;** www.themex.com), which serves a variety of the expected Mexican dishes (taco salads, fajitas, burritos), plus some seafood surprises (crab enchiladas, seviche, haddock Veracruz) as a tip of the sombrero to Maine. Large entrees run about $12 to $17, though you can spend less on a small plate or salad. More typical coastal dining is found in Ellsworth at the **Union River Lobster Pot,** 8 South St. (© **207/667-5077;** www.lobsterpot.com), featuring lobster dinners but also serving a basic menu of Maine seafood, steaks, chicken, and sandwiches.

To stock up for a picnic at Quoddy Head, make a beeline for **Bold Coast Smokehouse** (© **888/733-0807** or 207/733-8912; www.boldcoastsmokehouse.com) on Route 189 in Lubec; it's got to be the nation's easternmost smokehouse. Vinny and Holly Gartmayer smoke up hot salmon, gravlax, kabobs, and trout pâté, among other products. Another smokehouse, **Sullivan Harbor Farm,** is covered below.

Black Duck Inn   There isn't much to the little village of Corea, mostly just a clutch of fishing boats and some island views, but there is a bed-and-breakfast if you care to stay the night. The Black Duck consists of four no-frills rooms (two share a bathroom, while the others have private facilities), one suite, and one waterfront cottage rented out by the week. It's a simple place set among quiet scenery. Rooms here are uncluttered and dotted with antiques; three, including the studio apartment (which has a kitchenette) and the cottage, possess excellent vistas of the picturesque harbor and the lupine-strewn headland.

36 Crowley Island Rd. (P.O. Box 39), Corea ME 04624. ℂ **207/963-2689.** Fax 207/963-7495. www.black duck.com. 6 units (2 with shared bathroom), 1 cottage. $140–$165 double; weekly rates for cottage vary. Full breakfast included with rate. DISC, MC, V. Closed Dec to mid-May. Children 8 and older welcome. *In room:* No phone.

Captain Cates Bed & Breakfast   This trim blue house on a point of water, built by a sailor in the 1850s, is a simple yet accommodating place; five of the six units have ocean views, though all six of them do share three bathrooms. The J. W. Room, with an extra-long mahogany bed from 1865 and matching commode and dresser, sports water views, while the Olevia Room is furnished with a queen-size bed and late-19th-century maple French Provincial bedroom set. Up on the third floor, the Starboard Room is done in cream and blue-green tones. There are three more units with double beds or, in the case of the Puffin Room, a single bed. The lack of TVs and phones is made up for by a communal game room with a group tube and some puzzles.

Rte. 92 at Phinney Lane (P.O. Box 314), Machiasport, ME 04655. ℂ **207/255-8812.** Fax 207/255-6705. www.captaincates.com. High season 6 units (all share 3 bathrooms); Nov–Apr 3 units. $75–$95 double. AE, V. **Amenities:** 2 dining rooms; game room. *In room:* No phone.

Crocker House Country Inn   Built in 1884, this handsome shingled inn is off the beaten track on picturesque Hancock Point, across Frenchman Bay from Mount Desert Island. It's a cozy retreat, good for rest, relaxation, and quiet walks; it's only about a 4-minute walk from the water's edge. Rooms are tastefully decorated in comfortable country decor; there's nothing lavish here, but they do have phones. The common areas are more relaxed than fussy. The inn has a few bikes for guests to explore the point, the second-smallest post office in the U.S., or clay tennis courts (nearby). **Dinner** ★ here is a highlight: it's served in a fun atmosphere. Open daily from May through October and weekends in several other months, the kitchen serves mostly traditional favorites, such as oysters Rockefeller, scallops, fish, pasta, steak au poivre, and lamb.

967 Point Rd. (Box 171), Hancock Point, ME 04640. ℂ **877/715-6017** or 207/422-6806. Fax 207/422-3105. www.crockerhouse.com. 11 units. Mid-June to mid-Oct $110–$160 double; off season $85–$120 double. Rates include full breakfast. AE, DISC, MC, V. Closed Jan–Feb; open weekends only in Mar. **Amenities:** Dining room; free bikes. *In room:* A/C.

Harbor House on Sawyer Cove B&B ★   Once the local telegraph office and an outpost for ship equipment, the early-19th-century Harbor House may be Jonesport's most luxurious lodging choice. There are two suites, which are set above an antiques shop, and both feature truly impressive coastal scenery from their third-floor windows. The Beachrose Room is a funkily shaped space (narrow with low ceilings) with outstanding ocean views, while the Lupine Room features a king-size feather bed and private breakfast nook; both have private entrances. Breakfast is served on a wonderful inn porch, and a backyard picnic table is yet another perfect spot from which to take in the changing light over the reach and islands. Helpfully, it's open year-round.

27 Sawyer Sq. (P.O. Box 468), Jonesport, ME 04649. ℂ **207/497-5417.** Fax 207/497-3211. www.harborhs. com. 2 units. May–Oct $125 double; rest of the year $100 double. Rates include full breakfast. DISC, MC, V. *In room:* No phone.

Helen's Restaurant ⟨Finds⟩   **Diner** ★ This is the original Helen's, a cut-above-the-rest diner and one of the premier places in all of Maine to eat pie. (And, yes, there was a Helen.) You can get pork chops, fried fish, burgers, meatloaf, and other American-style square meals. But absolutely save room for the amazingly creamy and fruity pies; strawberry rhubarb or blueberry, when in season, are out of this world, but chocolate cream, banana cream, or just about anything else will satisfy the sweet tooth. Check for daily specials. There's another Helen's on the strip just north of Ellsworth.

28 E. Main St., Machias. (C) **207/255-8423.** Entrees $3–$16. DISC, MC, V. Daily 6am–7:30pm.

Home Port Inn ★   The 1880 Home Port was built as a family home, but converted into lodgings in 1982. On a quiet street in downtown Lubec, its rooms mostly possess tremendous views of both Cobscook Bay and the Bay of Fundy. The central living room and fireplace are the focal points; comfy guest rooms vary in size, with one occupying a former library and another a former dining room. Best bed? The Garden Overlook's king-size bed. Best view? The room known as the View, of course (though it only has a double bed). The inn restaurant is surprisingly good, serving passable seafood dinners nightly of smoked fish, lobsters, scallops, salmon, and crab, as well as landlubbing items such as chicken *cordon bleu* and steak au poivre. Note that this restaurant opens a month later (and closes a few weeks earlier) than the inn itself.

45 Main St. (P.O. Box 50), Lubec ME 04652. (C) **800/457-2077** or 207/733-2077. www.homeportinn.com. 7 units. $90–$105 double. Rates include continental breakfast. AE, DISC, MC, V. Closed mid-Oct to mid-May. **Amenities:** Restaurant. *In room:* No phone.

Le Domaine ★★ (Finds)   Set on Route 1 about 10 minutes east of Ellsworth, this inn somehow has the flair of a French *auberge*. While the highway in front can be a bit noisy, the garden and woodlands out back offer plenty of serenity. Rooms are comfortable and tastefully appointed without being pretentious; the innkeeper has combined several rooms to create two suites and added air-conditioning and phones to all units. Rooms are on the second floor, in the rear of the property; suites with private terraces face the woods. But the real draw is the **dining room** ★★, serving French country cooking in a handsome space of pine-wood floors and a big fireplace. Meals run to brandied pâté, filet mignon in Bordelaise sauce, grilled halibut, and quail wrapped in bacon; finish with custard-filled raspberry tarts or rich bread pudding. The wine list is great (and all French).

1513 U.S. Rte. 1 (P.O. Box 519), Hancock, ME 04640. (C) **800/554-8498** or 207/422-3395. Fax 207/422-3916. www.ledomaine.com. 5 units. June–Oct $200–$285 double; $285–$370 suite. Rates include full breakfast and dinner. AE, MC, V. Closed Nov–May. **Amenities:** Dining room. *In room:* A/C.

Little River Lodge   Overlooking Cutler's tiny, impressively situated harbor, this Victorian inn—once known as the Cutler Hotel—was built in the late 19th century to lodge steamship passengers bound from Boston to Canada. The inn has just five rooms, three of them facing the water; all have been decorated in nautical themes and simple, pleasing colors (forest green, eggshell blue) and stocked with old books and antiques. A warning—four of five rooms here are still furnished with twin, full, or double beds, though the Roosevelt Room (where T. R. himself is said to have slept) does contain a queen-size bed. Three of the units share a bathroom, but if you're wanting to stay in Cutler near the good coastal trails, this is really your only option.

Rte. 191 (P.O. Box 251), Cutler, ME 04626. (C) **207/259-4437.** www.cutlerlodge.com. 5 units (3 with shared bathroom). $110–$120 double (private bathroom); $80–$100 double (shared bathroom). Rates include breakfast. Some rooms 2-night minimum stay weekends. No credit cards. From Rte. 1 in E. Machias, turn onto Rte. 191 S. and continue 13 miles to hotel on left. **Amenities:** Dining room. *In room:* No phone.

Micmac Farm ★   Based in a 1763 home with intriguing history (the founder's family is buried in a cemetery on the premises), quiet Micmac Farm consists of just three units in a peaceful riverside setting: two rustic, wood-paneled "guesthouses" in the woods, furnished with two double beds apiece and kitchenettes, plus a more luxurious guest room located inside the main house with a big deck, king-size bed, television, and Jacuzzi tub. This third room also adjoins the home's library, which guests are welcome to use. An outdoor deck overlooks the Machias River, and it's a good spot for watching the water.

47 Micmac Lane (Rte. 92), Machiasport, ME 04655. (C) **207/255-3008.** www.micmacfarm.com. 3 units. Main house $125 double; cottages $80–$95 double or $495–$595 weekly. MC, V. Pets and children welcome in cottages. *In room:* TV (1 unit), kitchenette (2 units), coffeemaker (2 units), Jacuzzi (1 unit), no phone. From Rte. 1 in center of Machias, drive south and east on Rte. 92 (Elm St.) for 2 miles; turn left on Micmac Lane.

Milliken House B&B ★ (Value) Guests at this friendly B&B are greeted with glasses of port or sherry in a big living room sporting two fireplaces. It's a nice welcome, and the five rooms are equally nice, done up in marble-top furnishings and outfitted with the original owner's collection of books. (Benjamin Milliken had made a small fortune building a dock and outfitting the big ships passing in and out of this once-busy port during Eastport's 19th-c. heyday.) Expect small touches such as pillow-side chocolates and fresh flowers. All rooms feature televisions and fireplaces, something of a surprise given the low, low price. The house is located only 2 blocks from Eastport's historic district, as well, making it ideal for local explorations. Breakfast might run to buttermilk pancakes served with a berry sauce, crepes, or a quiche Lorraine, sided with homemade bread.

29 Washington St., Eastport, ME 04631. (C) **888/507-9370** or 207/853-2955. www.eastport-inn.com. 6 units. $75–$85 double. Rates include full breakfast. MC, V. Well-trained pets welcome. *In room:* TV, fireplace, no phone.

Peacock House Bed & Breakfast ★ (Value) The Peacock House was built in out-of-the-way Lubec by an English sea captain in 1860, yet has since hosted prominent Mainers including U.S. senators Margaret Chase Smith and Edmund Muskie. The three second-floor rooms are queen-size-bedded and simple; the Margaret Chase Smith Suite has a queen-size bed, while the king-size-bedded Meadow Suite has the inn's largest bathroom and a sitting area. (It's accessible for guests with limited mobility.) The Wedgwood Suite's queen-size bed is augmented by a daybed with trundle, and is best for small families. The Peacock Suite is the most romantic choice, with a gas fireplace, four-poster queen-size bed, wet bar, refrigerator, and TV with DVD player. Tinkle the keys of the living room's baby grand piano, if you like: It's allowed and even encouraged.

27 Summer St., Lubec, ME 04652. (C) **888/305-0036** or 207/733-2403. www.peacockhouse.com. 7 units. $90–$112 double. Rates include full breakfast. MC, V. No children 6 and under. *In room:* TV (some units), fridge (1 unit), no phone.

Redclyffe Shore Motor Inn ★ I don't recommend many motor inns or motels in this book, but this one packs a great deal more historic and scenic punch than most. The complex, consisting of a Gothic Revival main house dating from the 1860s (note the steep gables) and a cluster of motel units, perches on a cliff with awesome views of Passamaquoddy Bay and the St. Croix River. Book one of the so-called "patio rooms" with a private balcony for maximum gazing access. Whether in the main house or the motel section, all the double- and king-size-bedded rooms and suites here sport the basics: phones, televisions, and coffeemakers. The balcony rooms are a steal considering the views, and the glassed-in dining room—open every night, serving standard American meals—features yet another knockout ocean view. Remember, however, that there's no breakfast service at all here. You'll need to head elsewhere for that.

U.S. Rte. 1, Robbinston, ME 04671. ℂ **207/454-3270.** Fax 207/454-8723. www.redclyffeshoremotorinn. com. 16 units. $78 double. MC, V. Closed Nov to mid-May. **Amenities:** Dining room. *In room:* A/C (some units), TV, coffeemaker.

Riverside Inn ★ This far downeast, it isn't easy to find a frilly place, but the small three-room Riverside Inn outside of Machias does offer more than the usual motel in these parts does. The second-floor Mrs. Chase Room, named for the former captain's wife, has a claw-foot tub and skylight. The two-bedroom Lower Coach Suite features a wraparound deck overlooking the river and the inn's garden, while the popular Upper Coach Suite possesses even better views—from a private balcony—plus a small true kitchen. Rooms are uniformly attractive and clean. The **dining room** ★, a rarity around here, serves surprisingly fancy dinner entrees such as lobster and scallops in champagne sauce, almond-crusted fish filets, beef Wellington, pistachio-crusted pork medallions with a cranberry-plum chutney, and the like. (The dining room is closed in winter, though the inn remains open year-round.)

U.S. Rte. 1 (P.O. Box 373), E. Machias, ME 04630. ℂ **207/255-4134.** Fax 207/255-0577. www.riversideinn-maine.com. 4 units. $94–$129 double. Rates include breakfast. MC, V. **Amenities:** Dining room. *In room:* Kitchenette (1 unit), fridge (1 unit), no phone.

Sullivan Harbor Farm & Smokehouse (Finds) One of the last independently owned smokehouses in New England, this award-winning operation, run out of a farmhouse right on Route 1, specializes in delicious cuts of salmon, cured, hand-rubbed with salt and brown sugar, then cold-smoked over hickory smudge fires. They also produce gravlax, hot-roasted salmon, smoked scallops, smoked char, and pâté. If you're stumped for a place to stay near Mount Desert Island, consider renting one of three cottages on the smokehouse property; each is differently equipped—one has a full modern kitchen; another a washer/dryer, phone, and cable TV; and a third, simpler cottage comes with fewer extras. The cottages rent by the week in high summer season (shorter rentals possible in fall) from $975 to $1,700.

U.S. Rte. 1 (P.O. Box 96), Sullivan, ME 04664. ℂ **800/422-4014** or 207/422-2268. www.sullivanharborfarm. com. 3 cottages. $975–$1,700 weekly. 1-week minimum stay in summer, 3-night minimum stay (prorated rates) after Labor Day. MC, V. *In room:* TV (2 units), kitchenette (2 units), fireplace (2 units), no phone (2 units).

Todd House Bed & Breakfast A bright yellow house out on Todd's Head overlooking Cobscook and Passamaquoddy bays, this 1775 Cape features classic New England architectural touches such as a huge center chimney and a fireplace with bake oven. It served as everything from a former Mason's Hall and temporary military barracks; today, the six inn rooms come in various configurations. Two rooms have kitchenettes. The yard features cookout equipment, too, but the ocean views are the real draw. The inn is only about a $3/4$-mile walk from Eastport's burgeoning downtown district.

1 Capen Ave., Eastport, ME 04631. ℂ **207/853-2328.** Fax 207/853-2328. 6 units (2 with shared bathroom). $50–$90 double. Rates include self-service breakfast. MC, V. *In room:* Kitchenette (2 units), fridge (2 units), coffeemaker, no phone.

Weston House ★ A whitewashed, hillside 1810 Federal looking out onto the bay and Campobello, the Weston House features rooms with antiques and Asian furnishings, with classical music playing in the background. John James Audubon lodged here once upon a time, and today the three units (all sharing two bathrooms) are brightly furnished in prints and poster beds; one room has a television and a fireplace, as well. Breakfasts

are better than you might expect (coddled eggs, pancakes with apricot syrup, and the **255**
like); brunches are served on the weekend along with glasses of sherry, while picnic
lunches and dinners can be ordered by special arrangement. For relaxation, there's an
attractive patio with wicker furniture.

26 Boynton St., Eastport, ME 04631. © **207/853-2907.** www.westonhouse-maine.com. 3 units (all with
shared bathroom). $80–$90 double. Rates include full breakfast. No credit cards. *In room:* TV (1 unit), no
phone.

IN NEW BRUNSWICK

There's also camping at **Herring Cove Provincial Park** (© **506/752-7010**) for C$22 to
C$24 (US$19–US$22/£11–£12), with discounts for seniors.

Lupine Lodge ★ (Value) (Kids)   In 1915, cousins of the Roosevelts built this handsome
compound of log buildings not far from the Roosevelt cottage. A busy road runs between
the lodge and the water, but the buildings are located on a slight rise and have the feel of
being removed from the traffic. Guest rooms are in two long lodges adjacent to the main
building and restaurant. The rooms with bay views cost a bit more but are worth it—
they're slightly larger, and better furnished in a log-rustic style. All guests have queen-size-
bedded rooms (some rooms add another double bed or fireplace) and access to a deck
that overlooks the bay. You won't find phones, TVs, luxury bathrooms, or wireless Internet, but you will find a pleasing vibe—they welcome small children, and will pack a
lunch for your explorations, though they cannot accept pets. The lodge's attractive **dining room** ★ serves excellent meals.

610 Rte. 774, Welshpool, Campobello Island, NB E5E 1A5. © **888/912-8880** or 506/752-2555. www.
lupinelodge.com. 11 units. C$99–C$150 (US$89–US$135/£50–£75) double. MC, V. Closed Nov–Apr. **Amenities:** Restaurant. *In room:* No phone.

Owen House, A Country Inn & Gallery   This three-story clapboard captain's house
dates from 1835 and sits on 4 tree-filled hectares (10 acres) at the edge of the bay. The
first-floor common rooms are nicely decorated in a busy Victorian manner with Persian
and braided carpets and mahogany furniture; view the water from the nautical-feeling,
airy sunroom and its big windows. The guest rooms are a mixed lot, furnished with an
eclectic mélange of antique and modern furniture; some are bright and airy and filled
with salty air (room no. 1 is the largest, with waterfront views on two sides); others, like
room no. 5, are tucked under stairs and a bit dark, though the Owens are renovating the
house. Third-floor rooms share a single bathroom but also have excellent views. A filling
hot breakfast served family style is included in the room rates, and ask to see the owner's
in-house watercolor gallery if you're an art buff.

11 Welshpool St., Welshpool, Campobello, NB E5E 1G3. © **506/752-2977.** www.owenhouse.ca. 9 units
(2 with shared bathroom). C$107–C$210 (US$96–US$189/£54–£105) double. Rates include full breakfast.
MC, V. Closed Nov–Apr. No children 5 and under in Aug. *In room:* No phone.

11

Side Trips from the Maine Coast

Once ensconced on the coast of Maine, you'd be easily forgiven if you didn't wish to do anything more strenuous than turn the pages of a book while lying in a hammock. But if you're a back-roads adventurer, an outdoors enthusiast, or a connoisseur of gourmet meals, there are some additional interesting places to be found just a little bit farther afield.

Portsmouth, New Hampshire, for instance, is well worth a quick detour across the bridge from Kittery for its coffee shops, inns, boutiques, and pleasing snugness. And coastal New Brunswick, an hour or less from Eastport, is worth seeing for its pretty seaside villages, islands, and high tides. Finally, just inland from the midcoast section of Maine, huge Baxter State Park—featuring the lofty and impressive peak of Mount Katahdin—is one of Maine's finest moments.

I have described each of these three side trips below, going in order—as does this book—from south to north.

1 PORTSMOUTH, NEW HAMPSHIRE

Portsmouth ★★ is a civilized little seaside city of bridges, brick, and seagulls, and quite a little gem. Filled with elegant architecture that's more intimate than intimidating, this bonsai-size city projects a strong, proud sense of its heritage without being overly precious. Part of the city's appeal is its variety: Upscale coffee shops and art galleries stand alongside old-fashioned barbershops and tattoo parlors. Despite a steady influx of money in recent years, the town still retains an earthiness that serves as a tangy vinegar for more saccharine coastal spots. Portsmouth's humble waterfront must actually be sought out; when found, it's rather understated.

This city's history runs deep, a fact that is evident on even a quick walk through town. For the past 3 centuries, Portsmouth has been the hub of the coastal Maine/New Hampshire region's maritime trade. In the 1600s, Strawbery Banke (it wasn't called Portsmouth until 1653) was a major center for the export of wood and dried fish to Europe. Later, in the 19th century, it prospered as a center of regional trade. Just across the Piscataqua River in Maine (so important a connection that there are four bridges from Portsmouth to that state), the Portsmouth Naval Shipyard—founded way back in 1800—evolved into a prominent base for the building, outfitting, and repairing of U.S. Navy submarines. Today, Portsmouth's maritime tradition continues with a lively trade in bulk goods; look for the scrap metal and minerals stockpiled along the shores of the river on Market Street. The city's de facto symbol is the tugboat, one or two of which are almost always tied up in or near the waterfront's picturesque "tugboat alley."

Visitors to Portsmouth will discover a surprising number of experiences in such a small space, including good shopping in the boutiques that now occupy much of the historic

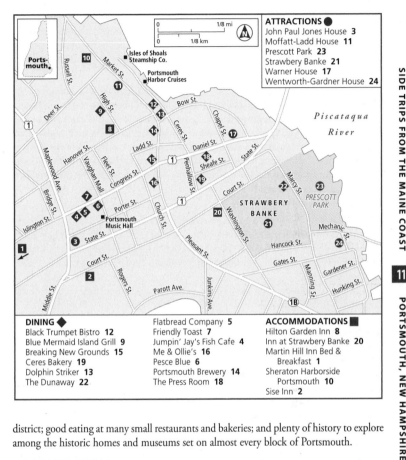

SIDE TRIPS FROM THE MAINE COAST

11

PORTSMOUTH, NEW HAMPSHIRE

ATTRACTIONS ●
John Paul Jones House **3**
Moffatt-Ladd House **11**
Prescott Park **23**
Strawbery Banke **21**
Warner House **17**
Wentworth-Gardner House **24**

DINING ◆
Black Trumpet Bistro **12**
Blue Mermaid Island Grill **9**
Breaking New Grounds **15**
Ceres Bakery **19**
Dolphin Striker **13**
The Dunaway **22**

Flatbread Company **5**
Friendly Toast **7**
Jumpin' Jay's Fish Cafe **4**
Me & Ollie's **16**
Pesce Blue **6**
Portsmouth Brewery **14**
The Press Room **18**

ACCOMMODATIONS ■
Hilton Garden Inn **8**
Inn at Strawbery Banke **20**
Martin Hill Inn Bed &
   Breakfast **1**
Sheraton Harborside
   Portsmouth **10**
Sise Inn **2**

district; good eating at many small restaurants and bakeries; and plenty of history to explore among the historic homes and museums set on almost every block of Portsmouth.

ESSENTIALS

GETTING THERE Portsmouth is served by exits 3 through 7 on I-95. The most direct access to downtown is via Market Street (exit 7), which is the last New Hampshire exit, just before crossing the big bridge and the river to Maine. Take that exit, then bear right (coming from the south) or left (from the north). You'll come straight into town.

Amtrak (© **800/872-7245;** www.amtrak.com) operates four to five trains daily from Boston's North Station to downtown Dover, New Hampshire; a one-way ticket is about $17 per person, and the trip takes about 1¹/₂ hours. You can then take the no. 2 **COAST** bus (© **603/743-5777;** www.coastbus.org) from Dover station to the center of downtown Portsmouth, a 45-minute trip that costs just $1 (50¢ for seniors).

The bus, for once, is not a bad choice. **Greyhound** (© **800/231-2222;** www.greyhound. com) and **C&J Trailways** (© **800/258-7111** or 603/430-1100; www.cjtrailways.com) each run about five buses daily from Boston's South Station to Portsmouth, plus one to three daily trips from Boston's Logan Airport. Each service has a different pickup point: Greyhound's is the main bus stop in Market Square, while C&J's is at a modern but distant bus station about 5 miles south at the former Pease air base (call a taxi or rent a car). The one-way cost for all three trips is about $16 per person; C&J purportedly has a no-cellphone-talking-on-the-bus rule.

A one-way Greyhound trip from New York City's Port Authority bus station to downtown Portsmouth is about $45 and takes about 6¹/₂ hours.

VISITOR INFORMATION The **Greater Portsmouth Chamber of Commerce,** 500 Market St. (© **603/436-3988;** www.portcity.org), has an information center between exit 7 and downtown across the road from the piles of salt and scrap metal. From Memorial Day to Columbus Day, it's open Monday through Wednesday from 8:30am to 5pm; Thursday and Friday, from 8:30am to 7pm; and Saturday and Sunday from 10am to 5pm. The rest of the year, it's open weekdays only, 8:30am to 5pm. During the summer, a second staffed booth opens in Market Square, right in front of the Breaking New Grounds coffee shop; hours are irregular.

PARKING Most of Portsmouth can be easily reconnoitered on foot, so you only need to park once. But mind the rules and signs; parking can be tight in and around the historic district in summer, and officers will ticket. The city's municipal parking garage nearly always has space and costs 75¢ per hour; it's located on Hanover Street, between Market and Fleet streets. The Strawbery Banke museum (see below) also provides limited parking for visitors.

There's also now a trackless **"trolley"** (© **603/743-5777**) circulating through central Portsmouth in a one-way loop from July to early September daily from 10:30am to 5:30pm. It hits all the key historical points and has traditionally been free to ride (that could change in the near future). Catch it at Market Square, Prescott Park, or Strawbery Banke.

A MAGICAL HISTORY TOUR

Portsmouth's 18th-century prosperity is evident in the Georgian-style homes that dot the city. Strawbery Banke occupies the core of the historic area and is well worth visiting. If you don't have the budget, time, or inclination to spend half a day at Strawbery Banke, a walking tour takes you past many other significant homes, some of which are maintained by various historical or colonial societies and are open to the public. A helpful map and brochure, *The Portsmouth Trail: An Historic Walking Tour,* is available free at information centers.

Tired from touring? Take a break at **Prescott Park ★★**, between Strawbery Banke and the water. It's one of the best municipal parks in New England. The water views, lemonade vendors, benches, grass, lovely gardens, and full card of festivals make it worth a visit. There's a full calendar of events at the park festival website, **www.prescottpark. org**. Be amazed.

John Paul Jones House ★ Scottish Revolutionary War hero John Paul ("I have not yet begun to fight") Jones is believed to have lived in this 1758 home during the war while here to oversee construction of his sloop, the *Ranger,* which was likely the first ship to sail under the U.S. flag (a model is on display). He took a ragtag crew of locals to England and gave them no end of bother. The house is immaculately restored and maintained by the Portsmouth Historical Society; costumed guides lead tours.

43 Middle St. © **603/436-8420.** Admission $8 adults, free for children. Daily 11am–5pm. (Last tour begins at 4:30pm.) Closed mid-Oct to mid-May.

(Finds) Exploring Near the Wentworth-Gardner House

Most travelers tend to visit just Strawbery Banke, do a little shopping at the downtown boutiques, grab a bite, and hustle onward to Maine. To get a fuller sense of historic Portsmouth, though, take the time to stroll a bit off the beaten track. The neighborhood around the Wentworth-Gardner House is a great area to snoop around in, too, with lanes too narrow for SUVs, twisting roads, and wooden houses in all shapes and sizes. It's a taste of the early 19th century.

Moffatt-Ladd House ★★ Built for a family of prosperous merchants and traders, this 1763 home is as notable for its elegant gardens as it is for the home's great hall and elaborate carvings. Now a National Historic Landmark, it belonged to a single family from 1763 until 1913, when it became a museum. As a result, many furnishings never left the premises; aficionados of Early American furniture and painting, take note.

154 Market St. (C) **603/436-8221.** Admission to house and gardens $6 adults, $2.50 children 11 and under; gardens only $2 per person. Mon–Sat 11am–5pm; Sun 1–5pm. Tours mid-June to mid-Oct; last tour at 4:30pm.

Strawbery Banke ★★★ In 1958, the city of Portsmouth was finalizing plans to raze this neighborhood (which was settled in 1653) to make way for urban renewal. A group of local citizens resisted the move, and they prevailed, establishing an outdoor history museum that's become one of the largest and best in New England. Today the attraction consists of 10 prime downtown acres and more than 40 historic buildings. Ten buildings have been restored with period furnishings; eight more feature exhibits. (The rest can only be viewed from the exterior, but are mostly very well restored.) While Strawbery Banke employs staffers to assume the character of historical residents, the emphasis is more on the buildings, architecture, and history than the costumed reenactors—as it should be.

The neighborhood surrounds an open lawn (formerly an inlet) and has a settled, picturesque quality. At three working crafts shops, watch coopers, boat builders, and potters at work. The most intriguing home is the split-personality Drisco House, half of which depicts life in the 1790s and half of which shows life in the 1950s, nicely demonstrating how houses grow and adapt to each era.

Hancock St. (C) **603/433-1100.** www.strawberybanke.org. Summer admission $15 adults, $10 children 5–17, free for children 4 and under, $40 per family; winter rates discounted. May–Oct open daily for self tours 10am–5pm; Nov–Apr Sat–Sun 10am–2pm, only on a 90-min. guided tour, offered on the hour; extra tours in Dec. Look for directional signs posted around town.

Warner House ★ This house, built in 1716, was the governor's mansion during the mid–18th century, when Portsmouth was the state capital. (Who knew?) After a period as a private home, it was opened to the public in the 1930s. This stately brick structure with graceful Georgian architectural elements is a favorite among architectural historians for its wall murals (said to be the oldest murals still in place in the U.S.), early wall marbleizing, and original white pine paneling.

150 Daniel St. (C) **603/436-8420.** www.warnerhouse.org. Admission $5 adults, $4 seniors, $2.50 children 7–12, free for children 6 and under. Mid-June to mid-Oct Mon–Sat 11am–4pm; Sun noon–4pm. Closed Nov to early June.

Packing a Picnic in Portsmouth

Portsmouth's **Prescott Park** is about as pretty a spot as you could expect to find for an alfresco bite, with views of the harbor, a well-kept green, free gardens, summer-long music festivals, and vendors dispensing slushies and other fun treats in the summer. And it's free. There are a few benches, but tote a blanket just in case—the lawn makes a great spot for splaying out and catching some rays. Get provisions nearby at the simple, aptly named **Portsmouth Provisions** (© 603/436-5104), 2 blocks away at 148 State St. It's open from early in the morning until almost midnight, daily. There's a selection of beers, an attached sandwich counter where locals eat lunch on the fly, and plenty of snacks. Or just hit the vendors in the park for a hot dog, ice cream, or a lemonade. For those with a sweet tooth, a summertime ice-cream shop has also opened its doors across the street in the Strawbery Banke complex.

Wentworth-Gardner House ★★★ Arguably the most handsome mansion in the Seacoast region, this is considered one of the nation's best examples of Georgian architecture. The 1760 home features many period elements, including pronounced *quoins* (blocks on the building's corners), pedimented window caps, plank sheathing (to make the home appear as if made of masonry), an elaborate doorway with Corinthian pilasters, a broken scroll, and a paneled door topped with a pineapple, the symbol of hospitality. Perhaps most memorable is its scale—though a grand home of the Colonial era, it's modest in scope; some architectural circles today may not consider it much more than a pool house.

50 Mechanic St. © 603/436-4406. Admission $5 adults, $2 children 6–14, free for children 5 and under. Tues–Sun noon–4pm. Closed mid-Oct to mid-June. From rose gardens on Marcy St. across from Strawbery Banke, walk south 1 block, turn left toward bridge, make a right before crossing bridge; house is down the block on your right.

BOAT TOURS

Portsmouth is especially attractive when seen from the water. A small fleet of tour boats ties up at Portsmouth, taking scenic tours of the Piscataqua River and the historic Isle of Shoals throughout the summer and fall.

The **Isles of Shoals Steamship Co.** ★★ (© 800/441-4620 or 603/431-5500; www.islesofshoals.com) sails from Barker Wharf on Market Street and is the most established of the city's tour companies. The firm takes a variety of tours on the 90-foot, three-deck *M/V Thomas Laighton* (a modern replica of a late-19th-c. steamship). Most popular are the excursions to the Isle of Shoals, at which passengers can disembark and wander about Star Island, a dramatic, rocky landmass that's part of an island cluster far out in the offshore swells. Reservations are strongly encouraged. Other popular trips include a sunset lighthouse cruise. Fares for the trips to the Isles of Shoals range from $25 to $33 per adult, depending on the length of the cruise; dinner cruises cost extra. Parking is an additional charge, as well.

Portsmouth Harbor Cruises ★ (© 800/776-0915 or 603/436-8084; www.portsmouthharbor.com) specializes in tours of the historic Piscataqua River aboard the *Heritage*, a

60-foot, 49-passenger cruise ship with plenty of open deck space. It leaves from the Ceres Street docks, beside the tugboats. Cruise past five old forts or enjoy the picturesque tidal estuary of inland Great Bay, a scenic trip upriver from Portsmouth. Trips run daily; reservations are suggested. Fares are $12 to $20 for adults, $10 to $18 for seniors, and $8 to $13 for children ages 2 to 12.

WHERE TO STAY

Downtown accommodations are preferable, as everything is within walking distance, but prices tend to be high. The newish **Courtyard Portsmouth,** 1000 Market St. (© **603/ 436-2121**), is big and modern, with business amenities and comfortable beds right off I-95 about 2 or 3 minutes' drive from downtown. But the service is highly variable; hopefully that will improve. It books up fast on summer weekends or when conventions come to town, so specify and confirm your room type in advance. Since 2006, there's also a **Hilton Garden Inn** (© **603/431-1499**) in a very central downtown location with a nice indoor pool.

For more downscale, budget-priced accommodations, less-stylish chain and family-owned hotels and motels clump up at the edges of town along I-95 and around the big traffic circle on the Route 1 bypass. I can't vouch for all of these; it's buyer beware.

Inn at Strawbery Banke ★ (Finds)   This historic little inn is tucked away in an 1814 home on Court Street, an ideal base for exploring Portsmouth: Strawbery Banke is just a block away, and Market Square (the center of the city's cafe action) is just 2 blocks away. The friendly innkeepers have done a nice job of taking a cozy antique home and making it comfortable for guests. Rooms are tiny and simply furnished, yet brightened up by stenciling, pencil-poster beds, wooden shutters, and their beautifully preserved pine floors; one has a bathroom down the hall. Two sitting rooms are stocked with TVs, phones (there are none in the rooms), and lots and lots of books, and you take full breakfast in a dining room each morning.

314 Court St., Portsmouth, NH 03801. © **800/428-3933** or 603/436-7242. www.innatstrawberybanke. com. 7 units (1 with detached bathroom). Mar–Sept $145–$150 double; Nov–Feb $100–$115 double. Rates include full breakfast. 2-night minimum stay Aug and Oct weekends. AE, DISC, MC, V. Children 10 and older welcome. *In room:* A/C, no phone.

Martin Hill Inn Bed & Breakfast ★★   This B&B in a residential neighborhood is just a short walk from downtown. The inn consists of two period buildings: a main house (built around 1815) and a second guesthouse built 35 years later. All rooms have queen-size beds, writing tables, and sofas or sitting areas, and are variously appointed with distinguished wallpapers, porcelains, antiques, love seats, four-poster or brass beds, and the like. The relaxing, expansive Greenhouse Room is basically a suite with its own sitting room and wicker-furnished sun porch. More good stuff: a stone path from the inn leads to a small, beautiful water garden, and the included full breakfast is a highlight. It might consist of johnnycakes (a delicious New England specialty of cornmeal pancakes), "goldenrod" eggs, quiche, nutty waffles, or cooked fruit. When checking out, remember there's an automatic $3 charge for housekeepers' tips.

404 Islington St., Portsmouth, NH 03801. © **603/436-2287.** 7 units. May–Oct $130–$210 double; rest of the year $115–$160 double. Holiday rates higher. Off-season discounts possible. 2-night minimum stay summer and holiday weekends. Rates include full breakfast. MC, V. No children 15 and under. *In room:* A/C.

Sheraton Harborside Portsmouth ★★ This five-story, in-town brick hotel is nicely located on the way into town—the attractions of downtown Portsmouth are virtually at your doorstep (Strawbery Banke is about a 10-min. walk, and waterfront bars are a block or two away). With plenty of parking both underground and across the street, a stay here makes for a relatively stress-free visit. The modern building was inspired by the low brick buildings of the city, and wraps around a circular courtyard; it's a well-maintained and -managed property popular with business travelers as well as leisure travelers looking for the amenities of a larger hotel, if a bit bland in its decor. Some rooms and suites have views of the working harbor.

250 Market St., Portsmouth, NH 03801. ✆ **888/627-7138** or 603/431-2300. Fax 603/431-7805. www.sheratonportsmouth.com. 200 units. $130–$310 double and suite; off-season discounts available. AE, DISC, MC, V. **Amenities:** Restaurant; fitness center; spa; business center; limited room service; executive rooms. *In room:* A/C, TV, dataport, minibar, coffeemaker, hair dryer, iron.

Sise Inn ★ A modern, elegant hotel in the guise of a country inn, this solid Queen Anne–style home was built for a prominent merchant in 1881; the hotel addition was constructed in the 1980s, amid other renovations. The effect is happily harmonious, with antique stained glass and copious oak trim meshing well with the more contemporary elements. An elevator serves the three floors; modern carpeting is throughout, but many rooms have antique armoires, updated Victorian styling, and whirlpool or soaking tubs. I like room no. 302, a bi-level, two-bedroom suite with a claw-foot tub; no. 406, a suite with soaking tub and private sitting room; no. 120, with its private patio; and no. 216 (in the carriage house), with an actual working sauna, a two-person whirlpool, and lovely natural light. This is a popular hotel for business travelers (partly thanks to Wi-Fi access).

40 Court St. (at Middle St.), Portsmouth, NH 03801. ✆ **877/747-3466** or 603/433-0200. Fax 603/433-1200. www.siseinn.com. 34 units. $120–$280 double and suite. Rates include continental breakfast. AE, DISC, MC, V. **Amenities:** Laundry service. *In room:* A/C, TV, hair dryer, iron/ironing board, Jacuzzi (some units).

Three Chimneys Inn ★★ About 20 minutes northwest of Portsmouth at the edge of the university town of Durham, this is a wonderful retreat. The main section of the inn dates to 1649, but later additions and a full-scale renovation in 1997 have given it more of a regal Georgian feel now. All of the units are above average in size, and have been lushly decorated with four-poster or canopied beds, mahogany armoires, and Belgian carpets. Most rooms sport either gas or Duraflame log fireplaces. One of my favorite rooms is the William Randolph Hearst Room, with photos of starlets on the walls and a massive bed that's a replica of one at San Simeon. Five rooms on the ground-floor level beneath the restored barn have private entrances, Jacuzzis, and gas fireplaces; these tend to be a bit more cave-like than the other units, but luxurious and romantic. This is a popular place for weddings on summer weekends, and is always booked up long in advance of University of New Hampshire events such as graduation, football games, and homecoming weekend. Be sure to book well ahead at those times.

17 Newmarket Rd., Durham, NH 03824. ✆ **888/399-9777** or 603/868-7800. Fax 603/868-2964. www.threechimneysinn.com. 23 units. $139–$239 double. MAP rates available. Rates include full breakfast. 2-night minimum stay on weekends Sept–Oct. AE, DISC, MC, V. Children 6 and older welcome. **Amenities:** 2 restaurants; bar. *In room:* A/C, TV, coffeemaker.

Wentworth by the Sea ★★★ The reopening of this historic resort in 2003 was a major event; it's now one of the top resorts in New England. The photogenic grand hotel, which opened on New Castle Island in 1874 but later shut down, was refurbished by the owners of the Samoset (p. ###) and is operated jointly with Marriott in professional, luxurious fashion. As befits an old hotel, rooms vary in size, but most are spacious with good views of ocean or harbor. Particularly interesting are the suites occupying the three turrets. Some rooms have gas-powered fireplaces or private balconies; all have luxury bath amenities, new bathroom fixtures, and beautiful detailing and furnishings. Families will appreciate that many contain two queen-size beds. Downhill, a set of new luxury suites beside the marina are truly outstanding, with water views, modern kitchens, and marble bathrooms with Jacuzzis. A full-service spa offers a range of treatments and body wraps.

Wentworth Rd. (P.O. Box 860), New Castle NH 03854. ℂ **866/240-6313** or 603/422-7322. Fax 603/422-7329. www.wentworth.com. 161 units. $229–$459 double and suite; off-season discounts possible. Packages available. AE, DISC, MC, V. **Amenities:** 2 restaurants; bar; indoor pool; outdoor pool; golf course privileges; spa. In room: A/C, TV, kitchenette (some units), coffeemaker, hair dryer, fireplace (some units), Jacuzzi (some units).

WHERE TO DINE

For two more dining options beyond those listed below, visit the **Wentworth by the Sea** resort (above) on Route 1B a few miles south of the city. There are two choices: a main dining room and a casual bar and grill. The **dining room** fare is top-rate, served beneath a remarkable (and original) frescoed dome; entrees might include grilled swordfish, lobster with filet mignon, seared yellowfin tuna, a clambake, a lobster pie, or something more Continental. There is a moderate dress code: Men are asked to wear a collared shirt. The **Latitudes** grill is simpler in menu, but offers something the main inn can't—an outdoor patio of tables with lovely views overlooking the water. It's softly lit at night.

Downtown Portsmouth now also has a branch of the terrific **Flatbread Company** (ℂ **603/436-7888**) pizzeria at 138 Congress St. It's *the* place to eat a terrific organic-wheat crust pizza.

Black Trumpet Bistro ★★ BISTRO/WINE BAR   When the former owners of this space decided to pack up and sell in early 2007, their own executive chef Evan Mallett jumped at the chance to buy it. He cooks exotically spiced comfort food in an intimate, two-story space within a former warehouse. The menu is subtly influenced by Spain and Latin America: you partake of starters that might include quahog chowder, tomatoey octopus with chorizo, bacalao salad, local mussels steamed in porter (a dark beer), or a Moroccan-spiced beet-root soup. Among the entrees, the Black Trumpet burger is fun, incorporating foraged mushrooms and Gouda cheese, as is an ostrich filet served with pine nuts in a Concord grape demiglace. The wine list is obviously strong. If they're full, just sit in the bar.

29 Ceres St. ℂ **603/431-0887**. www.blacktrumpetbistro.com. Reservations recommended. Main courses $16–$26. AE, DC, MC, V. Sun–Thurs 5:30–9:30pm; Fri–Sat 5:30–10pm.

Blue Mermaid Island Grill ★★ Finds   GLOBAL/ECLECTIC   The Blue Mermaid is a Portsmouth favorite for its good food, good value, and refusal to take itself too seriously. It's a short stroll from Market Square, in a historic area called the Hill, and is not pretentious—locals congregate here, Tom Waits tunes play in the background, and the service is casual but professional. The menu is adventurous in a low-key global way, leaning ever so slightly toward Mexico and the Caribbean—you might try a tortilla pizza or a salmon club sandwich for lunch, or a dinner of short ribs in guava-soy sauce, served with corn bread; Bimini-style grilled chicken with bananas and walnuts in bourbon

> **(Tips) Portsmouth: Coffee Capital**
>
> Portsmouth has perhaps the best cafe scene in northern New England, nearly comparable to Cambridge's or Boston's and better than Portland's or Burlington's. There are numerous places in the compact downtown alone where you can get a decent-to-very good cup of coffee and better-than-average baked goods; new coffeehouses open all the time. There's a Starbucks (of course), but my favorite spots to quaff a coffee drink or pot of tea with a book are, in this order: **Breaking New Grounds,** 14 Market Sq. ((C) **603/436-9555**), with outstanding espresso shakes, good tables for chatting out on the square, and late hours; and **Me and Ollie's,** 10 Pleasant St. ((C) **603/436-7777**), known locally for its good bread, sandwiches, and homemade granola.
>
> If you want a bit more of a bite to go with your coffee, Portsmouth's got that covered, too. Two outstanding places leap to mind. The tie-dyed **Friendly Toast,** 121 Congress St. ((C) **603/430-2154**), serves a variety of eggs and other breakfast dishes all day long, plus heartier items such as burgers. And the funky **Ceres Bakery,** 51 Penhallow St. ((C) **603/436-6518**), on a side street off the main square, has a handful of tiny interior tables; grab a sandwich, cookie, or slice of cake to go and walk to the waterfront rose gardens nearby.

sauce, sided with a sweet-potato hash; or beef medallions spiced up with horseradish cream and chipotle peppers. For fun, make a dinner out of small-plate offerings such as wontons, Jamaican beef patties, and the seafood-coconut wrap. They also cook seafood on a wood-fired grill, burgers, pasta, and pizzas; libations include local draft brews plus a full menu of coolers, mojitos, Goombay smashes, and margaritas.

409 The Hill (at Hanover and High sts., facing the municipal parking garage). (C) **603/427-2583.** www.bluemermaid.com. Reservations recommended for parties of 6 or more. Main courses $6–$12 lunch, $16–$22 dinner. AE, DISC, MC, V. Mon–Thurs 11:30am–9pm; Fri–Sat 11:30am–10pm; Sun 10am–9pm.

Dolphin Striker ★ NEW ENGLAND Housed in a historic brick warehouse in Portsmouth's most charming area, the Dolphin Striker serves traditional New England seafood dishes, some of them in new clothes, such as a mushroom-crusted filet of cod or a piece of salmon "lacquered" in tomatoey balsamic vinaigrette and then grilled. But the redoubtable Maine lobster potpie hasn't changed since, well, probably 1700. Seafood loathers can find refuge in a duet of organic beef (hanger steak and wine-braised ribs), a rack of lamb when it's on the menu, or the grilled duck breast with risotto and fruity sauce. The main dining room here has a rustic, public house atmosphere with wide pine-board floors and wooden furniture; downstairs is a comfortable pub known as the Spring Hill Tavern, with quite good acoustic acts. After 9pm, the Striker shelves the heavy fare and switches over to a lighter "tavern" menu.

15 Bow St. (C) **603/431-5222.** www.dolphinstriker.com. Reservations recommended. Main courses $21–$27 dinner. AE, DC, DISC, MC, V. Daily 5–11pm.

The Dunaway ★★★ NEW AMERICAN/FRENCH Right across the road from lovely little Prescott Park, restaurateur Jay McSharry's latest project is a very welcome addition to the Strawbery Banke complex. Dunaway chef Ben Hasty grew up on a farm in southern Maine and cooked at the prestigious The French Laundry in San Francisco and Arrows in Ogunquit before joining the Dunaway's opening team in 2005. His menu draws both on local ingredients (lobster, the catch of the day, Maine-raised organic beef) and techniques from faraway lands—chiefly, but not only, France. Witness entrees of sea bass, lemony stuffed sole, pan-roasted duck breast with duck bacon and polenta, and rib-eye with Calvados sauce. Many of the herbs, fruits, and vegetables are cultivated and plucked right from Strawbery Banke's gardens. But the real capping touch here is the elegant interior decor, which preserves the period feel of the building (lots of exposed wood and candles) yet also feels like a romantic night out.

66 Marcy St. (across from Prescott Park). *C* **603/373-6112.** www.dunawayrestaurant.com. Reservations recommended. Main courses $9–$18 lunch, $26–$36 dinner. AE, DC, DISC, MC, V. Mon–Thurs 5:30–9:30pm; Fri–Sat 5–10pm; Sun 5–9pm. Also, lunch daily 11:30am–2pm mid-Apr to Sept.

Jumpin' Jay's Fish Café ★★ SEAFOOD   One of Portsmouth's best eateries, Jay's is a hopping destination, and it's especially good for those travelers who want to eat seafood that has *not* been cooked in a deep-fryer. A sleek and spare dining room is dotted with splashes of color, with an open kitchen and polished-steel bar; locals seem to have fun eating here, and the place attracts a younger, hipper clientele than most other spots in town. The catch of the day is posted on blackboards; you pick your fish, then pair it with a sauce such as spicy orange-sesame glaze, lobster velouté, citrusy mustard sauce, or simple olive oil and herbs. Pasta dishes are also an option—you can add scallops, mussels, or even chicken.

150 Congress St. *C* **603/766-3474.** www.jumpinjays.com. Reservations recommended. Dinner main courses $19–$25. AE, DISC, MC, V. Mon–Thurs 5:30–9:30pm (closes 9pm in winter); Fri–Sat 5–10pm; Sun 5–9pm.

Pesce Blue ★★★ SEAFOOD/ITALIAN   Another upscale seafood eatery in downtown Portsmouth? Yes, and again it's a smashing success, thanks to a youthful drive that starts with ownership and trickles on down. Chef James Walter serves seafood and other dishes with a strong Italian accent. Lunch might be a piece of grilled flatbread topped with smoked salmon; a salad of mussels, San Marzano tomatoes, marinated olives, and capers; or a cut of pan-roasted haddock with baccala-whipped potatoes and ramps. Plenty of antipasti are available, as well. Dinner entrees could include a crispy piece of sockeye salmon, lasagna with house lamb sausage, oil-poached halibut, a mixed seafood grill, a wild boar steak, a small plate of tuna tartare with pickled apples and capers (the small plates are great), or salt-baked branzino. Desserts include mascarpone-ricotta cheesecake, fennel-flavored panna cotta, molten chocolate cake, gelati, and a lovely olive oil-orange cake topped with vanilla cream.

106 Congress St. *C* **603/430-7766.** www.pesceblue.com. Main courses $9–$21 lunch, $14–$30 dinner. AE, DISC, MC, V. Mon–Tues 5–9pm; Wed–Sun 11:45am–2pm and 5–9pm.

Portsmouth Brewery ★ ECLECTIC/PUB FARE   In the heart of the historic district (look for the tipping tankard suspended over the sidewalk), New Hampshire's first brewpub opened in 1991 and still draws a clientele loyal with its superb beers. The tin-ceiling, brick-wall dining room is open, airy, echoey, and redolent of hops. Brews are made in 200-gallon batches and include specialties such as Old Brown Dog ale and a delightfully creamy Black Cat Stout. An eclectic menu complements these robust beverages. It includes the expected pizzas, burgers, and sandwiches (including a steak bomb), but also offers a changing rotating of some pretty adventurous selections such as tamarind-grilled shrimp, crispy green tomatoes with Parmesan cheese, artichoke-stuffed ravioli, and cioppino. The food here is getting better every year; the beer is already excellent.

56 Market St. © **603/431-1115.** www.portsmouthbrewery.com. Reservations accepted for parties of 10 or more. Main courses $7–$22. AE, DC, DISC, MC, V. Daily 11:30am–12:30am.

The Press Room TAVERN FARE   Locals flock here more for convivial atmosphere and easy-on-the-budget prices than creative cuisine. An in-town favorite since 1976, the Press Room boasts that it was the first place in the area to serve Guinness beer, so it's appropriate that the place has a rustic, vaguely Gaelic charm. On cool days, a fire burns in the woodstove, and drinkers flex their elbows throwing darts in an atmosphere of brick walls, pine floors, and heavy wooden beams. Choose from a bar menu of inexpensive selections, such as burgers, fish and chips, and stir-fries. The jazz here is justifiably popular among locals (See "Portsmouth After Dark," below).

77 Daniel St. © **603/431-5186.** Reservations not accepted. Sandwiches $4–$7; main courses $8–$13. AE, DISC, MC, V. Sun–Thurs 5–11pm; Fri–Sat 11:30am–11pm.

Victory 96 State Street ★★ CONTINENTAL   Chef/owner Duncan Boyd, who opened this dining room and gentleman's bar in a brick corner space just off lovely Prescott Park, trained under legendary Boston grillman Jasper White and star chef Todd English. He learned very, very well: The food here emphasizes the New England harvest of clams, corn, cod, pumpkin, lobster, and so forth, and successfully carries a summery whiff of salty Cape Cod air throughout. The menus change seasonally. Starters run to such things as foie gras with brandied peaches and Pemaquid oysters on the half-shell; main courses have included leg of lamb, roasted venison, or roasted duck with a beach plum sauce. Finish with wild blueberry tarts, chocolate soufflé cake, or plates of artisanal cheeses. The bar area is a special treat, with lots of luxurious couches and chairs and its own menu of small plates and big burgers.

96 State St. © **603/766-0960.** www.96statestreet.com. Reservations recommended. Entrees $19–$27. AE, MC, V. Tues–Sun 5:30–9pm (lounge area from 5pm).

SHOPPING

Portsmouth's historic district is home to dozens of boutiques offering unique items. The fine contemporary **N.W. Barrett Gallery,** 53 Market St. (© **603/431-4262**), features the work of area craftspeople, with a classy selection of ceramic sculptures, glassware, lustrous woodworking, and handmade jewelry. The **Robert Lincoln Levy Gallery,** operated by the New Hampshire Art Association, 136 State St. (© **603/431-4230**), frequently changes exhibits and shows and is a good destination for some quality fine art produced by New Hampshire artists.

Chaise Lounge, 104 Congress St. (© **603/430-7872**), has a wonderfully eclectic range of home furnishings—sort of Empire meets modern—including wonderful photo lamps made in Brooklyn. **Nahcotta,** 110 Congress St. (© **603/433-1705**), is a gallery purveying high-end paintings and sculptures, many of which are quietly edgy and entertaining.

Bailey Works, 146 Congress St. (© **603/430-9577**), is an offbeat choice but young people might like to have a look. The company makes rugged, waterproof bike messenger–style bags in several styles and colors. The attention to detail is superb; the "253" style is quite popular.

(Tips)   **Seabrook Side Trip: Lobsters Galore!**

If you're driving Route 1 or Interstate 95 south of Portsmouth, heading to or from Massachusetts, make a detour to **Seabrook** for some of the best lobsters in New Hampshire—and the amazing spectacle of two (gently) competing shacks right across the road from each other.

Brown's (© 603/474-3331) got here first, and it's a bit more like the typically unadorned shack you'd find in, say, Downeast Maine. (Its patio also frames a view of Seabrook's infamous nuclear power plant—and, yes, it's active.) **Markey's** (© 603/474-2851) opened later and more closely resembles a small-town diner. The pounds frame both sides of state Route 286, easily reached from Portsmouth or Boston via the exits to Seabrook off both U.S. Route 1 and the New Hampshire Turnpike (I-95; drive east a few miles). From Hampton Beach, head south on coastal Route 1A a few miles and turn inland (west) on Route 286.

Paradiza, 63 Penhallow St. (© 603/431-0180), has an array of clever greeting cards, along with exotica such as soaps and bath products from Israel and Africa. **Macro Polo,** 89 Market St. (© 603/436-8338), specializes in retro-chic gifts, toys, dolls that will make you laugh out loud, magnets, and gadgets. It also recently opened two annexes, including a pet-accessories store next door called **Macro, Unleashed** (© 603/436-8887).

Finally, I'd be remiss if I didn't mention **Bull Moose Music** ★★, 82–86 Congress St. (© 603/422-9525). There's nothing glamorous about this cave-like space, but it is *the* place in northern New England to pick up new and used CDs, vintage (gasp) vinyl records, and rock memorabilia—often at special prices—and it's open until 11pm daily. I can't count the hours I've whiled away here, but I'd never call them wasted.

PORTSMOUTH AFTER DARK
Performing Arts
The Music Hall ★★   This historic theater dates back to 1878 and was restored to its former glory by a local arts group. A variety of shows are staged here, from film festivals and comedy revues to *The Nutcracker* and concerts by visiting symphonies and pop artists (David Crosby, Graham Nash). Call or check the website for a current calendar. 28 Chestnut St. © 603/436-2400. www.themusichall.org.

Bars & Clubs
Muddy River Smokehouse   Blues are the thing in Muddy River's upstairs eating room and downstairs lounge. Weekends offer reggae and blues, sometimes played by well-known performers from Boston and beyond. Cover charges vary; admission is free for some shows if you arrive early. I recommend the music here more than the barbecue, which is only middling. 21 Congress St. © 603/430-9582. www.muddyriver.com.

The Press Room ★   A popular local bar and restaurant (see "Where to Dine," above), the Press Room also offers casual entertainment almost every night, either upstairs or down. It's best known locally for its live jazz; the club brings in quality performers from Boston and beyond. You might also hear beat poetry or blues. 77 Daniel St. © 603/431-5186.

Spring Hill Tavern   Quality acoustic noodling, live jazz, classical guitar, and low-key rock is offered most evenings of the week here. It's the pub located right beneath the popular Dolphin Striker seafood restaurant (see "Where to Dine," above). 15 Bow St. ℂ 603/431-5222.

---

2 BAXTER STATE PARK & MOUNT KATAHDIN

There are two versions of the Maine Woods. There's the grand and unbroken forest threaded with tumbling rivers that unspools endlessly in the popular perception, and then there's the reality.

The perception is that this region is the last outpost of big wilderness in the East, with thousands of acres of unbroken forest, miles of free-running streams, and more azure lakes than you can shake a canoe paddle at. A look at a road map seems to confirm this, with only a few roads shown here and there amid terrain pocked with lakes; but undeveloped does not mean untouched.

The reality is that this forestland is a massive plantation, largely owned and managed by a handful of international paper and timber companies. An extensive network of small timber roads feeds off major arteries and opens the region to extensive clear-cutting. This is most visible from the air. In the early 1980s, *New Yorker* writer John McPhee noted that much of northern Maine "looks like an old and badly tanned pelt. The hair is coming out in tufts." That's even more the case today following the acceleration of timber harvesting thanks to technological advances in logging and demands for faster cutting to pay down large debts incurred during the large-scale buying and selling over the past decade and a half.

While the North Woods are not a vast, howling wilderness, the region still has fabulously remote enclaves where moose and loon predominate, and where the turf hasn't changed all that much since Thoreau paddled through in the mid–19th century and found it all "moosey and mossy." If you don't arrive expecting utter wilderness, you're less likely to be disappointed.

Baxter State Park is one of Maine's crown jewels, even more spectacular in some ways than Acadia National Park. This 200,000-plus-acre park in the remote north-central part of the state is unlike most state parks you may be accustomed to in New England—don't look for fancy bathhouses or groomed picnic areas. When you enter Baxter State Park, you enter near-wilderness.

Former Maine governor and philanthropist Percival Baxter single-handedly created the park, using his inheritance and investment profits to buy the property and donate it to the state in 1930. Baxter stipulated that it remain "forever wild." Caretakers have done a good job fulfilling his wishes: You won't find paved roads, RVs, or hookups at the campgrounds. (Size restrictions keep all RVs out.) Even cellphones are banned. You will find rugged backcountry and remote lakes. You'll also find Mount Katahdin, a granite monolith that rises above the sparkling lakes and boreal forests around it.

To the north and west of Baxter State Park lie several million acres of forestland owned by timber companies and managed for timber production. These concerns also control public recreation. If you drive on a logging road far enough, expect to run into a gate eventually; you'll be asked to pay a fee for day use or overnight camping on their lands.

Don't try to tour these woodlands by car. Industrial forestland is boring at best, downright depressing at its over-cut worst. A better strategy is to select one pond or river for

The Debate over Maine's North Woods

Much of Maine's outdoor recreation takes place on private lands—and that's especially true in the North Woods, 9 million acres of which are owned by fewer than two dozen **timber companies.** This sprawling, uninhabited land is increasingly at the heart of a simmering debate over land-use policies.

Hunters, fishermen, canoeists, rafters, bird-watchers, and hikers have been accustomed to having the run of much of this forest, with the tacit permission of most of the timber companies, many of which had long and historic ties to Maine's woodland communities because the companies were founded here.

But a lot has changed in recent years. One of the biggest factors has been the increasing **value of lakefront property,** which has suddenly made this land far more valuable as second-home property than as standing timber. A number of parcels have been sold off, and some formerly open land has been closed to visitors.

At the same time, **corporate turnovers** in the paper industry have led to increased debt loads and greater pressure from shareholders to produce more from the woodlands; this, in turn, has led to accelerated timber harvesting and big land sales, parcels sometimes changing hands at a dizzying speed. **Environmentalists** maintain this is a disaster in the making. They believe the forest can't provide jobs in the timber industry *or* remain a viable recreational destination if the state continues on its present course, and they believe that tree-cutting and herbicide spraying are both done far too recklessly. The timber companies deny this, insisting they're practicing responsible forestry.

A number of proposals to restore and conserve the forest have circulated in recent years, ranging from sweeping steps (such as establishing a new 2.6-million-acre **national park** here) to more modest notions such as encouraging timber companies to practice **sustainable forestry** and keep access open for recreation through tax incentives.

In the 1990s, statewide referendums calling for a clear-cutting ban and sweeping new timber-harvesting regulations were twice defeated, but the land-use issue still hasn't sorted itself out yet. The debate over the future of this forest isn't as volatile here as it is in the Pacific Northwest, where public lands are involved, but still—few residents around here lack opinions on the matter.

camping or fishing, then spend a couple of days getting to know the small area around it. Like a Hollywood set, buffer strips of trees have been left along the pond shores, streams, and rivers in this region, so it can feel like you're getting away from it all as you paddle along.

ESSENTIALS

GETTING THERE Baxter State Park is 85 miles north of Bangor. Take I-95 to Medway (exit 244), then head west 11 miles on Route 11/157 to the mill town of Millinocket, the last major stop for supplies. Go through town and follow signs to Baxter State Park.

> (**Tips**) **Grinning and Bearing It in Baxter**
>
> There are a few dozen black bears in Baxter State Park, and while they are not out
> to eat you, they do get ornery when disturbed, and they do get hungry at night.
> The park has published these tips to help you keep a safe distance:
>
> - Put all food and anything else with an odor (toothpaste, repellent, soap, deodor-
>   ant, perfume) in a sealed bag or container and keep it in the car.
> - If you're camping in the backcountry without a car, put all your food, dinner left-
>   overs, and other "smellable" things in a bag and hang it between two trees (far
>   from your tent) so that a bear can't reach it easily. Never keep any food in your
>   tent.
> - Take all your trash with you from the campsite when you leave.
> - Do not feed bears or any other animals in the park. They may bite that hand that
>   feeds them! And don't toss any food on the trail.

Another, less-used entrance is in the park's northeast corner. Follow I-95 to exit 259, then take Route 11 north through Patten and west on Route 159 to the park. Speed limit in the park is 20 mph; motorcycles and ATVs are not allowed here.

VISITOR INFORMATION   Baxter State Park provides maps and information from its **park headquarters** at 64 Balsam Dr. in Millinocket (© **207/723-5140;** www.baxter stateparkauthority.com). Note that no pets are allowed into the park, and all trash you generate must be brought back out. For information on canoeing and camping *outside* of Baxter State Park, contact **North Maine Woods, Inc.,** 92 Main St. (P.O. Box 421), Ashland, ME 04732 (© **207/435-6213;** www.northmainewoods.org). This is the con-sortium of paper companies, other landowners, and concerned individuals that controls and manages recreational access to private parcels of the Maine woods.

For help in finding cottages, rentals, and tour outfitters in the region, contact the **Katahdin Area Chamber of Commerce,** 1029 Central St., Millinocket, ME 04462 (© **207/723-4443;** www.katahdinmaine.com), open weekdays from 9am to 1pm.

FEES   Baxter State Park visitors driving cars with out-of-state license plates are charged a per-day fee of $12 per car. (It's free to Maine residents, as well as to any occupants of a rental car bearing Maine plates.) This fee is charged only once per stay if you're coming to camp; otherwise, you need to repay each day you enter the park.

GETTING OUTDOORS

BACKPACKING   The park maintains about 180 miles of backcountry hiking trails and more than 25 backcountry campsites, some of them accessible only by canoe. Most hik-ers coming to the park are intent on ascending **Mount Katahdin** (see below), Maine's highest peak; but dozens of other peaks are well worth scaling as well, and simply walking through the deep woods here is a sublime experience in stretches; you will hear no chain-saws. Reservations are required for backcountry camping; many of the best spots fill up quickly in early January when reservations open for a calendar year (see "Camping," below).

En route to Mount Katahdin, the Appalachian Trail winds through the "100-Mile Wilderness," a remote and bosky stretch where the trail crosses few roads and passes no settlements. It's the quiet habitat of loons and moose. Trail descriptions are available from the **Appalachian Trail Conference,** P.O. Box 807, Harpers Ferry, WV 25425 (© **304/ 535-6331;** www.appalachiantrail.org).

CAMPING Baxter State Park has eight **campgrounds** accessible by car and two more backcountry camping areas that must be walked into; most are open from mid-May until mid-October. Don't count on finding a spot if you show up without reservations in mid-summer; the park starts processing requests on a first-come, first-served basis the first week in January, and dozens of die-hard campers traditionally spend a cold night outside headquarters to secure the best spots. Call well in advance (as in, during the previous year) for the forms to mail in. Camping inside the park costs $9 to $18 per site, with some cabins and bunkhouses available at rates ranging from $10 to $30 per person. Reservations can be made by mail, in person at the headquarters in Millinocket (see "Visitor Information," above), or (sometimes) by phone—but *only* less than 14 days from arrival. Don't call them about any other dates.

North Maine Woods, Inc. (see above) also maintains a small network of **primitive campsites** on its 2-million-acre holdings. While you may have to drive through massive clear-cuts to reach them, some are positioned on secluded coves or picturesque points. A map showing logging road access and campsite locations is available for a small fee plus postage from the North Maine Woods headquarters (see "Visitor Information," above). Daily camping fees are minimal, though you must also pay an access fee to the lands.

CANOEING The state's premier canoe trip is the **Allagash River ★★**, starting west of Baxter State Park and running northward for nearly 100 miles, finishing at the village of Allagash. The **Allagash Wilderness Waterway** (© **207/941-4014**) was the first state-designated wild and scenic river in the country, protected from development since 1970. Most travelers spend between 7 and 10 days making the trip from Chamberlain Lake to Allagash. The trip begins on a chain of lakes involving light portaging. At Churchill Dam, a stretch of Class I–II white water runs for about 9 miles, then it's back to lakes and a mix of flatwater and mild rapids. Toward the end, there's a longish portage (about 450 ft.) around picturesque Allagash Falls before finishing up above the village of Allagash.

About 80 simple campsites are scattered along the route; most have outhouses, fire rings, and picnic tables. The camping fee is $5 per night, $4 for Maine residents.

HIKING With 180 miles of maintained backcountry trails and 46 peaks (including 18 that are higher than 3,000 ft.), Baxter State Park is a serious destination for serious hikers. The most imposing peak is 5,267-foot **Mount Katahdin ★★★**, the northern terminus of the **Appalachian Trail.** An ascent up this rugged, glacially scoured mountain is a trip you'll not soon forget. The raw drama and grandeur of the rocky, windswept summit is equal to anything you'll find in the White Mountains.

Allow at least 8 hours for the round-trip, and abandon your plans if the weather takes a turn for the worse while you're en route. The most popular route departs from **Roaring Brook Campground.** In fact, it's popular enough that it's often closed to day hikers— when the parking lot fills, hikers are shunted off to other trails. You ascend first to dramatic **Chimney Pond,** which is set like a jewel in a glacial cirque, then continue upward toward Katahdin's summit via one of two trails. (The **Saddle Trail** is the most forgiving, the **Cathedral Trail ★** the most dramatic.) From here, descent begins along the aptly named **Knife Edge,** a narrow, rocky spine between Baxter Peak and Pamola Peak. Do not take this trail if you are afraid of heights: In spots, the trail narrows to 2 or 3 feet with a drop of hundreds of feet on either side. Obviously, it's also not the spot to be if high winds move in or thunderstorms are threatening. From the Knife Edge, the trail follows a long and gentle ridge back down to Roaring Brook.

Katahdin draws the biggest crowds, but the park also maintains numerous other trails where you'll find more solitude and wildlife than on the main peak. One pleasant day hike is to the summit of **South Turner Mountain,** which offers wonderful views across to Mount Katahdin and blueberries for picking (in late summer). This trail also departs from Roaring Brook Campground, and requires about 3 to 4 hours for a round-trip. To the north, more good hikes begin at the **South Branch Pond Campground.** My advice? Talk to rangers and buy a trail map at park headquarters first.

WHITE-WATER RAFTING   One unique way to view Mount Katahdin is by rafting the west branch of the Penobscot River. Flowing along the park's southern border, this wild river has some of the most technically challenging white water in the East. At least a dozen rafting companies take trips on the Penobscot, with prices around $90 to $115 per person, including a lunch. Among the better-run outfitters in the area is **New England Outdoor Center** (✆ **800/766-7238;** www.neoc.com), on the river southeast of Millinocket. Its **River Driver Restaurant** ★ is among the best in Millinocket; the owners also run nearby **Twin Pine Camps,** a rustic lodge on the shores of Millinocket Lake with stellar views of Mount Katahdin (cabins for two start at around $120). For other rafting options, the trade group **Raft Maine** (✆ **800/723-8633;** www.raftmaine.com) in Bethel can connect you to one of its member outfitters.

3 ST. ANDREWS & GRAND MANAN ISLAND

Once you've reached the northernmost limits of coastal Maine, it's just a skip (well, boat ride) onward to the pleasures of maritime Canada. For a sampling of one pocket of briny goodness, head for the **Bay of Fundy.** Its top attractions close to Maine include Campobello, Deer Isle, Grand Manan, and St. Andrews.

Note that the bay is rich with plankton, and therefore rich with whales. Some 15 types of whales can be spotted in the bay, including finback, minke, humpback, the infrequent orca, and the endangered right whale. Whale-watching expeditions sail throughout the summer from Campobello Island, Deer Island, Grand Manan, St. Andrews, and St. George. Any visitor information center can point you in the right direction; the province's travel guide also lists many of the tours, which typically cost around C$40 to C$50 (US$32–US$40) for 2 to 4 hours of whale-watching.

ST. ANDREWS ★★

The lovely village of St. Andrews—or St. Andrews By-the-Sea, as the chamber of commerce persists in calling it—traces its roots back to the days of the Loyalists. After the American Revolution, New Englanders who supported the British in the struggle were made to feel unwelcome. They decamped first to lovely little Castine, Maine, which they presumed was safely on British soil. But it wasn't; the St. Croix River was later determined to be the border between Canada and the United States. Forced to uproot once again, the Loyalists dismantled their new homes, loaded the pieces aboard ships, and rebuilt them on the welcoming peninsula of St. Andrews, which is not so far away by water. Some of these remarkably resilient saltbox houses still stand in town today.

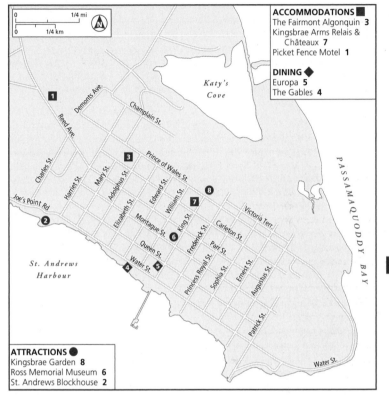

ACCOMMODATIONS ■
The Fairmont Algonquin **3**
Kingsbrae Arms Relais &
  Châteaux **7**
Picket Fence Motel **1**

DINING ◆
Europa **5**
The Gables **4**

Katy's
Cove

P A S S A M A Q U O D D Y   B A Y

Demonts Ave.
Reed Ave.
Champlain St.
Charles St.
Harriet St.
Mary St.
Adolphus St.
Elizabeth St.
Prince of Wales St.
Edward St.
Montague St.
William St.
King St.
Queen St.
Frederick St.
Carleton St.
Victoria Terr.
Water St.
Princess Royal St.
Parr St.
Sophia St.
Ernest St.
Augustus St.
Patrick St.
Water St.

Joe's Point Rd

St. Andrews
Harbour

ATTRACTIONS ●
Kingsbrae Garden **8**
Ross Memorial Museum **6**
St. Andrews Blockhouse **2**

This community later emerged as a fashionable summer resort in the late 19th century, when many of Canada's affluent and well-connected built homes and gathered annually here for social activities. Around this time, the Tudor-style Algonquin hotel (now known as the Fairmont Algonquin) was built on a low rise overlooking the town in 1889, and quickly became the town's social hub and defining landmark.

St. Andrews is beautifully sited at the tip of a long, wedge-shaped peninsula. Thanks to its location off the beaten track, the village hasn't been spoiled much by modern development, and walking the wide, shady streets—especially those around the Algonquin—invokes a more genteel era. Some 250 homes around the village are more than a century old. A number of appealing boutiques and shops are spread along Water Street, which stretches for some distance along the town's shoreline, and it's easy to grab a boat tour from the waterfront as well. I definitely recommend this town if you're seeking a tame, easy tourism dip into New Brunswick. Also don't miss the weekly farmer's market, held Thursday mornings in summer on the waterfront.

GETTING THERE   St. Andrews is located at the apex of Route 127, which dips southward from Route 1 between St. Stephen and St. George. It's an easy drive north from St. Stephen or south from Saint John (more scenic coming from Saint John), and the turn-off is well marked from either direction. In case you don't have wheels, **Acadien Bus Lines** (𝄪 **800/567-5151** or 506/529-3101; www.smtbus.com) runs one daily bus trip between St. Andrews and Saint John; the fare at press time was C$24 (US$22/£11) adult one-way, C$41 (US$37/£19) round-trip. Even better, the bus line offers discounts of 15% to 40% for children, students, and seniors.

VISITOR INFORMATION   St. Andrews' seasonal **Welcome Centre** (𝄪 **506/529-3556**) is located at 46 Reed Ave., on your left as you enter the village. It's in a handsome 1914 home overarched by broad-crowned trees. It's open daily from 8am to 8pm in July and August, from 9am to 5pm in May, June, and from September until it closes in early October. The rest of the year, contact the **Chamber of Commerce** in the same building (𝄪 **800/563-7397** or 506/529-3555) by writing P.O. Box 89, St. Andrews, NB E0G 2X0.

Exploring St. Andrews

The chamber of commerce produces two brochures, the *Town Map and Directory* and the *St. Andrews by-the-Sea Historic Guide,* both of which are free and can be found at the two visitor information centers. Also look for *A Guide to Historic St. Andrews,* produced by the St. Andrews Civic Trust. With these in hand you'll be able to launch an informed exploration. To make it even easier, many of the private dwellings in St. Andrews feature plaques with information on their origins. Look in particular for the saltbox-style homes, some of which are thought to be the original Loyalist structures that traveled here by barge.

The village's compact and handsome downtown flanks Water Street, a lengthy commercial street that parallels the bay. You'll find low, understated commercial architecture, much of it from the turn of the 20th century, that encompasses a gamut of styles. Allow an hour or so for browsing at boutiques and art galleries. There's also a mix of restaurants and inns.

Two blocks inland on King Street, you'll get a dose of local history at the **Ross Memorial Museum,** 188 Montague St. (𝄪 **506/529-5124**). The historic home was built in 1824; in 1945 the home was left to the town by Rev. Henry Phipps Ross and Sarah Juliette Ross, complete with their eclectic and intriguing collection of period furniture, carpets, and paintings. The museum is open June to early October, Monday through Saturday from 10am to 4:30pm. Admission is by donation.

Walk up the hill to the head of King Street, and you'll eventually come to the **Kingsbrae Garden** (see below).

On the west end of Water Street, you'll come to Joe's Point Road at the foot of Harriet Street. The stout wooden **blockhouse** that sits just off the water behind low grass-covered earthworks was built by townspeople during the War of 1812, when the British colonials anticipated a U.S. attack that never came. This structure is all that remains of the scattered fortifications created around town during that war.

Across the street from the blockhouse is the peaceful Centennial Gardens, established in 1967 to mark the centenary of Canadian confederation. The compact, tidy park has views of the bay and makes a pleasant spot for a picnic.

At the other end of Water Street, headed east from downtown, is the open space of Indian Point and the Passamaquoddy Ocean Park Campground. The views of the bay are panoramic; somehow it's even dramatic on foggy days, and swimming in these icy waters will earn you definite bragging rights.

Look for history right at your feet when exploring the park's rocky beaches: You'll sometimes turn up worn and rounded flint and coral that has washed ashore. It's not native, but rather imported—early traders sailing here from afar loaded up their holds with flint from Dover, England, and coral from the Caribbean to serve as ballast on their crossings. When they arrived, the ballast was just dumped offshore, and today it still churns up from the depths.

For a more protected swimming spot, wander down **Acadia Drive,** which runs downhill behind the Algonquin. You'll come to popular Katy's Cove, where floating docks form a sort of natural saltwater swimming pool along a lovely inlet. You'll find a snack bar, a playground, and an affable sense of gracious ease here, and it's a fine place for families to while away an afternoon. There's a small fee.

Boat Tours

St. Andrews is an excellent spot to launch an exploration of the bay, which is very much alive, biologically speaking. On the water you'll look for whales, porpoises, seals, and bald eagles, no matter which trip you select. Two to 3-hour tours generally run C$45 to C$50 (US$41–US$45/£23–£25) per adult, less for children.

Quoddy Link Marine (© 877/688-2600 or 506/529-2600) offers seasonal (late June to early Oct) whale-watching tours on a 17m (55-ft.) power catamaran, and the tour includes seafood snacks and use of binoculars; the tours take 2$\frac{1}{2}$ to 3 hours. Two-hour tours in search of wildlife aboard 7.2m (24-ft.) rigid-hull Zodiacs are offered by **Fundy Tide Runners** (© 506/529-4481); passengers wear flotation suits as they zip around the bay. This outfitter is open for a longer season than many others, from mid-May to mid-October.

For a more traditional experience, sign up for a trip aboard the 72-foot square-rigged cutter the *Jolly Breeze of St. Andrews* ★ with **Tall Ship Whale Watching** (© 506/529-8116). The outfit offers 3-hour tours under sail three times daily from mid-June through mid-October; tickets cost C$45 (US$41/£23) per adult, C$34 (US$31/£17) children 12 and under. A discount for families of four or more is available. Watch for seals, dolphins, and eagles—all have been sighted from the ship's deck.

Seascape Kayak Tours (© 866/747-1884 or 506/747-1884), in nearby Deer Island (see "Getting There," in the "Campobello Island" section in chapter 10), offers an upclose and personal view of the bay on half-day tours, with snacks provided during the 2$\frac{1}{2}$-hour run. No kayaking experience is needed. The trip costs C$59 (US$53/£30) adults, C$45 (US$41/£23) children. The outfit also offers a number of 3-day, 2-night trips for the serious kayaker throughout the summer; contact Seascape for more details.

Golf

In St. Andrews, the **Fairmont Algonquin** hotel's newly expanded and redesigned golf course is a beauty—easily among Eastern Canada's top 10, right behind the bigger-name stars on Cape Breton Island and Prince Edward Island. It features 9 newer inland holes (the front 9) and 9 older seaside holes that become increasingly spectacular as you approach the point of land separating New Brunswick from Maine. (All 18 of them are challenging, so bring your "A" game.) Service and upkeep are impeccable here, and there are both a snack bar on premises and a roving club car with sandwiches and drinks. Greens fees are C$79 to C$99 (US$80–US$89/£40–£50) for 18 holes (carts extra;

discount at twilight time). Lessons are offered, and there's a short-game practice area in addition to a driving range; call ☏ **888/460-8999** or 506/529-8165 for tee times.

What to See & Do

Atlantic Salmon Interpretive Centre   The splashy visitor center of the Atlantic Salmon Federation, sometimes called Salar's World after the main exhibit, is dedicated to educating the public about the increasingly rare and surprisingly intriguing Atlantic salmon. Located in a bright and airy post-and-beam facility, the center allows visitors to get oriented through exhibits, presentations, and viewing salmon through underwater windows or strolling the outdoor walkways along Chamcook Stream. Plan to spend about a half-hour here.

24 Chamcook Rd. (6.5km/4 miles from St. Andrews via Rte. 127). ☏ **506/529-1384.** Admission C$5 (US$4.50/£2.50) adults, C$3.50 (US$3.15/£1.75) seniors and college students, C$3 (US$2.70/£1.50) children, C$13 (US$12/£6.50) families. Daily 9am–5pm. Closed Oct to mid-May.

Kingsbrae Garden (Kids)   This 11-hectare (27-acre) public garden opened in 1998, using the former grounds of a long-gone estate. The designers incorporated the existing high hedges and trees, and have ambitiously planted open space around the mature plants. The entire project is very promising, and as the plantings take root and mature, it's certain to become a noted stop for garden lovers. The grounds include almost 2,000 varieties of trees (including old-growth forest), shrubs, and plants. Among the notable features: a day lily collection, an extensive rose garden, a small maze, a fully functional Dutch windmill that circulates water through the two duck ponds, and a children's garden with an elaborate Victorian-mansion playhouse.

With views over the lush lawns to the bay below, the on-site Garden Cafe is a pleasant place to stop for lunch. (Try the thick, creamy seafood chowder and one of the focaccia bread sandwiches.) There's also a gift shop and art gallery. Those with a horticultural bend should plan to spend at least a few hours here.

220 King St. ☏ **866/566-8687** or 506/529-3335. Admission C$9 (US$8/£4.50) adults, C$7.60 (US$6.85/£3.80) students and seniors, C$24 (US$21/£12) family, free for children 5 and under. Daily 9am–6pm. Closed early Oct to mid-May.

Ministers Island Historic Site/Covenhoven ★★   This rugged, 200-plus-hectare (500-acre) island is linked to the mainland by a sandbar at low tide, and the 2-hour tours are scheduled around the tides. (Call for upcoming times.) You'll meet your tour guide on the mainland side, then drive your car out convoy-style across the ocean floor to the magical island estate created in 1890 by Sir William Van Horne.

Van Horne was president of the Canadian Pacific Railway, and the person behind the extension of the rail line to St. Andrews. He then built a sandstone mansion (Covenhoven) with some 50 rooms (including 17 bedrooms), a circular bathhouse (where he indulged his passion for landscape painting), and one of Canada's largest and most impressive barns. The estate also features heated greenhouses, which produced grapes and mushrooms, along with peaches that weighed up to 2 pounds each. When Van Horne was home in Montreal, he had fresh dairy products and vegetables shipped daily (by rail, of course) so that he could enjoy fresh produce year-round. You'll learn all this, and more, on the tours.

Rte. 127 (northeast of St. Andrews), Chamcook. ☏ **506/529-5081.** Admission C$8 (US$7.20/£4) adults, C$7 (US$6.30/£3.50) seniors and students, C$25 (US$23/£13) family, free for children 6 and under. Closed mid-Oct to mid-May.

Those traveling on a budget instead of seeking the luxury digs below might head for the **Picket Fence Motel,** 102 Reed Ave. (© **506/529-8985**). This trim and tidy property is near the handsome, newly expanded Algonquin golf course (see "Golf," above) and within walking distance of St. Andrews' village center. Rooms cost C$69 to C$85 (US$62–US$77/£35–£43) double.

Or, for something slightly more upscale yet unlikely to break your bank, contact the **Europa ★★** restaurant (see "Where to Dine," below); the owners rent out a series of rooms, suites, and an apartment collectively rated at 3¹/₂ stars by Canada's government hotel-rating agency for C$69 to C$149 double (US$62–US$134/£35–£75). The suites and apartment have kitchenettes.

The Fairmont Algonquin ★★   The Algonquin dates from 1889. The original structure was destroyed by fire in 1914, but the surviving annexes were rebuilt in Tudor style; in 1993 an addition was built across the road, linked by a gatehouse-inspired bridge. The red-tile–roofed resort commands one's attention through its sheer size and aristocratic bearing (not to mention the kilt-wearing, bagpipe-playing staff). The inn is several long blocks, affording panoramic bay views from a second-floor roof garden and many rooms. The rooms have been refreshed, and are comfortable and tasteful. In addition to the outstanding seaside golf course (see "Golf," above), there's a full spa. Note that the hotel markets itself to bus tours and conferences, and if your timing is bad you might feel a bit overwhelmed by one or more of them.

184 Adolphus St., St. Andrews, NB E5B 1T7. © **800/441-1414** or 506/529-8823. Fax 506/529-7162. www. fairmont.com. 234 units. C$99–C$459 (US$89–US$413/£50–£230) double; C$299–C$1,169 (US$-69–US$1,052/£150–£585) suite. Rates include continental breakfast. AE, DC, MC, V. Valet parking. Small cats and dogs C$25 (US$24/£13) per night. **Amenities:** 2 restaurants; 2 bars; outdoor heated pool; golf course; 2 tennis courts; health club; spa; Jacuzzi; sauna; bike rentals; children's programs; game room; concierge; salon; massage; babysitting; laundry service; dry cleaning. *In room:* TV, dataport, minibar, coffeemaker, hair dryer, iron.

Kingsbrae Arms Relais & Châteaux ★★★   Kingsbrae Arms, part of the Relais & Châteaux network, is a five-star inn informed by an upscale European feel. The inn occupies an 1897 manor house built by prosperous jade merchants in 1897, and features a heated pool amid rose gardens at the foot of a lawn, and immediately next door are the 11-hectare (27-acre) Kingsbrae Horticultural Gardens; some rooms have wonderful views of the gardens, while others offer a view sweep of the bay. Guests will feel pampered, with amenities including high-thread-count sheets, plush robes, and a guest-services suite stocked with snacks and refreshments. Some rooms have Jacuzzis; all have gas fireplaces. Guests can also enjoy a five-course meal in the dining room during peak season. (This dining room is not open to the public.) Entrees on a given visit might include Fundy salmon, PEI mussels, roasted guinea hen, goat cheese in a hazelnut glacé New Zealand rack of lamb, or Alberta steaks.

219 King St., St. Andrews, NB E5B 1Y1. © **506/529-1897.** Fax 506/529-1197. www.kingsbrae.com. 8 units. C$650–C$1,094 (US$585–US$985/£325–£547) double. 2-night minimum; 3-night minimum July–Aug weekends. 5% room service charge additional. AE, MC, V. Closed Nov–Apr. Pets allowed with advance permission. **Amenities:** Babysitting; laundry service; dry cleaning. *In room:* A/C, TV, coffeemaker, hair dryer, iron/ironing board, Jacuzzi (some units).

Europa ★★ (Finds) CONTINENTAL   In an intriguing yellow building that once housed a movie theater and dance hall, Bavarian husband-and-wife transplants Markus and Simone Ritter whip up great French-, Swiss- and German-accented Continental cuisine for a 35-seat room. Starters include smoked salmon with rösti and capers; a house specialty of seared scallops in Mornay sauce, baked with cheese; French onion soup; and escargots. Main courses run to several versions of schnitzel (grilled pork or veal steak), each with distinct fillings, toppings, and sauces; beef stroganoff; duck a l'Orange; rack of lamb; haddock in lemon butter or champagne sauce; steak in béarnaise sauce; and tiger shrimp in mango-curry sauce. All are prepared with skill and restraint. Finish with chocolate mousse, homemade almond parfait, or one of about a dozen homemade ice creams or sorbets. The wine list is also surprisingly strong given that this is such a small, out-of-the-way town. All in all, consider this restaurant a gem—a should-get-there spot if you're at all in the area.

48 King St. (C) **506/529-3818.** Reservations recommended. Main courses C$18–C$27 (US$16–US$24/£9–£14). MC, V. Mid-May to Sept daily 5–9pm; Oct Tues–Sat 5–9pm; Nov to mid-Feb Thurs–Sat 5–9pm. Closed mid-Feb to mid-May.

The Gables SEAFOOD/PUB FARE   This informal eatery is located in a trim home with prominent gables fronting Water Street, though you enter down a narrow alley where sky and water views suddenly break through a soaring window from a spacious outside deck. Inside, expect a bright and lively local spot with a casual maritime decor and fare; outside there's a plastic-porch–furniture informality. Breakfast is served during peak season only, with homemade baked goods and rosemary potatoes. Lunch and dinner options include burgers, steaks, and seafood items such as breaded haddock, daily catches, and a lobster clubhouse—a chopped lobster salad with cheese, cucumber, lettuce, and tomato. There's a kids' menu, as well, while margaritas and sangria are available by the pitcher for the adults in the party. The view tends to pull rank on the menu, but if you like simple fare, both will satisfy.

143 Water St. (C) **506/529-3440.** Main courses C$3.95–C$6.95 (US$3.55–US$6.25/£2.80–£3.50) breakfast, C$7.50–C$25 (US$6.75–US$23/£3.75–£13) lunch and dinner. MC, V. July–Aug daily 8am–11pm; Sept–June daily 11am–9pm.

GRAND MANAN ISLAND ★

Geologically rugged, profoundly peaceable, and indisputably remote, this handsome island of 2,800 year-round residents is a 90-minute ferry ride from the port of Blacks Harbour, which is just southeast of St. George. Despite being located incredibly close to Maine (and the U.S.), Grand Manan is a much-prized destination for adventurous travelers—sometimes a highlight of their vacation. Yet the island also remains a mystifying puzzle for others who fail to be smitten by its rough-edged charm. Either this is your kind of place, or it isn't; perhaps there's no in between. The only way to find out is to visit.

Grand Manan is a special favorite both among serious **birders** and serious enthusiasts of Pulitzer Prize–winning novelist Willa Cather, who found her way from Nebraska and New York to a summer cottage here. Hiking the island's famous trails, don't be surprised to come across knots of very quiet people peering intently through binoculars. These are the birders, not the Cather fans. Nearly 300 different species of birds either nest here or stop by the island during their long migrations, and it's a good place to add mightily to your "life list," if you're into such a pursuit; with birds ranging from bald eagles to puffins (though you'll need to sign up for a boat tour to catch a glimpse at the latter) here, you're sure to see something with wings you've never seen before except in books.

Cather kept a cottage here and wrote some of her books while staying on the island. Her die-hard fans are as easy to spot as the birders, say locals, and something of a wild breed; during one Cather conference some years ago, several dozen got up, wrapped themselves in sheets, and danced around a bonfire during the summer solstice.

Essentials

GETTING THERE   Grand Manan is connected to Blacks Harbour on the mainland via frequent ferry service in summer. **Coastal Transport ferries** (© **506/642-0520;** www. coastaltransport.ca), each capable of hauling 60 cars, depart from the mainland and the island every 2 hours between 7:30am and 5:30pm during July and August; a ferry makes three to four daily trips the rest of the year. The round-trip fare is C$11 (US$9.45/£5.20) per passenger (C$5.30/US$4.80/£2.40 ages 5–12). Boarding the ferry on the mainland is free; you purchase tickets when you leave the island.

Reserve your return trip at least a day ahead to avoid getting stranded on the island, and get in line early to secure a spot. A good strategy for departing from Blacks Harbour is to bring a picnic lunch, arrive an hour or two early, put your car in line, and head to the grassy waterfront park adjacent to the wharf. It's an attractive spot; there's even an island to explore at low tide.

VISITOR INFORMATION   The island's **Visitor Information Centre,** Route 776, Grand Manan, NB E5G 4E9 (© **888/525-1655** or 506/662-3442), is open Monday to Friday in summer (8am–5pm except Sun, when it's open 9am–1pm) in the town of Grand Harbour. It's closed mid-September to early June; if so, ask at island stores or inns for a free island map published by the **Grand Manan Tourism Association** (www.grand manannb.com), which has a listing of key island phone numbers.

Exploring the Island

Start your explorations before you arrive. As you come abreast of the island aboard the ferry, head to the starboard side. You'll soon see **Seven Day's Work** in the rocky cliffs of Whale's Cove, where seven layers of hardened lava and sill (intrusive igneous rock) have come together in a sort of geological Dagwood sandwich.

You can begin to open the puzzle box that is local geology at the **Grand Manan Museum** (© **506/662-3424**) in Grand Harbour, one of three villages on the island's eastern shore. The museum's geology exhibit, located in the basement, offers pointers about what to look for as you roam the island. Birders will enjoy the Allan Moses collection upstairs, which features 230 stuffed and mounted birds in glass cases. The museum also has an impressive lighthouse lens from the Gannet Rock Lighthouse, and a collection of stuff that's washed ashore from the frequent shipwrecks. The museum is open from June to September Monday through Friday 10am to 4pm; it's also open Sundays 1 to 5pm in July and August. Admission is C$4 (US$3.60/£2) adults, C$2 (US$1.80/£1) seniors and students, and free for children 11 and under.

This relatively flat and compact island is perfect for exploring by bike; the only stretches to avoid are some of the faster, less scenic segments of Route 776. All the side roads offer **superb biking.** Especially nice is the **cross-island road ★★** (paved) to **Dark Harbour,** where you'll find a few cabins, dories, and salmon pens. The route is wild and hilly at times but offers a memorable descent to the ocean on the island's west side.

Bike rentals are available at **Adventure High** ★ (© **800/732-5492** or 506/662-3563) in North Head, not far from the ferry. (Day-trippers who are fit enough should consider leaving their cars at **Blacks Harbour** and exploring the island by bike alone, then returning on the last ferry.) Kevin Sampson's **Adventure High** also offers sea kayak tours of the island's shores for those who prefer a **cormorant's-eye view** ★ of the impressive cliffs. Bikes rent for C$22 (US$20/£11) per day, C$16 (US$14/£8) for a half-day. Kayak tours run from C$39 (US$35/£20) for a 2-hour sunset tour to C$99 (US$89/£50) for a full-day's excursion. He even rents out cabins.

While Grand Manan is very quiet, you can find more solitude and cross one more island off your life list on **White Head Island.** To get there, drive to Ingalls Head (follow Ingalls Head Rd. from Grand Harbour) and catch the half-hour ferry to this rocky island, home to about 200 locals. On the island, you can walk alongshore to the lighthouse guarding the way between Battle Beach and Sandy Cove. The ferry holds 10 cars, is free of charge, and sails up to 10 times daily in summer.

Hiking

Numerous hiking trails lace the island, and they offer a popular diversion throughout the summer. Trails can be found just about everywhere, but most are a matter of local knowledge. Don't hesitate to ask at your inn or the tourist information center, or to ask anyone you might meet on the street. *A Hiking Guide to New Brunswick* (Goose Lane Editions; © **506/450-4251**) lists 12 hikes with maps; this handy book is often sold on the ferry.

The most accessible clusters of trails are at the island's northern and southern tips. Head north up Whistle Road to Whistle Beach, and you'll find both the **Northwestern Coastal Trail** ★ and the **Seven Day's Work Trail** ★, both of which track along the rocky shoreline. Near the low lighthouse and towering radio antennae at Southwest Head (follow Rte. 776 to the end), trails radiate out along cliffs topped with scrappy forest; the views are remarkable when the fog's not in.

Whale-Watching & Boat Tours

A fine way to experience island ecology is to mosey offshore. Several outfitters offer complete nature tours, providing a nice sampling of the world above and beneath the sea. On an excursion you might see minke, finback, or humpback whales, along with exotic birds including puffins and phalaropes. **Sea Watch Tours** (© **506/662-8552**), run by Peter and Kenda Wilcox, operates a series of 5-hour excursions from mid-June to early August, with whale sightings guaranteed or your money back, aboard a 13m (42-ft.) vessel with canopy. The rate is C$59 (US$53/£30) for adults and C$39 (US$35/£20) per child.

Where to Stay

Anchorage Provincial Park ★ (© **506/662-7022**) has about 100 campsites scattered about forest and field, available late May to mid-September. There's a small beach and a hiking trail on the property, and it's well situated for exploring the southern part of the island. It's very popular midsummer; call before you board the ferry to ask about campsite availability. Sites are C$22 to C$35 (US$19–US$32/£11–£18), some with hookups for RVs and some better suited for a simple tent.

Inn at Whale Cove Cottages ★★ The Inn at Whale Cove is a delightful, family-run compound set in a grassy meadow overlooking a quiet and picturesque cove. The original building is a cozy 1816 farmhouse. It's been restored rustically with a nice selection of country antiques. The three guest rooms in here are comfortable (Sally's Attic has a small deck and a big view). Five cottages are scattered about the property, varying in size from one to four bedrooms. One of the older units was author Willa Cather's famous cottage, while the newer John's Flat and Cove View cottages are the most modern, with extra bedrooms, dining rooms, decks, televisions, and so forth. The grounds, especially the path down to the quiet beach, are wonderful. Innkeeper Laura Buckley received her culinary training in Toronto, and the **dining room** ★ demonstrates a deft touch with local ingredients. From June through mid-October, dinner is served nightly.

Whistle Rd. (P.O. Box 233), North Head, Grand Manan, NB E0G 2M0. ℂ **506/662-3181.** 3 rooms, 5 cottages (some only rented by week). C$105–C$150 (US$95–US$135/£53–£75) double or C$800–C$900 (US$720–US$810/£400–£450) weekly cottage. Rates include full breakfast. MC, V. All but 1 unit closed Nov–Apr. Pets accepted for C$5 (US$4.50/£2) per day. **Amenities:** Dining room. *In room:* TV (2 units), kitchenette (3 units), Jacuzzi (1 unit).

Shorecrest Lodge ★ ⓥalue ⓚids This century-old inn is a place to put your feet up and unwind. Located just a few hundred yards from the ferry, the inn is nicely decorated with a mix of modern furniture and eclectic country antiques. Most of the guest rooms have private bathrooms, a rarity for Grand Manan. The best might be room no. 8 with its burgundy leather chairs and great harbor view. Kids like the TV room in back, which also stocks games and a library that's long on local natural history. The country-style dining room has a fireplace and hardwood floors, and a menu of local fresh seafood, pizza, chicken, and beef tenderloin. Don't feel like sitting indoors? The lodge also maintains an outdoor grill area for firing up your own mini–Iron Chef competition.

100 Rte. 776, North Head, Grand Manan, NB E5G 1A1. ℂ **506/662-3216.** www.shorecrestlodge.com. 10 units (8 with private bathroom). C$65–C$119 (US$59–US$107/£33–£60) double. Rates include continental breakfast. MC, V. Closed Nov–May. **Amenities:** Restaurant; fitness room. *In room:* No phone.

Where to Dine

Options for dining out aren't exactly extravagant on Grand Manan. The inns listed above offer good meals, and you'll encounter a few more family restaurants and grocers along the road, as well. If you're here on Saturday morning, check out the weekly **farmer's market** in North Head.

In the mood for a dare? Try walking into **North Head Bakery** ★★, 199 Rte. 776 (ℂ **506/662-8862**), and walking out without buying anything. It cannot be done. This superb bakery (open Tues–Sat 6am–6pm) uses traditional baking methods and whole grains. Breads made daily include a crusty, seven-grain Saint John Valley bread and a delightful egg-and-butter bread. Nor should the chocolate-chip cookies be overlooked. The bakery is on Route 776 on the left when you're heading south from the ferry.

Fast Facts, Toll-Free Numbers & Websites

1 FAST FACTS: COASTAL MAINE

AMERICAN EXPRESS   American Express offers travel services, including check cashing and trip planning, through a number of affiliated agencies in the region. Call © **800/ 221-7282** for the nearest location.

AREA CODES   Maine's area code is **207.**

ATM NETWORKS & CASHPOINTS   See "Money & Costs," p. 40.

AUTOMOBILE ORGANIZATIONS   Motor clubs will supply maps, suggested routes, guidebooks, accident and bail-bond insurance, and emergency road service. The **American Automobile Association (AAA)** is the major auto club in the United States. If you belong to a motor club in your home country, inquire about AAA reciprocity before you leave. You may be able to join AAA even if you're not a member of a reciprocal club; to inquire, call AAA (© **800/222-4357;** www.aaa.com). AAA is actually an organization of regional motor clubs, so look under "AAA Automobile Club" in the White Pages of the telephone directory. AAA has a nationwide emergency road service telephone number (© 800/AAA-HELP [222-4357]).

BUSINESS HOURS   Banks are generally open Monday to Friday, 9am to 3pm. Drive-in teller hours are longer. Shops are usually open weekdays from 9am to 6pm, Saturdays from 10am to 6pm or 7pm, and Sundays from noon until 5pm or 6pm. In bigger cities or in shopping-mall or outlet-shop areas, these hours will be somewhat extended, as late as 9pm during peak summer shopping season.

CAR RENTALS   See "Toll-Free Numbers & Websites," p. 289.

DRINKING LAWS   The legal age for purchase and consumption of alcoholic beverages is 21; proof of age is required and often requested at bars, nightclubs, and restaurants, so it's always a good idea to bring ID when you go out.

Liquor of some sort is sold at special, state-operated stores; some supermarkets; and most convenience stores. Restaurants without liquor licenses sometimes allow patrons to bring in their own. Ask first. Bars sell liquor until 1am in Maine (and New Hampshire).

Do not carry open containers of alcohol in your car or any public area that isn't zoned for alcohol consumption. The police can fine you on the spot. And nothing will ruin your trip faster than getting a citation for DUI ("driving under the influence"), so don't even think about driving while intoxicated.

DRIVING RULES   See "Getting There & Getting Around," p. 33.

ELECTRICITY   Like Canada, the United States uses 110–120 volts AC (60 cycles), compared to 220–240 volts AC (50 cycles) in most of Europe, Australia, and New Zealand.

Downward converters that change 220–240 volts to 110–120 volts are difficult to find in the United States, so bring one with you.

If you're coming from Europe, bring a **connection kit** of the right power and phone adapters, a spare phone cord, and a spare Ethernet network cable—or find out whether your hotel supplies them to guests.

EMBASSIES & CONSULATES All embassies are located in the nation's capital, Washington, D.C. Some consulates are located in major U.S. cities, and most nations have a mission to the United Nations in New York City. If your country isn't listed below, call for directory information in Washington, D.C. (© **202/555-1212**), or check **www. embassy.org/embassies**.

The embassy of **Australia** is at 1601 Massachusetts Ave. NW, Washington, DC 20036 (© **202/797-3000;** www.austemb.org). There are consulates in New York, Honolulu, Houston, Los Angeles, and San Francisco.

The embassy of **Canada** is at 501 Pennsylvania Ave. NW, Washington, DC 20001 (© **202/682-1740;** www.canadianembassy.org). Other Canadian consulates are in Buffalo (New York), Detroit, Los Angeles, New York, and Seattle.

The embassy of **Ireland** is at 2234 Massachusetts Ave. NW, Washington, DC 20008 (© **202/462-3939;** www.irelandemb.org). Irish consulates are in Boston, Chicago, New York, San Francisco, and other cities. See website for complete listing.

The embassy of **New Zealand** is at 37 Observatory Circle NW, Washington, DC 20008 (© **202/328-4800;** www.nzemb.org). New Zealand consulates are in Los Angeles, Salt Lake City, San Francisco, and Seattle.

The embassy of the **United Kingdom** is at 3100 Massachusetts Ave. NW, Washington, DC 20008 (© **202/588-7800;** www.britainusa.com). Other British consulates are in Atlanta, Boston, Chicago, Cleveland, Houston, Los Angeles, New York, San Francisco, and Seattle.

EMERGENCIES For fire, police, and ambulance, find any phone and dial © **911.** If this fails, dial 0 (zero) and report an emergency.

GASOLINE (PETROL) At press time, in the U.S., the cost of gasoline (also known as gas, but never petrol) was fluctuating along with the global economy. Gas prices in Maine are about average for the U.S., in spots a bit higher. Taxes are included in the price listed on gas station signs. One U.S. gallon equals 3.8 liters or .85 imperial gallons. Fill-up locations are known as gas or service stations.

HOLIDAYS Banks, government offices, post offices, and many stores, restaurants, and museums are closed on the following legal national holidays: January 1 (New Year's Day), the third Monday in January (Martin Luther King, Jr., Day), the third Monday in February (Presidents' Day), the last Monday in May (Memorial Day), July 4 (Independence Day), the first Monday in September (Labor Day), the second Monday in October (Columbus Day), November 11 (Veterans Day/Armistice Day), the fourth Thursday in November (Thanksgiving Day), and December 25 (Christmas). The Tuesday after the first Monday in November is Election Day, a federal government holiday in presidential-election years (held every 4 years, and next in 2012).

Maine also celebrates **Patriot's Day** on a Monday in mid-April. All state offices are closed on this day. Most state offices also close on the day after Thanksgiving, which changes annually.

For more information on holidays see "The Maine Coast Calendar of Events" in chapter 3.

INSURANCE   Medical Insurance: Although it's not required of travelers, health insurance is highly recommended. Most health insurance policies cover you if you get sick away from home—but check your coverage before you leave.

International visitors to the U.S. should note that unlike many European countries, the United States does not usually offer free or low-cost medical care to its citizens or visitors. Doctors and hospitals are expensive, and in most cases will require advance payment or proof of coverage before they render their services. Good policies will cover the costs of an accident, repatriation, or death. Packages such as **Europ Assistance's "Worldwide Healthcare Plan"** are sold by European automobile clubs and travel agencies at attractive rates. **Worldwide Assistance Services, Inc.** (© **800/777-8710;** www.worldwideassistance.com) is the agent for Europ Assistance in the United States. Though lack of health insurance may prevent you from being admitted to a hospital in nonemergencies, don't worry about being left on a street corner to die: The American way is to fix you now and bill the daylights out of you later.

If you're ever hospitalized more than 150 miles from home, **MedjetAssist** (© **800/527-7478;** www.medjetassistance.com) will pick you up and fly you to the hospital of your choice in a medically equipped and staffed aircraft 24 hours day, 7 days a week. Annual memberships are $225 individual, $350 family; you can also purchase short-term memberships.

Canadians should check with their provincial health plan offices or call **Health Canada** (© **866/225-0709;** www.hc-sc.gc.ca) to find out the extent of their coverage and what documentation and receipts they must take home in case they are treated in the United States.

Travelers from the U.K. should carry their European Health Insurance Card (EHIC), which replaced the E111 form as proof of entitlement to free/reduced cost medical treatment abroad (© **0845/606-2030;** www.ehic.org.uk). Note, however, that the EHIC only covers "necessary medical treatment," and for repatriation costs, lost money, baggage, or cancellation, travel insurance from a reputable company should always be sought (www.travelinsuranceweb.com).

As a safety net, you may want to buy travel medical insurance, particularly if you're traveling to a remote or high-risk area where emergency evacuation might be necessary. If you require additional medical insurance, try **MEDEX Assistance** (© **410/453-6300;** www.medexassist.com) or **Travel Assistance International** (© **800/821-2828;** www.travelassistance.com; for general information on services, call the company's **Worldwide Assistance Services, Inc.,** at © **800/777-8710**).

Travel Insurance: The cost of travel insurance varies widely, depending on the destination, the cost and length of your trip, your age and health, and the type of trip you're taking, but expect to pay between 5% and 8% of the vacation itself. You can get estimates from various providers through **InsureMyTrip.com.** Enter your trip cost and dates, your age, and other information for prices from more than a dozen companies.

U.K. citizens and their families who make more than one trip abroad per year may find an annual travel insurance policy works out cheaper. Check **www.moneysupermarket.com**, which compares prices across a wide range of providers for single- and multitrip policies.

Most big travel agents offer their own insurance and will probably try to sell you their package when you book a holiday. Think before you sign. **Britain's Consumers' Association** recommends that you insist on seeing the policy and reading the fine print before buying travel insurance. The **Association of British Insurers** (✆ 020/7600-3333; www.abi.org.uk) gives advice by phone and publishes *Holiday Insurance*, a free guide to policy provisions and prices. You might also shop around for better deals: Try **Columbus Direct** (✆ 0870/033-9988; www.columbusdirect.net).

Trip-Cancellation Insurance: Trip-cancellation insurance will help retrieve your money if you have to back out of a trip or depart early, or if your travel supplier goes bankrupt. Trip cancellation traditionally covers such events as sickness, natural disasters, and State Department advisories. The latest news in trip-cancellation insurance is the availability of **expanded hurricane coverage** and the **"any-reason"** cancellation coverage—which costs more but covers cancellations made for any reason. You won't get back 100% of your prepaid trip cost, but you'll be refunded a substantial portion. **TravelSafe** (✆ 888/885-7233; www.travelsafe.com) offers both types of coverage. Expedia also offers any-reason cancellation coverage for its air-hotel packages. For details, contact one of the following recommended insurers: **Access America** (✆ 866/807-3982; www.accessamerica.com); **Travel Guard International** (✆ 800/826-4919; www.travelguard.com); **Travel Insured International** (✆ 800/243-3174; www.travelinsured.com); and **Travelex Insurance Services** (✆ 888/457-4602; www.travelex-insurance.com).

INTERNET ACCESS   Many public libraries in Maine have free terminals with Internet access, enabling travelers to check their e-mail through a Web-based e-mail service such as Yahoo! or Hotmail. Internet cafes have come and gone in the last few years; it's best to ask around locally, or try visiting **www.netcafeguide.com** or **www.cybercafe.com**.

LEGAL AID   If you are "pulled over" for a minor infraction (such as speeding), never attempt to pay the fine directly to a police officer; this could be construed as attempted bribery, a much more serious crime. Pay fines by mail, or directly into the hands of the clerk of the court. If accused of a more serious offense, say and do nothing before consulting a lawyer. Here the burden is on the state to prove a person's guilt beyond a reasonable doubt, and anyone has the right to remain silent, whether he or she is suspected of a crime or actually arrested. Once arrested, a person can make one telephone call to a party of his or her choice. International visitors should call your embassy or consulate.

LOST & FOUND   Be sure to tell all of your credit card companies the minute you discover your wallet has been lost or stolen, and file a report at the nearest police precinct. Your credit card company or insurer may require a police report number or record of the loss. Most credit card companies have an emergency toll-free number to call if your card is lost or stolen; they may be able to wire you a cash advance immediately or deliver an emergency credit card in a day or two.

Visa's U.S. emergency number is ✆ **800/847-2911** or 410/581-9994. American Express cardholders and traveler's check holders should call ✆ **800/221-7282.** MasterCard holders should call ✆ **800/307-7309** or 636/722-7111. For other credit cards, call the toll-free number directory at ✆ **800/555-1212.**

If you need emergency cash over the weekend when all banks and American Express offices are closed, you can have money wired to you via **Western Union** (✆ **800/325-6000;** www.westernunion.com).

MAIL   At press time, domestic postage rates were 27¢ for a postcard and 42¢ for a letter. For international mail, a first-class letter of up to 1 ounce costs 94¢ (72¢ to Canada and Mexico); a first-class postcard costs the same as a letter. For more information, go to **www.usps.com** and click on "Calculate Postage."

If you aren't sure what your address will be in the United States, mail can be sent to you, in your name, c/o General Delivery at the main post office of the city or region where you expect to be. (Call ✆ **800/275-8777** for information on the nearest post office.) The addressee must pick up mail in person and must produce proof of identity (driver's license, passport, and so on). Most post offices will hold your mail for up to 1 month, and are open Monday to Friday from 8am to 6pm, and Saturday from 9am to 3pm.

Always include zip codes when mailing items in the U.S. If you don't know your zip code, visit www.usps.com/zip4.

MAPS   All of the local tourism offices in Maine, as well as state-operated tourist offices, offer free maps at well-stocked visitor information centers; ask at the counter if you don't see them. For incredibly detailed maps, consider purchasing one or more of the **DeLorme** atlases, which depict every road and stream, along with many hiking trails and access points for canoes. DeLorme's headquarters and map store (✆ **800/561-5105** or 800/642-0970) are in Yarmouth (just north of Portland), but their products are available at bookstores and convenience stores throughout the region.

MEDICAL CONDITIONS   If you have a medical condition that requires **syringe-administered medications,** carry a valid signed prescription from your physician; syringes in carry-on baggage will be inspected. Insulin in any form should have the proper pharmaceutical documentation. If you have a disease that requires treatment with **narcotics,** you should also carry documented proof with you—smuggling narcotics aboard a plane carries severe penalties in the U.S.

For **HIV-positive visitors,** requirements for entering the United States are somewhat vague and change frequently. For up-to-the-minute information, contact **AIDSinfo** (✆ **800/448-0440** or 301/519-6616 outside the U.S.; www.aidsinfo.nih.gov) or the **Gay Men's Health Crisis** (✆ **212/367-1000;** www.gmhc.org).

NEWSPAPERS & MAGAZINES   The *Boston Globe, Wall Street Journal,* and the *New York Times* are distributed throughout Maine, though they can be quite hard to find in small villages. Almost every small city and town has a daily or weekly newspaper covering local happenings. These are good sources of information for small-town events and specials at local restaurants—the day-to-day things that slip through the cracks at the tourist bureaus.

The three largest papers in the region are the *Portland Press Herald* (Portland), the *Portsmouth Herald* (Portsmouth, New Hampshire), and the *Bangor Daily News* (Bangor). Portland and Portsmouth also share a free alternative weekly paper, the *Phoenix,* that is a very handy source of information on concerts and shows at local clubs, and the *Portland Press Herald* maintains an active website (**http://pressherald.mainetoday.com**) that's good for getting a sense of the state before you arrive.

PASSPORTS   The websites listed provide downloadable passport applications as well as the current fees for processing applications. For an up-to-date, country-by-country listing of passport requirements around the world, go to the "International Travel" tab of the U.S. State Department at **http://travel.state.gov**. International visitors to the U.S. can obtain a visa application at the same website. *Note:* Children are required to present a passport when entering the United States at airports. More information on obtaining a passport for a minor can be found at http://travel.state.gov. Allow plenty of time before your trip to apply for a passport; processing normally takes 4 to 6 weeks (3 weeks for expedited service) but can take longer during busy periods (especially spring). And keep in mind that if you need a passport in a hurry, you'll pay a higher processing fee.

For Residents of Australia: You can pick up an application from your local post office or any branch of Passports Australia, but you must schedule an interview at the passport office to present your application materials. Call the **Australian Passport Information Service** at © **131-232,** or visit the government website at www.passports.gov.au.

For Residents of Canada: Passport applications are available at travel agencies throughout Canada or from the central **Passport Office,** Department of Foreign Affairs and International Trade, Ottawa, ON K1A 0G3 (© **800/567-6868;** www.ppt.gc.ca). *Note:* Canadian children who travel must have their own passport. However, if you hold a valid Canadian passport issued before December 11, 2001, that bears the name of your child, the passport remains valid for you and your child until it expires.

For Residents of Ireland: You can apply for a 10-year passport at the **Passport Office,** Setanta Centre, Molesworth Street, Dublin 2 (© **01/671-1633;** www.irlgov.ie/iveagh). Those under age 18 and over 65 must apply for a 3-year passport. You can also apply at 1A South Mall, Cork (© **21/494-4700**) or at most main post offices.

For Residents of New Zealand: You can pick up a passport application at any New Zealand Passports Office or download it from their website. Contact the **Passports Office** at © **0800/225-050** in New Zealand or 04/474-8100, or log on to www.passports.govt.nz.

For Residents of the United Kingdom: To pick up an application for a standard 10-year passport (5-year passport for children under 16), visit your nearest passport office, major post office, or travel agency. Or contact the **United Kingdom Passport Service** at © **0870/521-0410,** or search its website at www.ukpa.gov.uk.

POLICE   For police, dial © **911.** If this fails, dial 0 (zero) and report an emergency.

SMOKING   Smoking is now banned in all workplaces and public places (restaurants, bars, offices, hotel lobbies) in Maine.

TAXES   The United States has no value-added tax (VAT) or other indirect tax at the national level. Every state, county, and city may levy its own local tax on all purchases, including hotel and restaurant checks and airline tickets. These taxes will not appear on price tags.

At press time, state sales tax in Maine is 5% on goods, 7% on lodging, and 10% on auto rentals.

TELEPHONES   Many convenience groceries and packaging services sell **prepaid calling cards** in denominations up to $50; for international visitors these can be the least expensive way to call home. Many public pay phones at airports now accept American Express, MasterCard, and Visa credit cards. **Local calls** made from pay phones in most locales cost either 25¢ or 35¢ (no pennies, please). Most long-distance and international calls can be dialed directly from any phone. **For calls within the United States and to Canada,** dial 1 followed by the area code and the seven-digit number. **For other international calls,** dial 011 followed by the country code, city code, and the number you are calling.

Calls to area codes **800, 888, 877,** and **866** are toll-free. However, calls to area codes **700** and **900** (chat lines, bulletin boards, "dating" services, and so on) can be very expensive—usually a charge of 95¢ to $3 or more per minute, and they sometimes have minimum charges that can run as high as $15 or more.

For **reversed-charge or collect calls,** and for person-to-person calls, dial the number 0 then the area code and number; an operator will come on the line, and you should specify whether you are calling collect, person-to-person, or both. If your operator-assisted call is international, ask for the overseas operator.

For **local directory assistance** ("information"), dial 411; for long-distance information, dial 1, then the appropriate area code and 555-1212.

TELEGRAPH, TELEX & FAX   **Telegraph and telex services** are provided primarily by **Western Union** (✆ **800/325-6000;** www.westernunion.com). You can telegraph (wire) money, or have it telegraphed to you, very quickly over the Western Union system, but this service can cost as much as 15% to 20% of the amount sent. Most hotels have **fax machines** available for guest use (be sure to ask about the charge to use it). Many hotel rooms are wired for guests' fax machines.

TIME   The continental United States is divided into four time zones: Eastern Standard Time (EST), Central Standard Time (CST), Mountain Standard Time (MST), and Pacific Standard Time (PST); in addition, Alaska and Hawaii each have their own time zones.

All of the Maine coast is in the **Eastern Standard Time zone.** When it's noon in Bar Harbor and Portland, it's 11am in Chicago (CST), 10am in Denver (MST), 9am in Los Angeles (PST), and 5pm in London (GMT).

Daylight saving time is in effect from 1am on the second Sunday in March to 1am on the first Sunday in November, except in Arizona, Hawaii, the U.S. Virgin Islands, and Puerto Rico. Daylight saving time moves the clock 1 hour ahead of standard time.

TIPPING   Tips are a very important part of certain workers' income, and gratuities are the standard way of showing appreciation for services provided. (However, tipping is certainly not compulsory if service is poor.) In hotels, tip **bellhops** at least $1 per bag ($2–$3 if you have a lot of luggage) and tip the **chamber staff** $1 to $2 per day (more if you've left a disaster area for him or her to clean up). Tip the **doorman** or **concierge** only if he or she has provided you with some specific service (for example, calling a cab for you or obtaining difficult-to-get theater tickets). Tip the **valet-parking attendant** $1 every time you get your car.

In restaurants, bars, and nightclubs, tip **service staff** 15% to 20% of the check, tip **bartenders** 10% to 15%, tip **checkroom attendants** $1 per garment, and tip **valet-parking attendants** $1 per vehicle.

As for other service personnel, tip **cabdrivers** 15% of the fare; tip **skycaps** at airports at least $1 per bag ($2–$3 if you have a lot of luggage); and tip **hairdressers** and **barbers** 15% to 20%.

TOILETS   You won't find public toilets or "restrooms" on the streets in most U.S. cities but they can be found in hotel lobbies, bars, restaurants, museums, department stores, railway and bus stations, and service stations. Large hotels and fast-food restaurants are often the best bet for clean facilities. Restaurants and bars in resorts or heavily visited areas may reserve their restrooms for patrons.

(manned 24 hr.).

U.S. Passport Agency: ☎ **202/647-0518.**

U.S. Centers for Disease Control International Traveler's Hotline: ☎ **404/332-4559.**

VISAS For information about U.S. visas, go to **http://travel.state.gov** and click on "Visas." Or go to one of the following websites:

Australian citizens can obtain up-to-date visa information from the **U.S. Embassy Canberra,** Moonah Place, Yarralumla, ACT 2600 (☎ **02/6214-5600**) or by checking the U.S. Diplomatic Mission's website at **http://usembassy-australia.state.gov/ consular**.

British subjects can obtain up-to-date visa information by calling the **U.S. Embassy Visa Information Line** (☎ **0891/200-290**) or by visiting the "Visas to the U.S." section of the American Embassy London's website at **www.usembassy.org.uk**.

Irish citizens can obtain up-to-date visa information through the **Embassy of the USA Dublin,** 42 Elgin Rd., Dublin 4, Ireland (☎ **353/1-668-8777**), or by checking the "Consular Services" section of the website at **http://dublin.usembassy.gov**.

Citizens of **New Zealand** can obtain up-to-date visa information by contacting the **U.S. Embassy New Zealand,** 29 Fitzherbert Terrace, Thorndon, Wellington (☎ **644/ 472-2068**), or get the information directly from the website at **http://wellington.us embassy.gov**.

2 TOLL-FREE NUMBERS & WEBSITES

MAJOR U.S. AIRLINES

(*flies internationally as well)

American Airlines*
☎ 800/433-7300 (in U.S. and Canada)
☎ 020/7365-0777 (in U.K.)
www.aa.com

ATA Airlines
☎ 800/435-9282
www.ata.com

Continental Airlines*
☎ 800/523-3273 (in U.S. and Canada)
☎ 084/5607-6760 (in U.K.)
www.continental.com

Delta Air Lines*
☎ 800/221-1212 (in U.S. and Canada)
☎ 084/5600-0950 (in U.K.)
www.delta.com

Northwest Airlines
☎ 800/225-2525 (in U.S.)
☎ 870/0507-4074 (in U.K.)
www.nwa.com

Pan Am Clipper Connection
☎ 800/359-7262
www.flypanam.com

United Airlines*
☎ 800/864-8331 (in U.S. and Canada)
☎ 084/5844-4777 in U.K.
www.united.com

US Airways*
☎ 800/428-4322 (in U.S. and Canada)
☎ 084/5600-3300 (in U.K.)
www.usairways.com

(into Boston)

Aer Lingus
☎ 800/474-7424 (in U.S. and Canada)
☎ 087/0876-5000 (in U.K.)
www.aerlingus.com

Air France
☎ 800/237-2747 (in U.S.)
☎ 800/375-8723 (U.S. and Canada)
☎ 087/0142-4343 (in U.K.)
www.airfrance.com

Air New Zealand
☎ 800/262-1234 (in U.S.)
☎ 800/663-5494 (in Canada)
☎ 0800/028-4149 (in U.K.)
www.airnewzealand.com

Alitalia
☎ 800/223-5730 (in U.S.)
☎ 800/361-8336 (in Canada)
☎ 087/0608-6003 (in U.K.)
www.alitalia.com

American Airlines
☎ 800/433-7300 (in U.S. and Canada)
☎ 020/7365-0777 (in U.K.)
www.aa.com

Bahamasair
☎ 800/222-4262 (in U.S.)
☎ 242/300-8359 (in Family Islands)
☎ 242/377-5505 (in Nassau)
www.bahamasair.com

British Airways
☎ 800/247-9297 (in U.S. and Canada)
☎ 087/0850-9850 (in U.K.)
www.british-airways.com

Continental Airlines
☎ 800/523-3273 (in U.S. and Canada)
☎ 084/5607-6760 (in U.K.)
www.continental.com

Delta Air Lines
☎ 800/221-1212 (in U.S. and Canada)
☎ 084/5600-0950 (in U.K.)
www.delta.com

Finnair
☎ 800/950-5000 (in U.S. and Canada)
☎ 087/0241-4411 (in U.K.)
www.finnair.com

Icelandair
☎ 800/223-5500, ext. 2 prompt 1 (in U.S. and Canada)
☎ 084/5758-1111 (in U.K.)
www.icelandair.com
www.icelandair.co.uk (in U.K.)

Japan Airlines
☎ 012/025-5931 (international)
www.jal.co.jp

Lufthansa
☎ 800/399-5838 (in U.S.)
☎ 800/563-5954 (in Canada)
☎ 087/0837-7747 (in U.K.)
www.lufthansa.com

Qantas Airways
☎ 800/227-4500 (in U.S.)
☎ 084/5774-7767 (in U.K. and Canada)
☎ 13 13 13 (in Australia)
www.qantas.com

South African Airways
☎ 271/1978-5313 (international)
☎ 0861 FLYSAA (086/135-9122) (in South Africa)
www.flysaa.com

Swiss Air
☎ 877/359-7947 (in U.S. and Canada)
☎ 084/5601-0956 (in U.K.)
www.swiss.com

Turkish Airlines
☎ 90 212 444 0 849
www.thy.com

United Airlines*
☎ 800/864-8331 (in U.S. and Canada)
☎ 084/5844-4777 (in U.K.)
www.united.com

US Airways*
☎ 800/428-4322 (in U.S. and Canada)
☎ 084/5600-3300 (in U.K.)
www.usairways.com

Virgin Atlantic Airways
☎ 800/821-5438 (in U.S. and Canada)
☎ 087/0574-7747 (in U.K.)
www.virgin-atlantic.com

BUDGET AIRLINES

AirTran Airways
ⓒ 800/247-8726
www.airtran.com

ATA Airlines
ⓒ 800/435-9282
www.ata.com

JetBlue Airways
ⓒ 800/538-2583 (in U.S.)
ⓒ 801/365-2525 (in U.K. and Canada)
www.jetblue.com

Skybus
ⓒ no phone
www.skybus.com

Spirit Airlines
ⓒ 800/772-7117
www.spiritair.com

Southwest Airlines
ⓒ 800/435-9792 (in U.S., U.K., and Canada)
www.southwest.com

CAR-RENTAL AGENCIES

Alamo
ⓒ 800/GO-ALAMO (800/462-5266)
www.alamo.com

Avis
ⓒ 800/331-1212 (in U.S. and Canada)
ⓒ 084/4581-8181 (in U.K.)
www.avis.com

Budget
ⓒ 800/527-0700 (in U.S.)
ⓒ 087/0156-5656 (in U.K.)
ⓒ 800/268-8900 (in Canada)
www.budget.com

Dollar
ⓒ 800/800-4000 (in U.S.)
ⓒ 800/848-8268 (in Canada)
ⓒ 080/8234-7524 (in U.K.)
www.dollar.com

Enterprise
ⓒ 800/261-7331 (in U.S.)
ⓒ 514/355-4028 (in Canada)
ⓒ 012/9360-9090 (in U.K.)
www.enterprise.com

Hertz
ⓒ 800/645-3131
ⓒ 800/654-3001 (for international reservations)
www.hertz.com

National
ⓒ 800/CAR-RENT (800/227-7368)
www.nationalcar.com

Rent-A-Wreck
ⓒ 800/535-1391
www.rentawreck.com

Thrifty
ⓒ 800/367-2277
ⓒ 918/669-2168 (international)
www.thrifty.com

MAJOR HOTEL & MOTEL CHAINS

Best Western International
ⓒ 800/780-7234 (in U.S. and Canada)
ⓒ 0800/393-130 (in U.K.)
www.bestwestern.com

Clarion Hotels
ⓒ 800/CLARION (252-7466) or
    877/424-6423 (in U.S. and Canada)
ⓒ 0800/444-444 (in U.K.)
www.choicehotels.com

Comfort Inns
ⓒ 800/228-5150
ⓒ 0800/444-444 (in U.K.)
www.comfortinnchoicehotels.com

Courtyard by Marriott
ⓒ 888/236-2427 (in U.S.)
ⓒ 0800/221-222 (in U.K.)
www.marriott.com/courtyard

Days Inn
- ☎ 800/329-7466 (in U.S.)
- ☎ 0800/280-400 (in U.K.)
- www.daysinn.com

Doubletree Hotels
- ☎ 800/222-TREE (800/222-8733) (in U.S. and Canada)
- ☎ 087/0590-9090 (in U.K.)
- www.doubletree.com

Econo Lodges
- ☎ 800/55-ECONO (800/552-3666)
- www.choicehotels.com

Embassy Suites
- ☎ 800/EMBASSY (800/362-2779)
- www.embassysuites.hilton.com

Fairfield Inn by Marriott
- ☎ 800/228-2800 (in U.S. and Canada)
- ☎ 0800/221-222 (in U.K.)
- www.marriott.com/fairfieldinn

Hampton Inn
- ☎ 800/HAMPTON (800/426-4766)
- www.hamptoninn.hilton.com

Hilton Hotels
- ☎ 800/HILTONS (800/445-8667) (in U.S. and Canada)
- ☎ 087/0590-9090 (in U.K.)
- www.hilton.com

Holiday Inn
- ☎ 800/315-2621 (in U.S. and Canada)
- ☎ 0800/405-060 (in U.K.)
- www.holidayinn.com

Howard Johnson
- ☎ 800/446-4656 (in U.S. and Canada)
- www.hojo.com

Hyatt
- ☎ 888/591-1234 (in U.S. and Canada)
- ☎ 084/5888-1234 (in U.K.)
- www.hyatt.com

La Quinta Inns and Suites
- ☎ 800/642-4271 (in U.S. and Canada)
- www.lq.com

Marriott
- ☎ 877/236-2427 (in U.S. and Canada)
- ☎ 0800/221-222 (in U.K.)
- www.marriott.com

Motel 6
- ☎ 800/4MOTEL6 (800/466-8356)
- www.motel6.com

Quality
- ☎ 877/424-6423 (in U.S. and Canada)
- ☎ 0800/444-444 (in U.K.)
- www.qualityinn.choicehotels.com

Radisson Hotels & Resorts
- ☎ 888/201-1718 (in U.S. and Canada)
- ☎ 0800/374-411 (in U.K.)
- www.radisson.com

Ramada Worldwide
- ☎ 888/2-RAMADA (888/272-6232) (in U.S. and Canada)
- ☎ 080/8100-0783 (in U.K.)
- www.ramada.com

Red Roof Inns
- ☎ 866/686-4335 (in U.S. and Canada)
- ☎ 614/601-4075 (international)
- www.redroof.com

Residence Inn by Marriott
- ☎ 800/331-3131
- ☎ 800/221-222 (in U.K.)
- www.marriott.com/residenceinn

Rodeway Inns
- ☎ 877/424-6423
- www.rodewayinn.choicehotels.com

Sheraton Hotels & Resorts
- ☎ 800/325-3535 (in U.S.)
- ☎ 800/543-4300 (in Canada)
- ☎ 0800/3253-5353 (in U.K.)
- www.starwoodhotels.com/sheraton

Super 8 Motels
- ☎ 800/800-8000
- www.super8.com

Travelodge
- ☎ 1-800-578-7878
- www.travelodge.com

INDEX

See also Accommodations and Restaurant indexes, below.

The new way to get AROUND town.

Make the most of your stay. Go Day by Day!

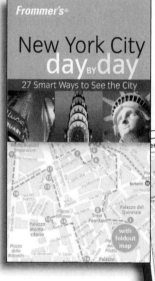

The all-new Day by Day series shows you the best places to visit and the best way to see them.

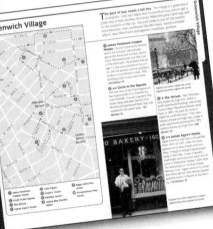

- Full-color throughout, with hundreds of photos and maps
- Packed with 1–to–3–day itineraries, neighborhood walks, and thematic tours
- Museums, literary haunts, offbeat places, and more
- Star-rated hotel and restaurant listings
- Sturdy foldout map in reclosable plastic wallet
- Foldout front covers with at-a-glance maps and info

The best trips start here. **Frommer's**®

A Branded Imprint of ⓦ**WILEY**
Now you know.

FROMMER'S® COMPLETE TRAVEL GUIDES

FROMMER'S® DAY BY DAY GUIDES

PAULINE FROMMER'S GUIDES: SEE MORE. SPEND LESS.

FROMMER'S® PORTABLE GUIDES

Acapulco, Ixtapa & Zihuatanejo
Amsterdam
Aruba, Bonaire & Curacao
Australia's Great Barrier Reef
Bahamas
Big Island of Hawaii
Boston
California Wine Country
Cancún
Cayman Islands
Charleston
Chicago
Dominican Republic

Florence
Las Vegas
Las Vegas for Non-Gamblers
London
Maui
Nantucket & Martha's Vineyard
New Orleans
New York City
Paris
Portland
Puerto Rico
Puerto Vallarta, Manzanillo &
    Guadalajara

Rio de Janeiro
San Diego
San Francisco
Savannah
St. Martin, Sint Maarten, Anguilla &
    St. Bart's
Turks & Caicos
Vancouver
Venice
Virgin Islands
Washington, D.C.
Whistler

FROMMER'S® CRUISE GUIDES

Alaska Cruises & Ports of Call

Cruises & Ports of Call

European Cruises & Ports of Call

FROMMER'S® NATIONAL PARK GUIDES

Algonquin Provincial Park
Banff & Jasper
Grand Canyon

National Parks of the American West
Rocky Mountain
Yellowstone & Grand Teton

Yosemite and Sequoia & Kings
    Canyon
Zion & Bryce Canyon

FROMMER'S® WITH KIDS GUIDES

Chicago
Hawaii
Las Vegas
London

National Parks
New York City
San Francisco

Toronto
Walt Disney World® & Orlando
Washington, D.C.

FROMMER'S® PHRASEFINDER DICTIONARY GUIDES

Chinese
French

German
Italian

Japanese
Spanish

SUZY GERSHMAN'S BORN TO SHOP GUIDES

France
Hong Kong, Shanghai & Beijing
Italy

London
New York
Paris

San Francisco
Where to Buy the Best of Everything,

FROMMER'S® BEST-LOVED DRIVING TOURS

Britain
California
France
Germany

Ireland
Italy
New England
Northern Italy

Scotland
Spain
Tuscany & Umbria

THE UNOFFICIAL GUIDES®

Adventure Travel in Alaska
Beyond Disney
California with Kids
Central Italy
Chicago
Cruises
Disneyland®
England
Hawaii

Ireland
Las Vegas
London
Maui
Mexico's Best Beach Resorts
Mini Mickey
New Orleans
New York City
Paris

San Francisco
South Florida including Miami &
    the Keys
Walt Disney World®
Walt Disney World® for
    Grown-ups
Walt Disney World® with Kids
Washington, D.C.

SPECIAL-INTEREST TITLES

Athens Past & Present
Best Places to Raise Your Family
Cities Ranked & Rated
500 Places to Take Your Kids Before They Grow Up
Frommer's Best Day Trips from London
Frommer's Best RV & Tent Campgrounds in the U.S.A.

Frommer's Exploring America by RV
Frommer's NYC Free & Dirt Cheap
Frommer's Road Atlas Europe
Frommer's Road Atlas Ireland
Retirement Places Rated